Zenescope Entertainment F

Grimm Fairy Tales™

VOLUME THREE

ARCANE ACRE

zenescope

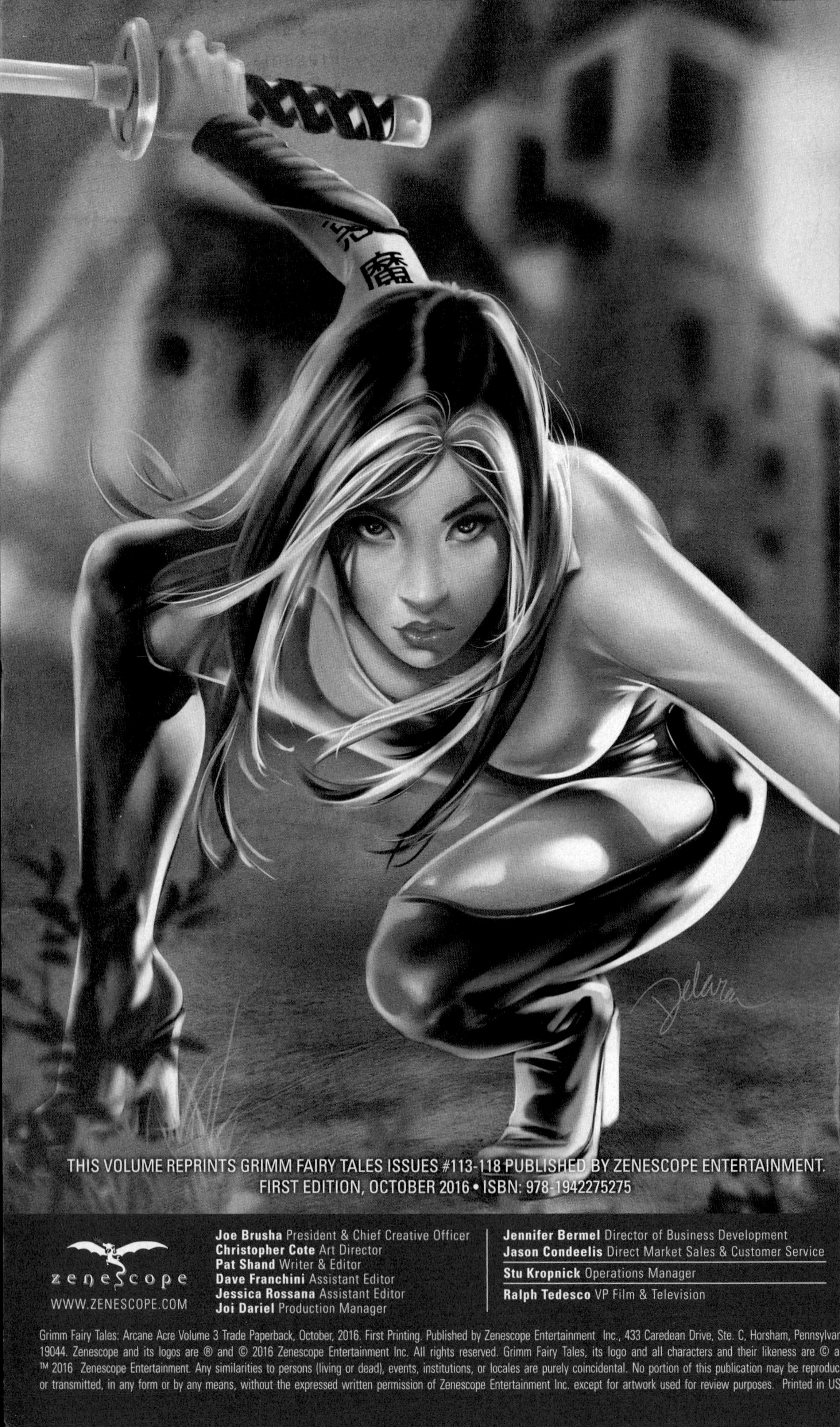

THIS VOLUME REPRINTS GRIMM FAIRY TALES ISSUES #113-118 PUBLISHED BY ZENESCOPE ENTERTAINMENT.
FIRST EDITION, OCTOBER 2016 • ISBN: 978-1942275275

zenescope
WWW.ZENESCOPE.COM

Joe Brusha President & Chief Creative Officer
Christopher Cote Art Director
Pat Shand Writer & Editor
Dave Franchini Assistant Editor
Jessica Rossana Assistant Editor
Joi Dariel Production Manager

Jennifer Bermel Director of Business Development
Jason Condeelis Direct Market Sales & Customer Service
Stu Kropnick Operations Manager
Ralph Tedesco VP Film & Television

Grimm Fairy Tales: Arcane Acre Volume 3 Trade Paperback, October, 2016. First Printing. Published by Zenescope Entertainment Inc., 433 Caredean Drive, Ste. C, Horsham, Pennsylvar 19044.

VOLUME **THREE**

Grimm Fairy Tales™

ARCANE ACRE

GRIMM FAIRY TALES CREATED BY
JOE BRUSHA
RALPH TEDESCO

STORY
JOE BRUSHA
RALPH TEDESCO
PAT SHAND

ART DIRECTION & TRADE DESIGN
CHRISTOPHER COTE

EDITORS
PAT SHAND
NICOLE GLADE

THE STORY SO FAR...

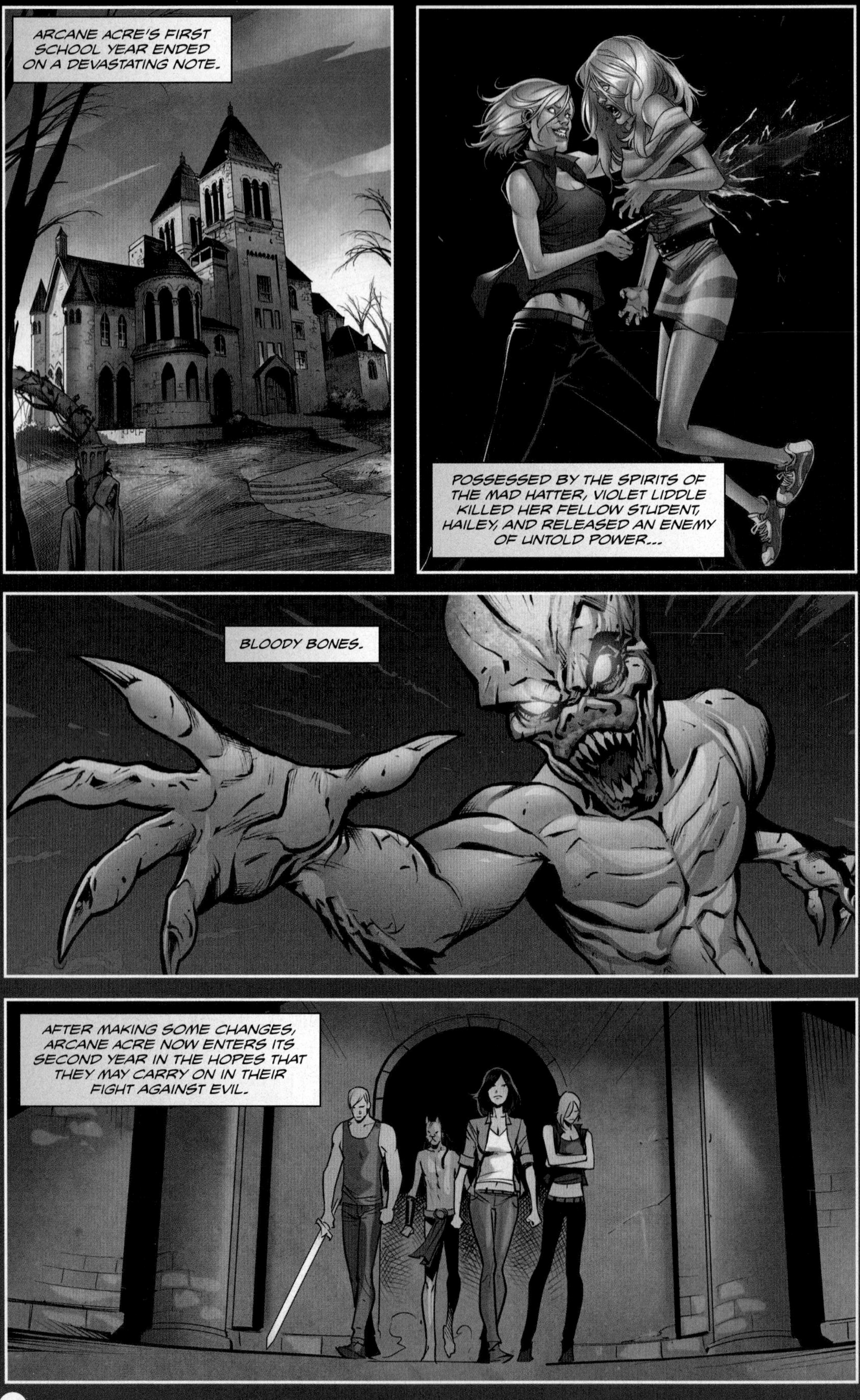
ARCANE ACRE'S FIRST SCHOOL YEAR ENDED ON A DEVASTATING NOTE.
POSSESSED BY THE SPIRITS OF THE MAD HATTER, VIOLET LIDDLE KILLED HER FELLOW STUDENT, HAILEY, AND RELEASED AN ENEMY OF UNTOLD POWER...
BLOODY BONES.
AFTER MAKING SOME CHANGES, ARCANE ACRE NOW ENTERS ITS SECOND YEAR IN THE HOPES THAT THEY MAY CARRY ON IN THEIR FIGHT AGAINST EVIL.

THE CAST

STUDENTS

Skye

Wulf

Ali

Hailey

Wiglaf

Lance

Mary

Phil

FACULTY

Sela

Shang

Belinda

Adraste

Kiera

Bolder

Masumi

VILLAINS

Bloody Bones

Maka

Warlord of Oz

Voodoo

Harbingers

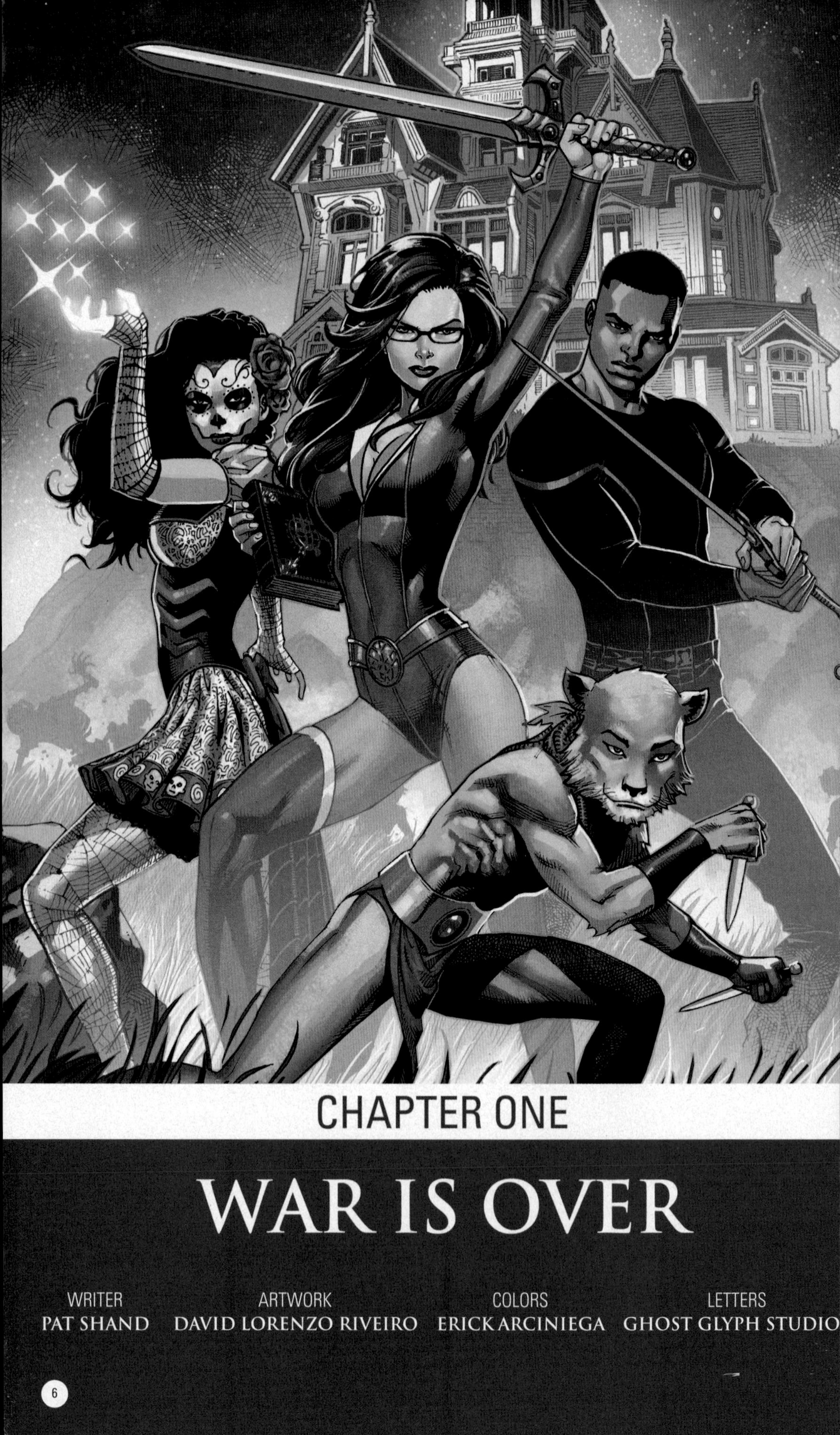

CHAPTER ONE

WAR IS OVER

WRITER
PAT SHAND

ARTWORK
DAVID LORENZO RIVEIRO

COLORS
ERICK ARCINIEGA

LETTERS
GHOST GLYPH STUDIO

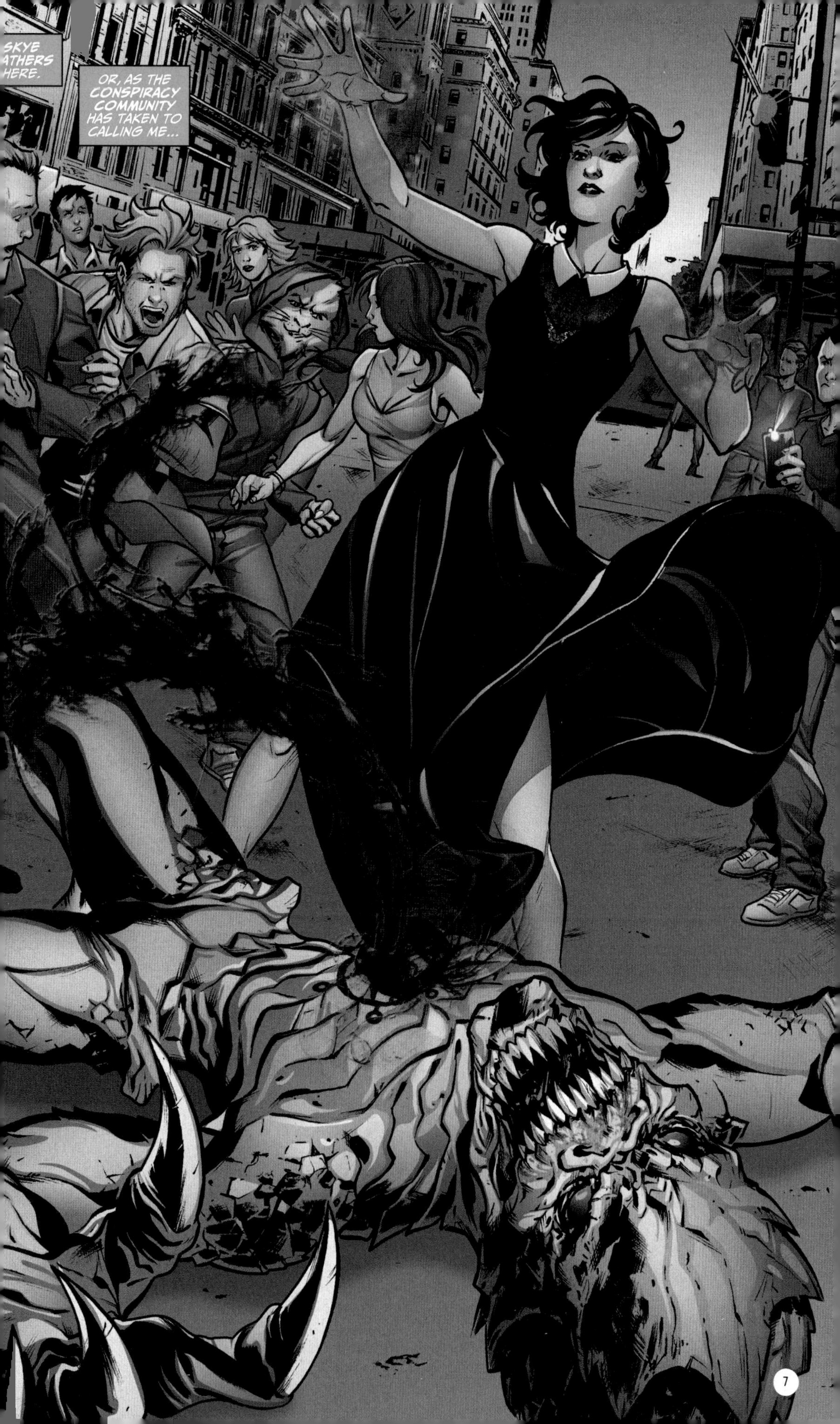
SKYE ATHERS HERE.
OR, AS THE CONSPIRACY COMMUNITY HAS TAKEN TO CALLING ME...

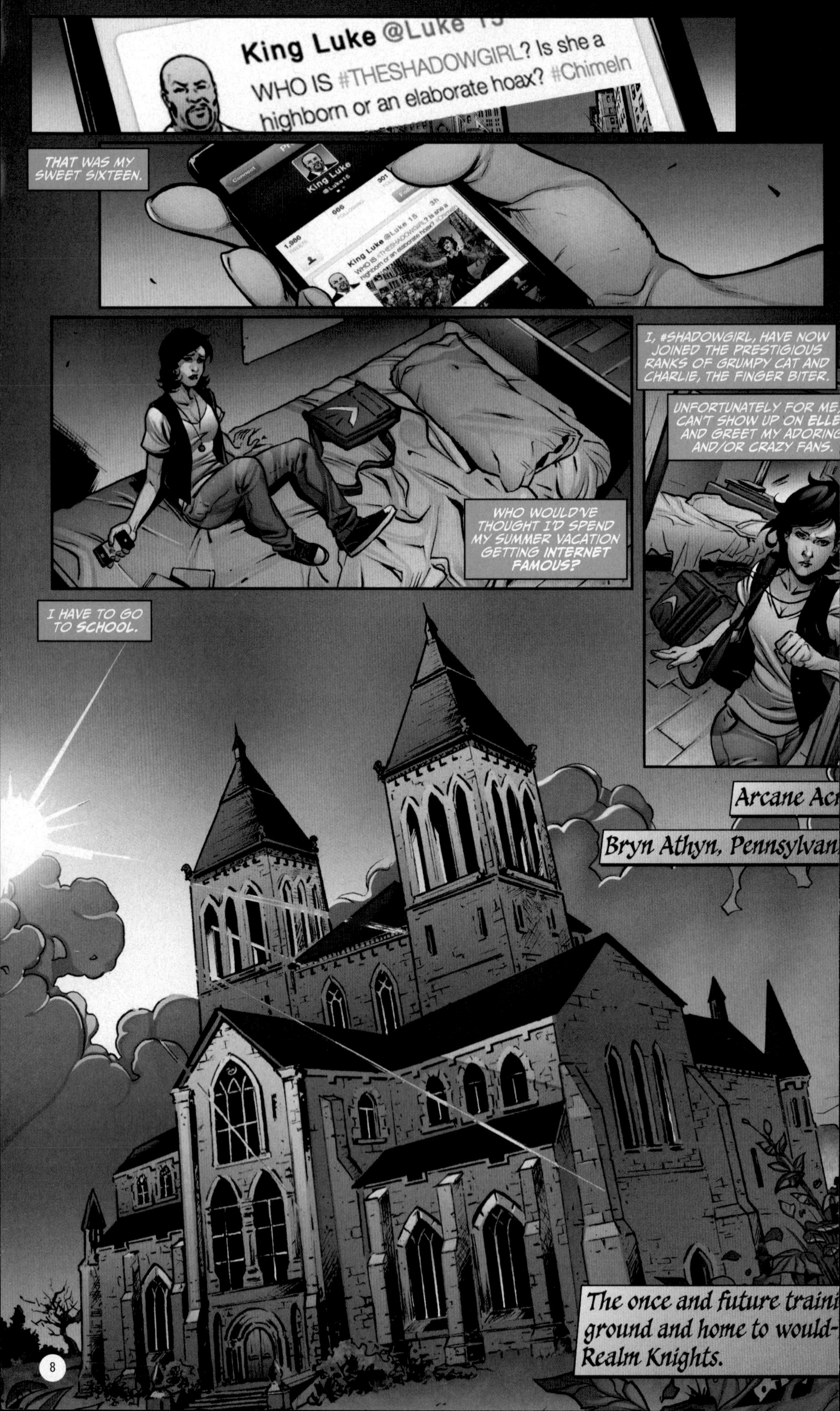
King Luke @Luke 15
WHO IS #THESHADOWGIRL? Is she a highborn or an elaborate hoax? #ChimeIn
THAT WAS MY SWEET SIXTEEN.
WHO WOULD'VE THOUGHT I'D SPEND MY SUMMER VACATION GETTING INTERNET FAMOUS?
I, #SHADOWGIRL, HAVE NOW JOINED THE PRESTIGIOUS RANKS OF GRUMPY CAT AND CHARLIE, THE FINGER BITER.
UNFORTUNATELY FOR ME, I CAN'T SHOW UP ON ELLEN AND GREET MY ADORING AND/OR CRAZY FANS.
I HAVE TO GO TO SCHOOL.
Arcane Ac
Bryn Athyn, Pennsylvan
The once and future traini ground and home to would- Realm Knights.

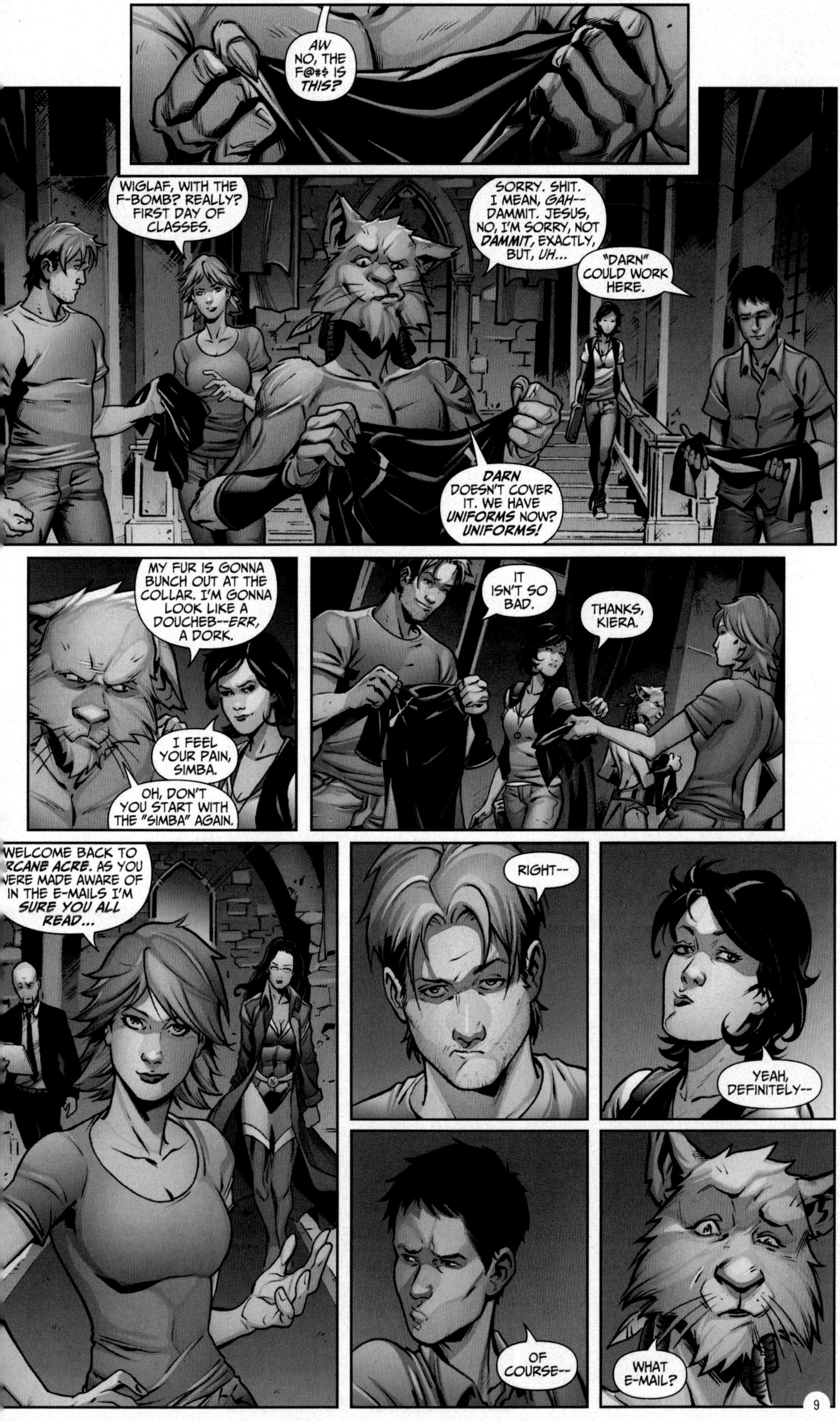
AW NO, THE F@#$ IS THIS?
WIGLAF, WITH THE F-BOMB? REALLY? FIRST DAY OF CLASSES.
SORRY. SHIT. I MEAN, GAH-- DAMMIT. JESUS, NO, I'M SORRY, NOT DAMMIT, EXACTLY, BUT, UH...
"DARN" COULD WORK HERE.
DARN DOESN'T COVER IT. WE HAVE UNIFORMS NOW? UNIFORMS!
MY FUR IS GONNA BUNCH OUT AT THE COLLAR. I'M GONNA LOOK LIKE A DOUCHEB--ERR, A DORK.
I FEEL YOUR PAIN, SIMBA.
OH, DON'T YOU START WITH THE "SIMBA" AGAIN.
IT ISN'T SO BAD.
THANKS, KIERA.
WELCOME BACK TO RCANE ACRE. AS YOU ERE MADE AWARE OF IN THE E-MAILS I'M SURE YOU ALL READ...
RIGHT--
YEAH, DEFINITELY--
OF COURSE--
WHAT E-MAIL?

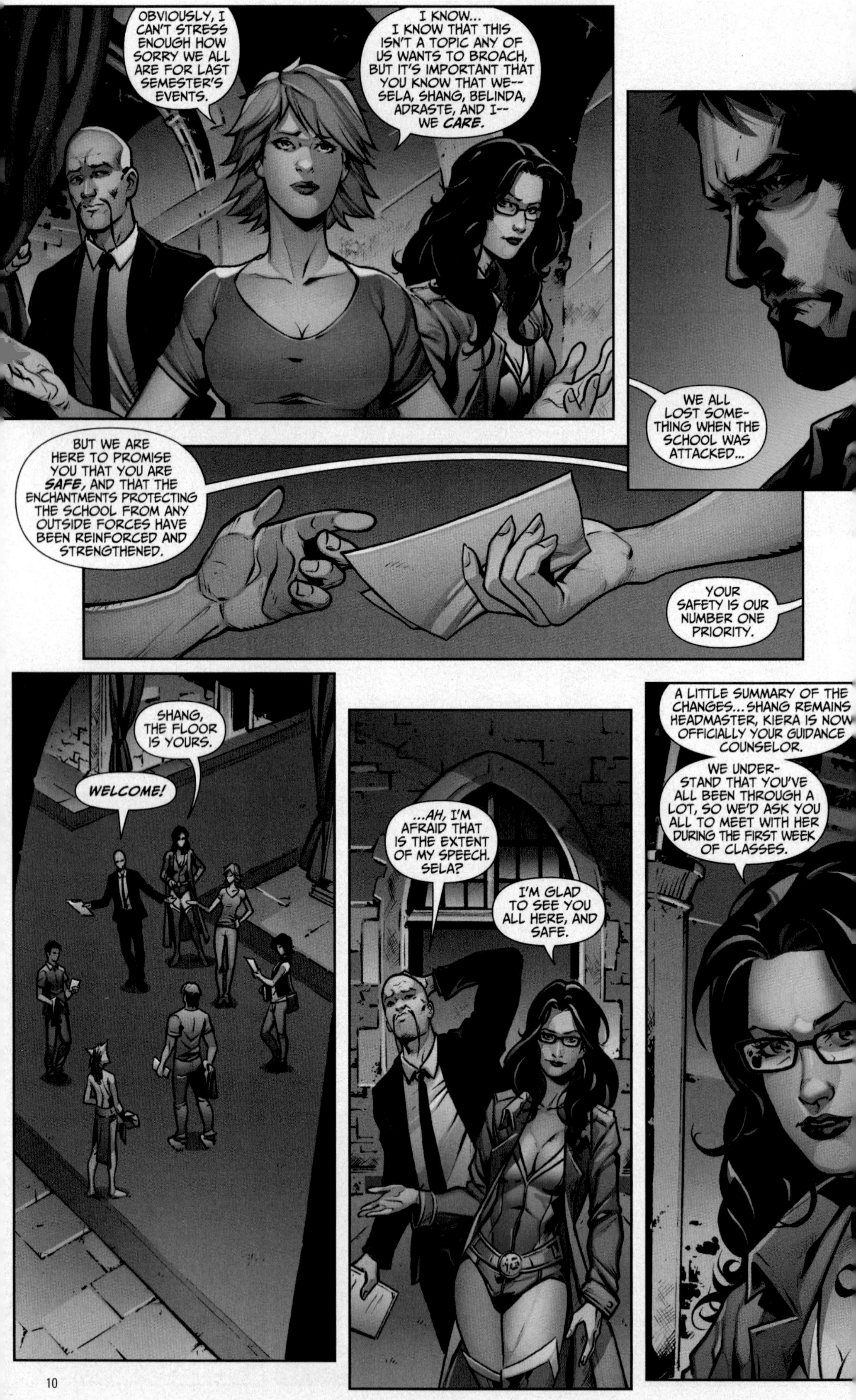
OBVIOUSLY, I CAN'T STRESS ENOUGH HOW SORRY WE ALL ARE FOR LAST SEMESTER'S EVENTS.
I KNOW... I KNOW THAT THIS ISN'T A TOPIC ANY OF US WANTS TO BROACH, BUT IT'S IMPORTANT THAT YOU KNOW THAT WE-- SELA, SHANG, BELINDA, ADRASTE, AND I-- WE CARE.
WE ALL LOST SOMETHING WHEN THE SCHOOL WAS ATTACKED...
BUT WE ARE HERE TO PROMISE YOU THAT YOU ARE SAFE, AND THAT THE ENCHANTMENTS PROTECTING THE SCHOOL FROM ANY OUTSIDE FORCES HAVE BEEN REINFORCED AND STRENGTHENED.
YOUR SAFETY IS OUR NUMBER ONE PRIORITY.
SHANG, THE FLOOR IS YOURS.
WELCOME!
...AH, I'M AFRAID THAT IS THE EXTENT OF MY SPEECH. SELA?
I'M GLAD TO SEE YOU ALL HERE, AND SAFE.
A LITTLE SUMMARY OF THE CHANGES... SHANG REMAINS HEADMASTER, KIERA IS NOW OFFICIALLY YOUR GUIDANCE COUNSELOR.
WE UNDERSTAND THAT YOU'VE ALL BEEN THROUGH A LOT, SO WE'D ASK YOU ALL TO MEET WITH HER DURING THE FIRST WEEK OF CLASSES.

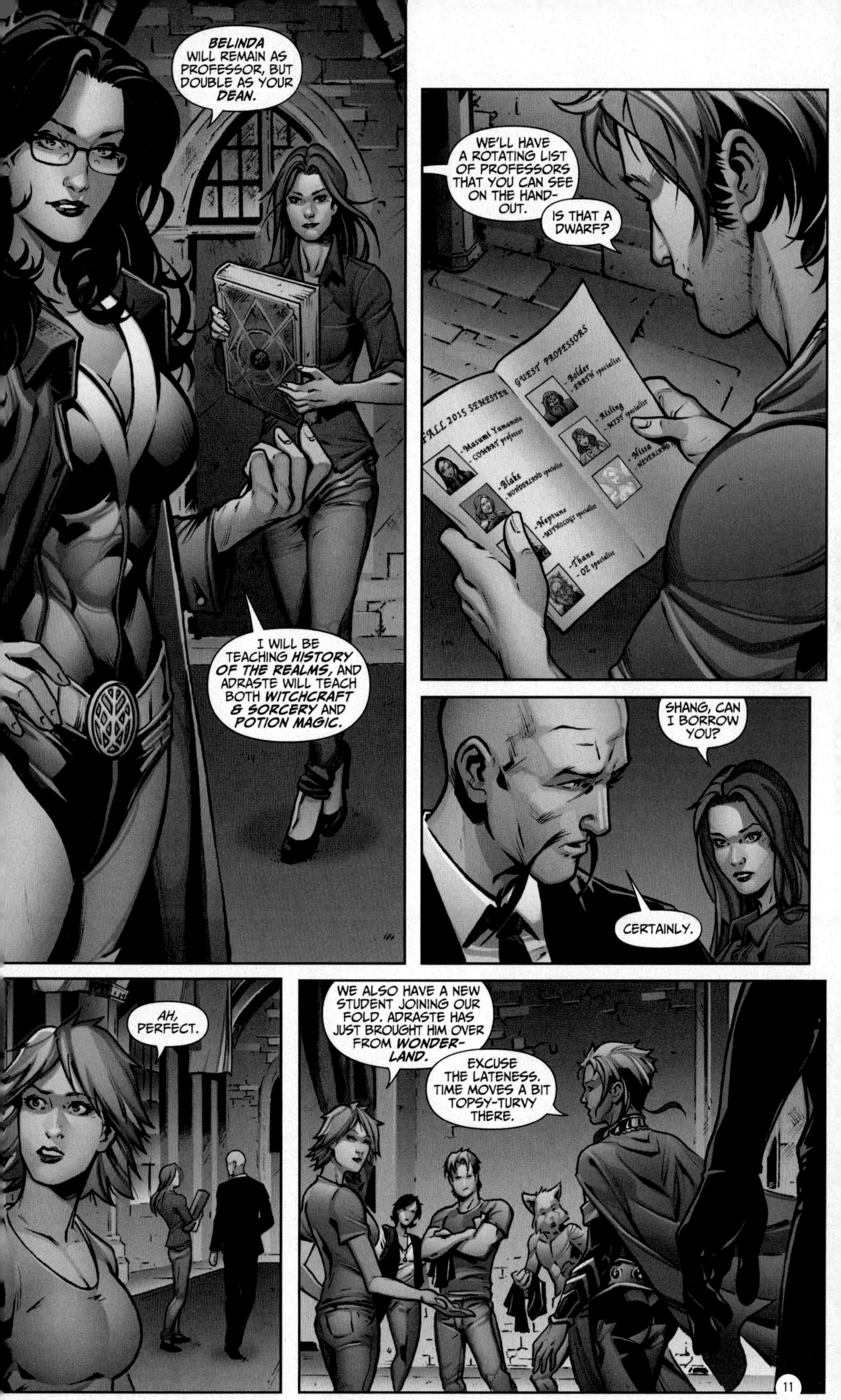
BELINDA WILL REMAIN AS PROFESSOR, BUT DOUBLE AS YOUR DEAN.
I WILL BE TEACHING HISTORY OF THE REALMS, AND ADRASTE WILL TEACH BOTH WITCHCRAFT & SORCERY AND POTION MAGIC.
WE'LL HAVE A ROTATING LIST OF PROFESSORS THAT YOU CAN SEE ON THE HAND-OUT.
IS THAT A DWARF?
FALL 2015 SEMESTER
-Masumi Yamamoto
-COMBAT professor
-Blake
-WONDERLAND specialist
-Neptune
-MYTHOLOGY specialist
-Thane
-OZ specialist
GUEST PROFESSORS
-Bolder
-EARTH specialist
-Aisling
-MYST specialist
SHANG, CAN I BORROW YOU?
CERTAINLY.
AH, PERFECT.
WE ALSO HAVE A NEW STUDENT JOINING OUR FOLD. ADRASTE HAS JUST BROUGHT HIM OVER FROM WONDERLAND.
EXCUSE THE LATENESS. TIME MOVES A BIT TOPSY-TURVY THERE.

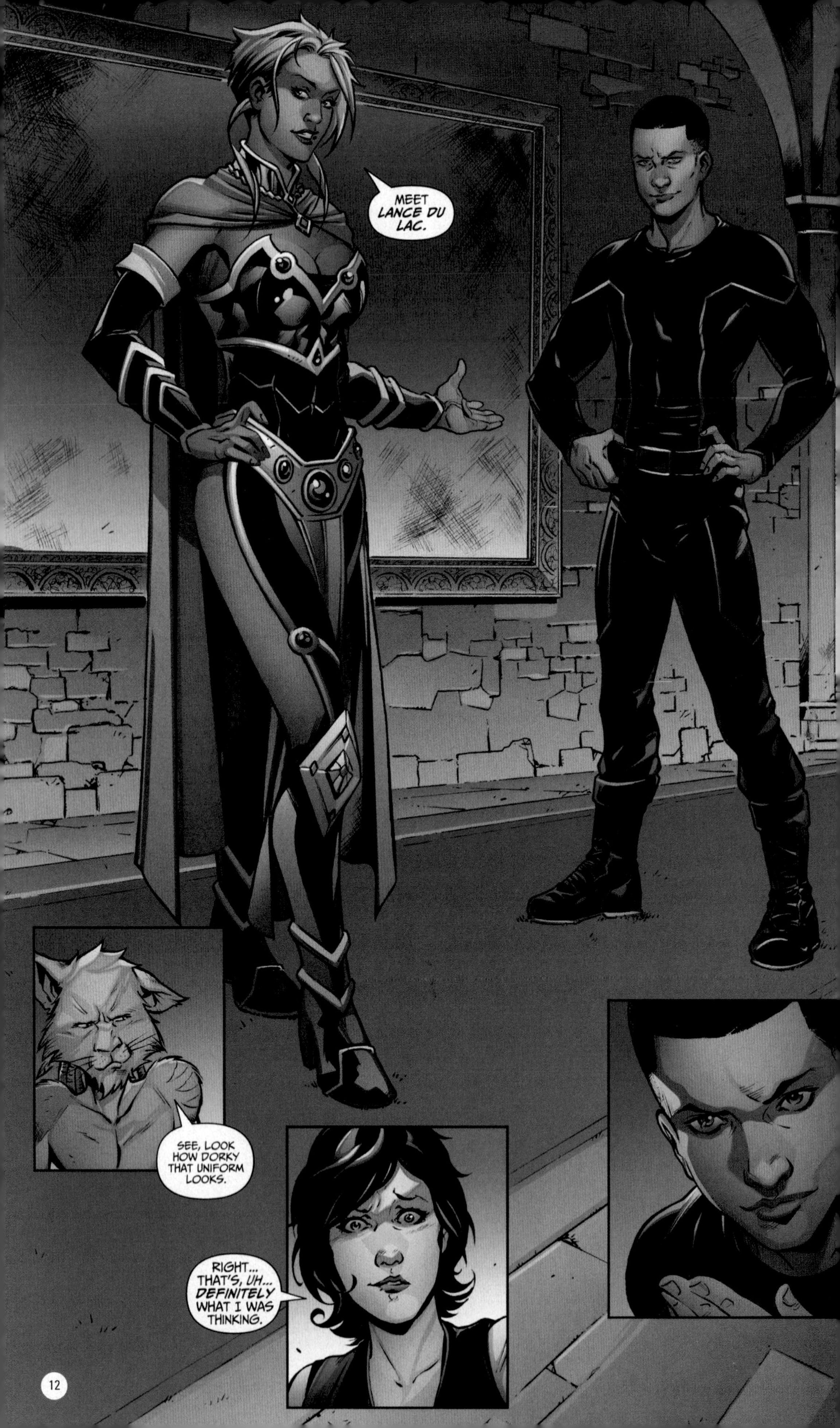
MEET *LANCE DU LAC.*
SEE, LOOK HOW DORKY THAT UNIFORM LOOKS.
RIGHT... THAT'S, *UH*... ***DEFINITELY*** WHAT I WAS THINKING.

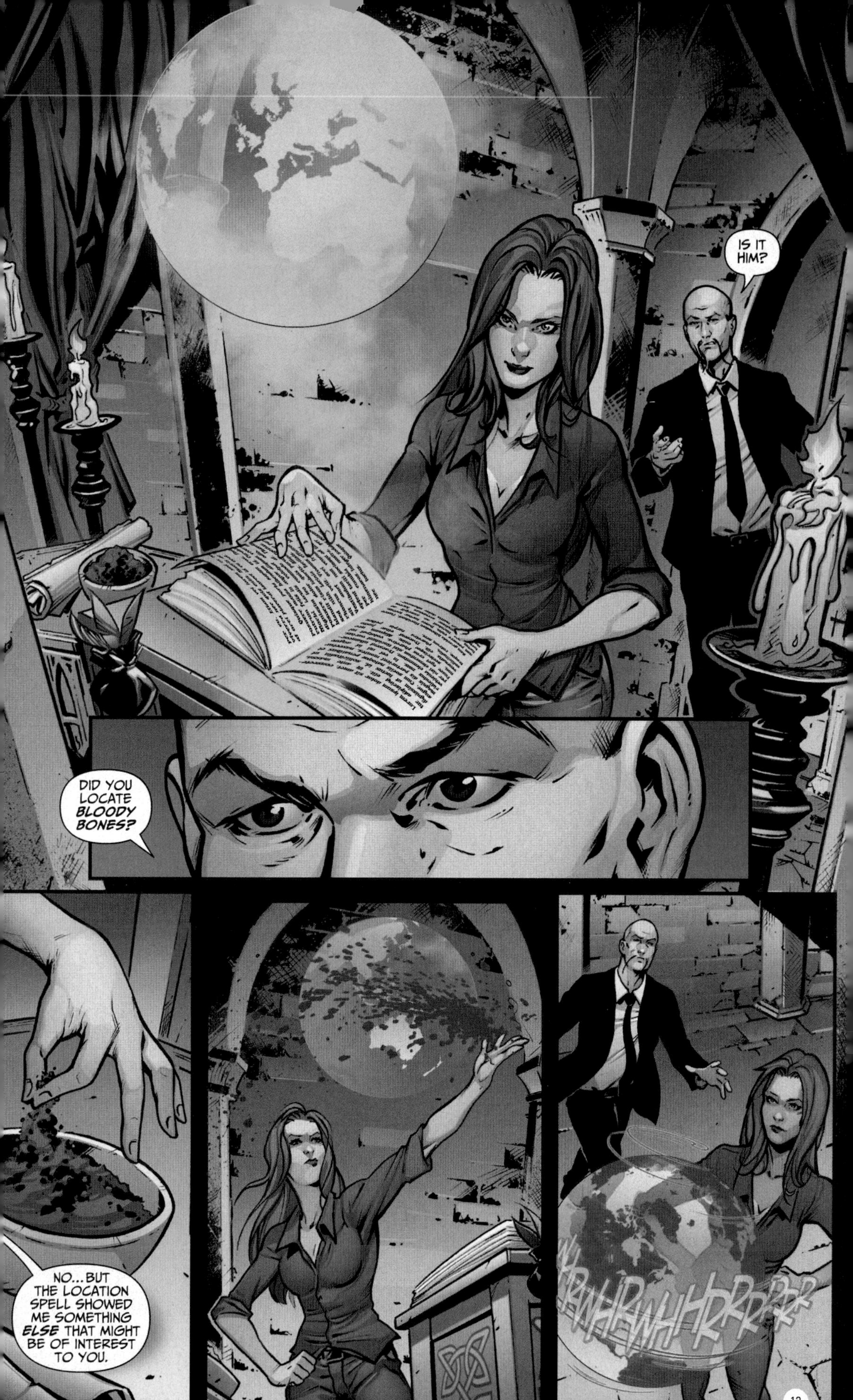
IS IT HIM?
DID YOU LOCATE BLOODY BONES?
NO...BUT THE LOCATION SPELL SHOWED ME SOMETHING ELSE THAT MIGHT BE OF INTEREST TO YOU.
WHRWHRWHRRRRRR

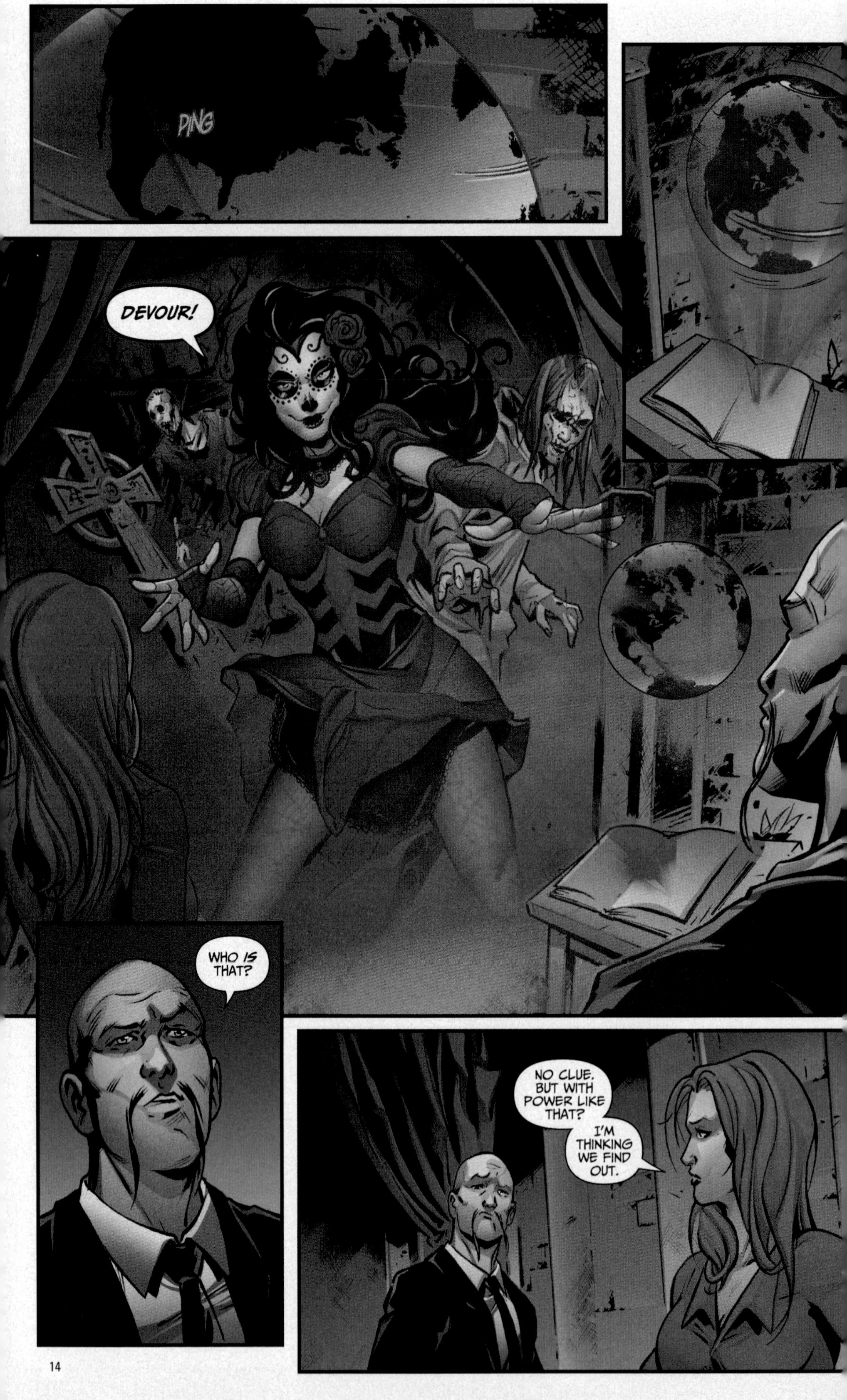
PING
DEVOUR!
WHO IS THAT?
NO CLUE. BUT WITH POWER LIKE THAT?
I'M THINKING WE FIND OUT.

IT'S SCARY HOW MUCH A YEAR CAN CHANGE YOU.

CHANGE EVERYTHING, REALLY.

ST YEAR, WULF WAS THE LAST PERSON CALL MY FRIEND. HE GOT EXPELLED FOR TRYING TO KILL BELINDA.

THERE'LL BE SOME RULES IN MY CLASSROOM, Y'HEAR? FIRST, ANY JOKES MADE AT MY EXPENSE'LL GET YE A TRIP TO THE DEAN, WITH MY RECOMMENDATION TO, UH...TO PUT YE ON TOILET CLEANIN' DUTY! PUN INTENDED!

AND SECOND, ANY JOKES MADE AT THE EXPENSE OF MY BEARD WILL BE CONSIDERED A RACIAL SLUR. I'M A PROUD DWARF, MIND YE, THIS BEARD'S MORE'N JUST SOME WHISKERS ON MY FACE— IT'S SACRED, INNIT? NOW, I'VE BEEN CALLED UPON TO TEACH YOU ABOUT THE EARTH... THE NEXUS, OUR WORLD WHICH SITS BETWEEN THE FOUR REALMS DEPICTED... SEE, THERE'S

NOW, HE AND WIGLAF ARE MY CLOSEST FRIENDS.

LAST YEAR, ALI WAS THE ONLY PERSON I TRUSTED. I LIKED HIM...AND I KNEW HE LIKED ME FROM THE WAY HE LOOKED AT ME.

HE NEVER LOOKS AT ME ANYMORE.

DAMN, YOU'RE GETTING GOOD, BRO--YOU CAUGHT ME SLIPPING WITH THAT SWEEP THING YOU DID.

WHEN I THINK ABOUT WHERE WE'VE BEEN AND HOW FAR WE'VE COME, IT'S HARD NOT TO WONDER WHERE WE'RE GOING TO GO.

15

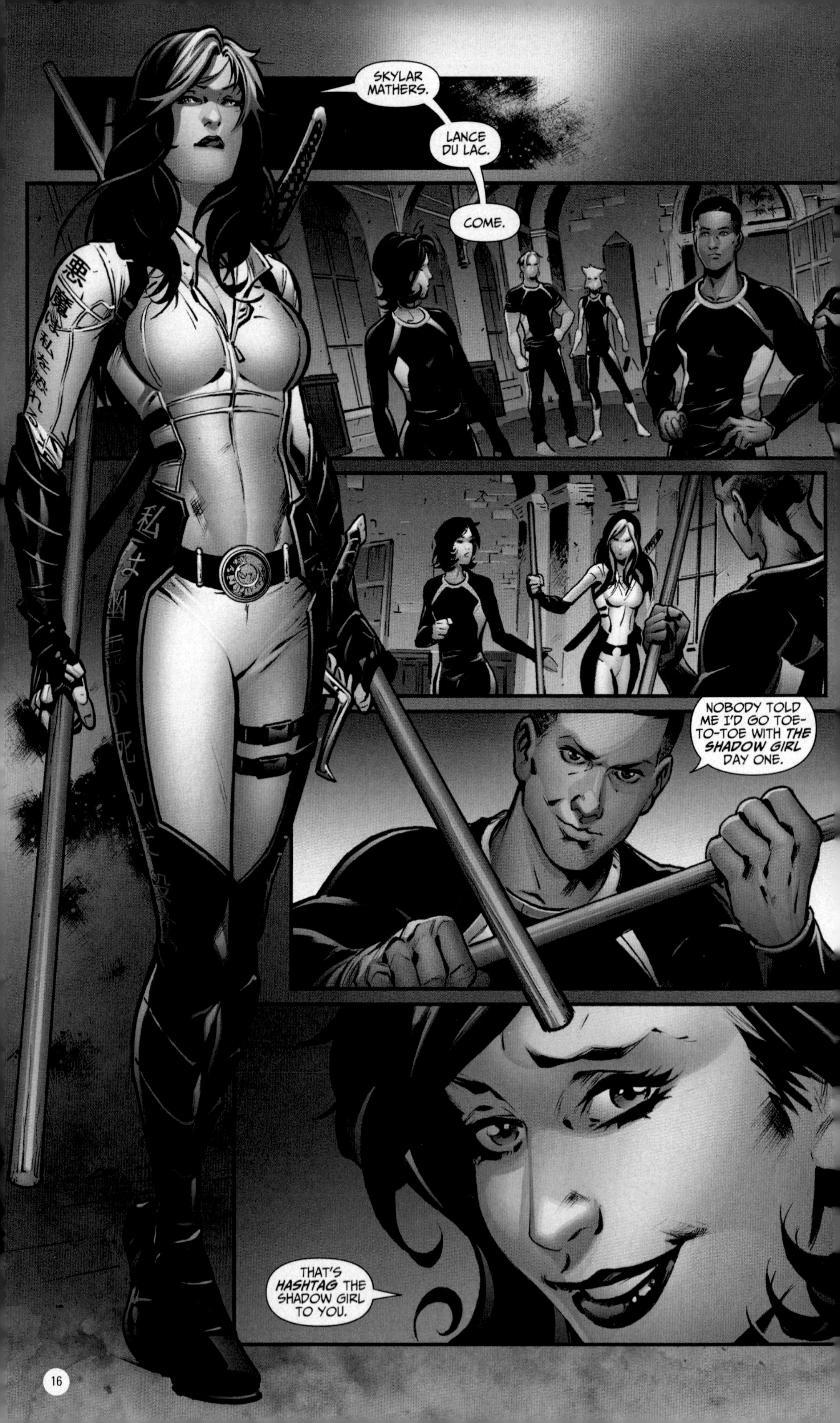
SKYLAR MATHERS.
LANCE DU LAC.
COME.
NOBODY TOLD ME I'D GO TOE-TO-TOE WITH ***THE SHADOW GIRL*** DAY ONE.
THAT'S ***HASHTAG*** THE SHADOW GIRL TO YOU.

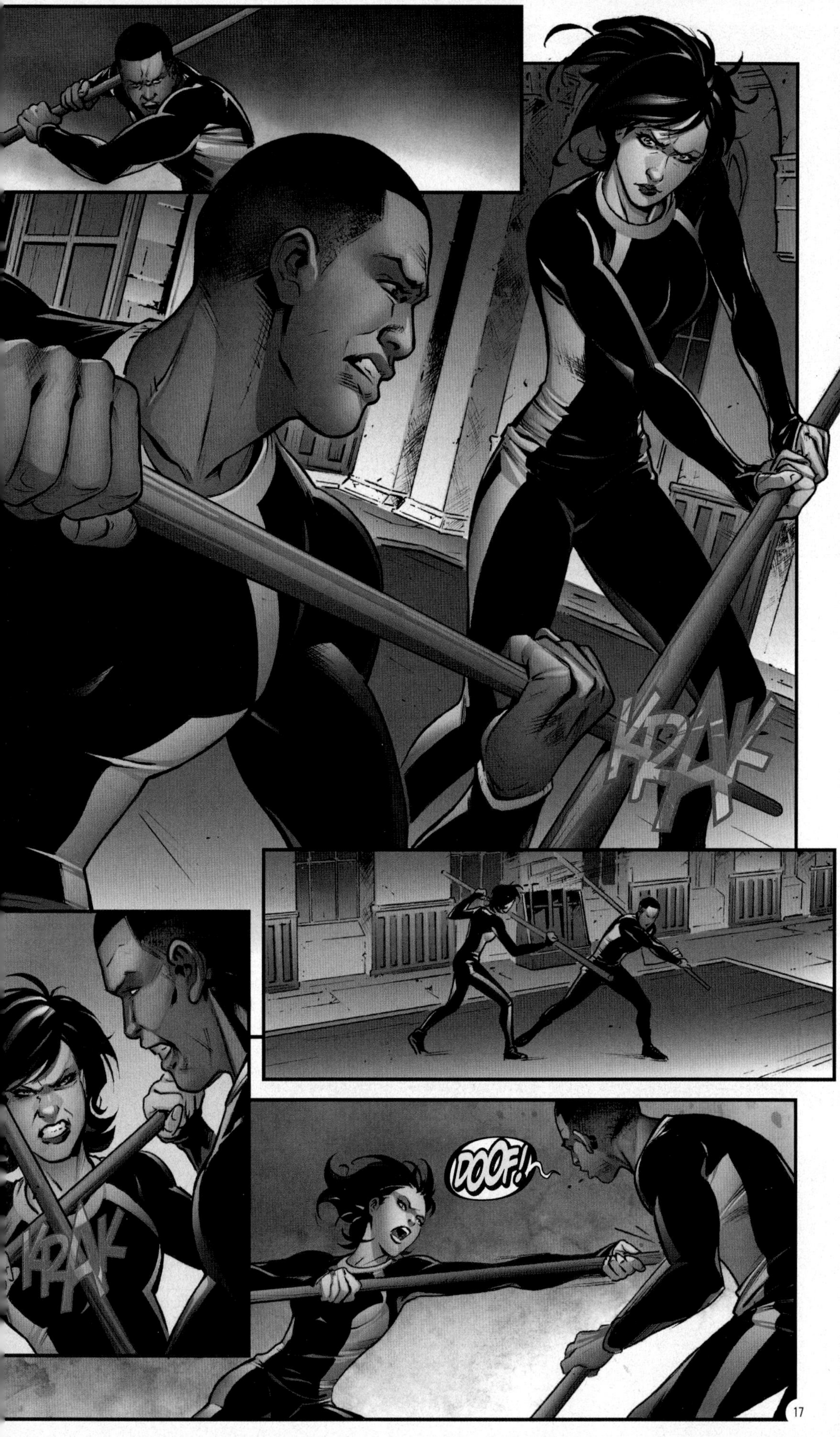
KRAK
KRAK
DOOF!

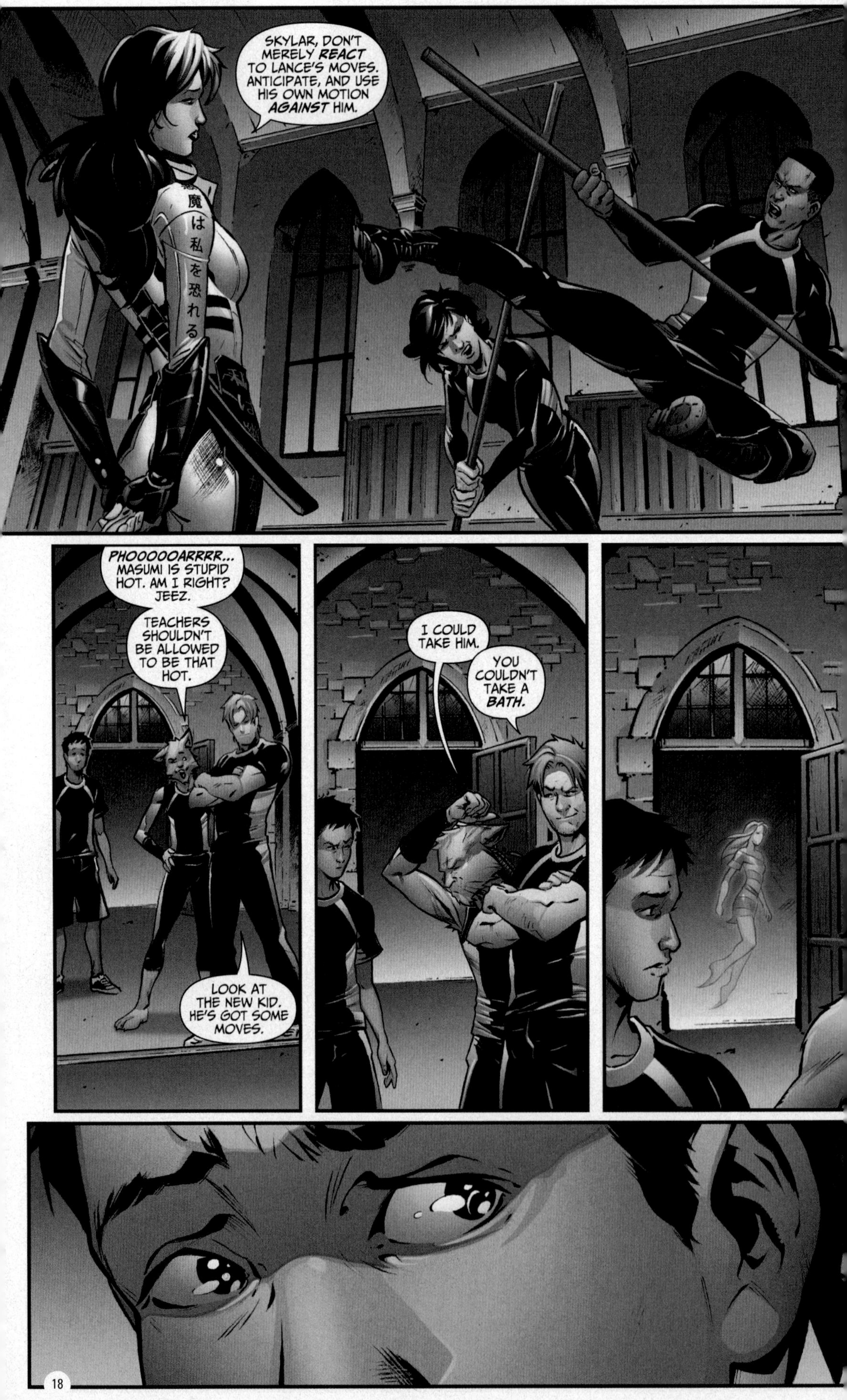
SKYLAR, DON'T MERELY REACT TO LANCE'S MOVES. ANTICIPATE, AND USE HIS OWN MOTION AGAINST HIM.
PHOOOOOARRRR... MASUMI IS STUPID HOT. AM I RIGHT? JEEZ.
TEACHERS SHOULDN'T BE ALLOWED TO BE THAT HOT.
LOOK AT THE NEW KID. HE'S GOT SOME MOVES.
I COULD TAKE HIM.
YOU COULDN'T TAKE A BATH.

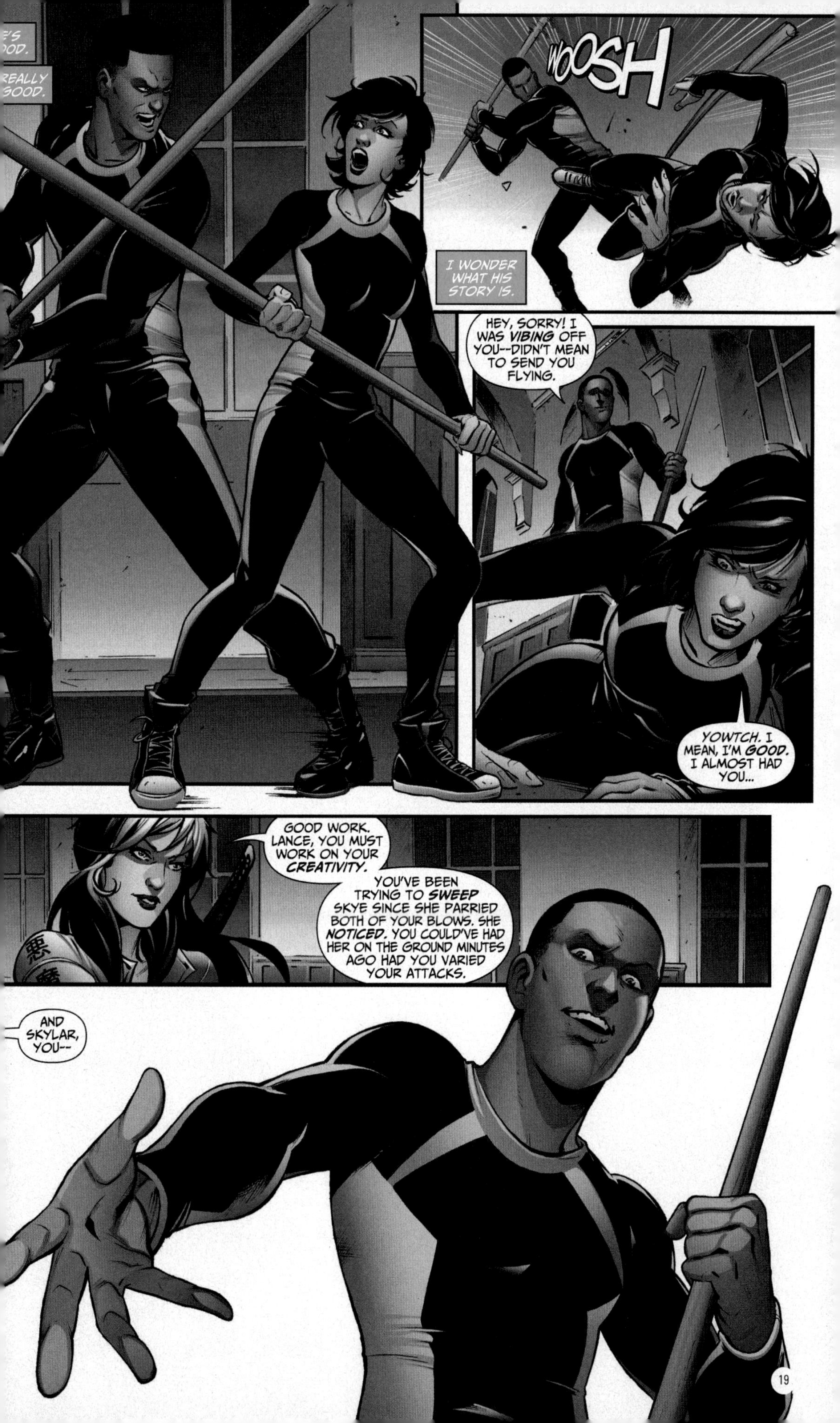

'S
OOD.
REALLY
GOOD.
WOOSH
I WONDER WHAT HIS STORY IS.
HEY, SORRY! I WAS VIBING OFF YOU--DIDN'T MEAN TO SEND YOU FLYING.
YOWTCH. I MEAN, I'M GOOD. I ALMOST HAD YOU...
GOOD WORK. LANCE, YOU MUST WORK ON YOUR CREATIVITY.
YOU'VE BEEN TRYING TO SWEEP SKYE SINCE SHE PARRIED BOTH OF YOUR BLOWS. SHE NOTICED. YOU COULD'VE HAD HER ON THE GROUND MINUTES AGO HAD YOU VARIED YOUR ATTACKS.
AND SKYLAR, YOU--

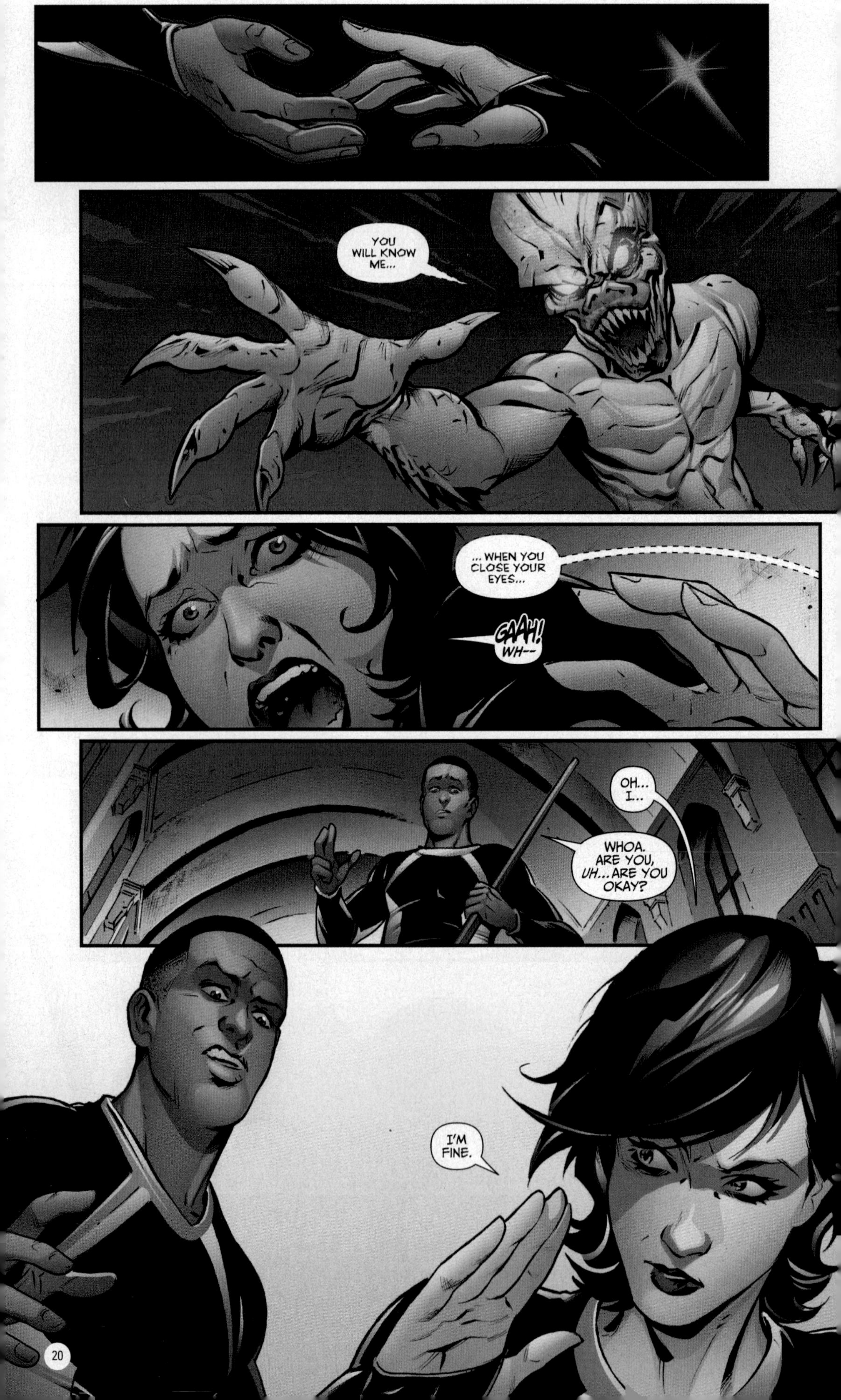

YOU WILL KNOW ME...
...WHEN YOU CLOSE YOUR EYES...
GAAH! WH--
OH... I...
WHOA. ARE YOU, UH... ARE YOU OKAY?
I'M FINE.

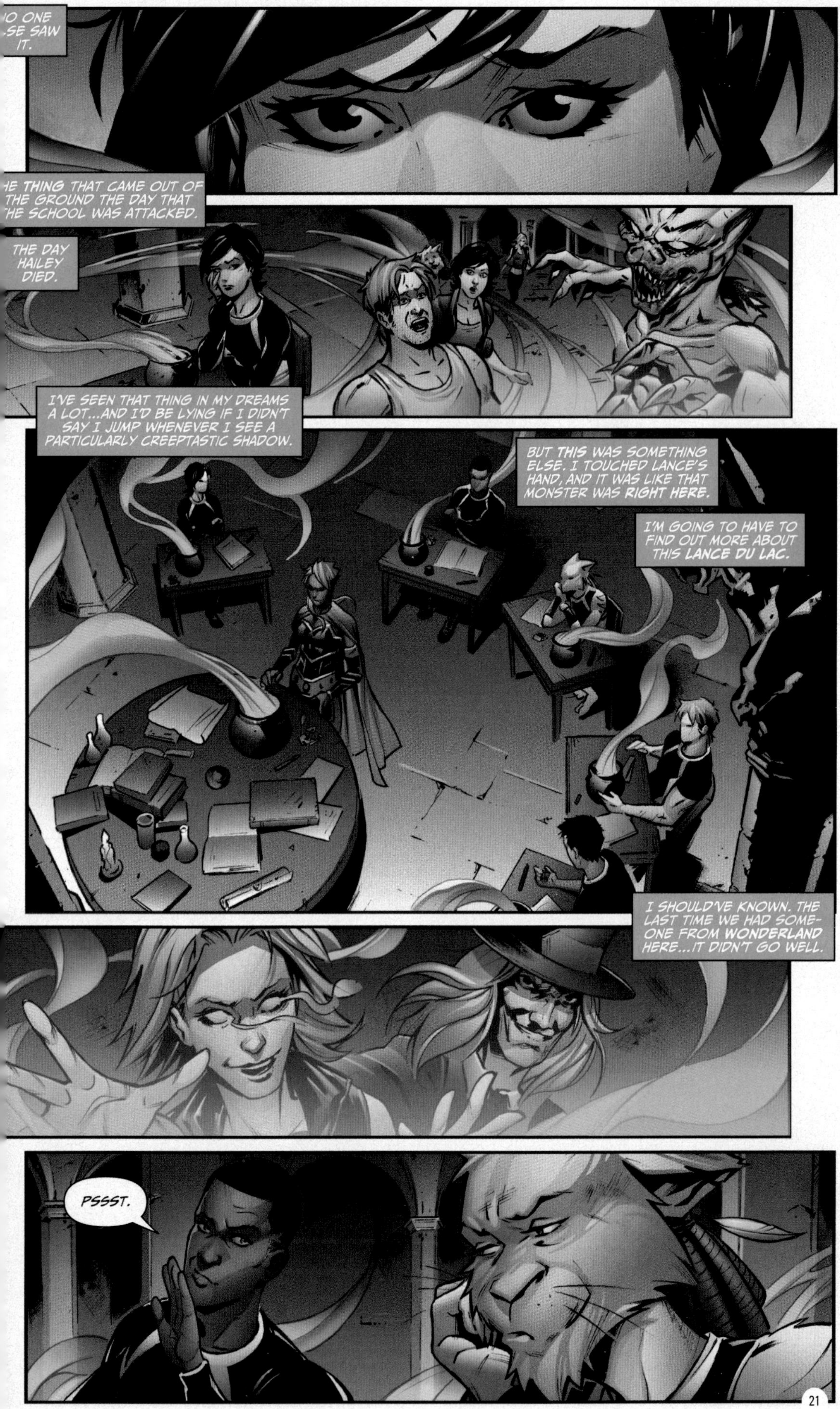
NO ONE ELSE SAW IT.
THE THING THAT CAME OUT OF THE GROUND THE DAY THAT THE SCHOOL WAS ATTACKED.
THE DAY HAILEY DIED.
I'VE SEEN THAT THING IN MY DREAMS A LOT...AND I'D BE LYING IF I DIDN'T SAY I JUMP WHENEVER I SEE A PARTICULARLY CREEPTASTIC SHADOW.
BUT THIS WAS SOMETHING ELSE. I TOUCHED LANCE'S HAND, AND IT WAS LIKE THAT MONSTER WAS RIGHT HERE.
I'M GOING TO HAVE TO FIND OUT MORE ABOUT THIS LANCE DU LAC.
I SHOULD'VE KNOWN. THE LAST TIME WE HAD SOME-ONE FROM WONDERLAND HERE...IT DIDN'T GO WELL.
PSSST.

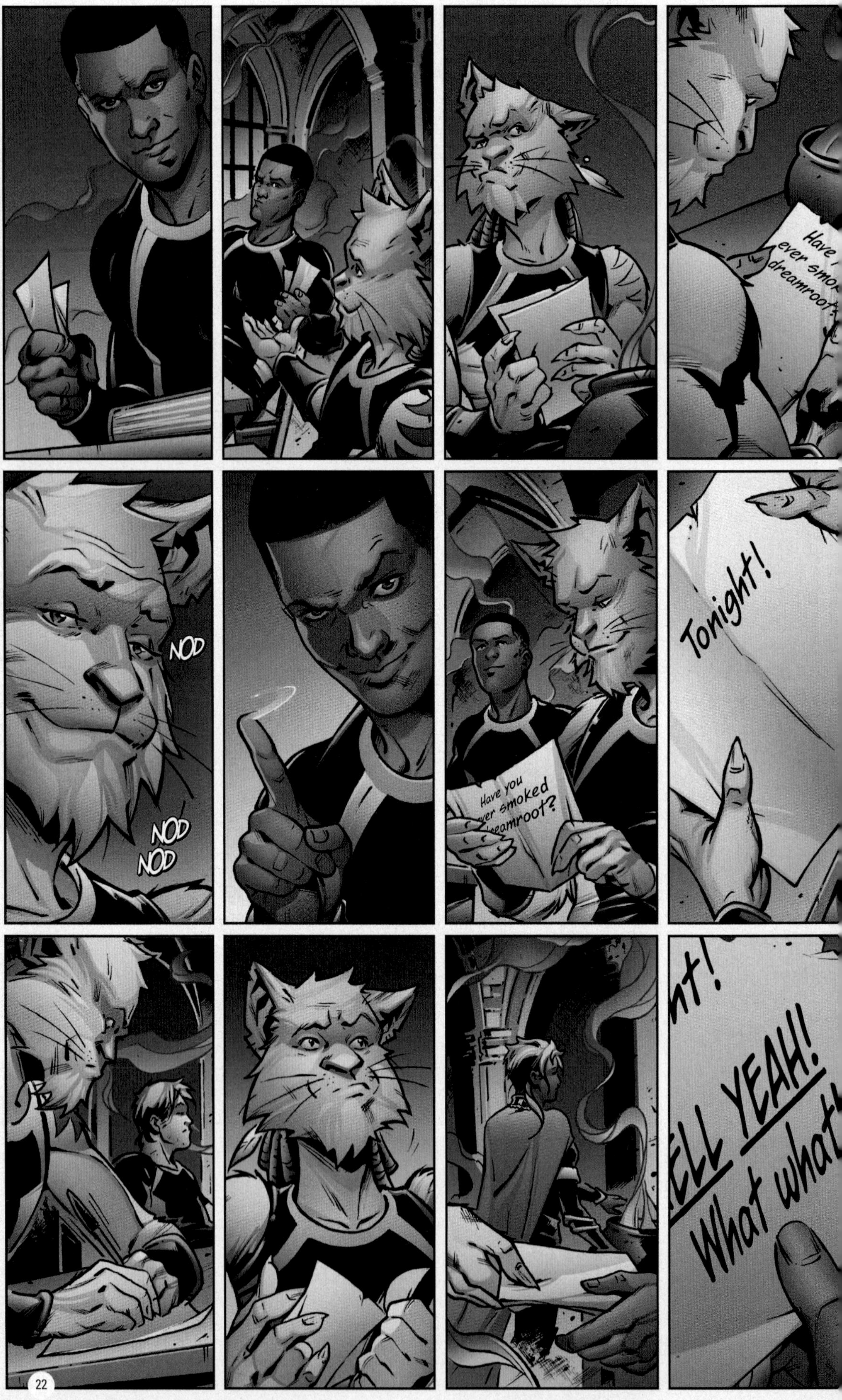
Have
ever smo
dreamroot?
NOD
NOD
NOD
Have you
ver smoked
eamroot?
Tonight!
nt!
ELL YEAH!
What what

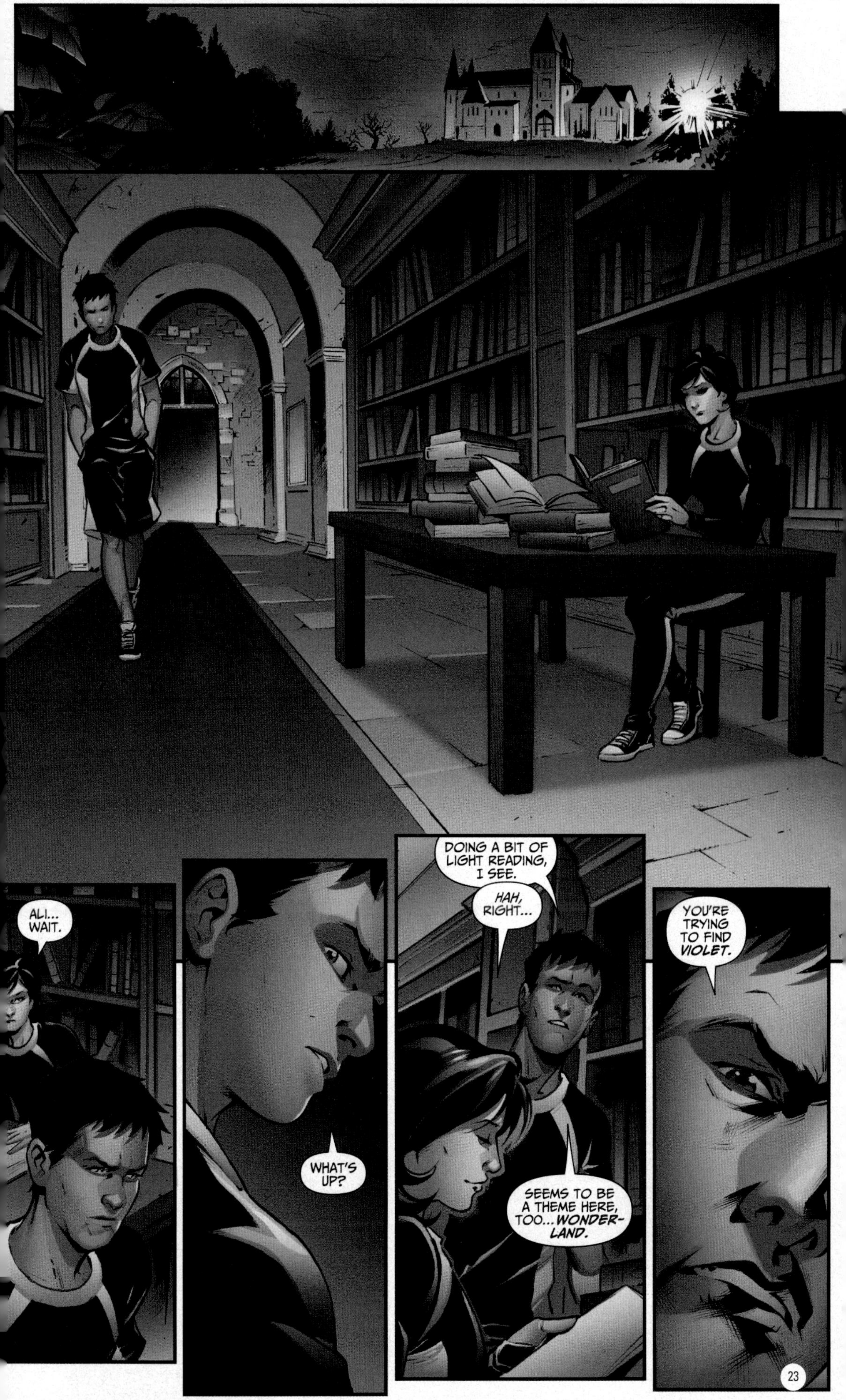
ALI... WAIT.
WHAT'S UP?
DOING A BIT OF LIGHT READING, I SEE.
HAH, RIGHT...
SEEMS TO BE A THEME HERE, TOO... WONDER-LAND.
YOU'RE TRYING TO FIND VIOLET.

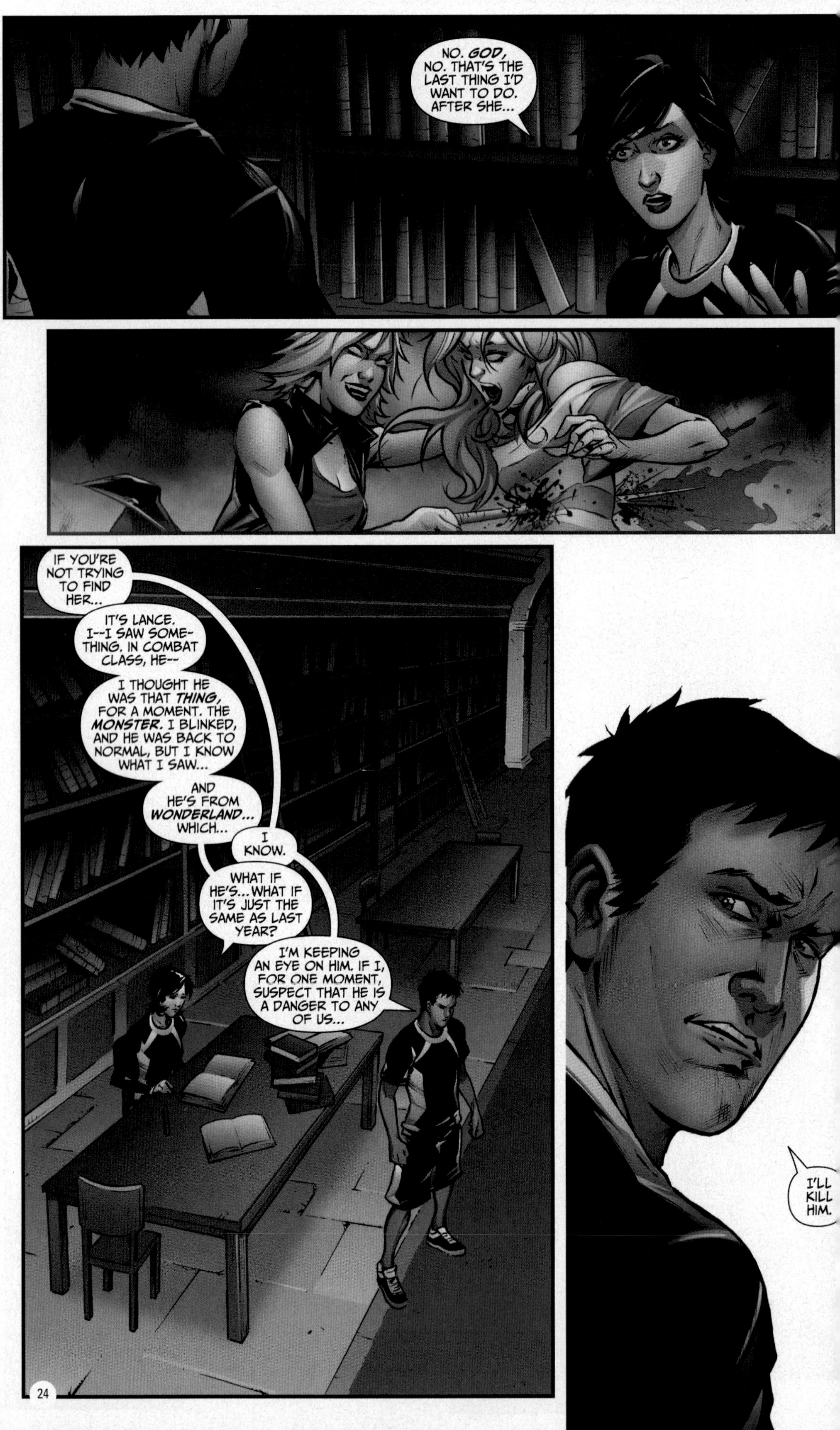
NO. GOD, NO. THAT'S THE LAST THING I'D WANT TO DO. AFTER SHE...
IF YOU'RE NOT TRYING TO FIND HER...
IT'S LANCE. I--I SAW SOMETHING. IN COMBAT CLASS, HE--
I THOUGHT HE WAS THAT THING, FOR A MOMENT. THE MONSTER. I BLINKED, AND HE WAS BACK TO NORMAL, BUT I KNOW WHAT I SAW...
AND HE'S FROM WONDERLAND... WHICH...
I KNOW.
WHAT IF HE'S... WHAT IF IT'S JUST THE SAME AS LAST YEAR?
I'M KEEPING AN EYE ON HIM. IF I, FOR ONE MOMENT, SUSPECT THAT HE IS A DANGER TO ANY OF US...
I'LL KILL HIM.

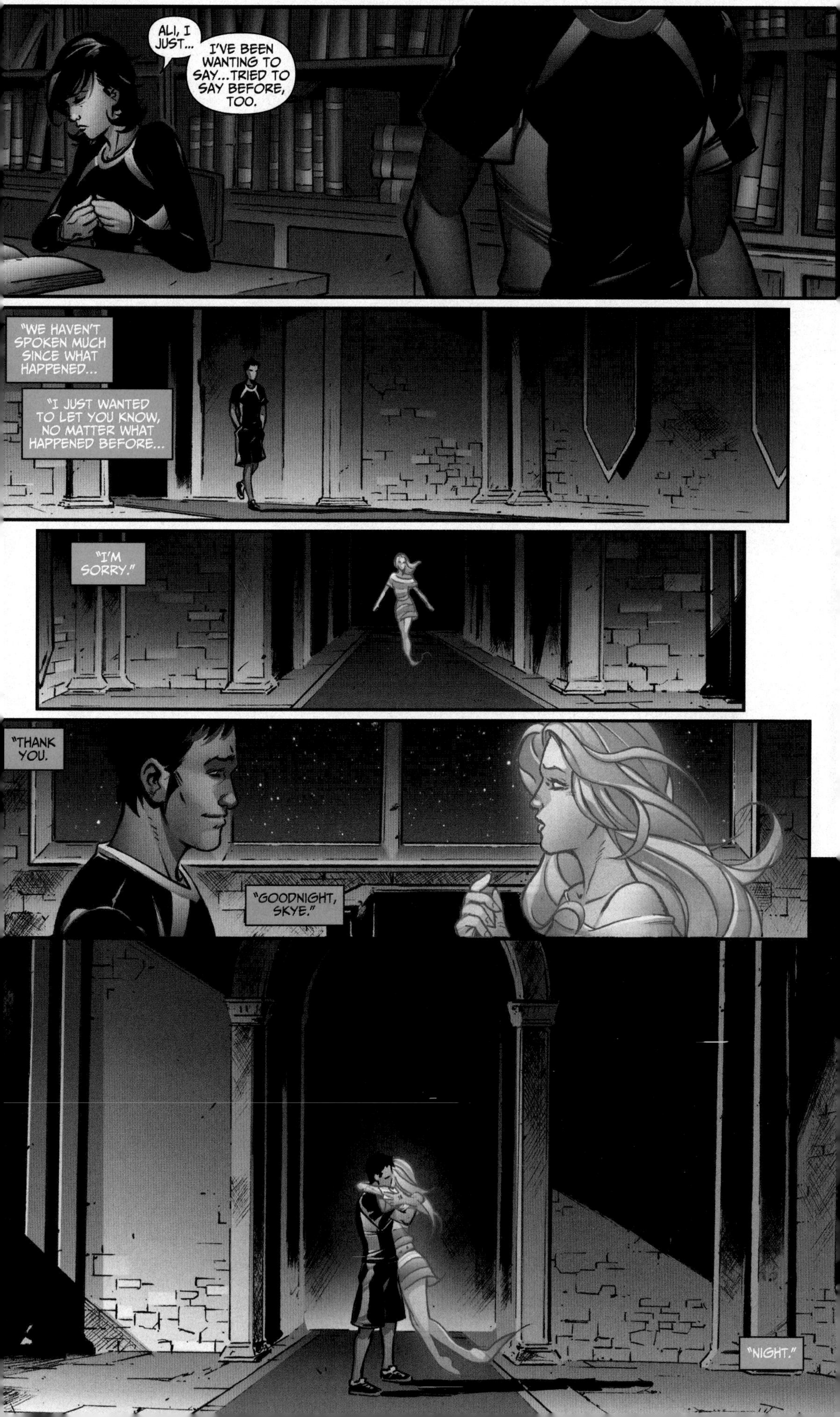
ALI, I JUST...
I'VE BEEN WANTING TO SAY...TRIED TO SAY BEFORE, TOO.
"WE HAVEN'T SPOKEN MUCH SINCE WHAT HAPPENED...
"I JUST WANTED TO LET YOU KNOW, NO MATTER WHAT HAPPENED BEFORE...
"I'M SORRY."
"THANK YOU.
"GOODNIGHT, SKYE."
"NIGHT."

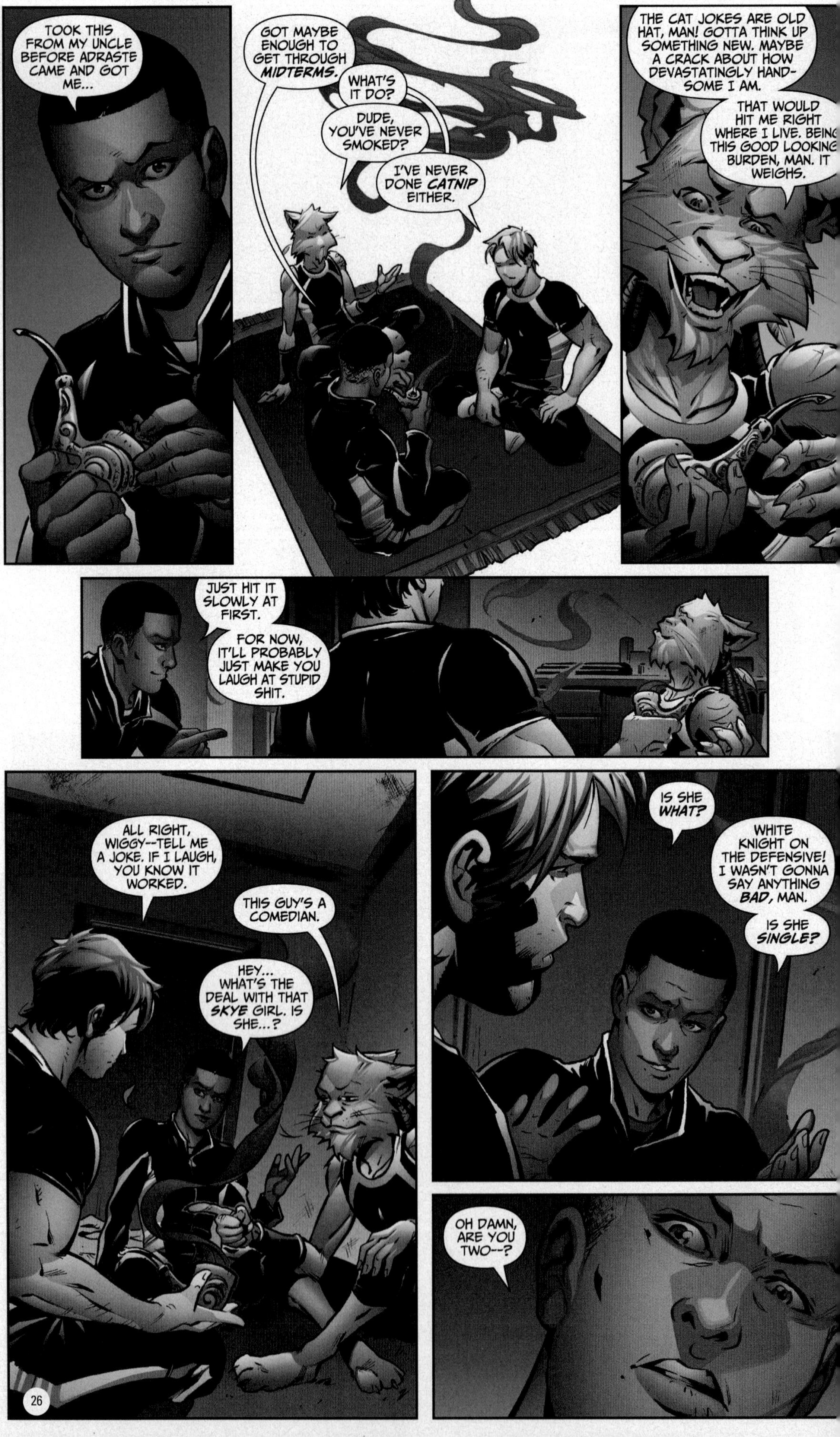

TOOK THIS FROM MY UNCLE BEFORE ADRASTE CAME AND GOT ME...
GOT MAYBE ENOUGH TO GET THROUGH MIDTERMS.
WHAT'S IT DO?
DUDE, YOU'VE NEVER SMOKED?
I'VE NEVER DONE CATNIP EITHER.
THE CAT JOKES ARE OLD HAT, MAN! GOTTA THINK UP SOMETHING NEW. MAYBE A CRACK ABOUT HOW DEVASTATINGLY HANDSOME I AM.
THAT WOULD HIT ME RIGHT WHERE I LIVE. BEING THIS GOOD LOOKING BURDEN, MAN. IT WEIGHS.
JUST HIT IT SLOWLY AT FIRST.
FOR NOW, IT'LL PROBABLY JUST MAKE YOU LAUGH AT STUPID SHIT.
ALL RIGHT, WIGGY--TELL ME A JOKE. IF I LAUGH, YOU KNOW IT WORKED.
THIS GUY'S A COMEDIAN.
HEY... WHAT'S THE DEAL WITH THAT SKYE GIRL. IS SHE...?
IS SHE WHAT?
WHITE KNIGHT ON THE DEFENSIVE! I WASN'T GONNA SAY ANYTHING BAD, MAN.
IS SHE SINGLE?
OH DAMN, ARE YOU TWO--?

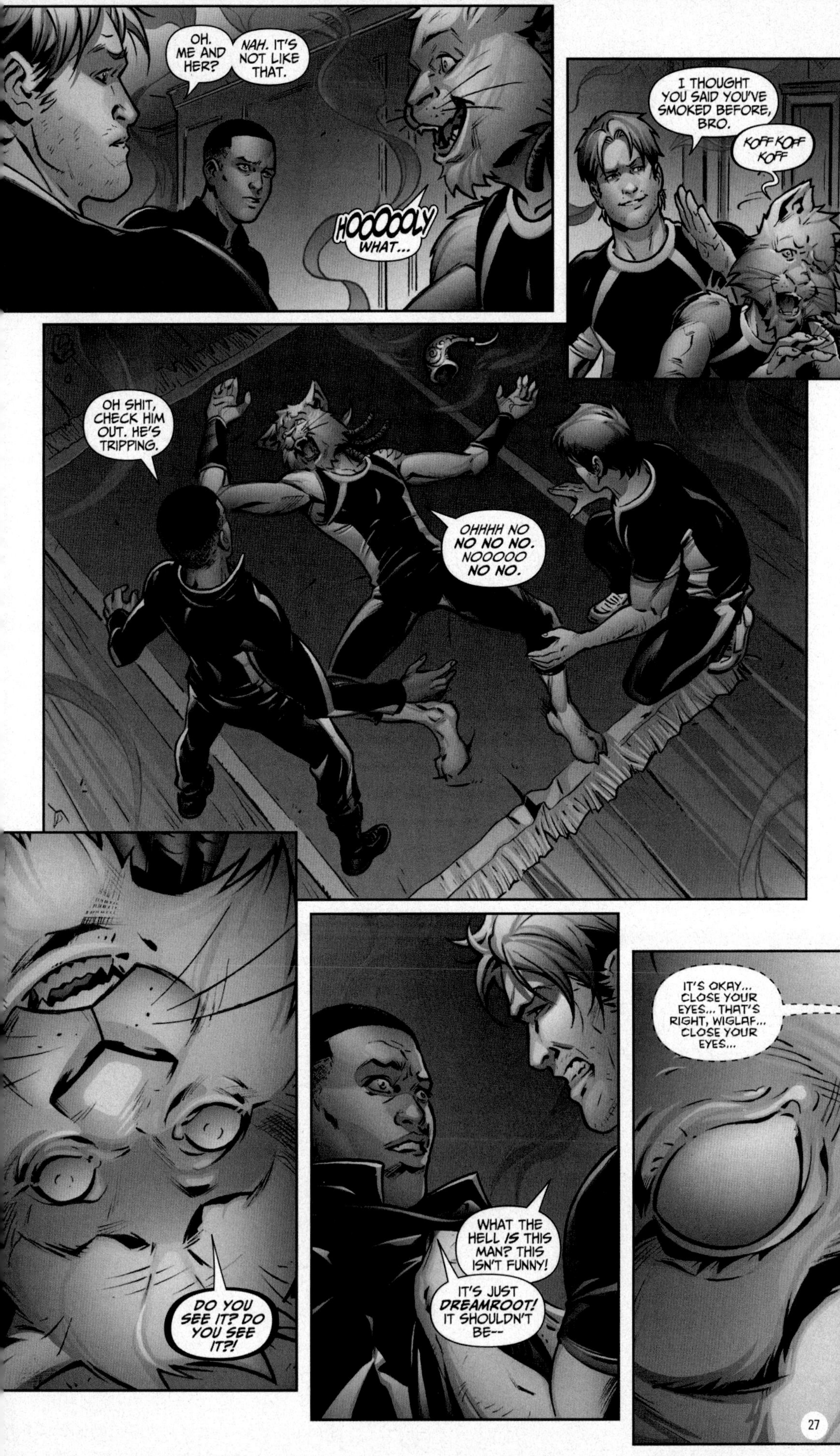
OH. ME AND HER?
NAH. IT'S NOT LIKE THAT.
HOOOOOLY WHAT...
I THOUGHT YOU SAID YOU'VE SMOKED BEFORE, BRO.
KOFF KOFF KOFF
OH SHIT, CHECK HIM OUT. HE'S TRIPPING.
OHHHH NO NO NO NO. NOOOOO NO NO.
DO YOU SEE IT? DO YOU SEE IT?!
WHAT THE HELL IS THIS MAN? THIS ISN'T FUNNY!
IT'S JUST DREAMROOT! IT SHOULDN'T BE--
IT'S OKAY... CLOSE YOUR EYES... THAT'S RIGHT, WIGLAF... CLOSE YOUR EYES...

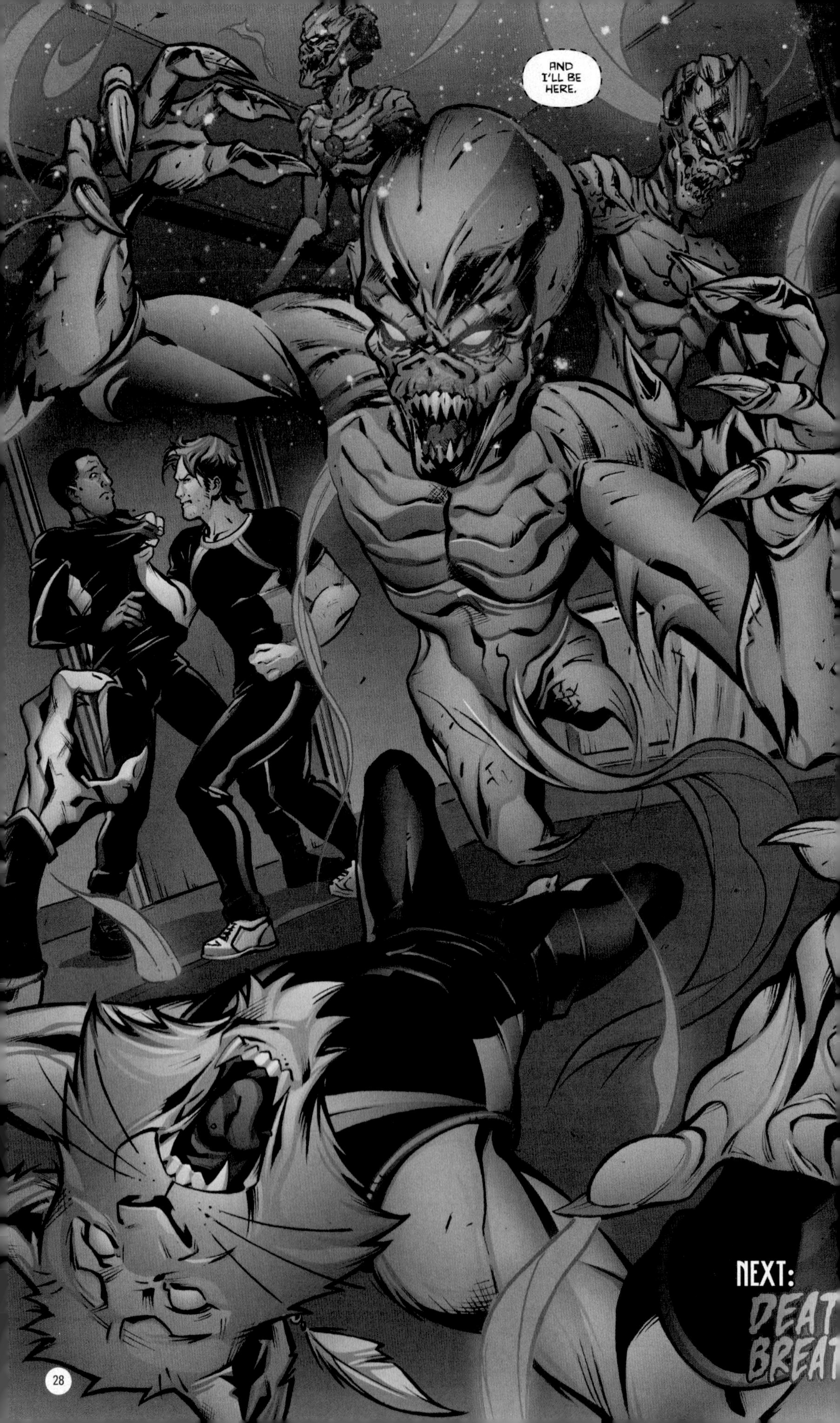
AND I'LL BE HERE.
NEXT:
DEAT
BREAT

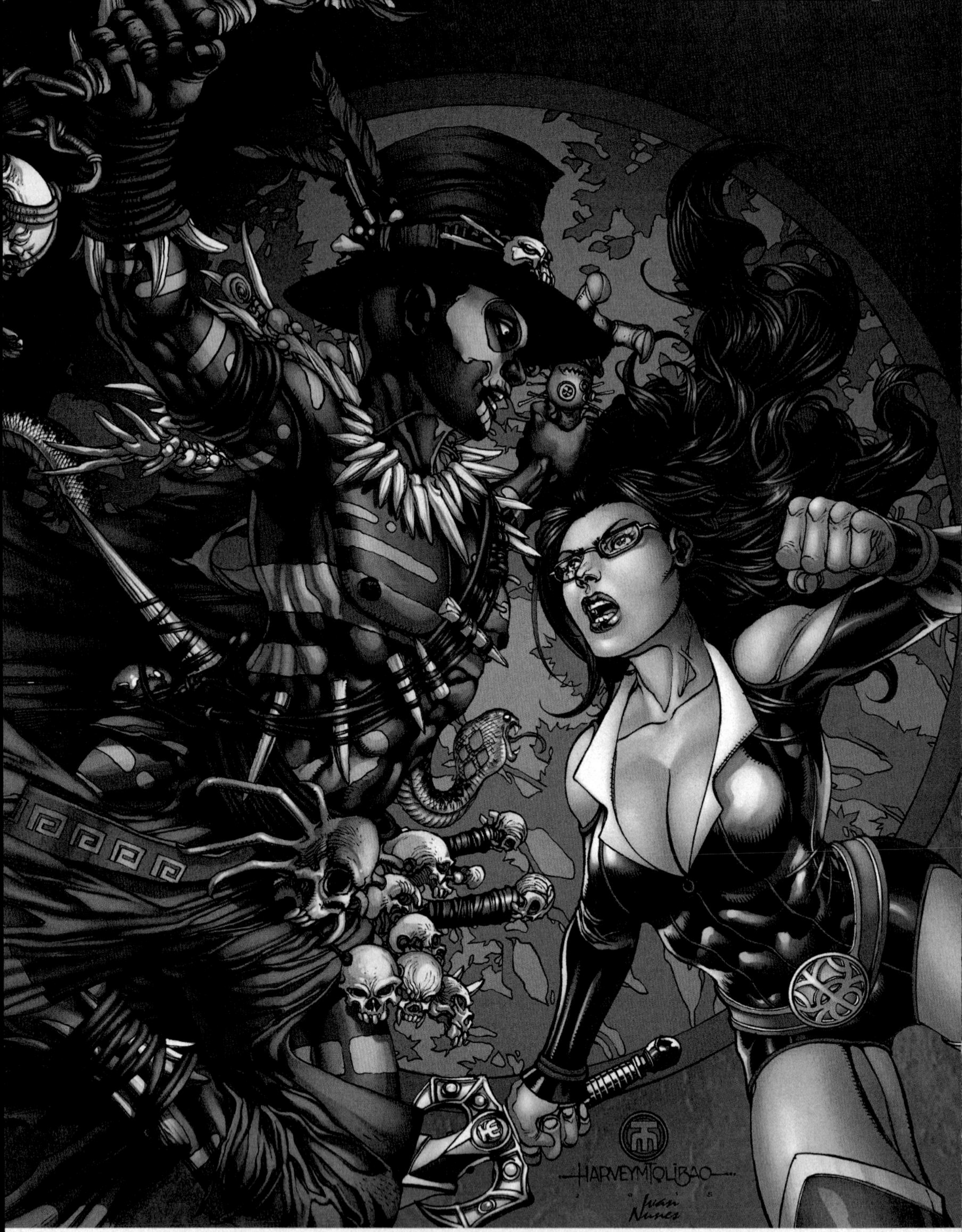
HARVEYMTOLIBAO
Juan Nunez

CHAPTER TWO

DEATH BREATH

WRITER
PAT SHAND

ARTWORK
DAVID LORENZO RIVEIRO

COLORS
ERICK ARCINIEGA

LETTERS
GHOST GLYPH STUDIO

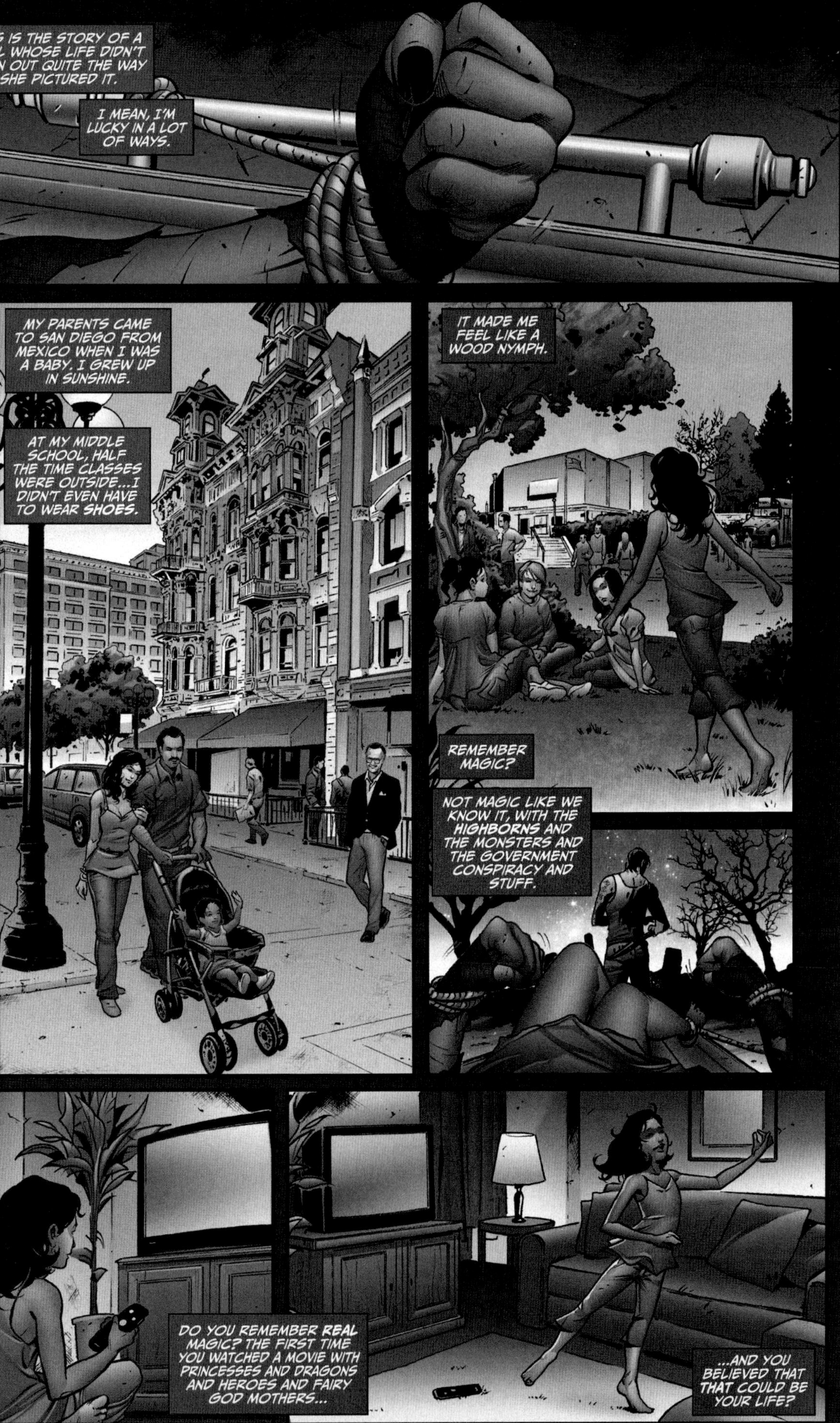

S IS THE STORY OF A
L WHOSE LIFE DIDN'T
N OUT QUITE THE WAY
SHE PICTURED IT.
I MEAN, I'M LUCKY IN A LOT OF WAYS.
MY PARENTS CAME TO SAN DIEGO FROM MEXICO WHEN I WAS A BABY. I GREW UP IN SUNSHINE.
AT MY MIDDLE SCHOOL, HALF THE TIME CLASSES WERE OUTSIDE...I DIDN'T EVEN HAVE TO WEAR SHOES.
IT MADE ME FEEL LIKE A WOOD NYMPH.
REMEMBER MAGIC?
NOT MAGIC LIKE WE KNOW IT, WITH THE HIGHBORNS AND THE MONSTERS AND THE GOVERNMENT CONSPIRACY AND STUFF.
DO YOU REMEMBER REAL MAGIC? THE FIRST TIME YOU WATCHED A MOVIE WITH PRINCESSES AND DRAGONS AND HEROES AND FAIRY GOD MOTHERS...
...AND YOU BELIEVED THAT THAT COULD BE YOUR LIFE?

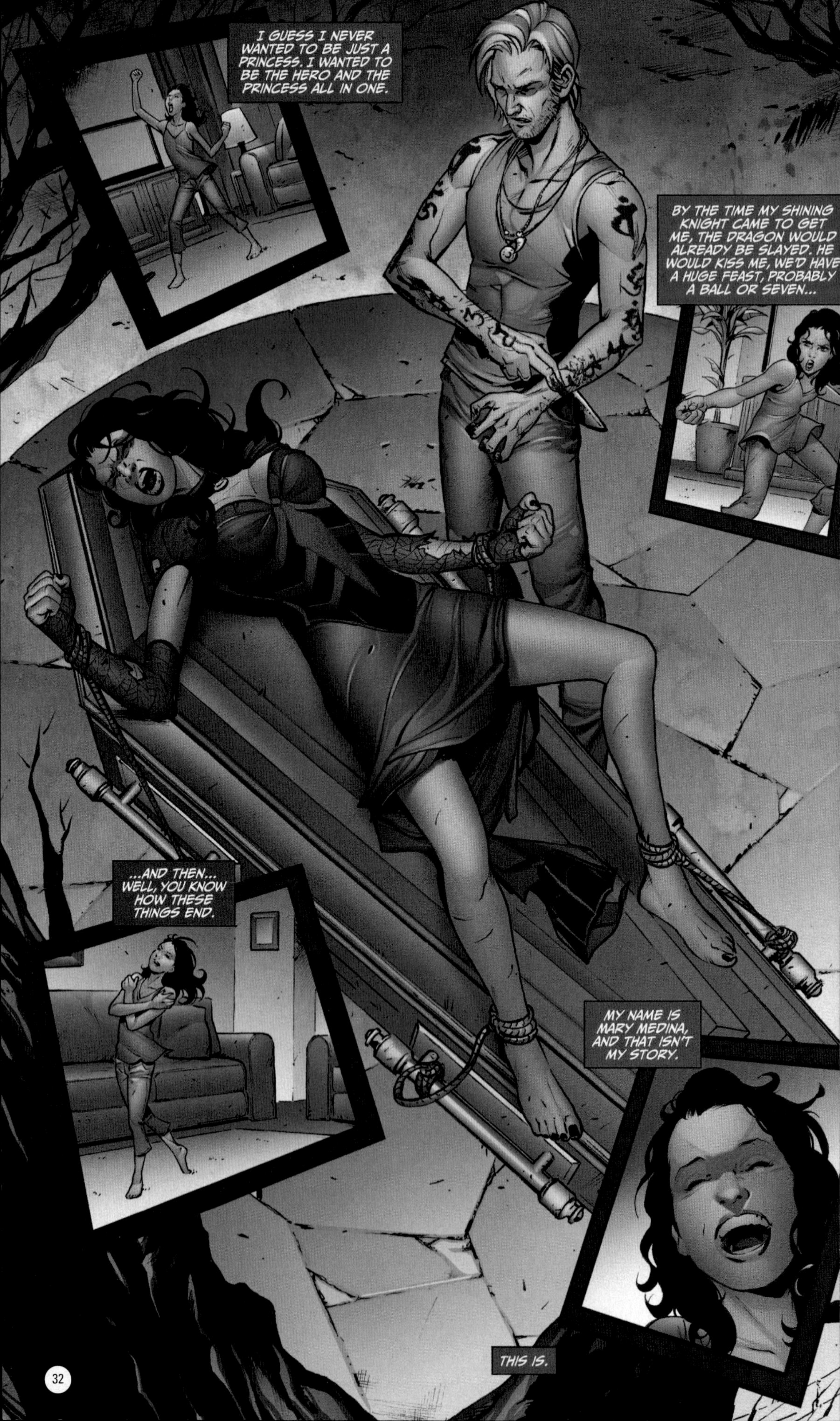
I GUESS I NEVER WANTED TO BE JUST A PRINCESS. I WANTED TO BE THE HERO AND THE PRINCESS ALL IN ONE.
BY THE TIME MY SHINING KNIGHT CAME TO GET ME, THE DRAGON WOULD ALREADY BE SLAYED. HE WOULD KISS ME, WE'D HAVE A HUGE FEAST, PROBABLY A BALL OR SEVEN...
...AND THEN... WELL, YOU KNOW HOW THESE THINGS END.
MY NAME IS MARY MEDINA, AND THAT ISN'T MY STORY.
THIS IS.

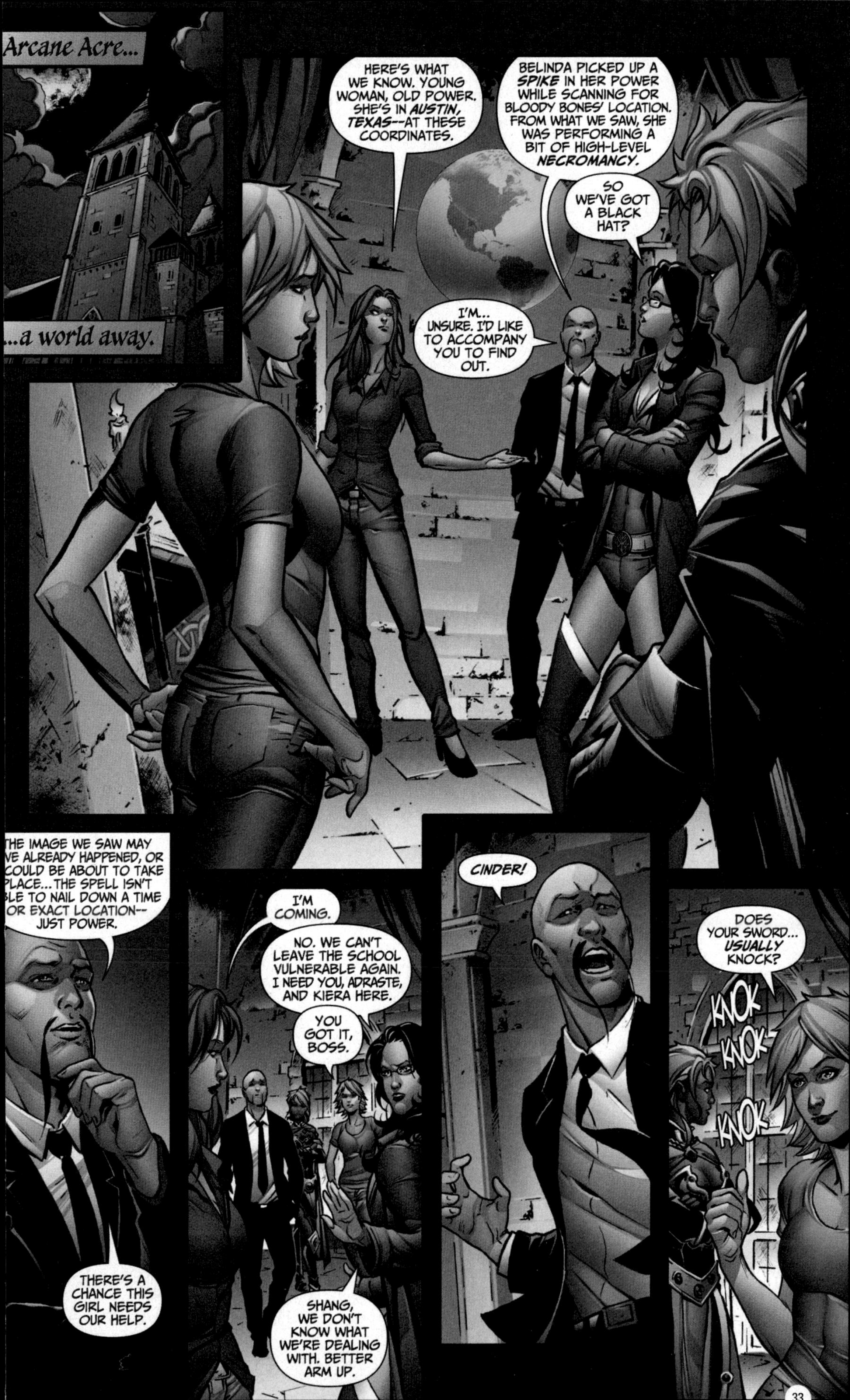

Arcane Acre...
...a world away.
HERE'S WHAT WE KNOW. YOUNG WOMAN, OLD POWER. SHE'S IN AUSTIN, TEXAS--AT THESE COORDINATES.
BELINDA PICKED UP A SPIKE IN HER POWER WHILE SCANNING FOR BLOODY BONES' LOCATION. FROM WHAT WE SAW, SHE WAS PERFORMING A BIT OF HIGH-LEVEL NECROMANCY.
SO WE'VE GOT A BLACK HAT?
I'M... UNSURE. I'D LIKE TO ACCOMPANY YOU TO FIND OUT.
THE IMAGE WE SAW MAY VE ALREADY HAPPENED, OR COULD BE ABOUT TO TAKE PLACE... THE SPELL ISN'T BLE TO NAIL DOWN A TIME OR EXACT LOCATION-- JUST POWER.
THERE'S A CHANCE THIS GIRL NEEDS OUR HELP.
I'M COMING.
NO. WE CAN'T LEAVE THE SCHOOL VULNERABLE AGAIN. I NEED YOU, ADRASTE, AND KIERA HERE.
YOU GOT IT, BOSS.
SHANG, WE DON'T KNOW WHAT WE'RE DEALING WITH. BETTER ARM UP.
CINDER!
DOES YOUR SWORD... USUALLY KNOCK?
KNOK
KNOK
KNOK

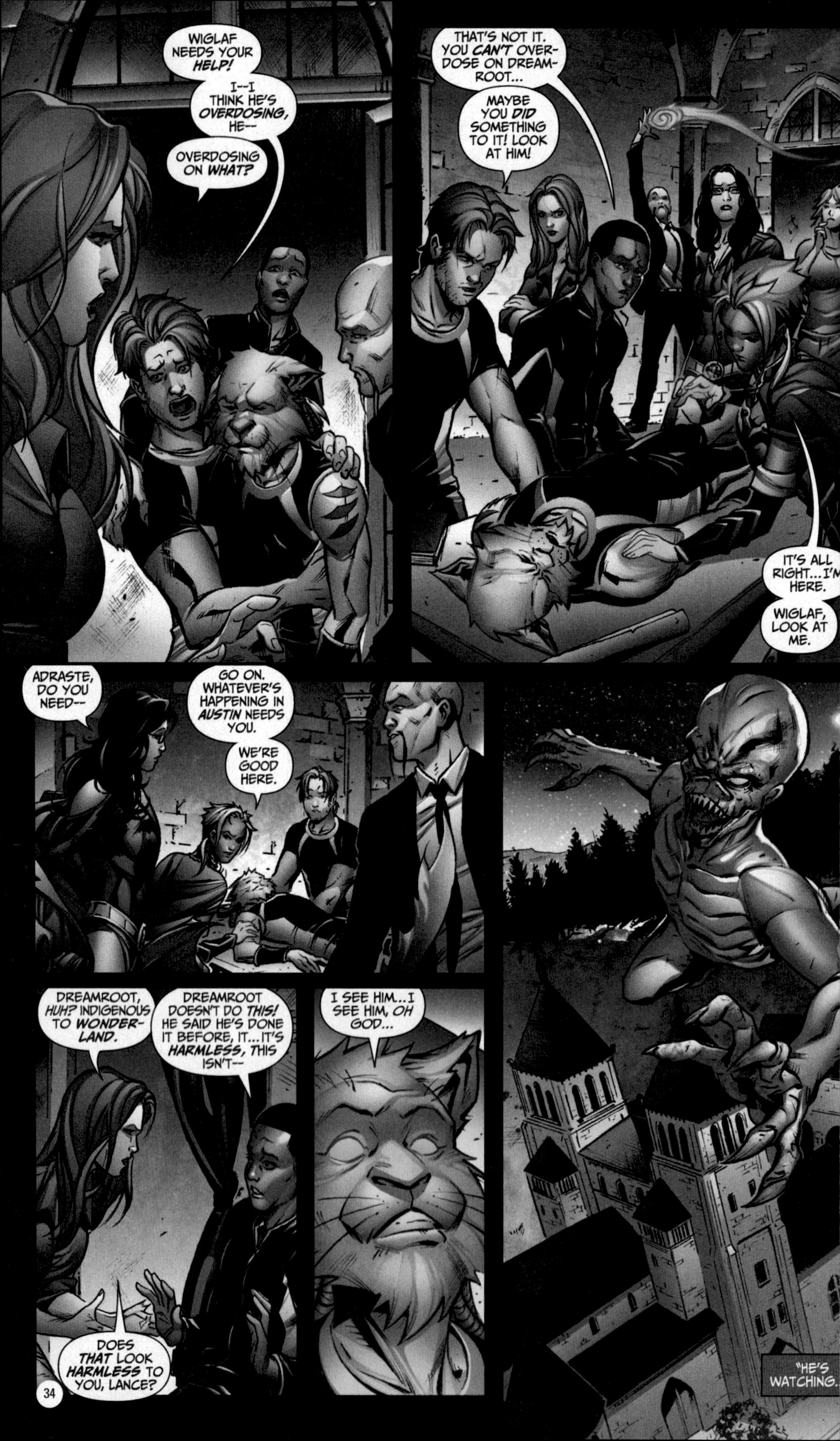
WIGLAF NEEDS YOUR HELP!
I--I THINK HE'S OVERDOSING, HE--
OVERDOSING ON WHAT?
THAT'S NOT IT. YOU CAN'T OVERDOSE ON DREAMROOT...
MAYBE YOU DID SOMETHING TO IT! LOOK AT HIM!
IT'S ALL RIGHT... I'M HERE.
WIGLAF, LOOK AT ME.
ADRASTE, DO YOU NEED--
GO ON. WHATEVER'S HAPPENING IN AUSTIN NEEDS YOU.
WE'RE GOOD HERE.
DREAMROOT, HUH? INDIGENOUS TO WONDERLAND.
DREAMROOT DOESN'T DO THIS! HE SAID HE'S DONE IT BEFORE, IT... IT'S HARMLESS, THIS ISN'T--
DOES THAT LOOK HARMLESS TO YOU, LANCE?
I SEE HIM... I SEE HIM, OH GOD...
"HE'S WATCHING.

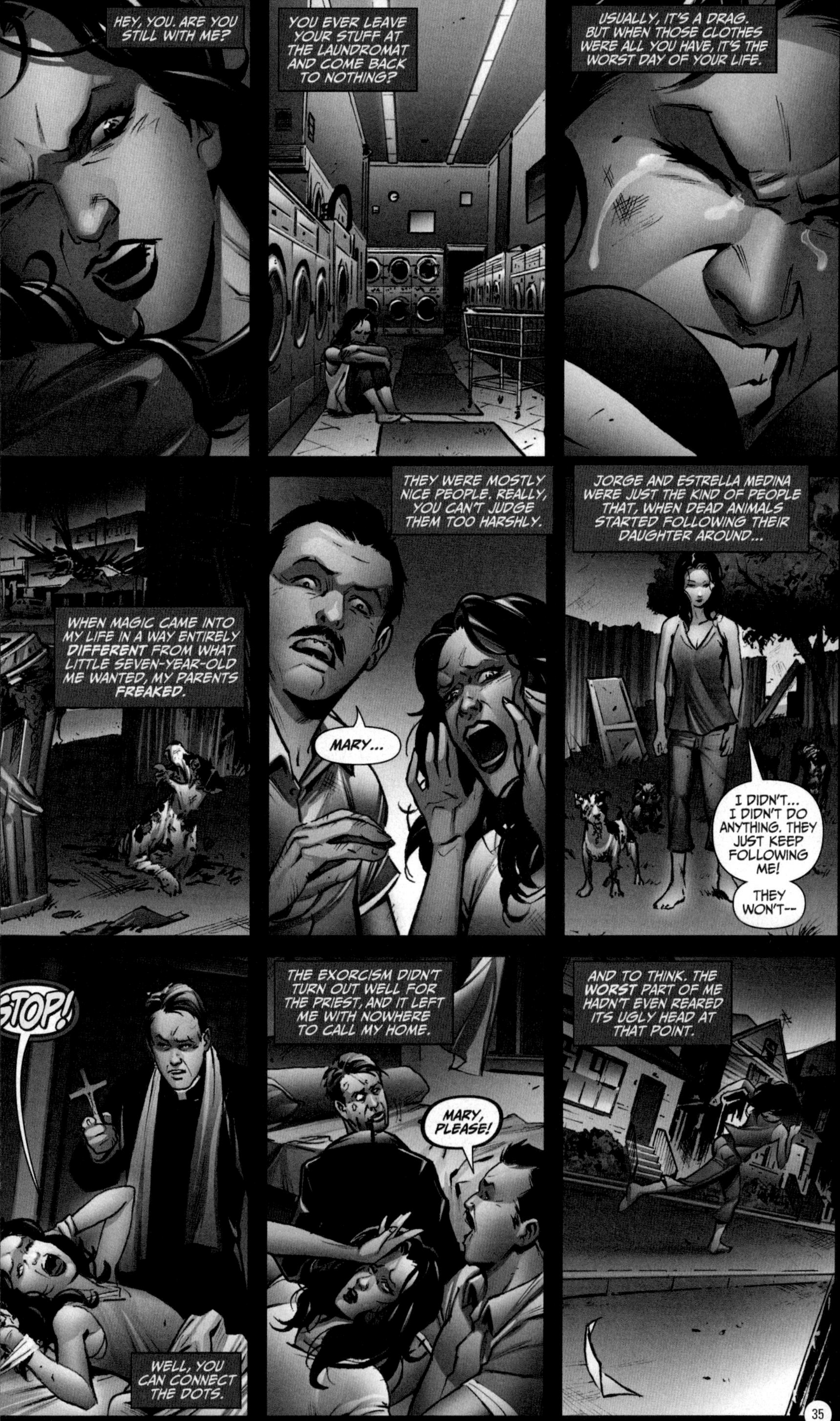

HEY, YOU. ARE YOU STILL WITH ME?
YOU EVER LEAVE YOUR STUFF AT THE LAUNDROMAT AND COME BACK TO NOTHING?
USUALLY, IT'S A DRAG. BUT WHEN THOSE CLOTHES WERE ALL YOU HAVE, IT'S THE WORST DAY OF YOUR LIFE.
WHEN MAGIC CAME INTO MY LIFE IN A WAY ENTIRELY DIFFERENT FROM WHAT LITTLE SEVEN-YEAR-OLD ME WANTED, MY PARENTS FREAKED.
THEY WERE MOSTLY NICE PEOPLE. REALLY, YOU CAN'T JUDGE THEM TOO HARSHLY.
MARY...
JORGE AND ESTRELLA MEDINA WERE JUST THE KIND OF PEOPLE THAT, WHEN DEAD ANIMALS STARTED FOLLOWING THEIR DAUGHTER AROUND...
I DIDN'T... I DIDN'T DO ANYTHING. THEY JUST KEEP FOLLOWING ME!
THEY WON'T--
STOP!
WELL, YOU CAN CONNECT THE DOTS.
THE EXORCISM DIDN'T TURN OUT WELL FOR THE PRIEST, AND IT LEFT ME WITH NOWHERE TO CALL MY HOME.
MARY, PLEASE!
AND TO THINK. THE WORST PART OF ME HADN'T EVEN REARED ITS UGLY HEAD AT THAT POINT.

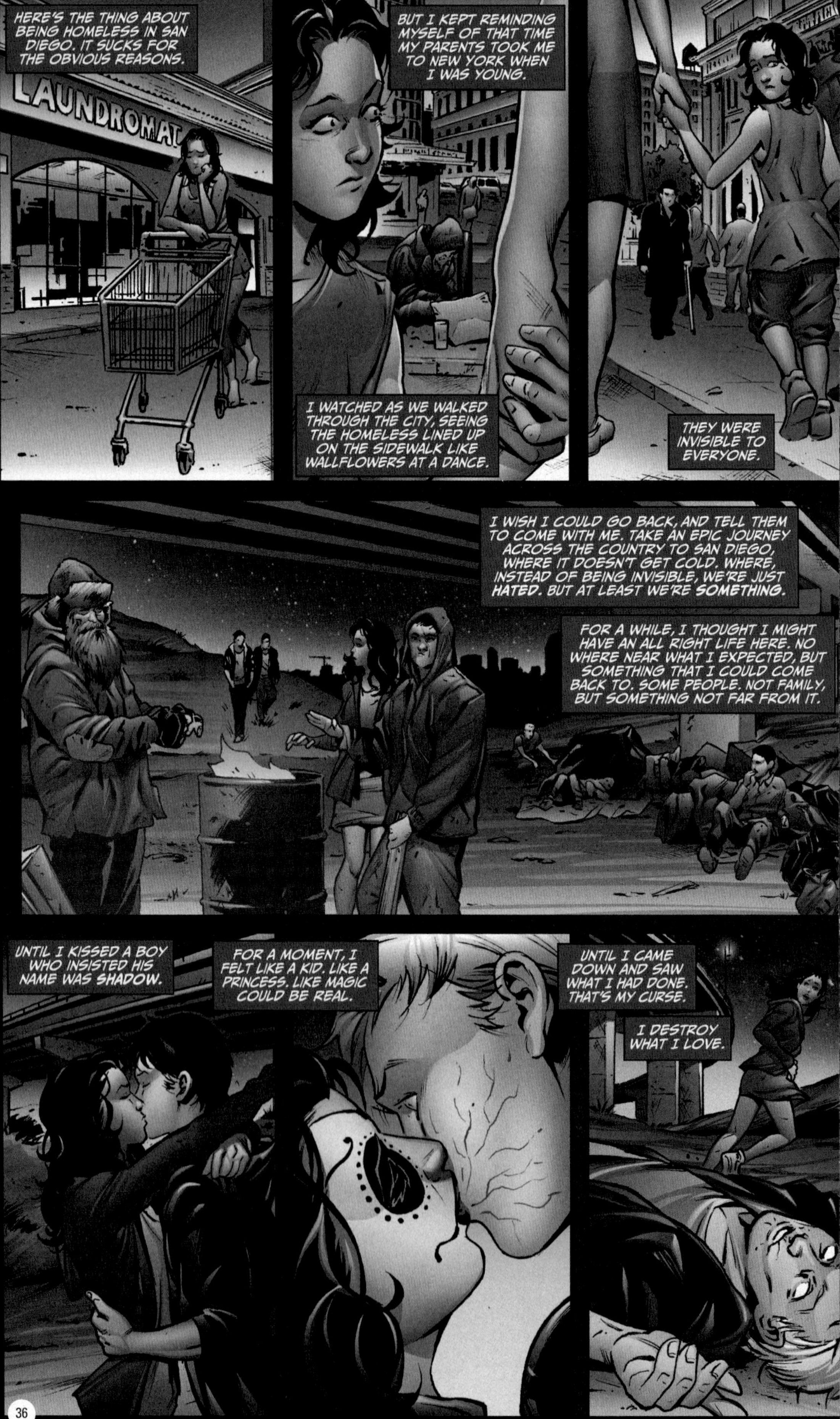
HERE'S THE THING ABOUT BEING HOMELESS IN SAN DIEGO. IT SUCKS FOR THE OBVIOUS REASONS.
LAUNDROMAT
BUT I KEPT REMINDING MYSELF OF THAT TIME MY PARENTS TOOK ME TO NEW YORK WHEN I WAS YOUNG.
I WATCHED AS WE WALKED THROUGH THE CITY, SEEING THE HOMELESS LINED UP ON THE SIDEWALK LIKE WALLFLOWERS AT A DANCE.
THEY WERE INVISIBLE TO EVERYONE.
I WISH I COULD GO BACK, AND TELL THEM TO COME WITH ME. TAKE AN EPIC JOURNEY ACROSS THE COUNTRY TO SAN DIEGO, WHERE IT DOESN'T GET COLD. WHERE, INSTEAD OF BEING INVISIBLE, WE'RE JUST **HATED**. BUT AT LEAST WE'RE **SOMETHING**.
FOR A WHILE, I THOUGHT I MIGHT HAVE AN ALL RIGHT LIFE HERE. NO WHERE NEAR WHAT I EXPECTED, BUT SOMETHING THAT I COULD COME BACK TO. SOME PEOPLE. NOT FAMILY, BUT SOMETHING NOT FAR FROM IT.
UNTIL I KISSED A BOY WHO INSISTED HIS NAME WAS **SHADOW**.
FOR A MOMENT, I FELT LIKE A KID. LIKE A PRINCESS. LIKE MAGIC COULD BE REAL.
UNTIL I CAME DOWN AND SAW WHAT I HAD DONE. THAT'S MY CURSE.
I DESTROY WHAT I LOVE.

I LIVED ALONE ON THE STREETS FOR A WHILE. THERE WERE A FEW NIGHTS WHERE IT GOT BAD...WHERE I GOT BAD.

BUT I ALWAYS ENDED UP OKAY, I SUPPOSE. WHATEVER THAT MEANS.

UNTIL HE CAME ALONG.

HE TOLD ME HE KNEW WHAT I WAS. HE'D BEEN WATCHING ME SINCE THE PRIEST WAS REPORTED DEAD. HE SAW WHAT I DID TO SHADOW. HE COULD HELP ME.

I DON'T KNOW IF I EVER BELIEVED HIM, BUT I DIDN'T CARE ENOUGH ABOUT MYSELF TO WORRY WHAT WOULD HAPPEN IF I FOLLOWED HIM.

I KNOW YOU FEEL THEM.

THE DEAD, ROTTING BENEATH US.

I FELT AS IF I WERE IN HIS TRUNK FOR DAYS. MAYBE I WAS.

MAKE THEM RISE! MAKE THEM MINE TO COMMAND.

WH-- WHY? WHY DO YOU--

HE TOOK ME OUT, HIT ME OVER THE HEAD--NOT FOR THE FIRST TIME--AND I WOKE UP TIED TO A COFFIN.

JUST DO IT!

AND THAT'S KINDA HOW THIS WHOLE THING REALLY STARTS, ISN'T IT?

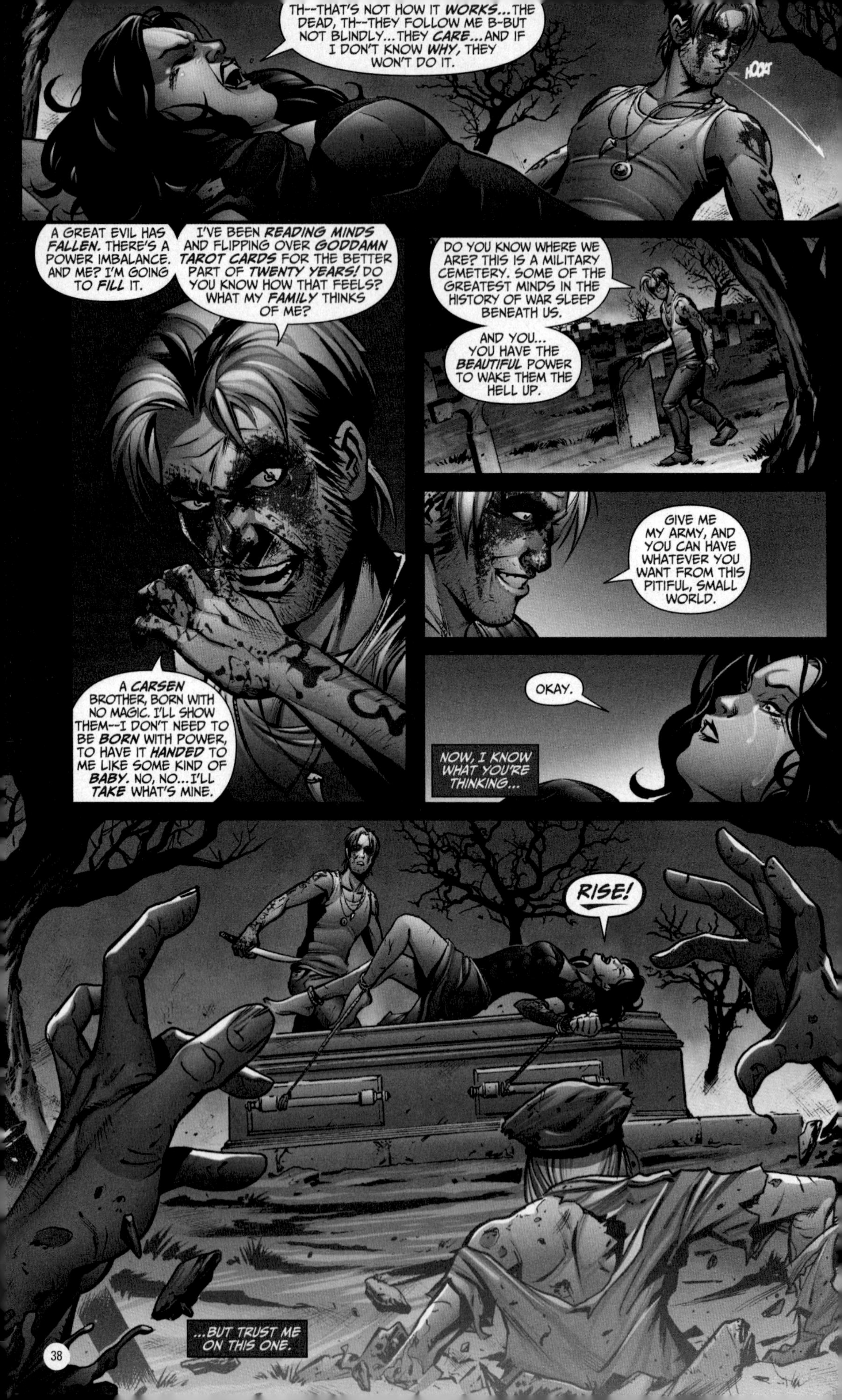
TH--THAT'S NOT HOW IT WORKS...THE DEAD, TH--THEY FOLLOW ME B-BUT NOT BLINDLY...THEY CARE...AND IF I DON'T KNOW WHY, THEY WON'T DO IT.
A GREAT EVIL HAS FALLEN. THERE'S A POWER IMBALANCE. AND ME? I'M GOING TO FILL IT.
I'VE BEEN READING MINDS AND FLIPPING OVER GODDAMN TAROT CARDS FOR THE BETTER PART OF TWENTY YEARS! DO YOU KNOW HOW THAT FEELS? WHAT MY FAMILY THINKS OF ME?
A CARSEN BROTHER, BORN WITH NO MAGIC. I'LL SHOW THEM--I DON'T NEED TO BE BORN WITH POWER, TO HAVE IT HANDED TO ME LIKE SOME KIND OF BABY. NO, NO...I'LL TAKE WHAT'S MINE.
DO YOU KNOW WHERE WE ARE? THIS IS A MILITARY CEMETERY. SOME OF THE GREATEST MINDS IN THE HISTORY OF WAR SLEEP BENEATH US.
AND YOU... YOU HAVE THE BEAUTIFUL POWER TO WAKE THEM THE HELL UP.
GIVE ME MY ARMY, AND YOU CAN HAVE WHATEVER YOU WANT FROM THIS PITIFUL, SMALL WORLD.
OKAY.
NOW, I KNOW WHAT YOU'RE THINKING...
RISE!
...BUT TRUST ME ON THIS ONE.

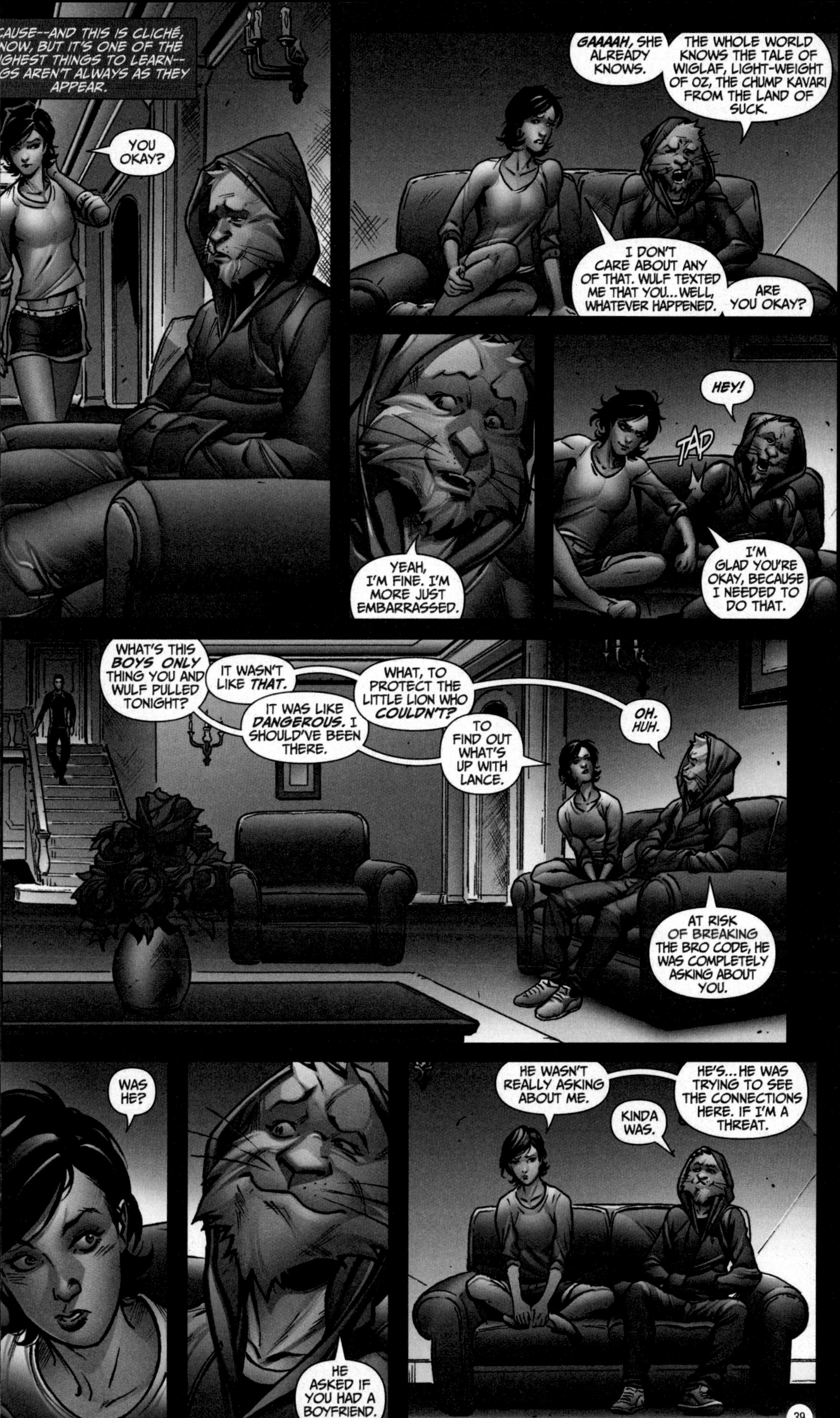
CAUSE--AND THIS IS CLICHÉ, NOW, BUT IT'S ONE OF THE UGHEST THINGS TO LEARN-- GS AREN'T ALWAYS AS THEY APPEAR.
YOU OKAY?
GAAAAH, SHE ALREADY KNOWS.
THE WHOLE WORLD KNOWS THE TALE OF WIGLAF, LIGHT-WEIGHT OF OZ, THE CHUMP KAVARI FROM THE LAND OF SUCK.
I DON'T CARE ABOUT ANY OF THAT. WULF TEXTED ME THAT YOU...WELL, WHATEVER HAPPENED.
ARE YOU OKAY?
YEAH, I'M FINE. I'M MORE JUST EMBARRASSED.
HEY!
TAP
I'M GLAD YOU'RE OKAY, BECAUSE I NEEDED TO DO THAT.
WHAT'S THIS BOYS ONLY THING YOU AND WULF PULLED TONIGHT?
IT WASN'T LIKE THAT.
WHAT, TO PROTECT THE LITTLE LION WHO COULDN'T?
IT WAS LIKE DANGEROUS. I SHOULD'VE BEEN THERE.
TO FIND OUT WHAT'S UP WITH LANCE.
OH. HUH.
AT RISK OF BREAKING THE BRO CODE, HE WAS COMPLETELY ASKING ABOUT YOU.
WAS HE?
HE ASKED IF YOU HAD A BOYFRIEND.
HE WASN'T REALLY ASKING ABOUT ME.
KINDA WAS.
HE'S...HE WAS TRYING TO SEE THE CONNECTIONS HERE. IF I'M A THREAT.

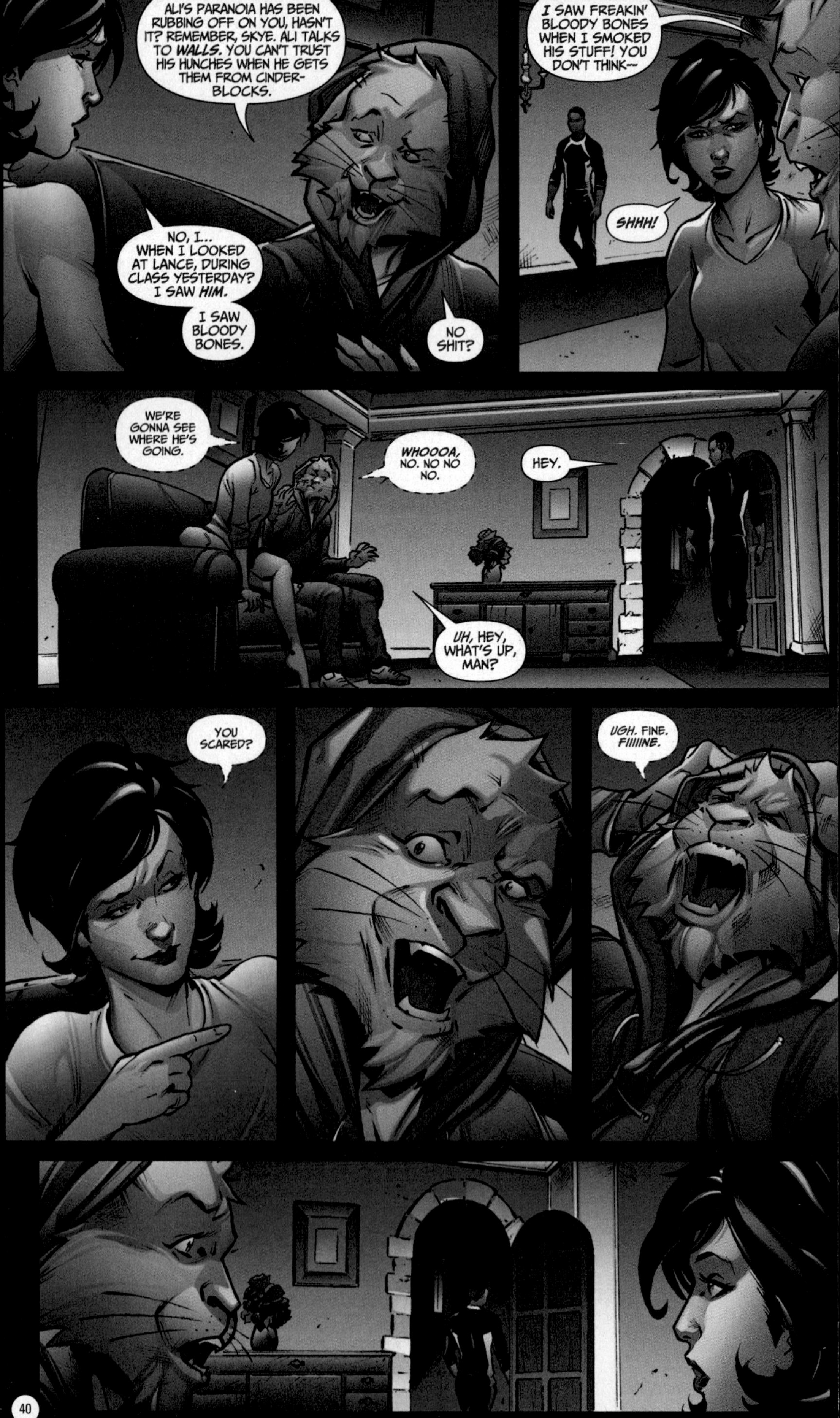
ALI'S PARANOIA HAS BEEN RUBBING OFF ON YOU, HASN'T IT? REMEMBER, SKYE. ALI TALKS TO *WALLS*. YOU CAN'T TRUST HIS HUNCHES WHEN HE GETS THEM FROM CINDER-BLOCKS.
NO, I... WHEN I LOOKED AT LANCE, DURING CLASS YESTERDAY? I SAW *HIM*.
I SAW BLOODY BONES.
NO SHIT?
I SAW FREAKIN' BLOODY BONES WHEN I SMOKED HIS STUFF! YOU DON'T THINK--
SHHH!
WE'RE GONNA SEE WHERE HE'S GOING.
WHOOOA, NO. NO NO NO.
HEY.
UH, HEY, WHAT'S UP, MAN?
YOU SCARED?
UGH. FINE. *FIIIIINE.*

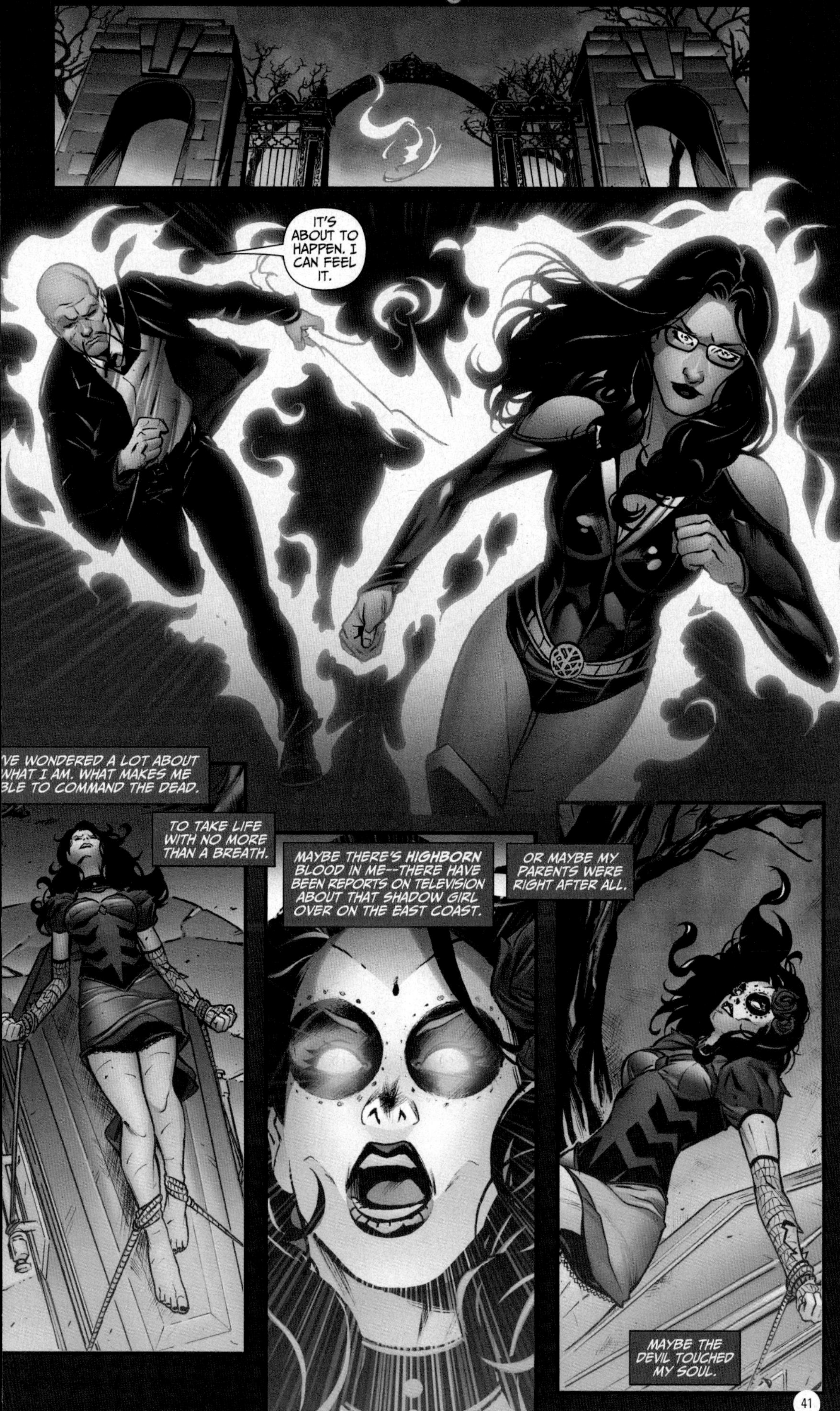

IT'S ABOUT TO HAPPEN. I CAN FEEL IT.
'VE WONDERED A LOT ABOUT WHAT I AM. WHAT MAKES ME BLE TO COMMAND THE DEAD.
TO TAKE LIFE WITH NO MORE THAN A BREATH.
MAYBE THERE'S HIGHBORN BLOOD IN ME--THERE HAVE BEEN REPORTS ON TELEVISION ABOUT THAT SHADOW GIRL OVER ON THE EAST COAST.
OR MAYBE MY PARENTS WERE RIGHT AFTER ALL.
MAYBE THE DEVIL TOUCHED MY SOUL.

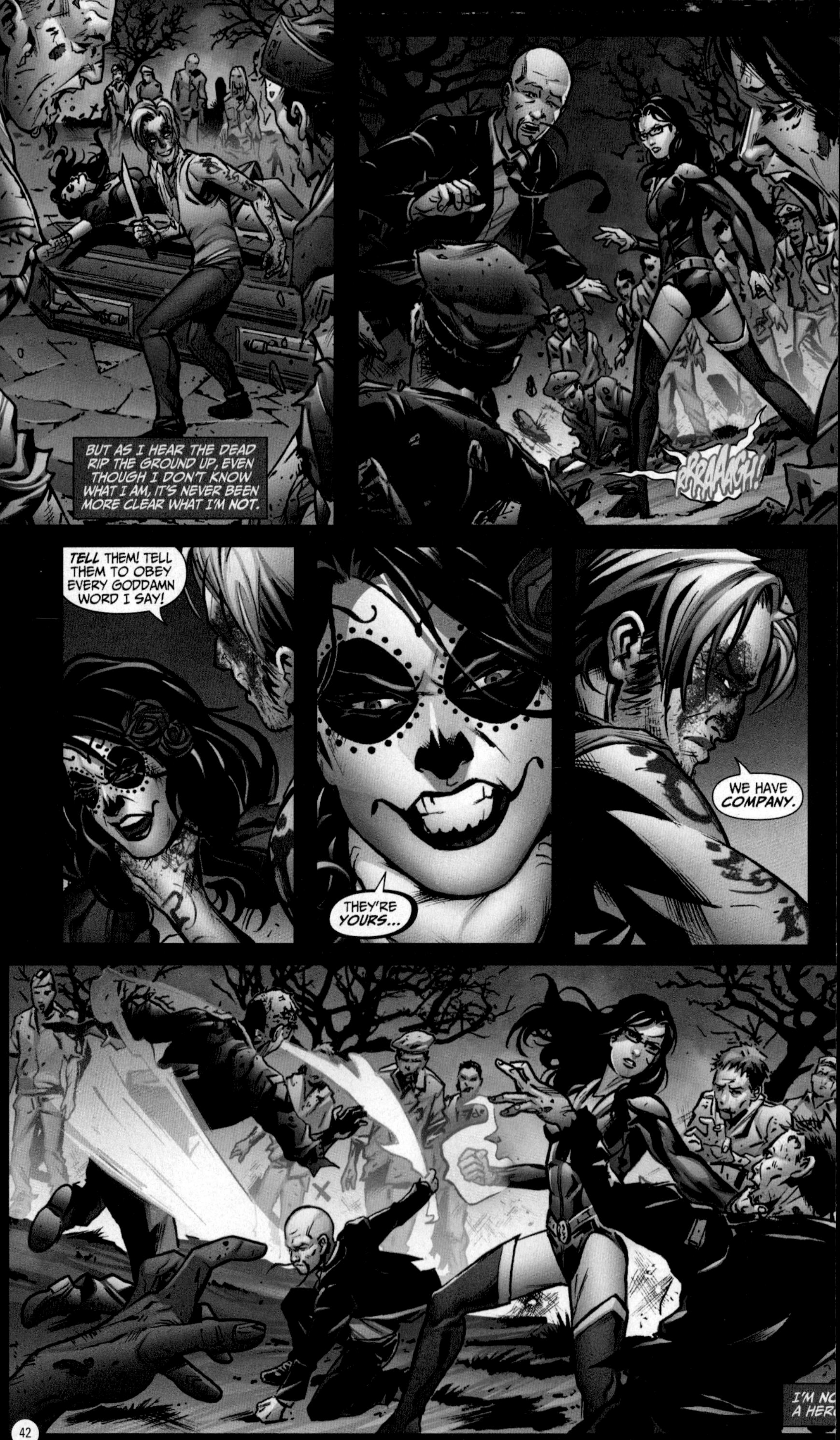
BUT AS I HEAR THE DEAD RIP THE GROUND UP, EVEN THOUGH I DON'T KNOW WHAT I AM, IT'S NEVER BEEN MORE CLEAR WHAT I'M **NOT**.
RRAAAGH!
TELL THEM! TELL THEM TO OBEY EVERY GODDAMN WORD I SAY!
THEY'RE **YOURS**...
WE HAVE **COMPANY**.
I'M NO
A HER

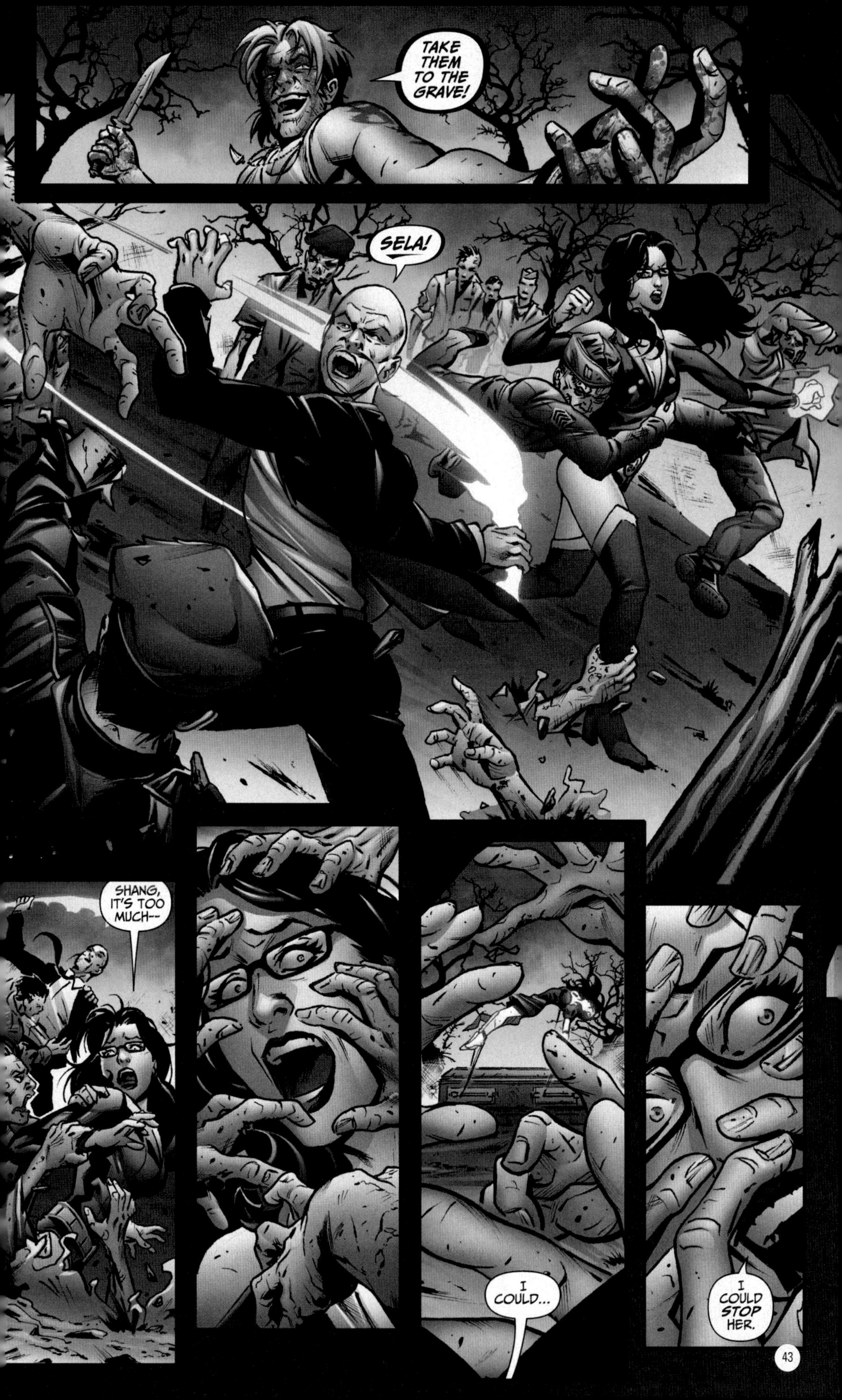
TAKE THEM TO THE GRAVE!
SELA!
SHANG, IT'S TOO MUCH--
I COULD...
I COULD STOP HER.

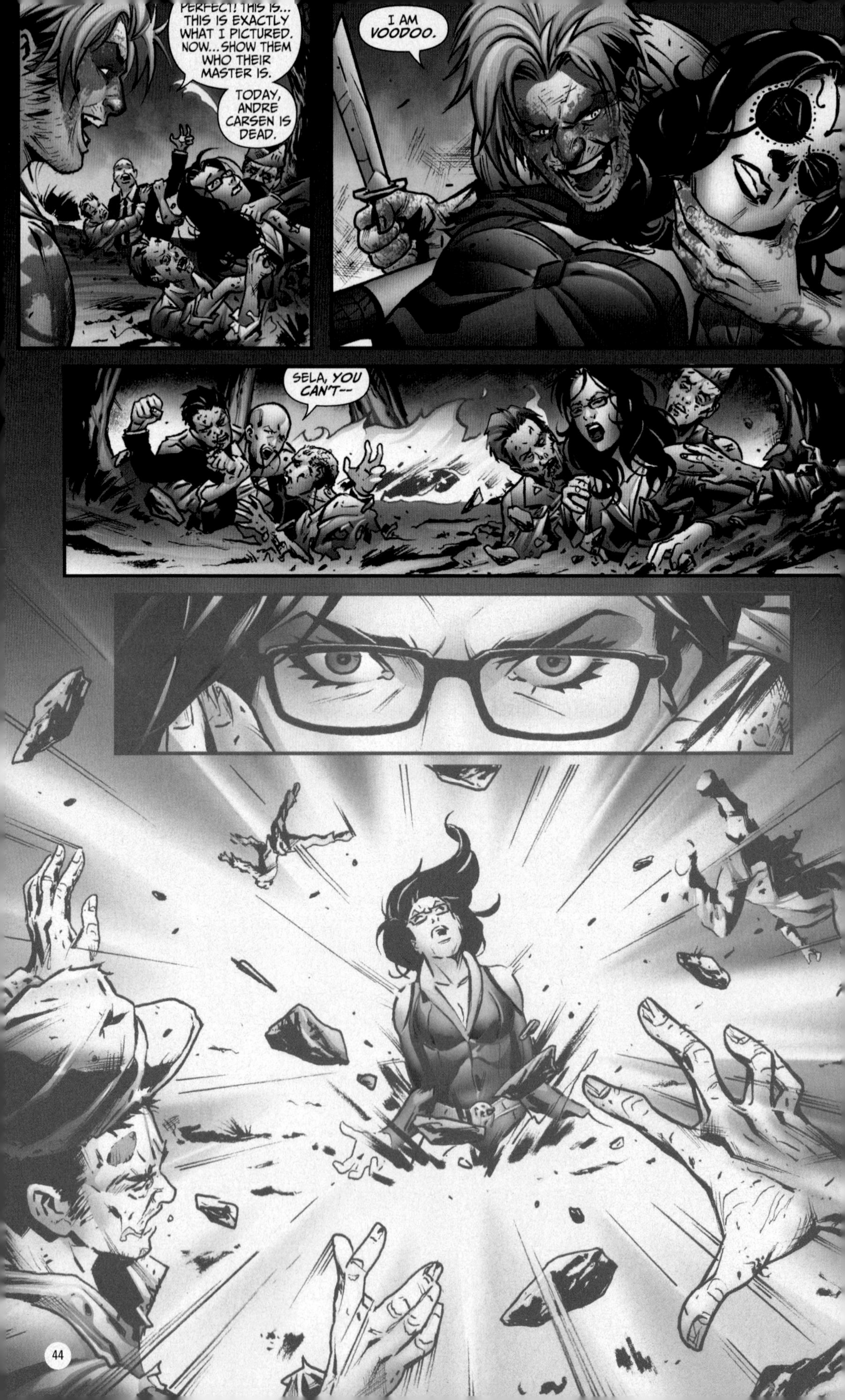
PERFECT! THIS IS... THIS IS EXACTLY WHAT I PICTURED. NOW...SHOW THEM WHO THEIR MASTER IS.
TODAY, ANDRE CARSEN IS DEAD.
I AM *VOODOO.*
SELA, *YOU* CAN'T--

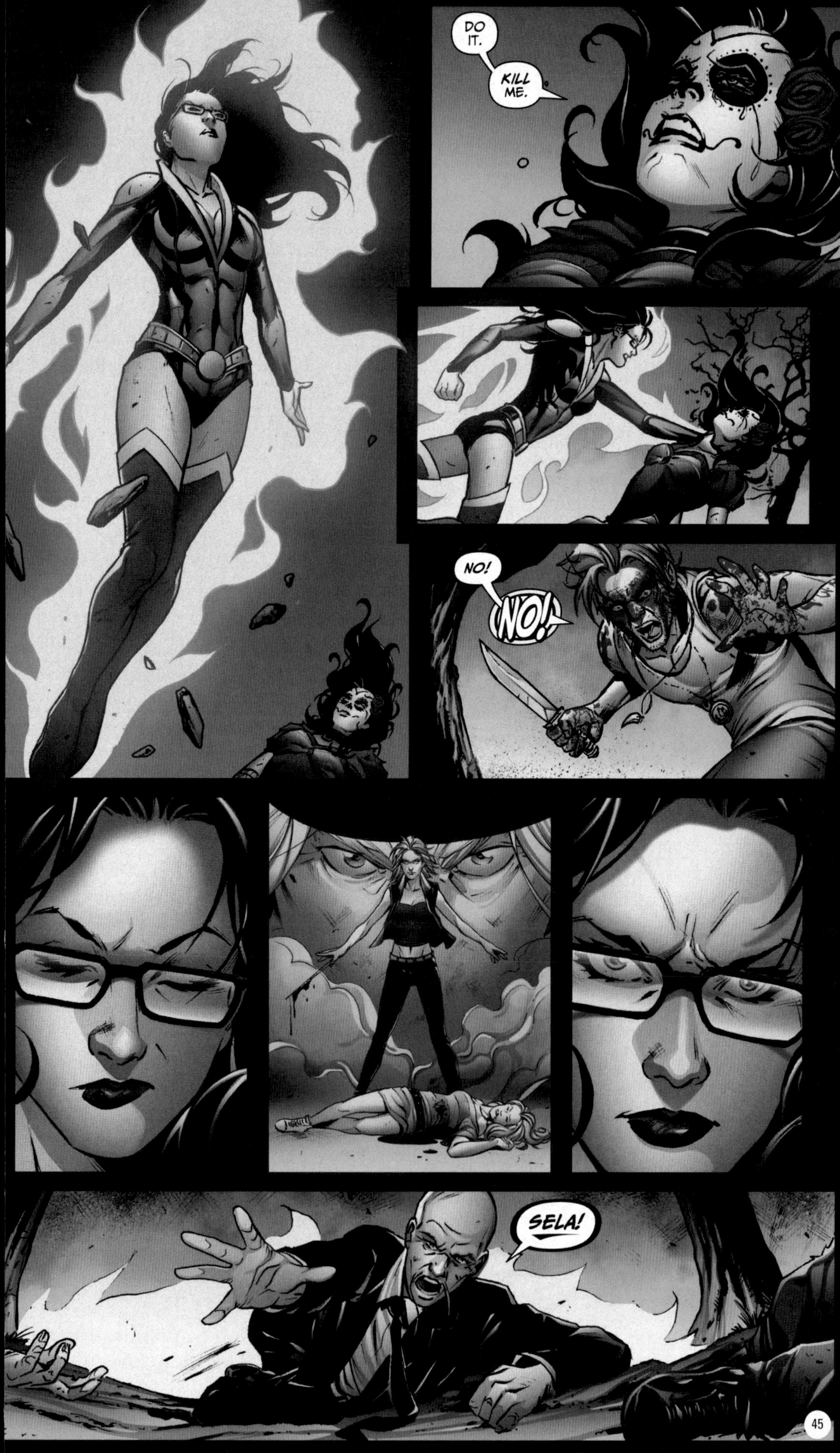
DO IT.
KILL ME.
NO!
NO!
SELA!

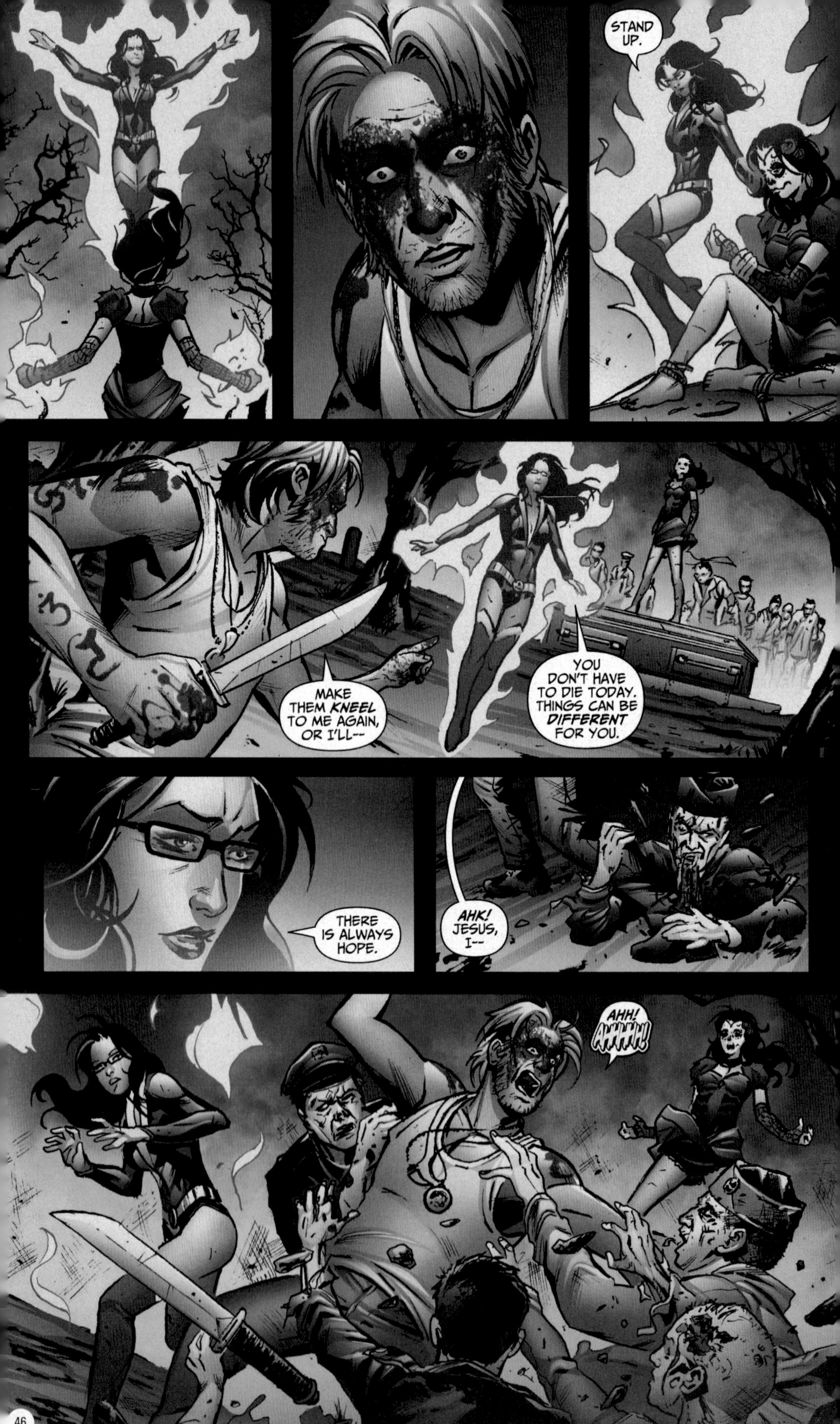
STAND UP.
MAKE THEM KNEEL TO ME AGAIN, OR I'LL--
YOU DON'T HAVE TO DIE TODAY. THINGS CAN BE DIFFERENT FOR YOU.
THERE IS ALWAYS HOPE.
AHK! JESUS, I--
AHH! AHHHH!

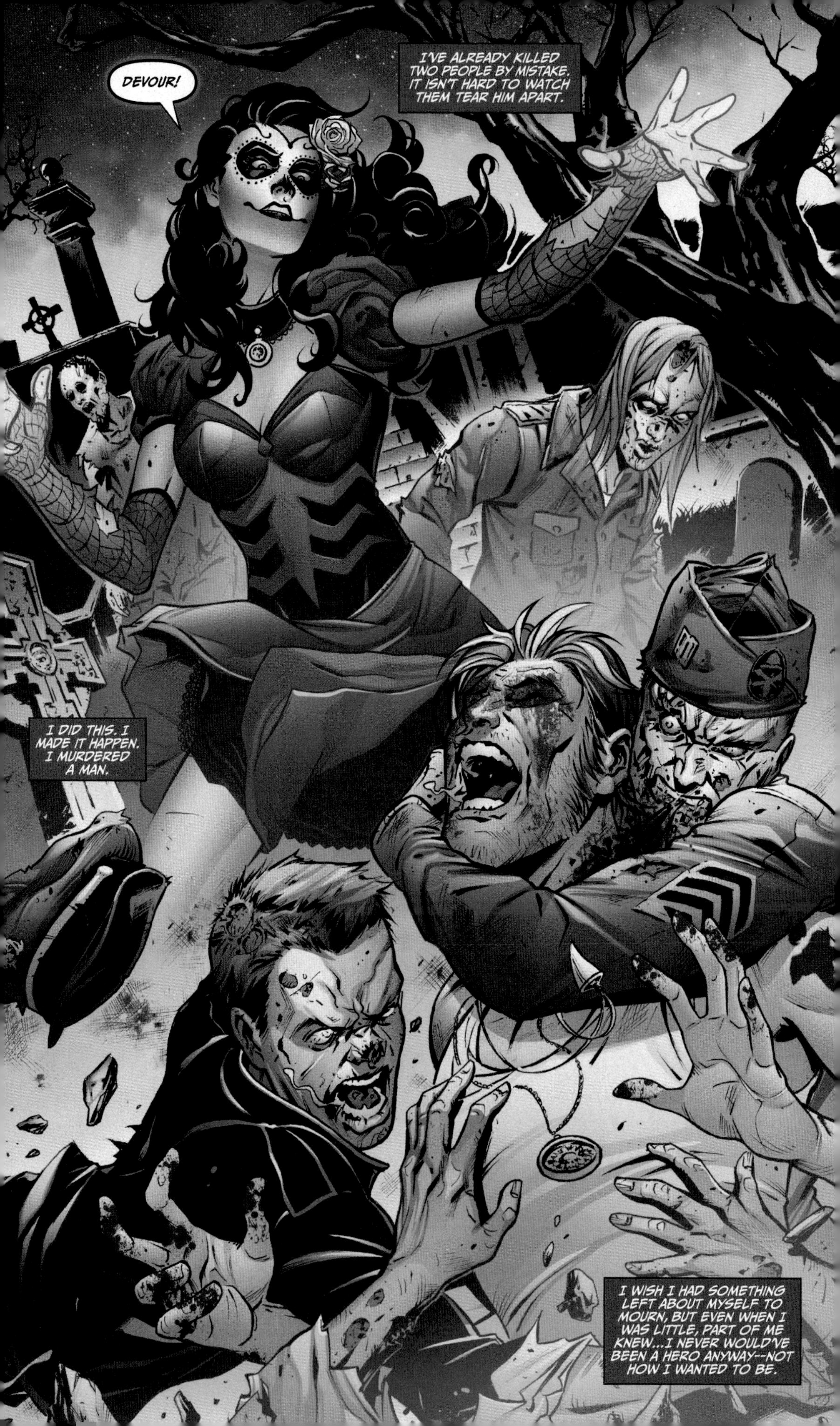
DEVOUR!
I'VE ALREADY KILLED TWO PEOPLE BY MISTAKE. IT ISN'T HARD TO WATCH THEM TEAR HIM APART.
I DID THIS. I MADE IT HAPPEN. I MURDERED A MAN.
I WISH I HAD SOMETHING LEFT ABOUT MYSELF TO MOURN, BUT EVEN WHEN I WAS LITTLE, PART OF ME KNEW...I NEVER WOULD'VE BEEN A HERO ANYWAY--NOT HOW I WANTED TO BE.

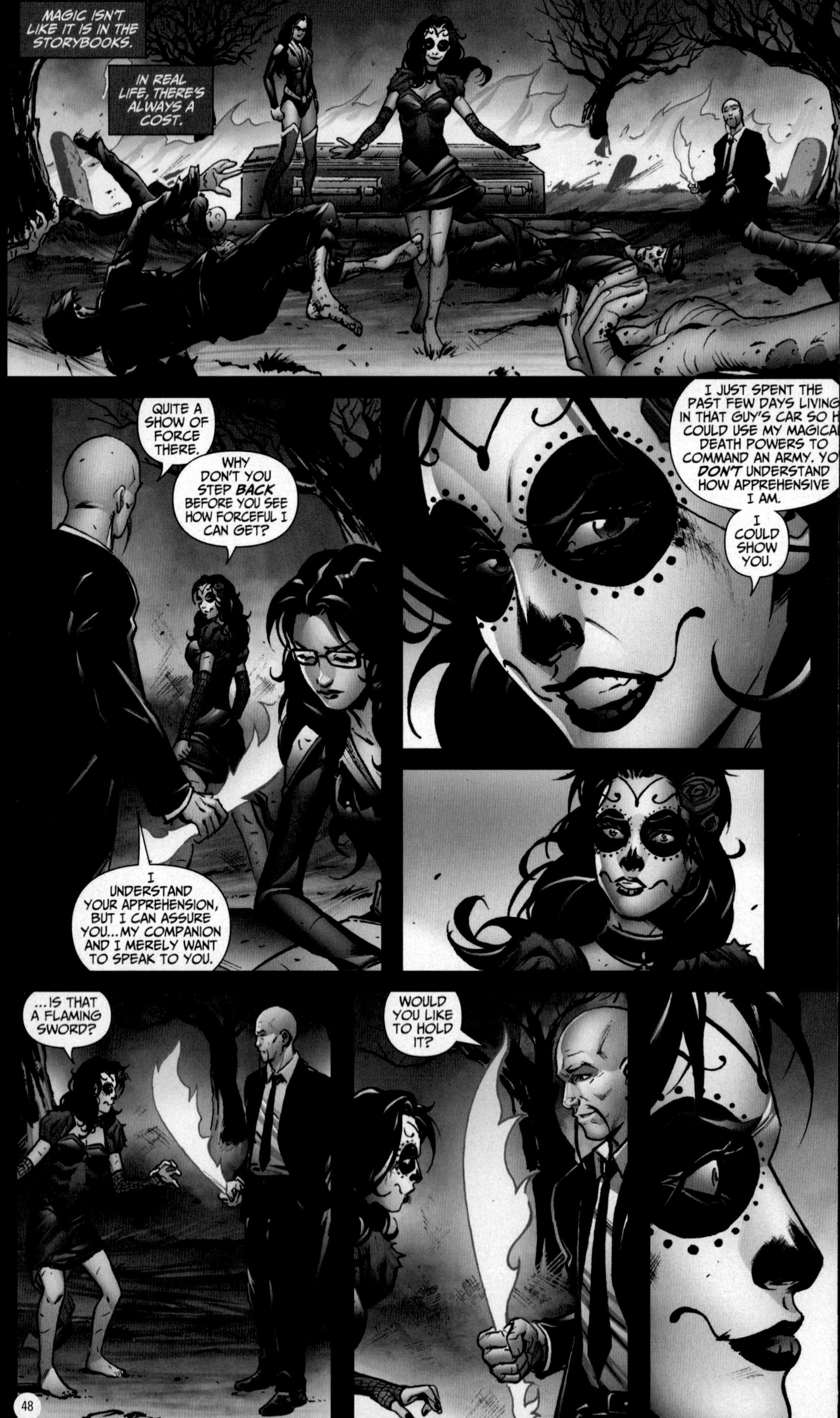

MAGIC ISN'T LIKE IT IS IN THE STORYBOOKS.
IN REAL LIFE, THERE'S ALWAYS A COST.
QUITE A SHOW OF FORCE THERE.
WHY DON'T YOU STEP BACK BEFORE YOU SEE HOW FORCEFUL I CAN GET?
I UNDERSTAND YOUR APPREHENSION, BUT I CAN ASSURE YOU...MY COMPANION AND I MERELY WANT TO SPEAK TO YOU.
I JUST SPENT THE PAST FEW DAYS LIVING IN THAT GUY'S CAR SO H COULD USE MY MAGICAL DEATH POWERS TO COMMAND AN ARMY. YO DON'T UNDERSTAND HOW APPREHENSIVE I AM.
I COULD SHOW YOU.
...IS THAT A FLAMING SWORD?
WOULD YOU LIKE TO HOLD IT?

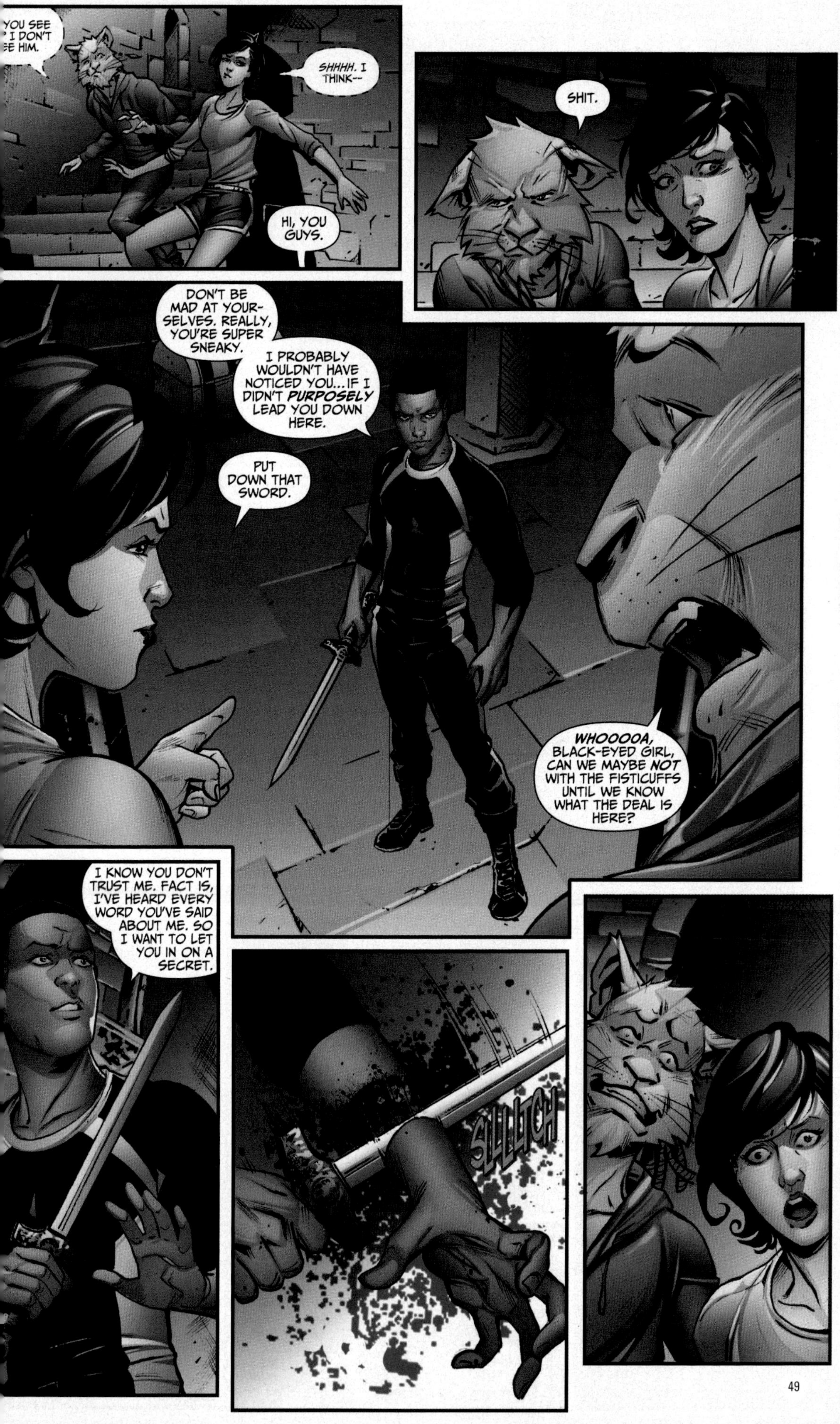

YOU SEE
I DON'T
EE HIM.
SHHHH. I THINK--
HI, YOU GUYS.
SHIT.
DON'T BE MAD AT YOUR-SELVES. REALLY, YOU'RE SUPER SNEAKY.
I PROBABLY WOULDN'T HAVE NOTICED YOU...IF I DIDN'T *PURPOSELY* LEAD YOU DOWN HERE.
PUT DOWN THAT SWORD.
WHOOOOA, BLACK-EYED GIRL, CAN WE MAYBE ***NOT*** WITH THE FISTICUFFS UNTIL WE KNOW WHAT THE DEAL IS HERE?
I KNOW YOU DON'T TRUST ME. FACT IS, I'VE HEARD EVERY WORD YOU'VE SAID ABOUT ME. SO I WANT TO LET YOU IN ON A SECRET.
SLLLLTCH

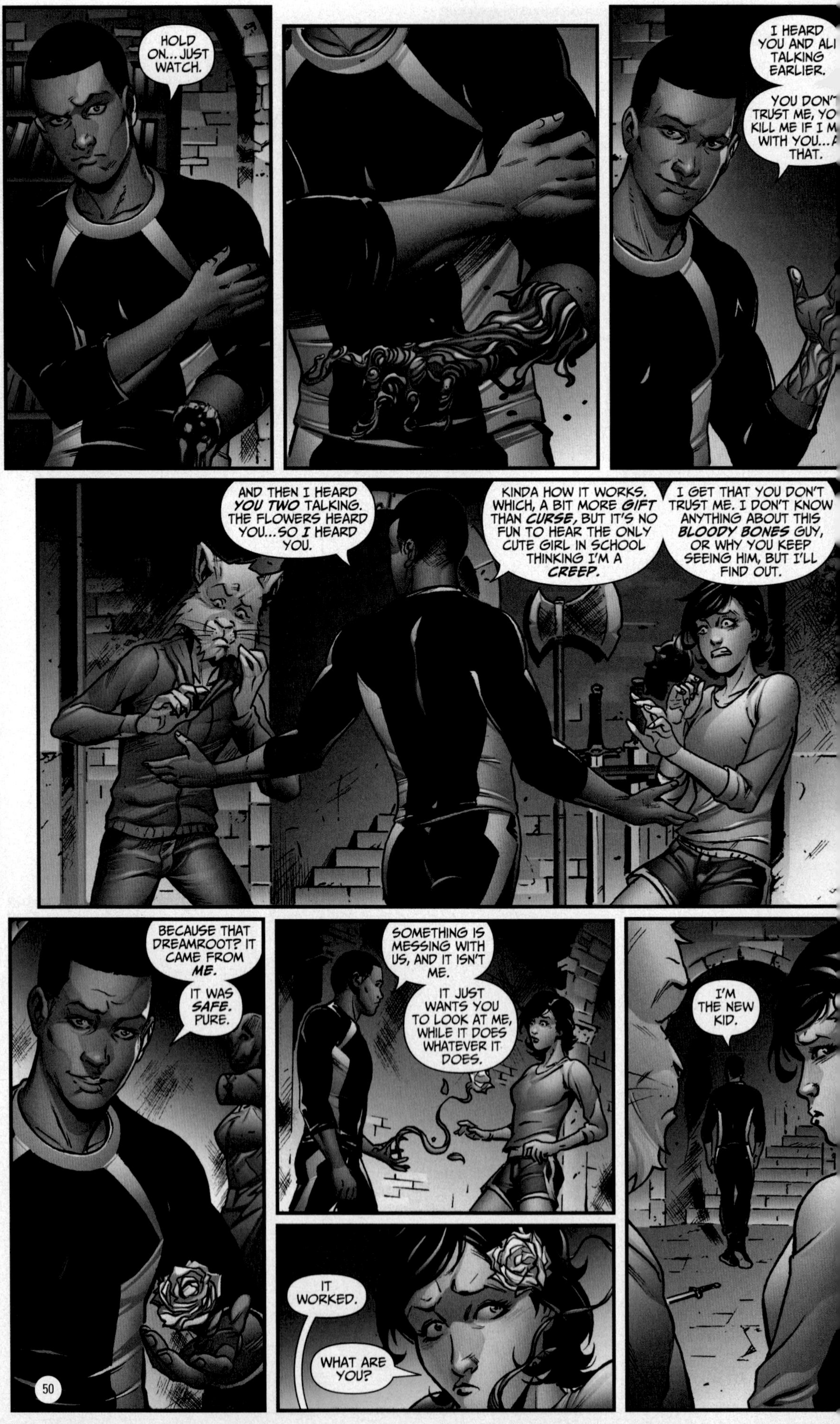

HOLD ON... JUST WATCH.
I HEARD YOU AND ALI TALKING EARLIER.
YOU DON'T TRUST ME, YO KILL ME IF I M WITH YOU... THAT.
AND THEN I HEARD YOU TWO TALKING. THE FLOWERS HEARD YOU... SO I HEARD YOU.
KINDA HOW IT WORKS. WHICH, A BIT MORE GIFT THAN CURSE, BUT IT'S NO FUN TO HEAR THE ONLY CUTE GIRL IN SCHOOL THINKING I'M A CREEP.
I GET THAT YOU DON'T TRUST ME. I DON'T KNOW ANYTHING ABOUT THIS BLOODY BONES GUY, OR WHY YOU KEEP SEEING HIM, BUT I'LL FIND OUT.
BECAUSE THAT DREAMROOT? IT CAME FROM ME.
IT WAS SAFE. PURE.
SOMETHING IS MESSING WITH US, AND IT ISN'T ME.
IT JUST WANTS YOU TO LOOK AT ME, WHILE IT DOES WHATEVER IT DOES.
IT WORKED.
WHAT ARE YOU?
I'M THE NEW KID.

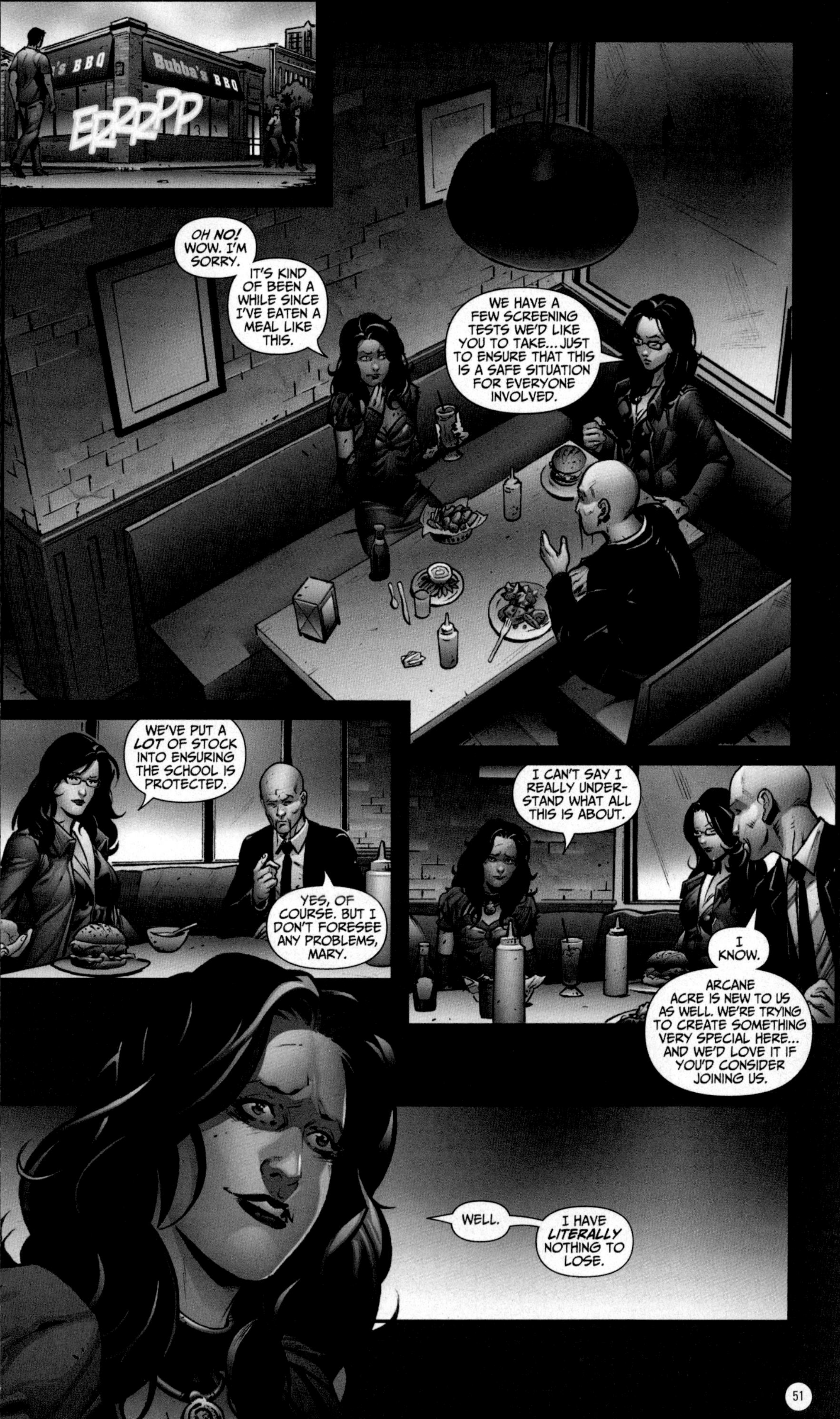

Bubba's BBQ
's BBQ
ERRRPP
OH NO! WOW. I'M SORRY.
IT'S KIND OF BEEN A WHILE SINCE I'VE EATEN A MEAL LIKE THIS.
WE HAVE A FEW SCREENING TESTS WE'D LIKE YOU TO TAKE... JUST TO ENSURE THAT THIS IS A SAFE SITUATION FOR EVERYONE INVOLVED.
WE'VE PUT A LOT OF STOCK INTO ENSURING THE SCHOOL IS PROTECTED.
YES, OF COURSE. BUT I DON'T FORESEE ANY PROBLEMS, MARY.
I CAN'T SAY I REALLY UNDERSTAND WHAT ALL THIS IS ABOUT.
I KNOW.
ARCANE ACRE IS NEW TO US AS WELL. WE'RE TRYING TO CREATE SOMETHING VERY SPECIAL HERE... AND WE'D LOVE IT IF YOU'D CONSIDER JOINING US.
WELL.
I HAVE LITERALLY NOTHING TO LOSE.

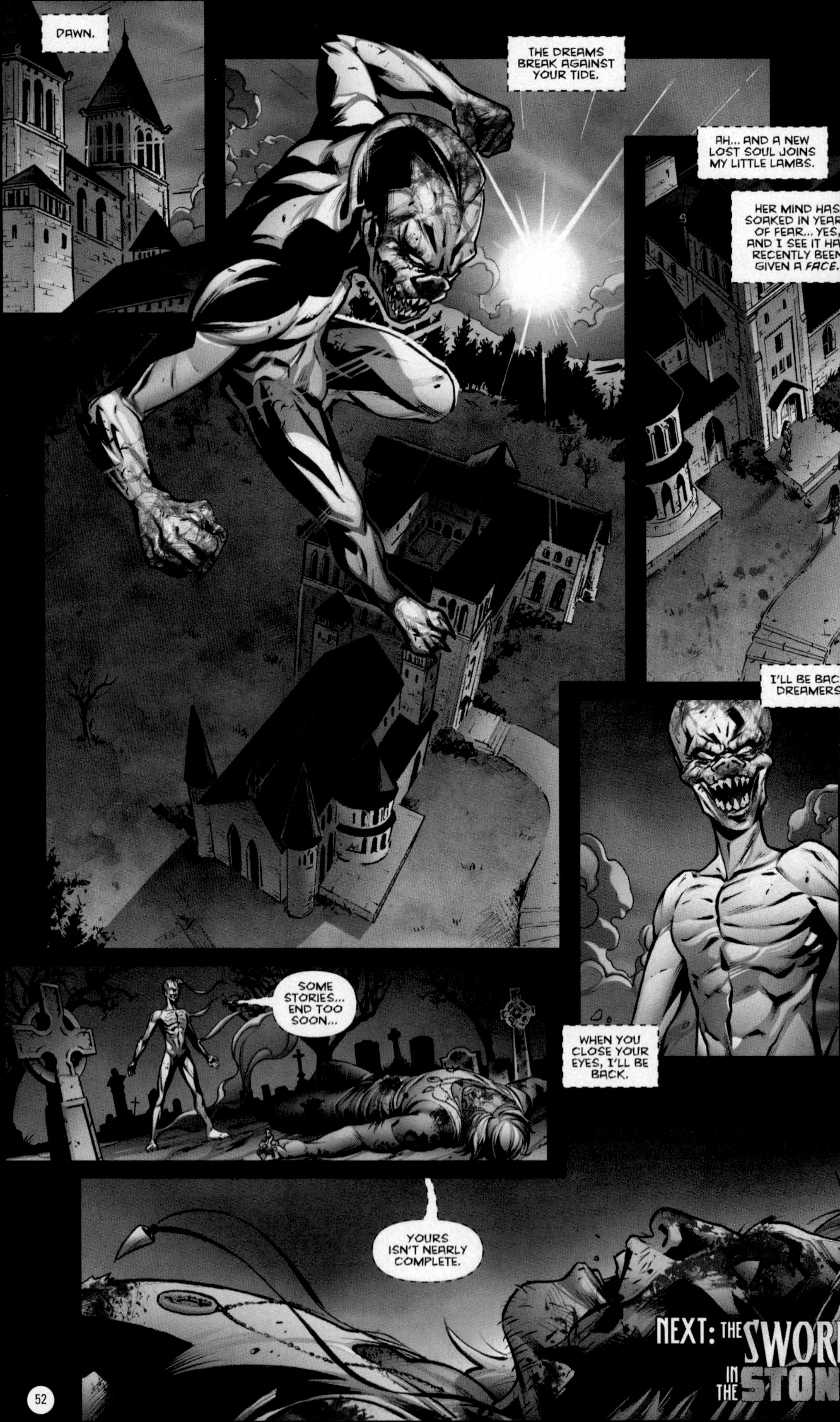

DAWN.
THE DREAMS BREAK AGAINST YOUR TIDE.
AH... AND A NEW LOST SOUL JOINS MY LITTLE LAMBS.
HER MIND HAS SOAKED IN YEAR OF FEAR... YES, AND I SEE IT HA RECENTLY BEEN GIVEN A *FACE.*
I'LL BE BAC DREAMERS
WHEN YOU CLOSE YOUR EYES, I'LL BE BACK.
SOME STORIES... END TOO SOON...
YOURS ISN'T NEARLY COMPLETE.
NEXT: THE SWORI IN THE STON

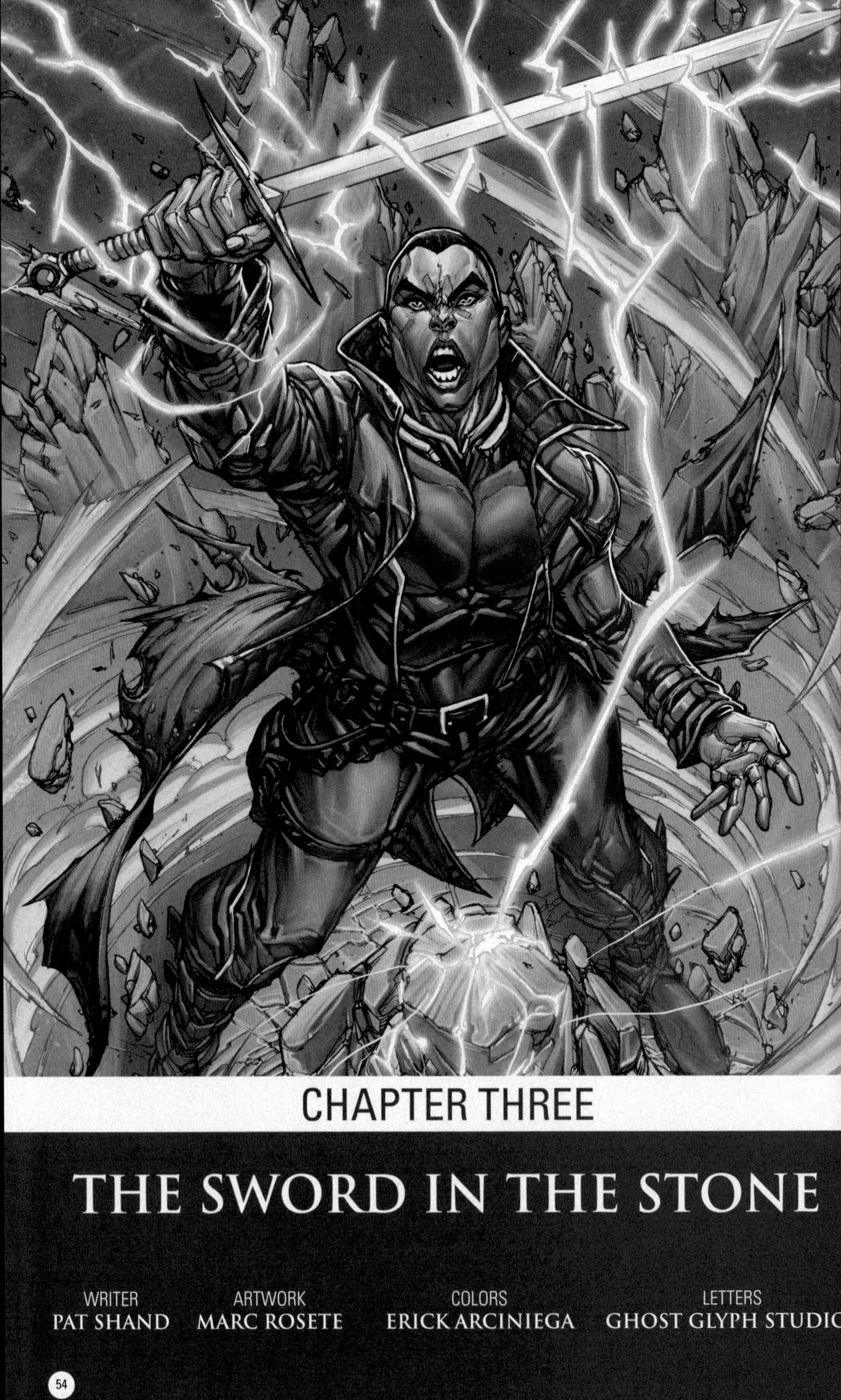

CHAPTER THREE

THE SWORD IN THE STONE

WRITER
PAT SHAND

ARTWORK
MARC ROSETE

COLORS
ERICK ARCINIEGA

LETTERS
GHOST GLYPH STUDIO

LET ME BE VERY CLEAR ABOUT THIS. WE DO **NOT** NEED ANOTHER **SHADOW GIRL** INCIDENT.

GREEK "GODS": ZEUS, NEPTUNE, HADES, AND THE PANTHEON

"I DON'T MEAN TO SINGLE YOU OUT, SKYE--WHEN YOU TOOK DOWN THAT HARBINGER, YOU SAVED THE DAY."

"BUT HIGHBORNS AREN'T EXACTLY **PUBLIC DARLINGS** SINCE WE WERE DISCOVERED, AND **HIBOCORP** HAS ALREADY DEMONSTRATED WHAT THE GOVERNMENT WOULD LIKE TO DO TO US."

GREEK "GODS": ZEUS, NEPTUNE, AND THE PANTH

BUT, AT THE SAME TIME, IT'S IMPORTANT THAT WE DON'T SEPARATE OURSELVES FROM SOCIETY. IF WE ARE TO PROTECT THIS WORLD, AS TRUE REALM KNIGHTS...

WE MUST BE PART OF IT.

YOU'RE G ON A TRIP."

DUDE, LOOK AT YOUR TEXTS.

Wiglaf: So Lance is some kind of plant guy.

Wulf: ?

Swear, Skye and I followed him but he knew we were coming, so he cut his arm off, and it regrew out of plants and shit.

WTF?

ikr?

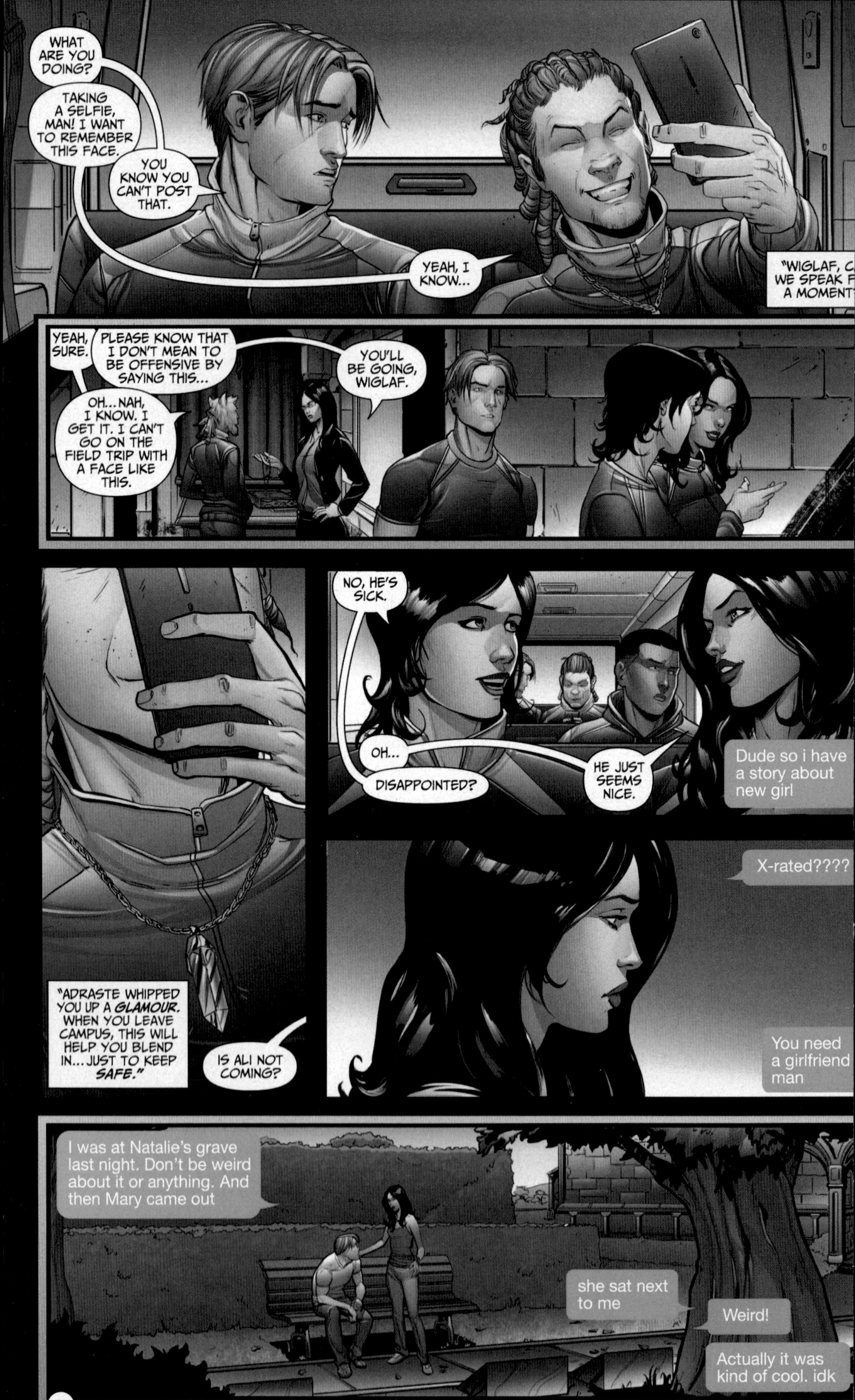

WHAT ARE YOU DOING?
TAKING A SELFIE, MAN! I WANT TO REMEMBER THIS FACE.
YOU KNOW YOU CAN'T POST THAT.
YEAH, I KNOW...
"WIGLAF, C
WE SPEAK F
A MOMENT
YEAH, SURE.
PLEASE KNOW THAT I DON'T MEAN TO BE OFFENSIVE BY SAYING THIS...
YOU'LL BE GOING, WIGLAF.
OH...NAH, I KNOW. I GET IT. I CAN'T GO ON THE FIELD TRIP WITH A FACE LIKE THIS.
"ADRASTE WHIPPED YOU UP A GLAMOUR. WHEN YOU LEAVE CAMPUS, THIS WILL HELP YOU BLEND IN... JUST TO KEEP SAFE."
IS ALI NOT COMING?
NO, HE'S SICK.
OH...
DISAPPOINTED?
HE JUST SEEMS NICE.
Dude so i have a story about new girl
X-rated????
You need a girlfriend man
I was at Natalie's grave last night. Don't be weird about it or anything. And then Mary came out
she sat next to me
Weird!
Actually it was kind of cool. idk

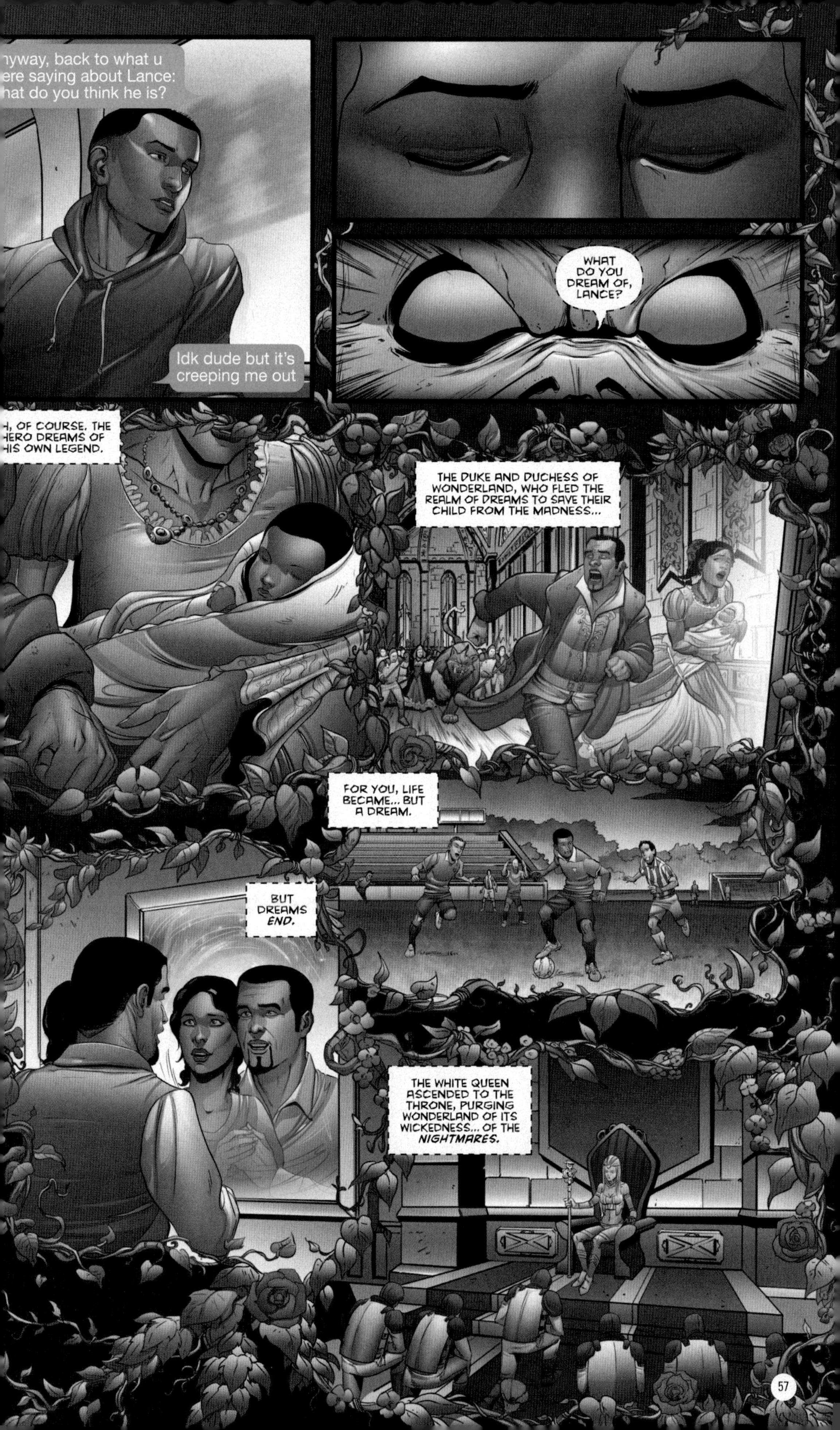

nyway, back to what u ere saying about Lance: hat do you think he is?
Idk dude but it's creeping me out
WHAT DO YOU DREAM OF, LANCE?
H, OF COURSE. THE HERO DREAMS OF HIS OWN LEGEND.
THE DUKE AND DUCHESS OF WONDERLAND, WHO FLED THE REALM OF DREAMS TO SAVE THEIR CHILD FROM THE MADNESS...
FOR YOU, LIFE BECAME... BUT A DREAM.
BUT DREAMS *END.*
THE WHITE QUEEN ASCENDED TO THE THRONE, PURGING WONDERLAND OF ITS WICKEDNESS... OF THE *NIGHTMARES.*

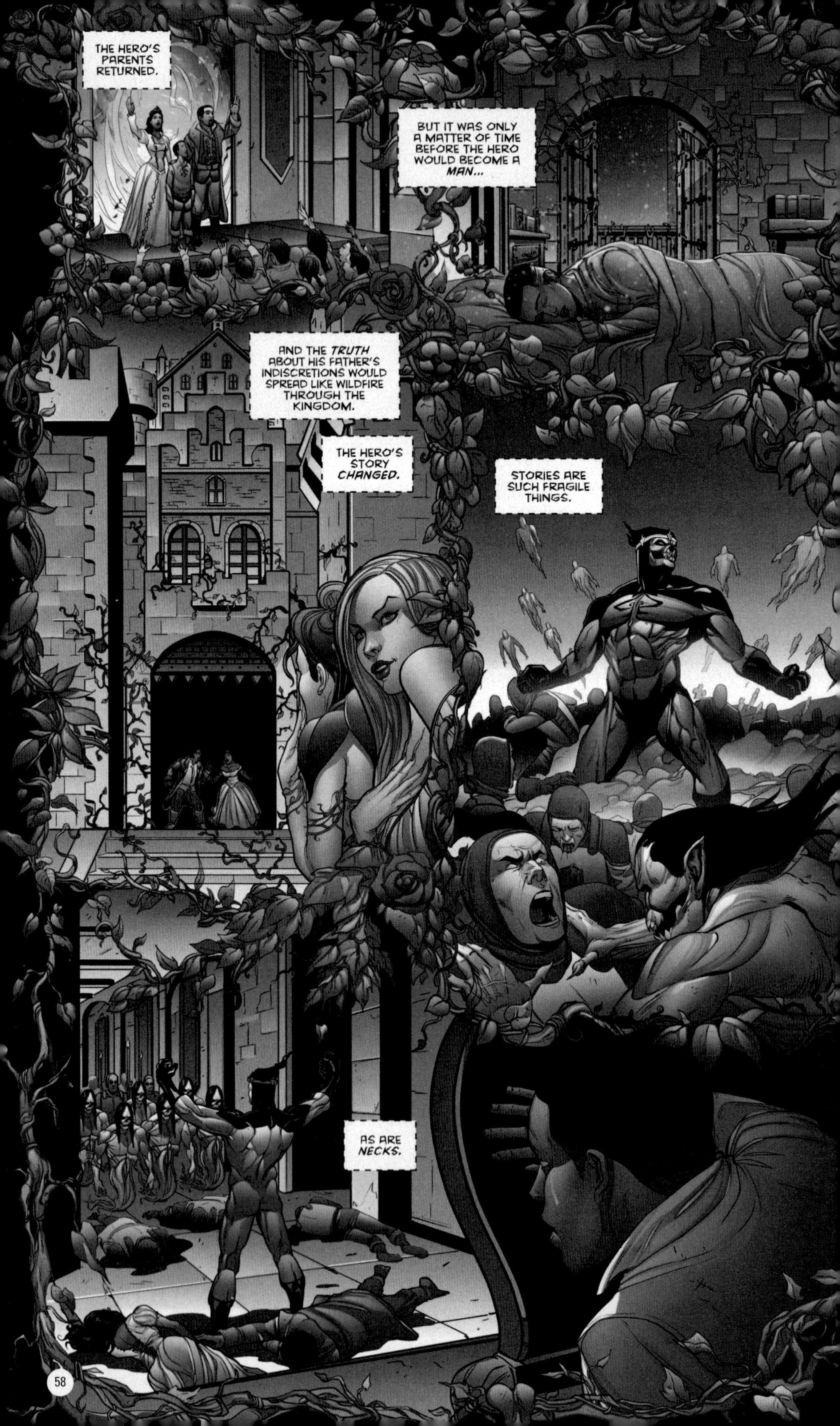
THE HERO'S PARENTS RETURNED.
BUT IT WAS ONLY A MATTER OF TIME BEFORE THE HERO WOULD BECOME A *MAN*...
AND THE *TRUTH* ABOUT HIS FATHER'S INDISCRETIONS WOULD SPREAD LIKE WILDFIRE THROUGH THE KINGDOM.
THE HERO'S STORY *CHANGED.*
STORIES ARE SUCH FRAGILE THINGS.
AS ARE *NECKS.*

THE *ACE OF SPADES*--A WORTHY ANTAGONIST FOR YOUR TALE!--LED AN ARMY AGAINST YOUR PARENTS. HE DIDN'T WANT THE THRONE.

HE WANTED TO PAINT THE TOWN RED WITH THOSE WHO BELIEVED IN THE WHITE QUEEN.

THE HERO OF THE STORY WAS NEXT IN LINE FOR THE THRONE.

YOUR FATHER WAS *WEAK*...HE BROUGHT THIS UPON US!

I'LL SLIT YOUR THROAT BEFORE I SEE A *FLOWER CHILD* ASCEND TO THE THRONE. *BE GONE!*

BUT THE THRONE, LIKE THE HERO, WAS *BROKEN*.

WHAT HAPPENS NEXT, I KNOW NOT.

WAKE UP...

DOES THE HERO ALLOW HIMSELF TO BE TAKEN AWAY INTO A GROUP OF MISFITS, LEARNING FROM OLD MEN AND OLD WOMEN WHO SHOULD'VE LONG SINCE BEEN BURIED?

OR DOES HE FIND THE BLADE THAT ONLY *HE* CAN HOLD... AND DO TO THE *ACE OF SPADES* WHAT WAS DONE TO HIS PARENTS, RETURNING EVERY FELL BLOW IN KIND?

WAKE UP, LANCE. WE'RE HERE.

AND *THIS*-- THIS HELMET WAS WORN BY ARES, *GOD OF WAR*. HE WENT BY *MARS* AT THE TIME HE WORE IT, HOWEVER.

I DON'T MEAN TO BE IMMODEST ABOUT MY PLACE IN HISTORY BUT, IN INTEREST OF PAINTING THE ENTIRE PICTURE, IF YOU'D ALL OBSERVE THE DENT ON THIS HELMET?

I STILL REMEMBER THE WAY THE HILT OF THE BLADE SHOOK IN MY HANDS AS I CLOBBERED THAT IDIOT OVER THE HEAD.

AH, THIS IS A--A *CREATIVE WRITING* CLASS! THEATRICAL, AH-- STORYTELLING, AND SO FORTH...

GOOD GOING, SHANG.

RIGHT THIS WAY. I BELIEVE THEY'VE STRUNG UP THE BONES OF A *SHADOW DRAGON*, MISTAKING IT FOR *TWO DIFFERENT DINOSAURS!*

THE THINGS PEOPLE ALLOW THEMSELVES TO BELIEVE...

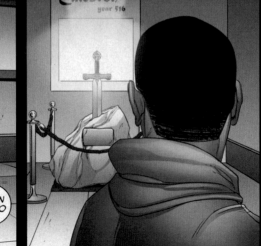

Calesvol,
year 516

Calesvol,
year 516

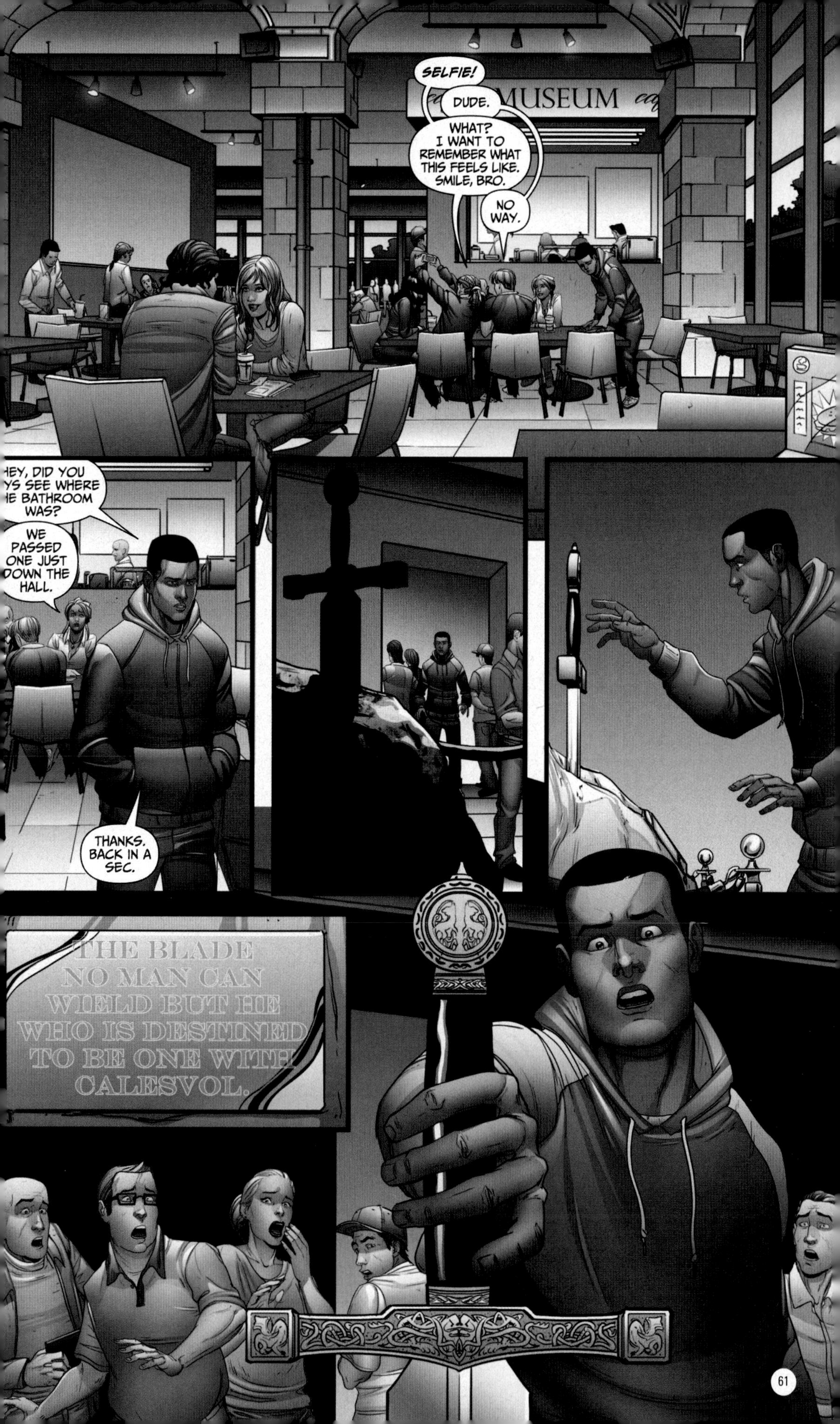
MUSEUM
SELFIE!
DUDE.
WHAT? I WANT TO REMEMBER WHAT THIS FEELS LIKE. SMILE, BRO.
NO WAY.
HEY, DID YOU GUYS SEE WHERE THE BATHROOM WAS?
WE PASSED ONE JUST DOWN THE HALL.
THANKS. BACK IN A SEC.
THE BLADE NO MAN CAN WIELD BUT HE WHO IS DESTINED TO BE ONE WITH CALESVOL.

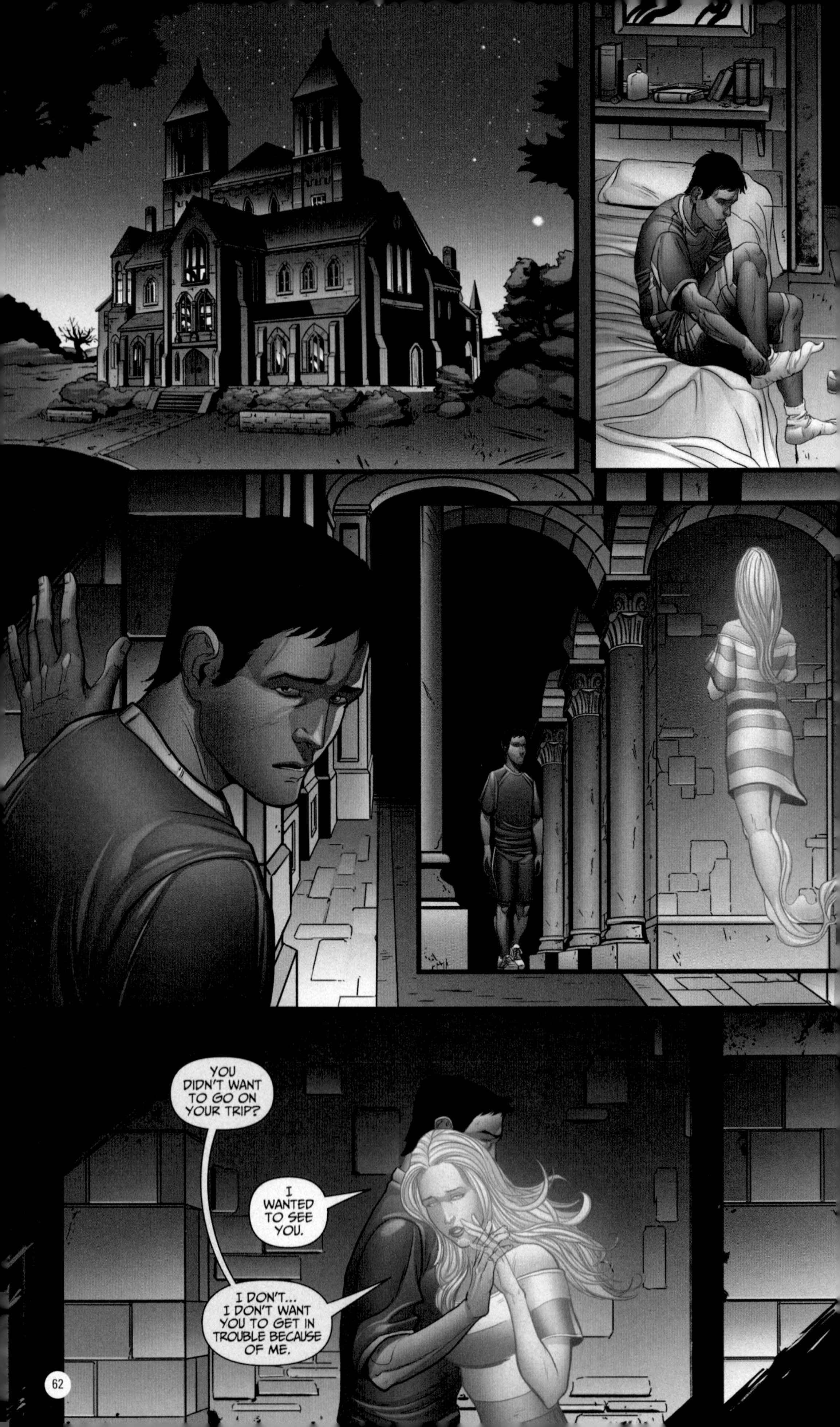
YOU DIDN'T WANT TO GO ON YOUR TRIP?
I WANTED TO SEE YOU.
I DON'T... I DON'T WANT YOU TO GET IN TROUBLE BECAUSE OF ME.

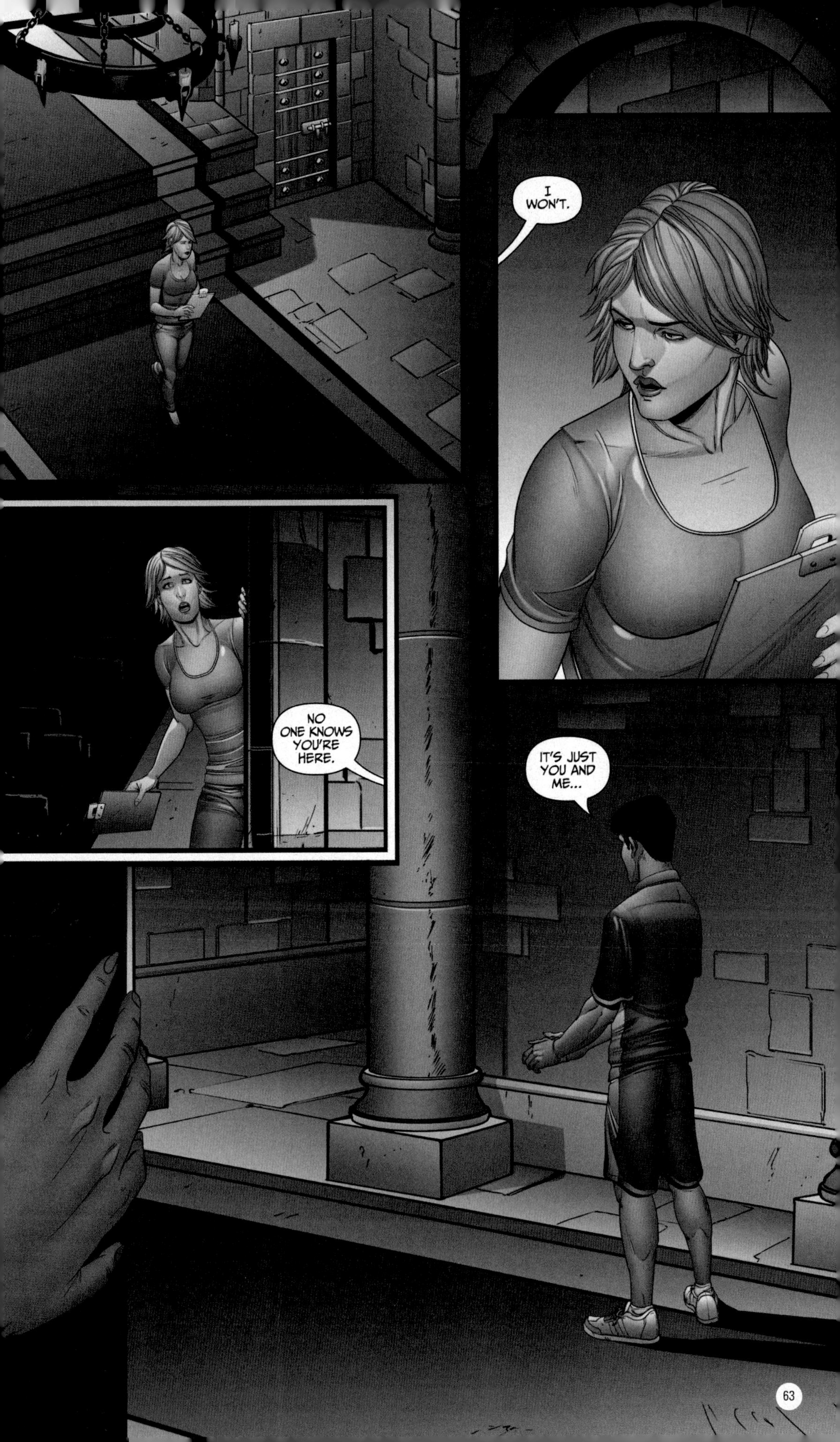
I WON'T.
NO ONE KNOWS YOU'RE HERE.
IT'S JUST YOU AND ME...

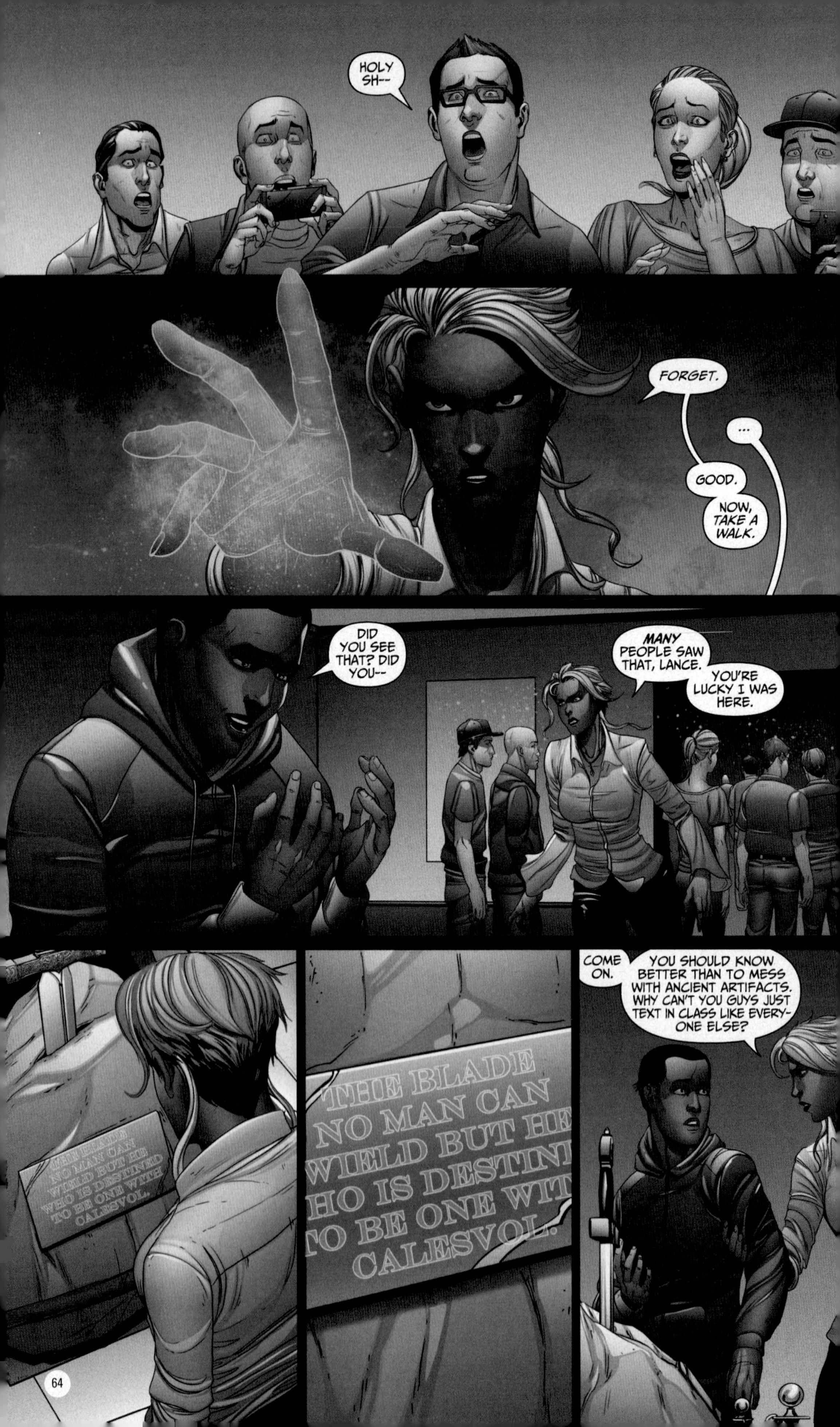
HOLY SH--
FORGET.
...
GOOD.
NOW, TAKE A WALK.
DID YOU SEE THAT? DID YOU--
MANY PEOPLE SAW THAT, LANCE.
YOU'RE LUCKY I WAS HERE.
THE BLADE NO MAN CAN WIELD BUT HE WHO IS DESTINED TO BE ONE WITH CALESVOL.
THE BLADE NO MAN CAN WIELD BUT HE WHO IS DESTINED TO BE ONE WITH CALESVOL.
COME ON.
YOU SHOULD KNOW BETTER THAN TO MESS WITH ANCIENT ARTIFACTS. WHY CAN'T YOU GUYS JUST TEXT IN CLASS LIKE EVERY-ONE ELSE?

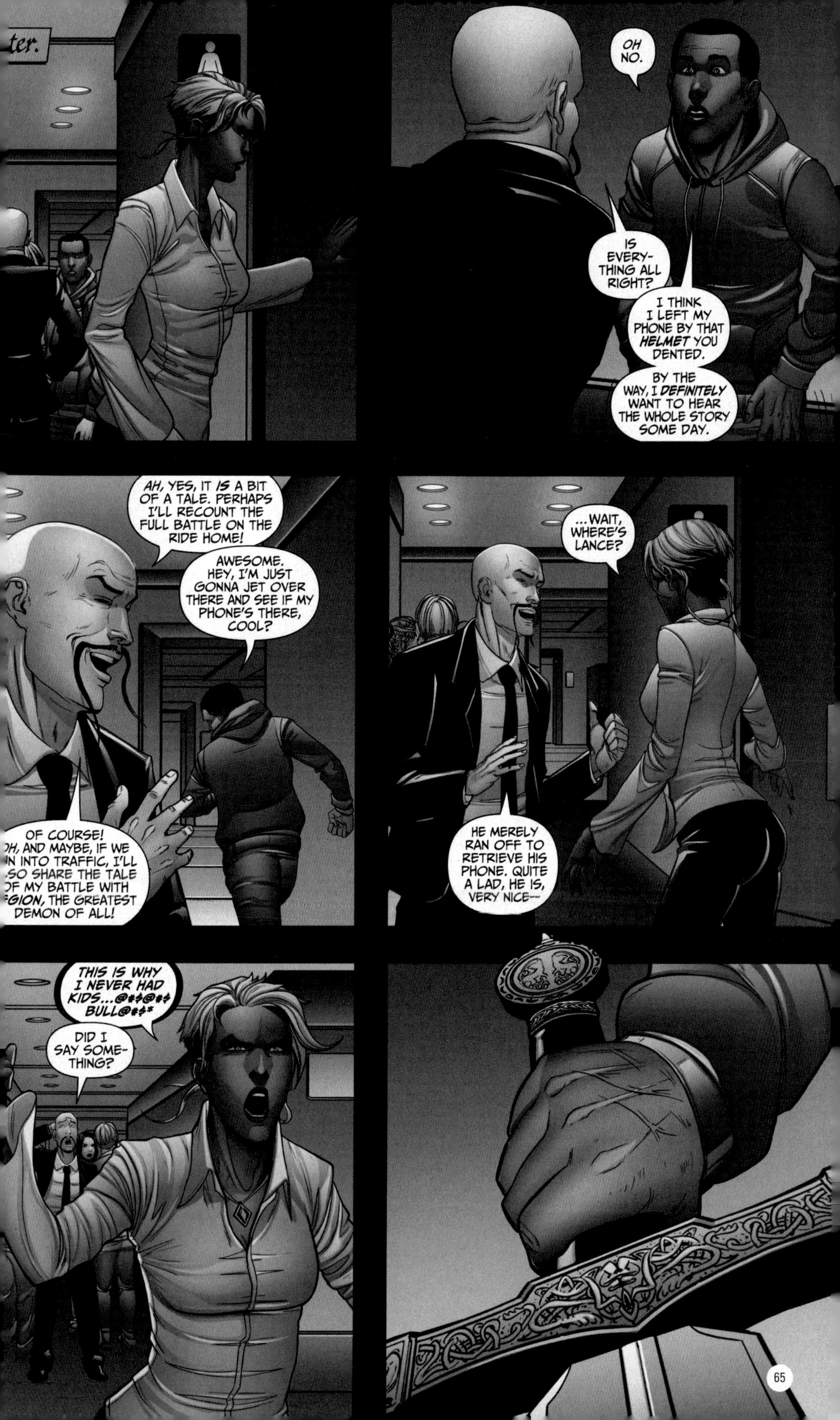
ter.
OH NO.
IS EVERYTHING ALL RIGHT?
I THINK I LEFT MY PHONE BY THAT HELMET YOU DENTED.
BY THE WAY, I DEFINITELY WANT TO HEAR THE WHOLE STORY SOME DAY.
AH, YES, IT IS A BIT OF A TALE. PERHAPS I'LL RECOUNT THE FULL BATTLE ON THE RIDE HOME!
AWESOME. HEY, I'M JUST GONNA JET OVER THERE AND SEE IF MY PHONE'S THERE, COOL?
OF COURSE! OH, AND MAYBE, IF WE RUN INTO TRAFFIC, I'LL ALSO SHARE THE TALE OF MY BATTLE WITH LEGION, THE GREATEST DEMON OF ALL!
...WAIT, WHERE'S LANCE?
HE MERELY RAN OFF TO RETRIEVE HIS PHONE. QUITE A LAD, HE IS, VERY NICE--
THIS IS WHY I NEVER HAD KIDS...@#$@#$ BULL@#$*
DID I SAY SOMETHING?

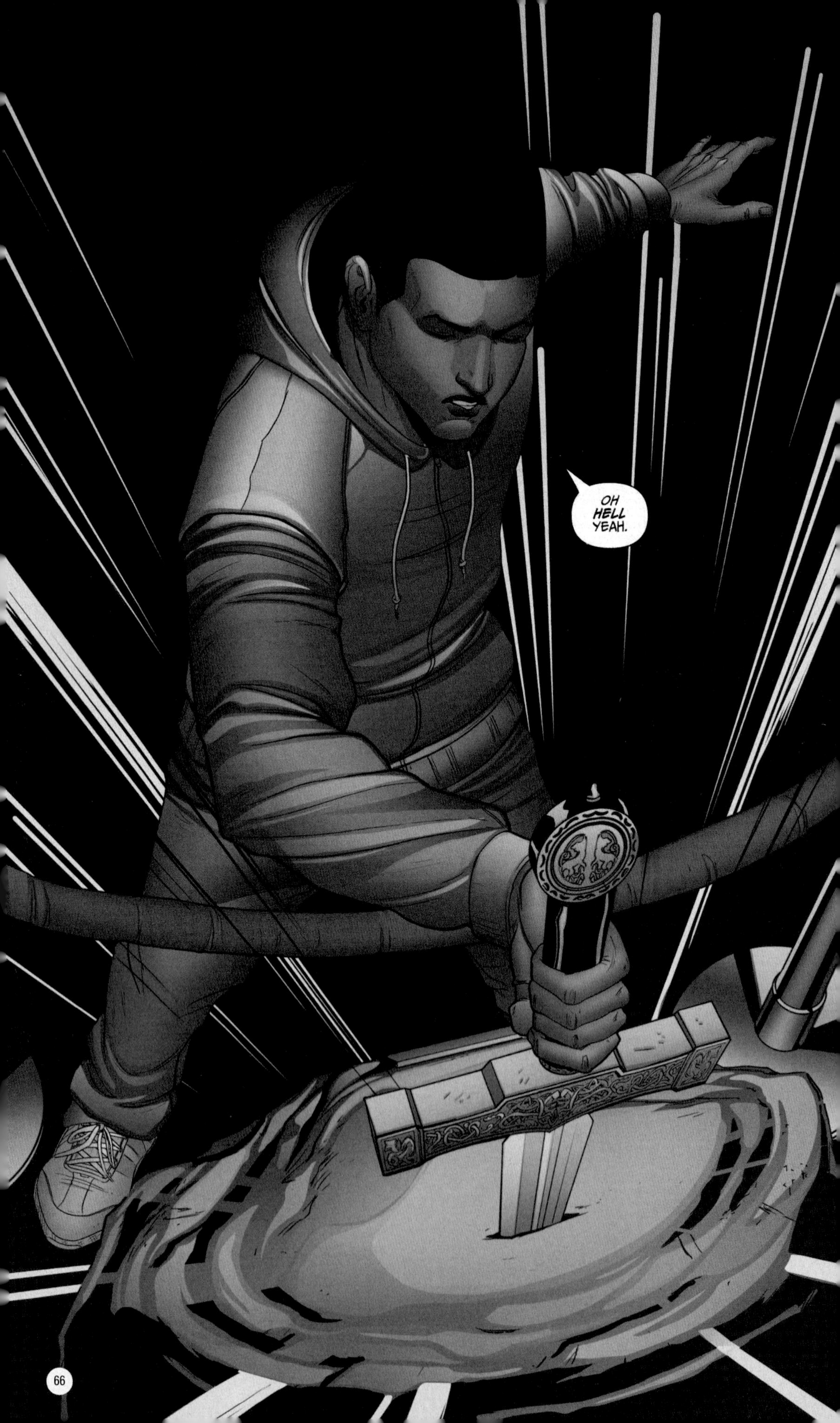
OH HELL YEAH.

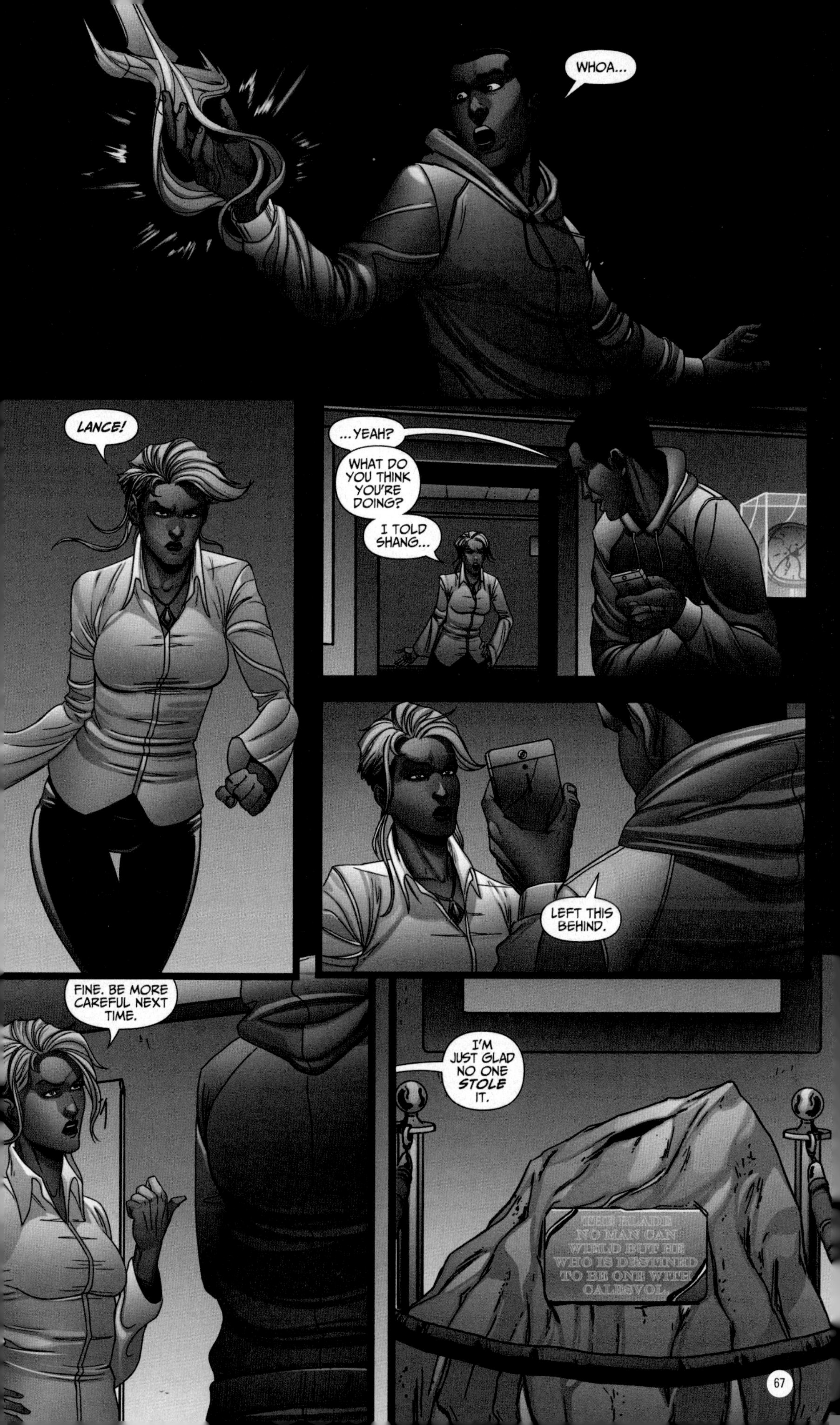
WHOA...
LANCE!
...YEAH?
WHAT DO YOU THINK YOU'RE DOING?
I TOLD SHANG...
LEFT THIS BEHIND.
FINE. BE MORE CAREFUL NEXT TIME.
I'M JUST GLAD NO ONE STOLE IT.
THE BLADE NO MAN CAN WIELD BUT HE WHO IS DESTINED TO BE ONE WITH CALESVOL.

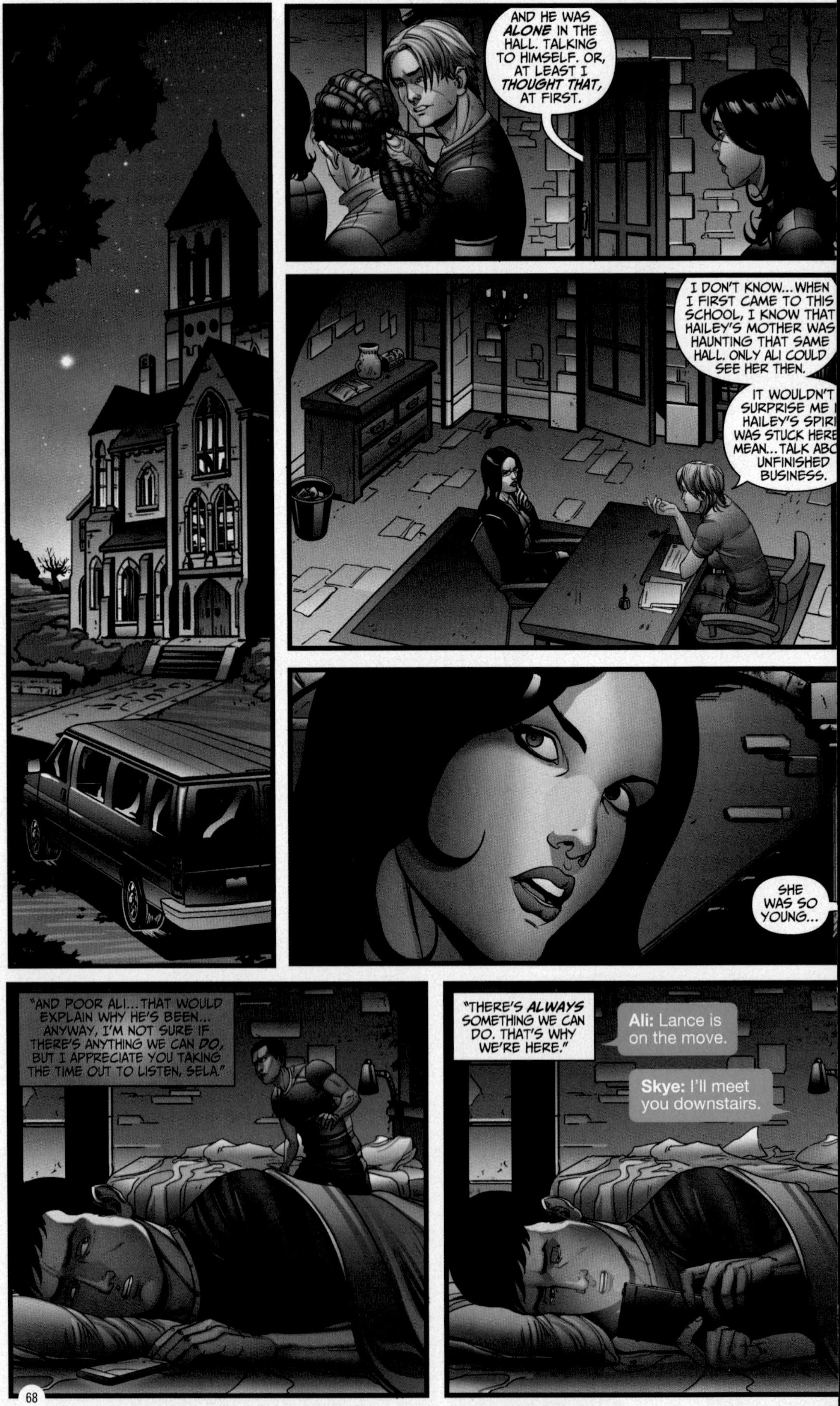

AND HE WAS ALONE IN THE HALL. TALKING TO HIMSELF. OR, AT LEAST I THOUGHT THAT, AT FIRST.
I DON'T KNOW...WHEN I FIRST CAME TO THIS SCHOOL, I KNOW THAT HAILEY'S MOTHER WAS HAUNTING THAT SAME HALL. ONLY ALI COULD SEE HER THEN.
IT WOULDN'T SURPRISE ME I HAILEY'S SPIRI WAS STUCK HERE MEAN...TALK ABO UNFINISHED BUSINESS.
SHE WAS SO YOUNG...
"AND POOR ALI...THAT WOULD EXPLAIN WHY HE'S BEEN... ANYWAY, I'M NOT SURE IF THERE'S ANYTHING WE CAN DO, BUT I APPRECIATE YOU TAKING THE TIME OUT TO LISTEN, SELA."
"THERE'S ALWAYS SOMETHING WE CAN DO. THAT'S WHY WE'RE HERE."
Ali: Lance is on the move.
Skye: I'll meet you downstairs.

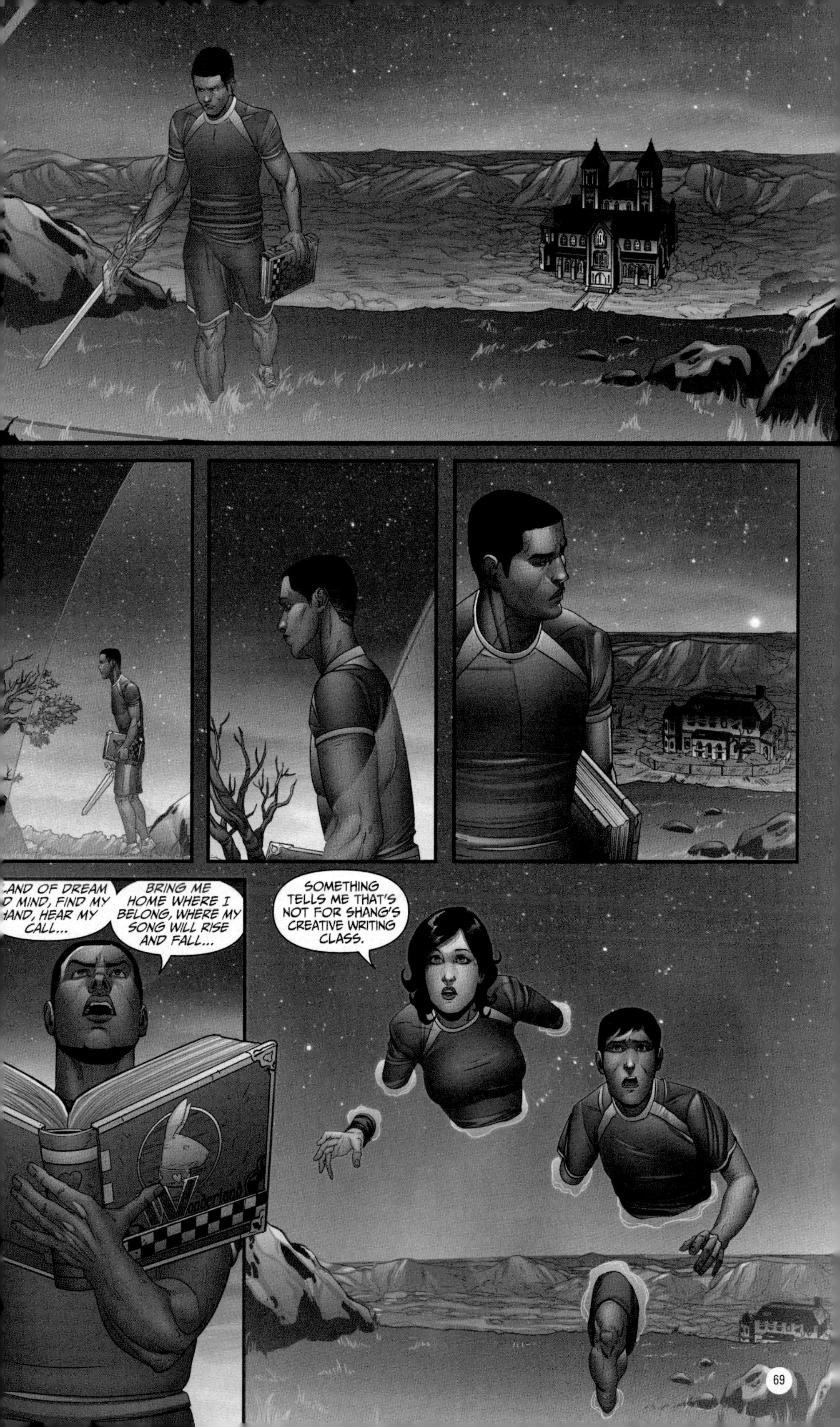
LAND OF DREAM
D MIND, FIND MY
HAND, HEAR MY
CALL...
BRING ME HOME WHERE I BELONG, WHERE MY SONG WILL RISE AND FALL...
SOMETHING TELLS ME THAT'S NOT FOR SHANG'S CREATIVE WRITING CLASS.
Wonderland

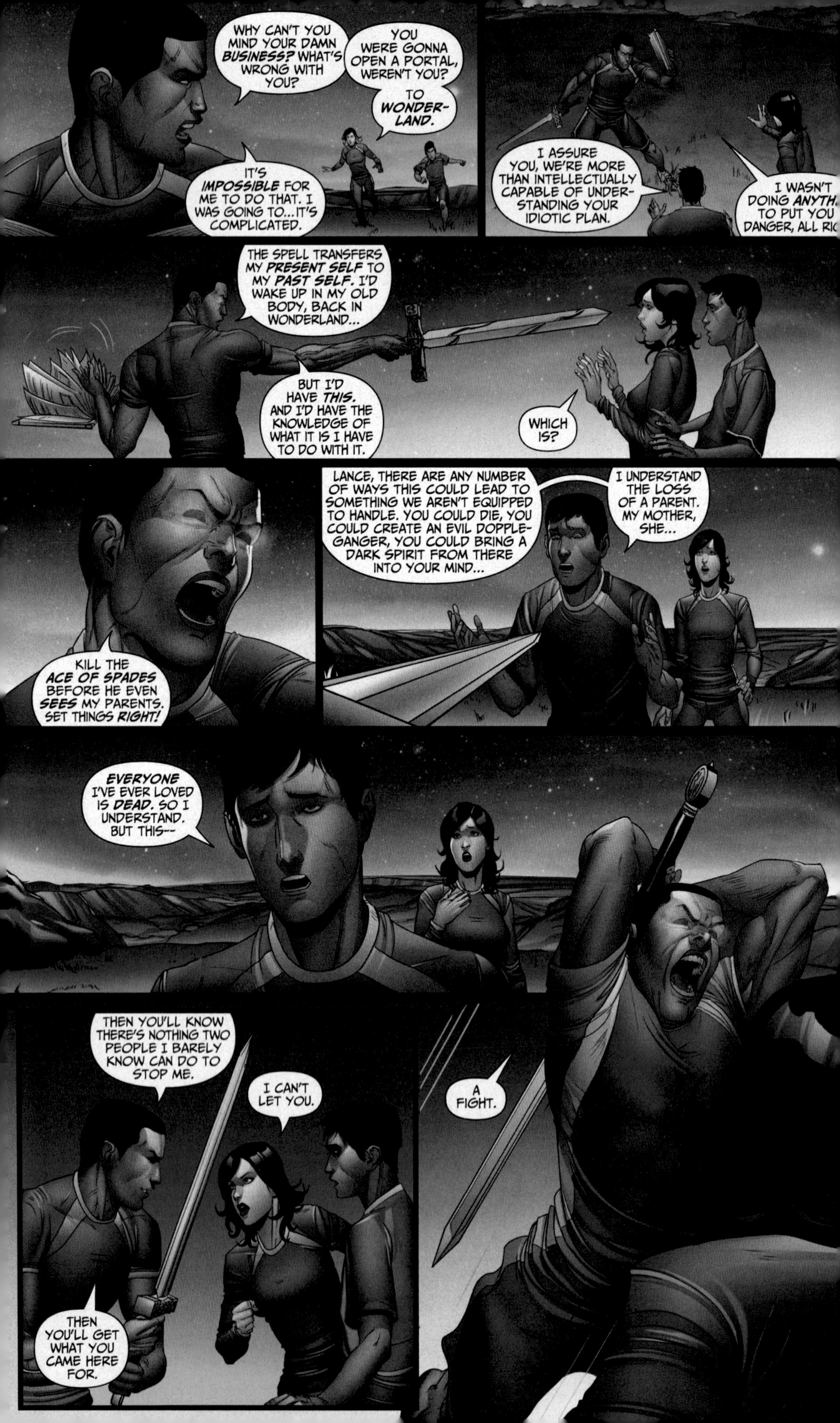
WHY CAN'T YOU MIND YOUR DAMN *BUSINESS?* WHAT'S WRONG WITH YOU?
YOU WERE GONNA OPEN A PORTAL, WEREN'T YOU?
TO *WONDER-LAND.*
IT'S *IMPOSSIBLE* FOR ME TO DO THAT. I WAS GOING TO... IT'S COMPLICATED.
I ASSURE YOU, WE'RE MORE THAN INTELLECTUALLY CAPABLE OF UNDER-STANDING YOUR IDIOTIC PLAN.
THE SPELL TRANSFERS MY *PRESENT SELF* TO MY *PAST SELF.* I'D WAKE UP IN MY OLD BODY, BACK IN WONDERLAND...
BUT I'D HAVE *THIS.* AND I'D HAVE THE KNOWLEDGE OF WHAT IT IS I HAVE TO DO WITH IT.
WHICH IS?
KILL THE *ACE OF SPADES* BEFORE HE EVEN *SEES* MY PARENTS. SET THINGS *RIGHT!*
LANCE, THERE ARE ANY NUMBER OF WAYS THIS COULD LEAD TO SOMETHING WE AREN'T EQUIPPED TO HANDLE. YOU COULD DIE, YOU COULD CREATE AN EVIL DOPPLE-GANGER, YOU COULD BRING A DARK SPIRIT FROM THERE INTO YOUR MIND...
I UNDERSTAND THE LOSS OF A PARENT. MY MOTHER, SHE...
EVERYONE I'VE EVER LOVED IS *DEAD.* SO I UNDERSTAND. BUT THIS--
THEN YOU'LL KNOW THERE'S NOTHING TWO PEOPLE I BARELY KNOW CAN DO TO STOP ME.
I CAN'T LET YOU.
THEN YOU'LL GET WHAT YOU CAME HERE FOR.
A FIGHT.

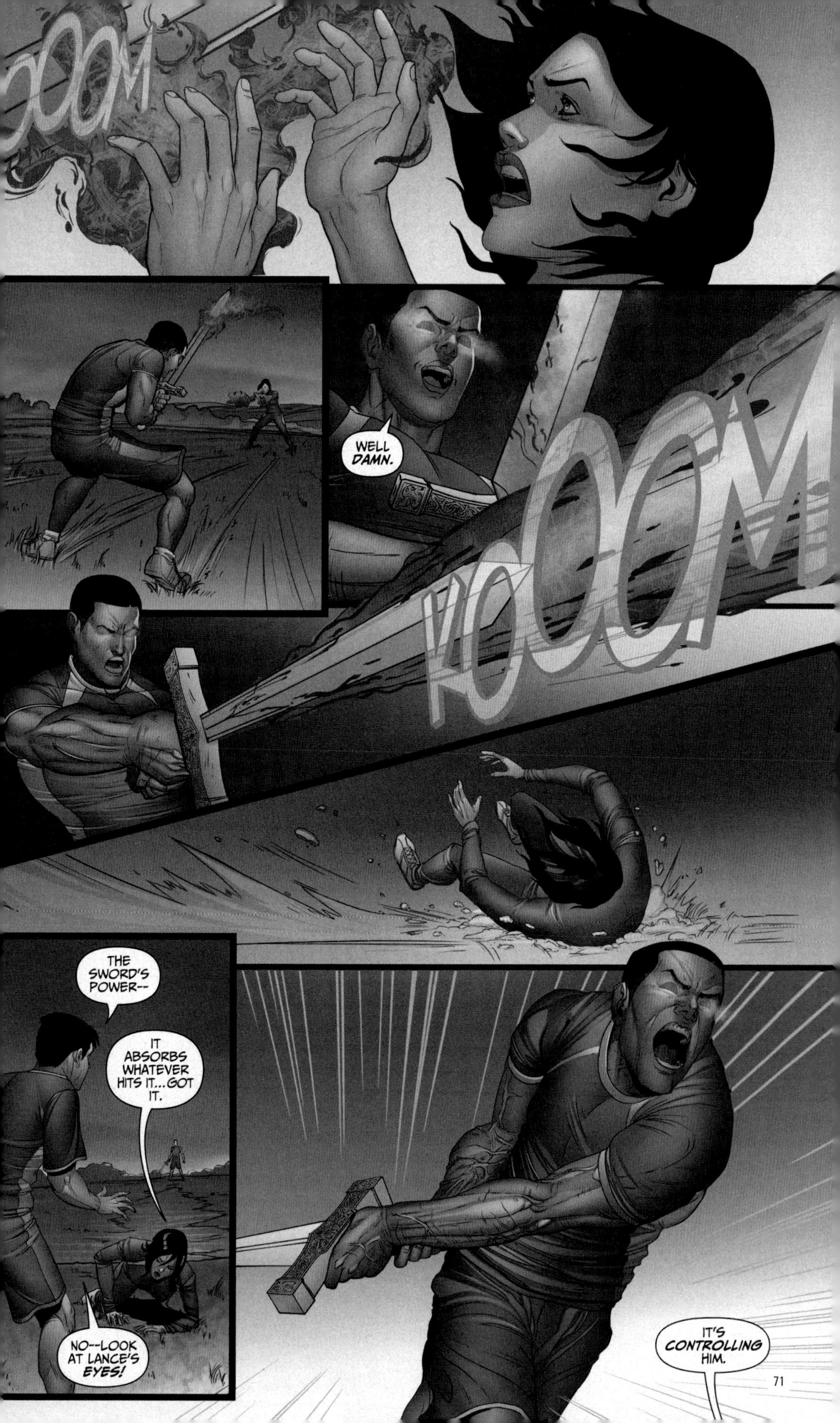

OOOM
WELL DAMN.
KOOOM
THE SWORD'S POWER--
IT ABSORBS WHATEVER HITS IT...GOT IT.
NO--LOOK AT LANCE'S EYES!
IT'S CONTROLLING HIM.

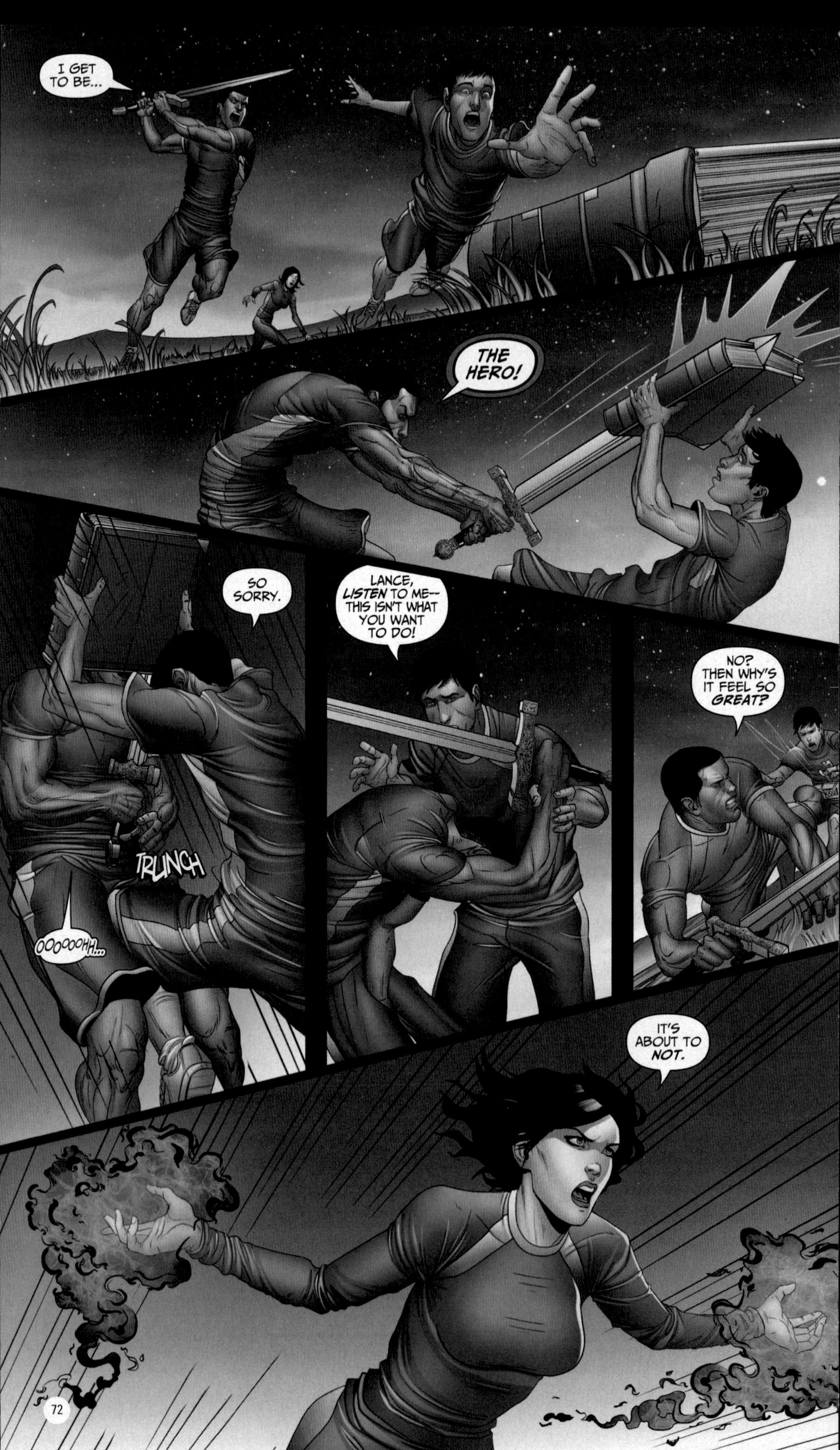
I GET TO BE...
THE HERO!
SO SORRY.
TRUNCH
OOOOOHH...
LANCE, LISTEN TO ME-- THIS ISN'T WHAT YOU WANT TO DO!
NO? THEN WHY'S IT FEEL SO GREAT?
IT'S ABOUT TO NOT.

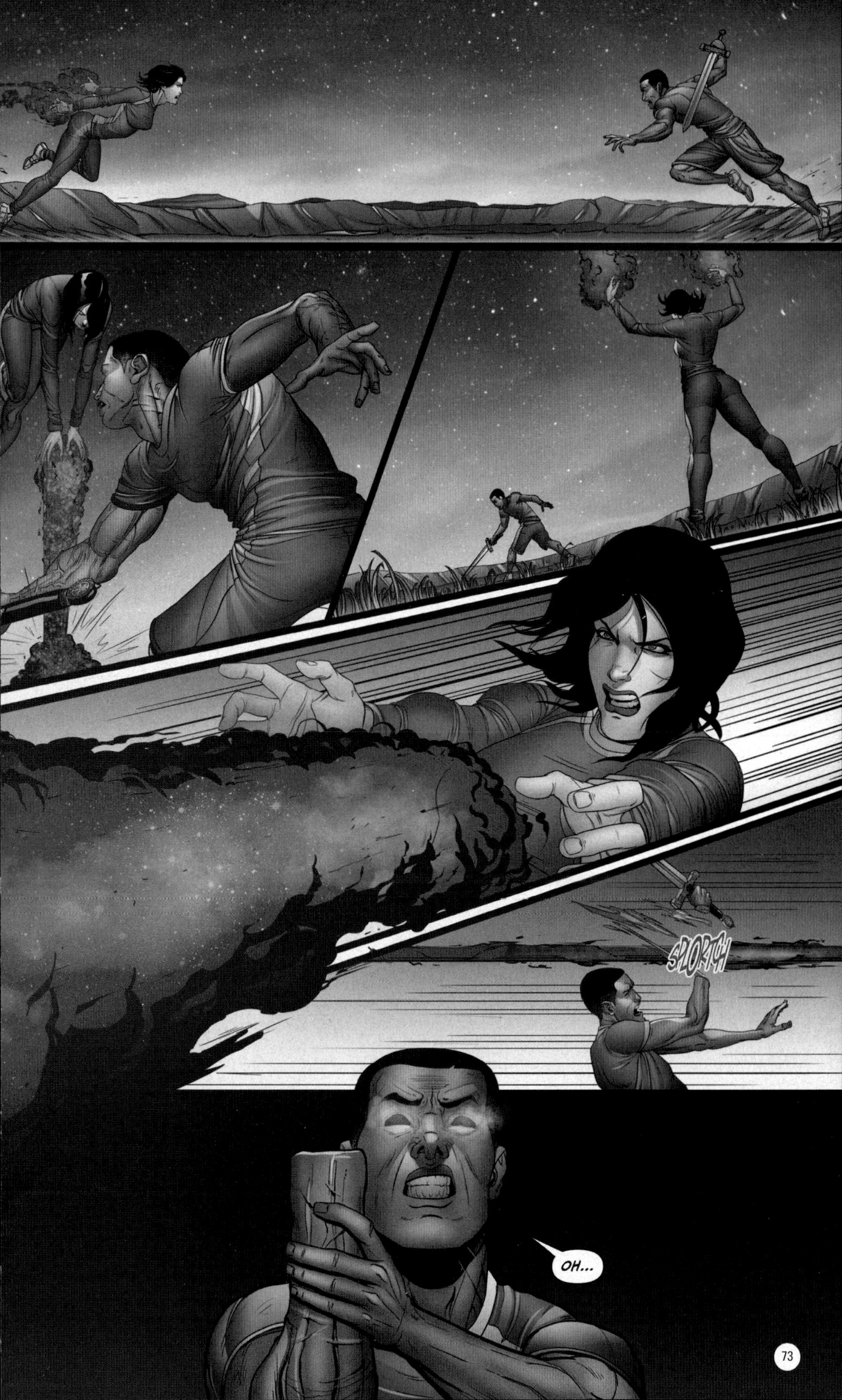
SPLORTCH
OH...

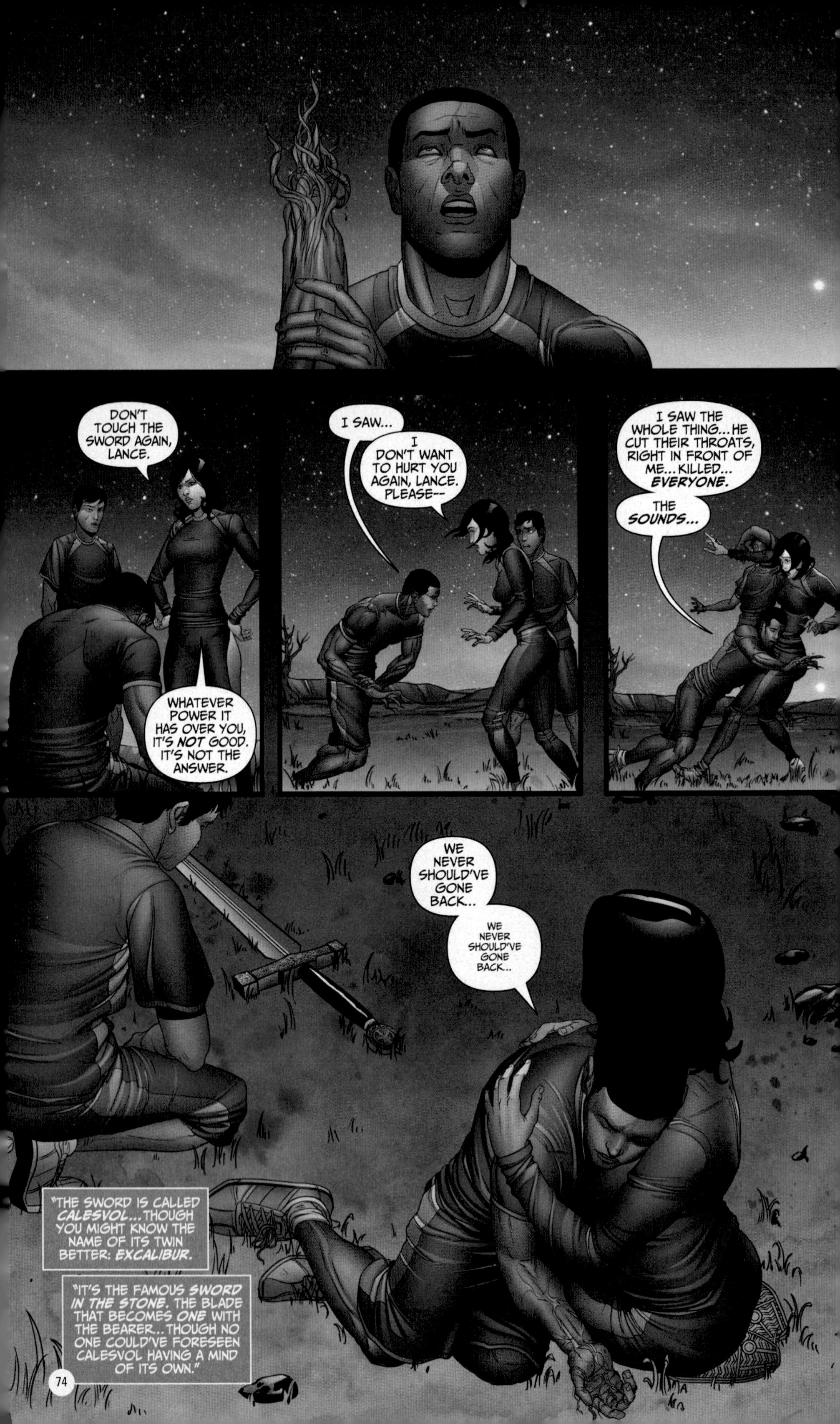
DON'T TOUCH THE SWORD AGAIN, LANCE.
WHATEVER POWER IT HAS OVER YOU, IT'S NOT GOOD. IT'S NOT THE ANSWER.
I SAW...
I DON'T WANT TO HURT YOU AGAIN, LANCE. PLEASE--
I SAW THE WHOLE THING... HE CUT THEIR THROATS, RIGHT IN FRONT OF ME... KILLED... EVERYONE.
THE SOUNDS...
WE NEVER SHOULD'VE GONE BACK..
WE NEVER SHOULD'VE GONE BACK...
"THE SWORD IS CALLED CALESVOL... THOUGH YOU MIGHT KNOW THE NAME OF ITS TWIN BETTER: EXCALIBUR.
"IT'S THE FAMOUS SWORD IN THE STONE. THE BLADE THAT BECOMES ONE WITH THE BEARER... THOUGH NO ONE COULD'VE FORESEEN CALESVOL HAVING A MIND OF ITS OWN."

...SAID, WE ST KEEP S BLADE ER CLOSE WATCH.

ONCE IT'S BEEN TAKEN FROM THE STONE, IT CAN-NOT BE PUT BACK.

IT IS OUR DUTY TO KEEP THIS WEAPON AWAY FROM WHATEVER WICKED THING IS PULLING OUR STRINGS.

YOU THINK IT'S HIM, DON'T YOU.

BLOODY BONES. I DO.

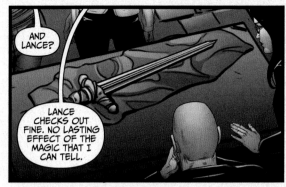

AND LANCE?

LANCE CHECKS OUT FINE. NO LASTING EFFECT OF THE MAGIC THAT I CAN TELL.

BUT WHATEVER CURSE IS PUT ON THE BLADE... T'S NOTHING I RECOGNIZE.

NOR I.

HEY, ALI...CAN I TALK TO YOU?

SORRY. I'M NOT FEELING WELL.

I HEARD ABOUT YOU. YOUR POWER OVER SPIRITS. YOU CAN SEE THINGS THAT WE CAN'T.

OH MY GOD. ALI, CAN SHE... CAN SHE SEE ME?

YOUR POINT, MARY?

I KNOW THAT WE'RE NOT ALONE HERE. I CAN'T SEE HER, BUT I KNOW. I HAVE POWER OVER THE DEAD, TOO.

I CAN CONTROL THEIR BODIES...AND YOU CAN BOND WITH THEIR MINDS.

WHAT ARE YOU SAYING?

I'M SAYING...HER SPIRIT IS HERE, RIGHT?

WHAT IF I CAN GIVE HER A BODY?

WHAT IF AILEY DIDN'T HAVE TO BE DEAD?

I FEAR SOMETHING DARK IS COMING.

NO, THAT'S NOT IT. HONESTLY...

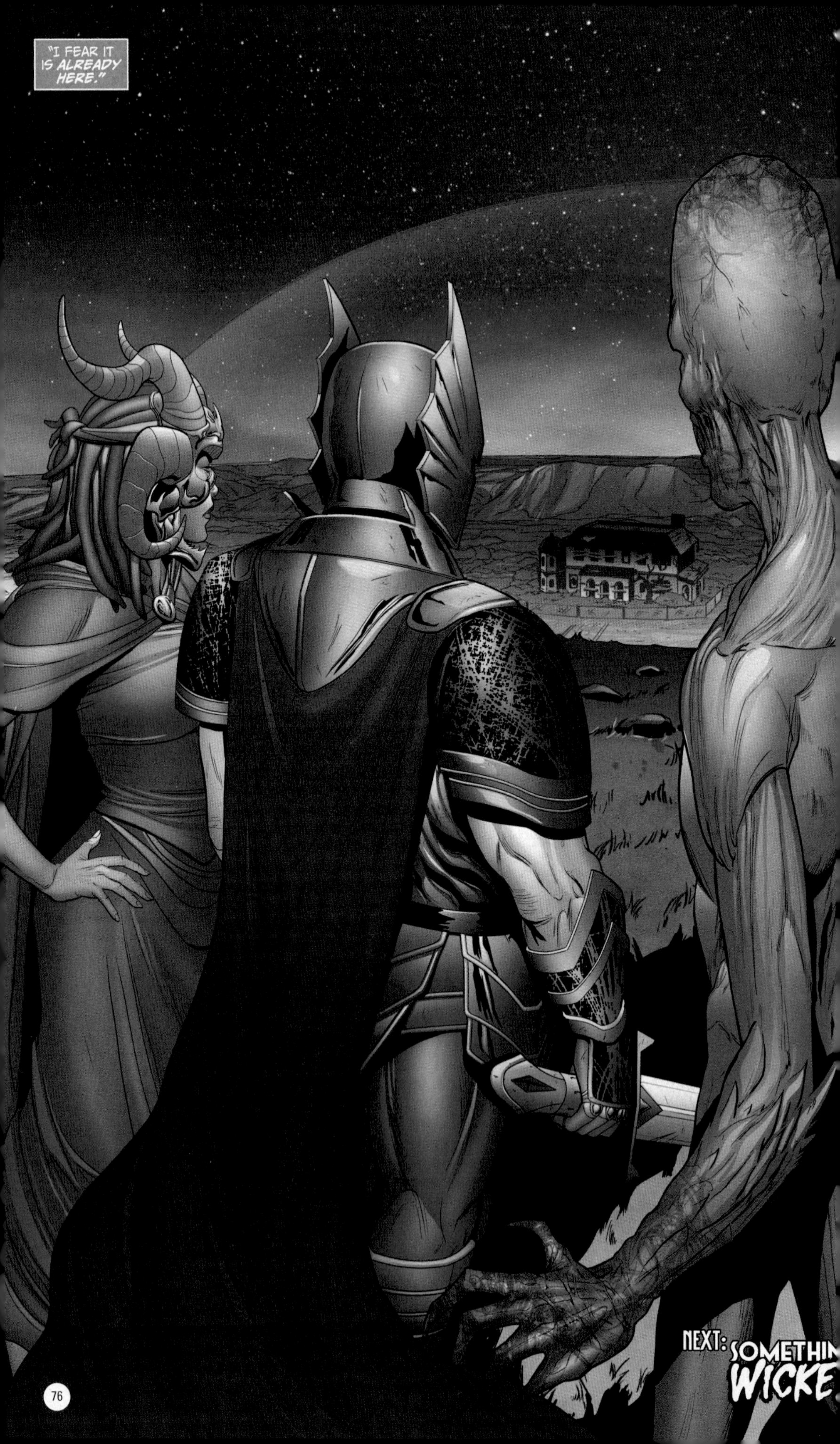
"I FEAR IT IS *ALREADY* HERE."
NEXT: SOMETHIN WICKE

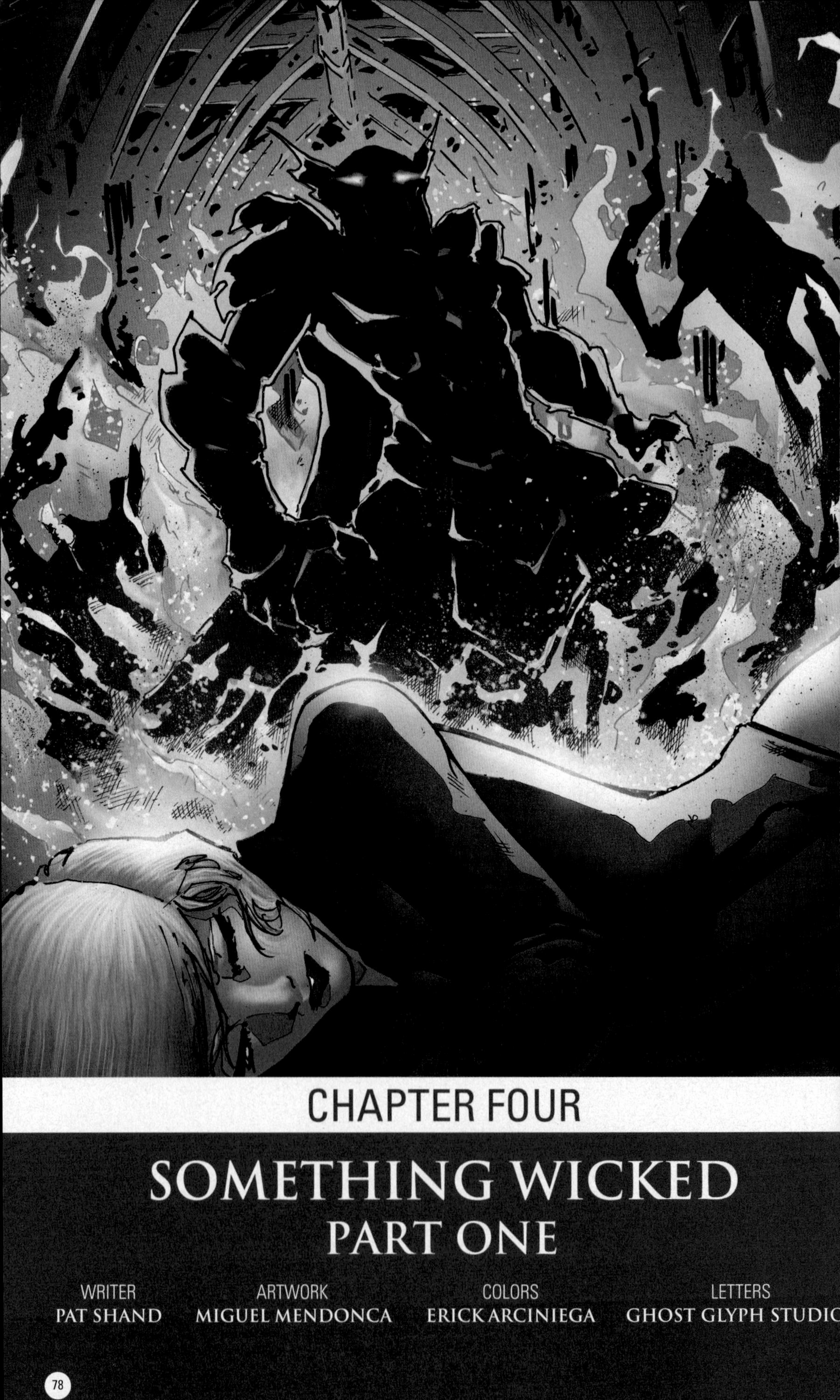

CHAPTER FOUR

SOMETHING WICKED
PART ONE

WRITER
PAT SHAND

ARTWORK
MIGUEL MENDONCA

COLORS
ERICK ARCINIEGA

LETTERS
GHOST GLYPH STUDIO

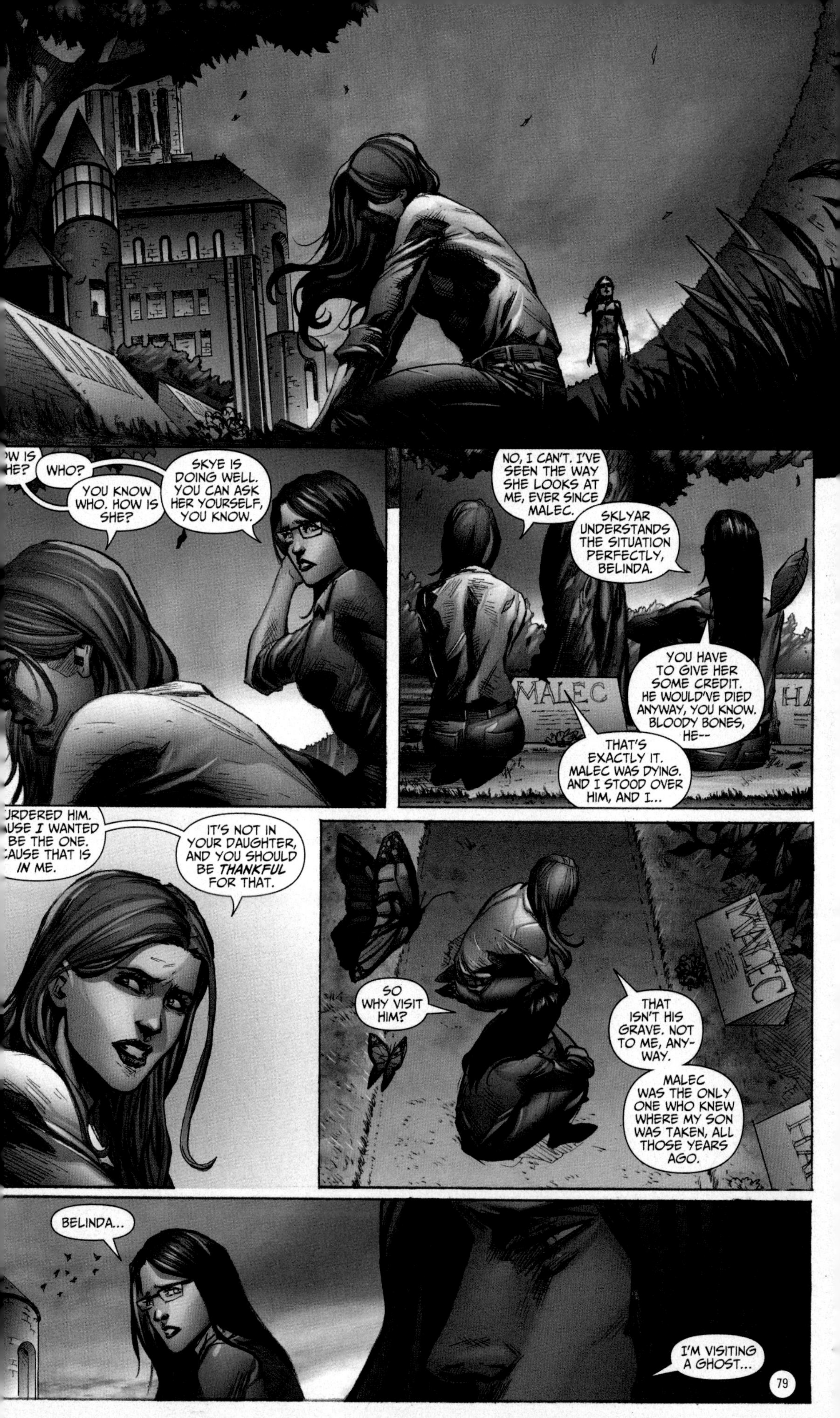

W IS HE?
WHO?
YOU KNOW WHO. HOW IS SHE?
SKYE IS DOING WELL. YOU CAN ASK HER YOURSELF, YOU KNOW.
NO, I CAN'T. I'VE SEEN THE WAY SHE LOOKS AT ME, EVER SINCE MALEC.
SKLYAR UNDERSTANDS THE SITUATION PERFECTLY, BELINDA.
MALEC
YOU HAVE TO GIVE HER SOME CREDIT. HE WOULD'VE DIED ANYWAY, YOU KNOW. BLOODY BONES, HE--
THAT'S EXACTLY IT. MALEC WAS DYING. AND I STOOD OVER HIM, AND I...
URDERED HIM. USE *I* WANTED BE THE ONE. CAUSE THAT IS *IN* ME.
IT'S NOT IN YOUR DAUGHTER, AND YOU SHOULD BE ***THANKFUL*** FOR THAT.
SO WHY VISIT HIM?
THAT ISN'T HIS GRAVE. NOT TO ME, ANY-WAY.
MALEC WAS THE ONLY ONE WHO KNEW WHERE MY SON WAS TAKEN, ALL THOSE YEARS AGO.
MALEC
BELINDA...
I'M VISITING A GHOST...

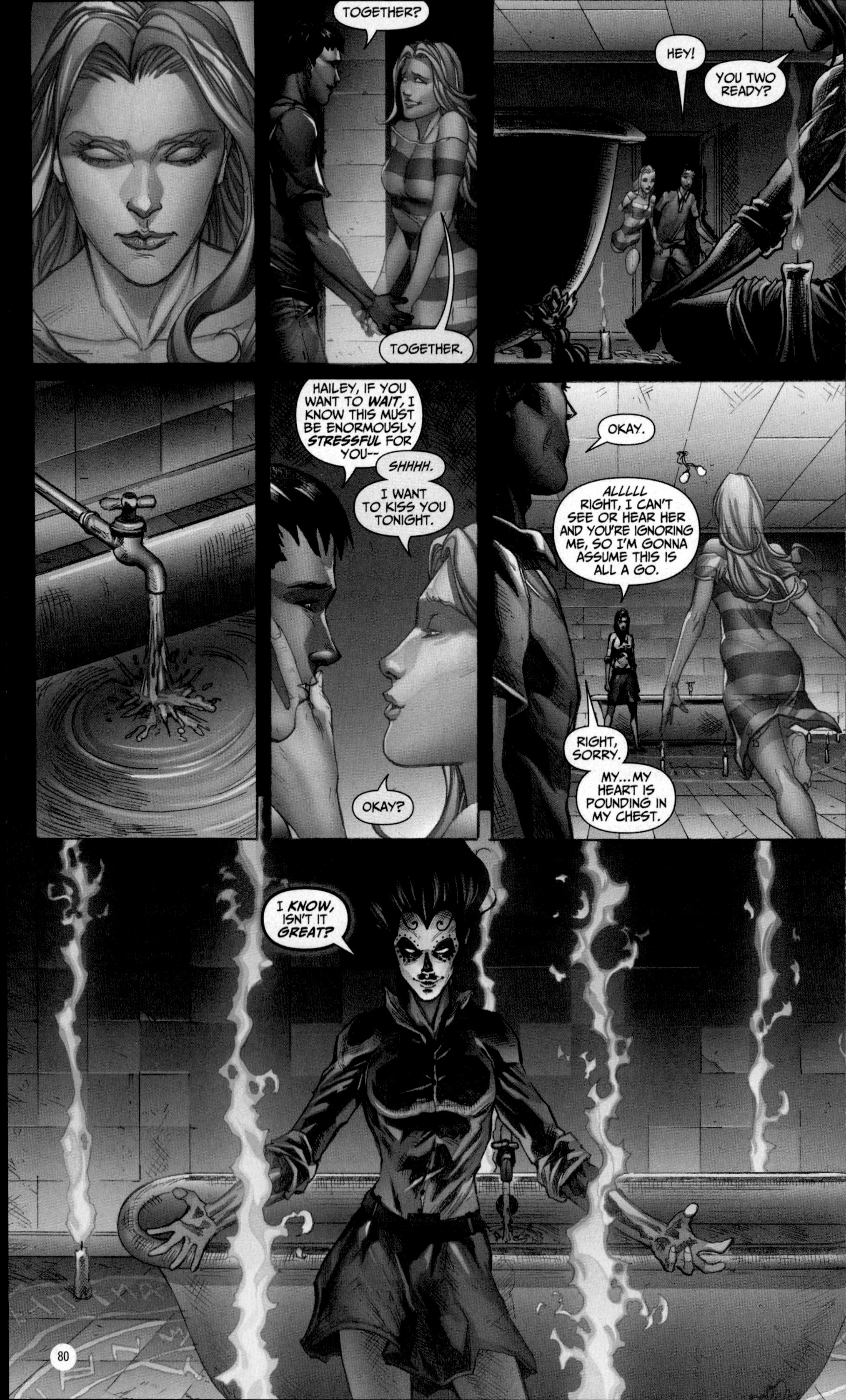
TOGETHER?
TOGETHER.
HEY!
YOU TWO READY?
HAILEY, IF YOU WANT TO WAIT, I KNOW THIS MUST BE ENORMOUSLY STRESSFUL FOR YOU--
SHHHH.
I WANT TO KISS YOU TONIGHT.
OKAY?
OKAY.
ALLLLL RIGHT, I CAN'T SEE OR HEAR HER AND YOU'RE IGNORING ME, SO I'M GONNA ASSUME THIS IS ALL A GO.
RIGHT, SORRY.
MY... MY HEART IS POUNDING IN MY CHEST.
I KNOW, ISN'T IT GREAT?

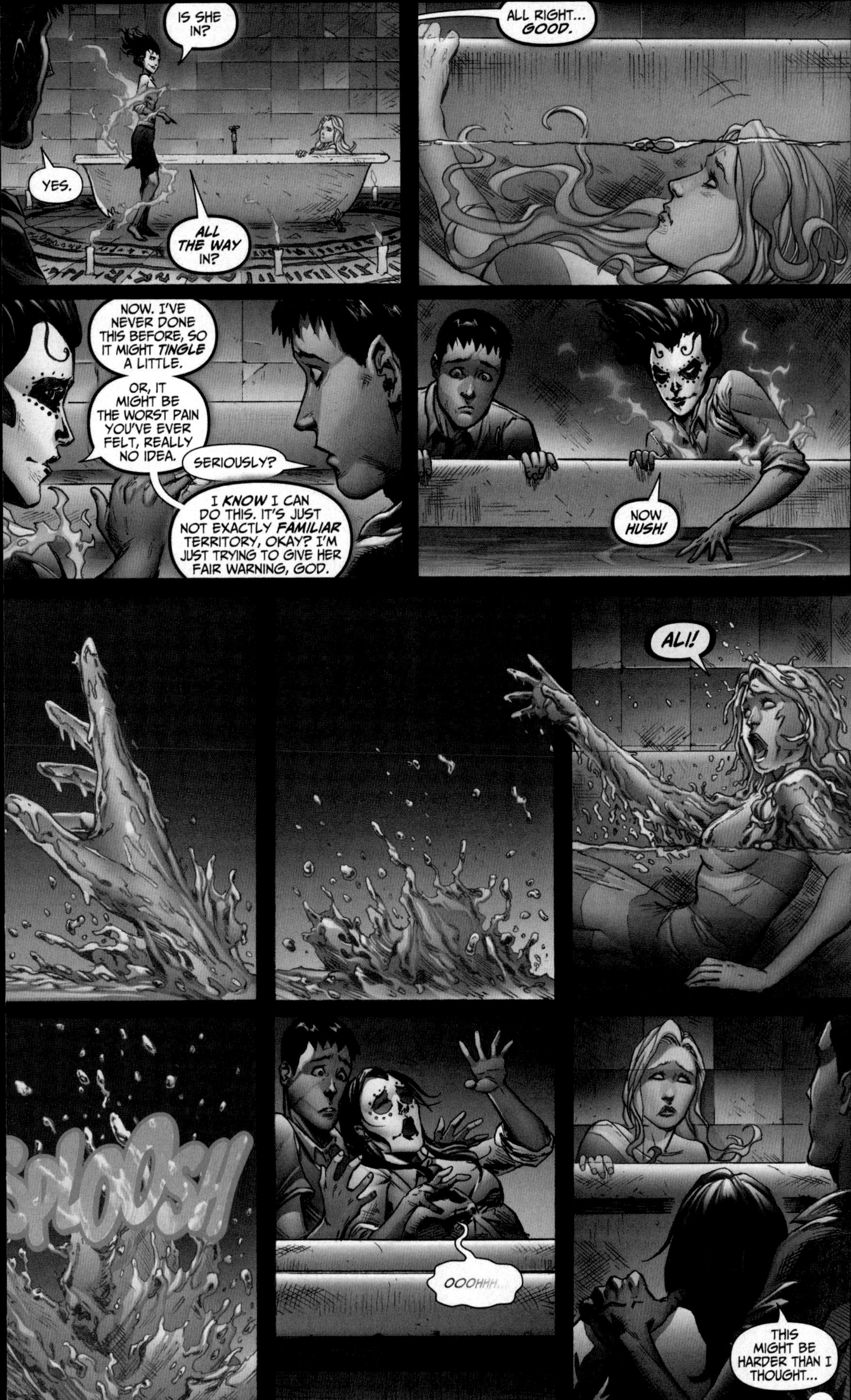

IS SHE IN?
YES.
ALL THE WAY IN?
ALL RIGHT... GOOD.
NOW. I'VE NEVER DONE THIS BEFORE, SO IT MIGHT TINGLE A LITTLE.
OR, IT MIGHT BE THE WORST PAIN YOU'VE EVER FELT, REALLY NO IDEA.
SERIOUSLY?
I KNOW I CAN DO THIS. IT'S JUST NOT EXACTLY FAMILIAR TERRITORY, OKAY? I'M JUST TRYING TO GIVE HER FAIR WARNING, GOD.
NOW HUSH!
ALI!
SPLOOSH
OOOHHH...
THIS MIGHT BE HARDER THAN I THOUGHT...

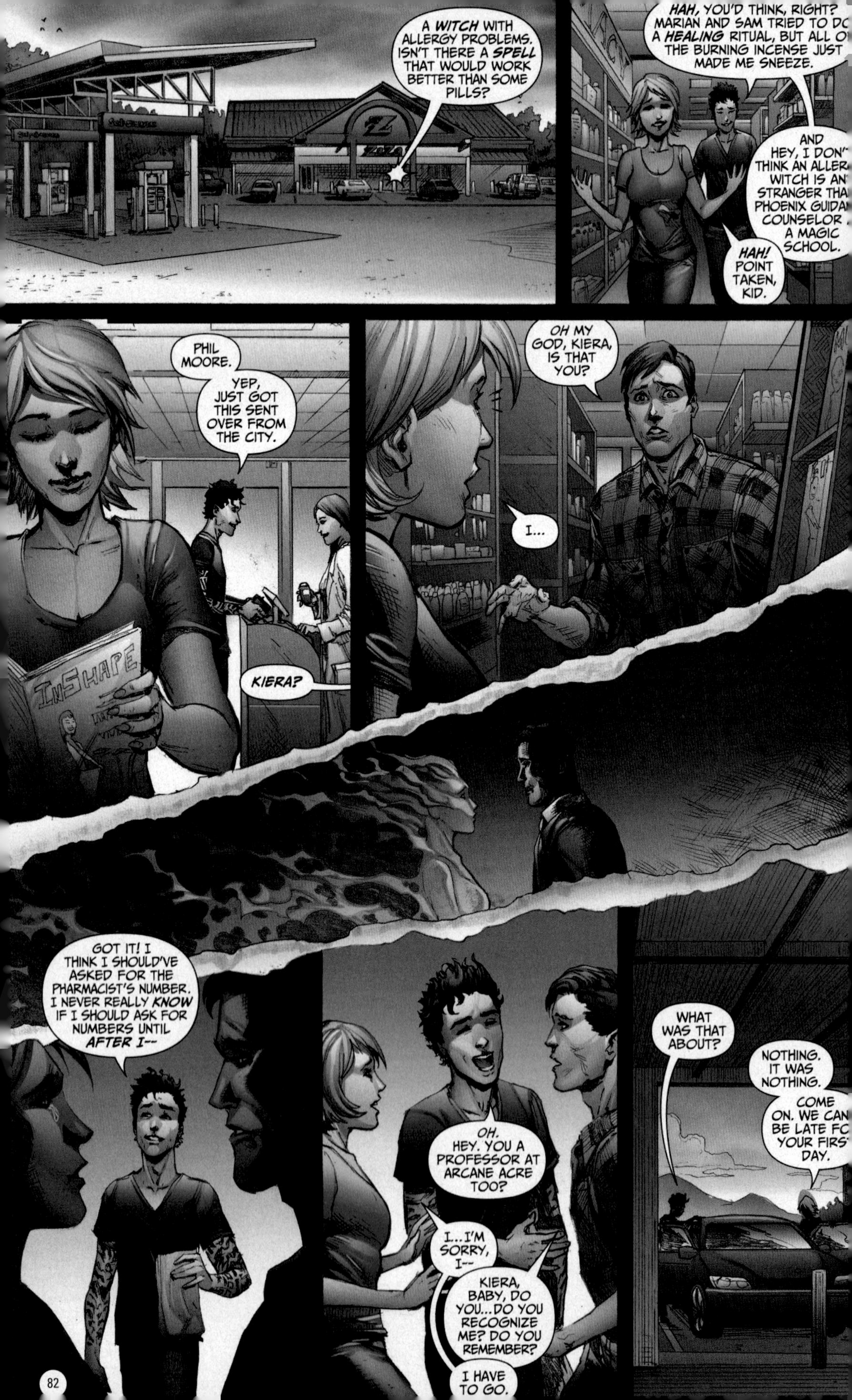
A WITCH WITH ALLERGY PROBLEMS. ISN'T THERE A SPELL THAT WOULD WORK BETTER THAN SOME PILLS?
HAH, YOU'D THINK, RIGHT? MARIAN AND SAM TRIED TO DO A HEALING RITUAL, BUT ALL OF THE BURNING INCENSE JUST MADE ME SNEEZE.
AND HEY, I DON'T THINK AN ALLERGY WITCH IS ANY STRANGER THAN A PHOENIX GUIDANCE COUNSELOR AT A MAGIC SCHOOL.
HAH! POINT TAKEN, KID.
PHIL MOORE.
YEP, JUST GOT THIS SENT OVER FROM THE CITY.
KIERA?
OH MY GOD, KIERA, IS THAT YOU?
I...
GOT IT! I THINK I SHOULD'VE ASKED FOR THE PHARMACIST'S NUMBER. I NEVER REALLY KNOW IF I SHOULD ASK FOR NUMBERS UNTIL AFTER I--
OH. HEY. YOU A PROFESSOR AT ARCANE ACRE TOO?
I...I'M SORRY, I--
KIERA, BABY, DO YOU...DO YOU RECOGNIZE ME? DO YOU REMEMBER?
I HAVE TO GO.
WHAT WAS THAT ABOUT?
NOTHING. IT WAS NOTHING.
COME ON. WE CAN'T BE LATE FOR YOUR FIRST DAY.

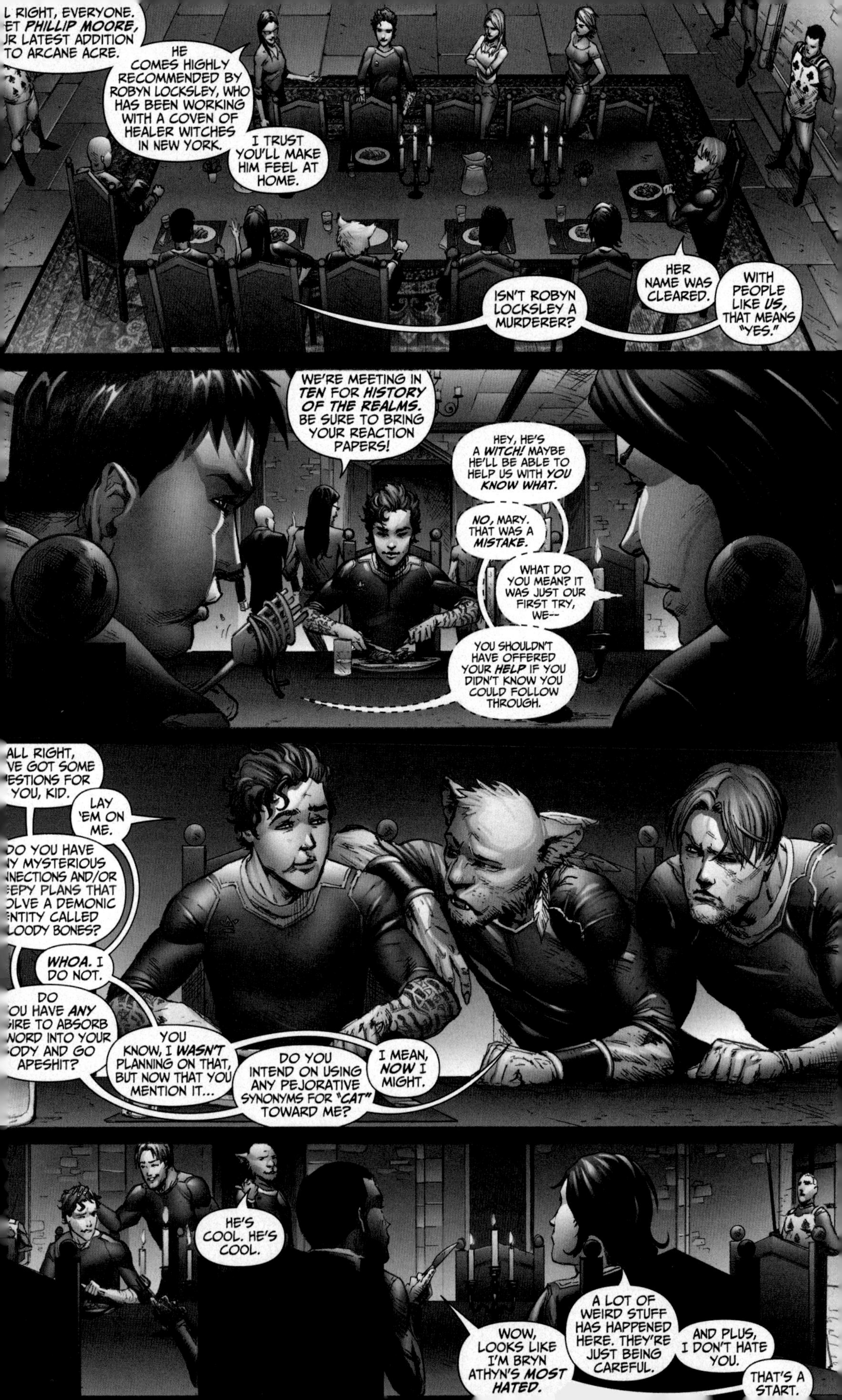

L RIGHT, EVERYONE. ET PHILLIP MOORE, JR LATEST ADDITION TO ARCANE ACRE.
HE COMES HIGHLY RECOMMENDED BY ROBYN LOCKSLEY, WHO HAS BEEN WORKING WITH A COVEN OF HEALER WITCHES IN NEW YORK.
I TRUST YOU'LL MAKE HIM FEEL AT HOME.
ISN'T ROBYN LOCKSLEY A MURDERER?
HER NAME WAS CLEARED.
WITH PEOPLE LIKE US, THAT MEANS "YES."
WE'RE MEETING IN TEN FOR HISTORY OF THE REALMS. BE SURE TO BRING YOUR REACTION PAPERS!
HEY, HE'S A WITCH! MAYBE HE'LL BE ABLE TO HELP US WITH YOU KNOW WHAT.
NO, MARY. THAT WAS A MISTAKE.
WHAT DO YOU MEAN? IT WAS JUST OUR FIRST TRY, WE--
YOU SHOULDN'T HAVE OFFERED YOUR HELP IF YOU DIDN'T KNOW YOU COULD FOLLOW THROUGH.
ALL RIGHT, VE GOT SOME ESTIONS FOR YOU, KID.
LAY 'EM ON ME.
DO YOU HAVE Y MYSTERIOUS NNECTIONS AND/OR EEPY PLANS THAT OLVE A DEMONIC NTITY CALLED LOODY BONES?
WHOA. I DO NOT.
DO OU HAVE ANY SIRE TO ABSORB WORD INTO YOUR ODY AND GO APESHIT?
YOU KNOW, I WASN'T PLANNING ON THAT, BUT NOW THAT YOU MENTION IT...
DO YOU INTEND ON USING ANY PEJORATIVE SYNONYMS FOR "CAT" TOWARD ME?
I MEAN, NOW I MIGHT.
HE'S COOL. HE'S COOL.
WOW, LOOKS LIKE I'M BRYN ATHYN'S MOST HATED.
A LOT OF WEIRD STUFF HAS HAPPENED HERE. THEY'RE JUST BEING CAREFUL.
AND PLUS, I DON'T HATE YOU.
THAT'S A START.

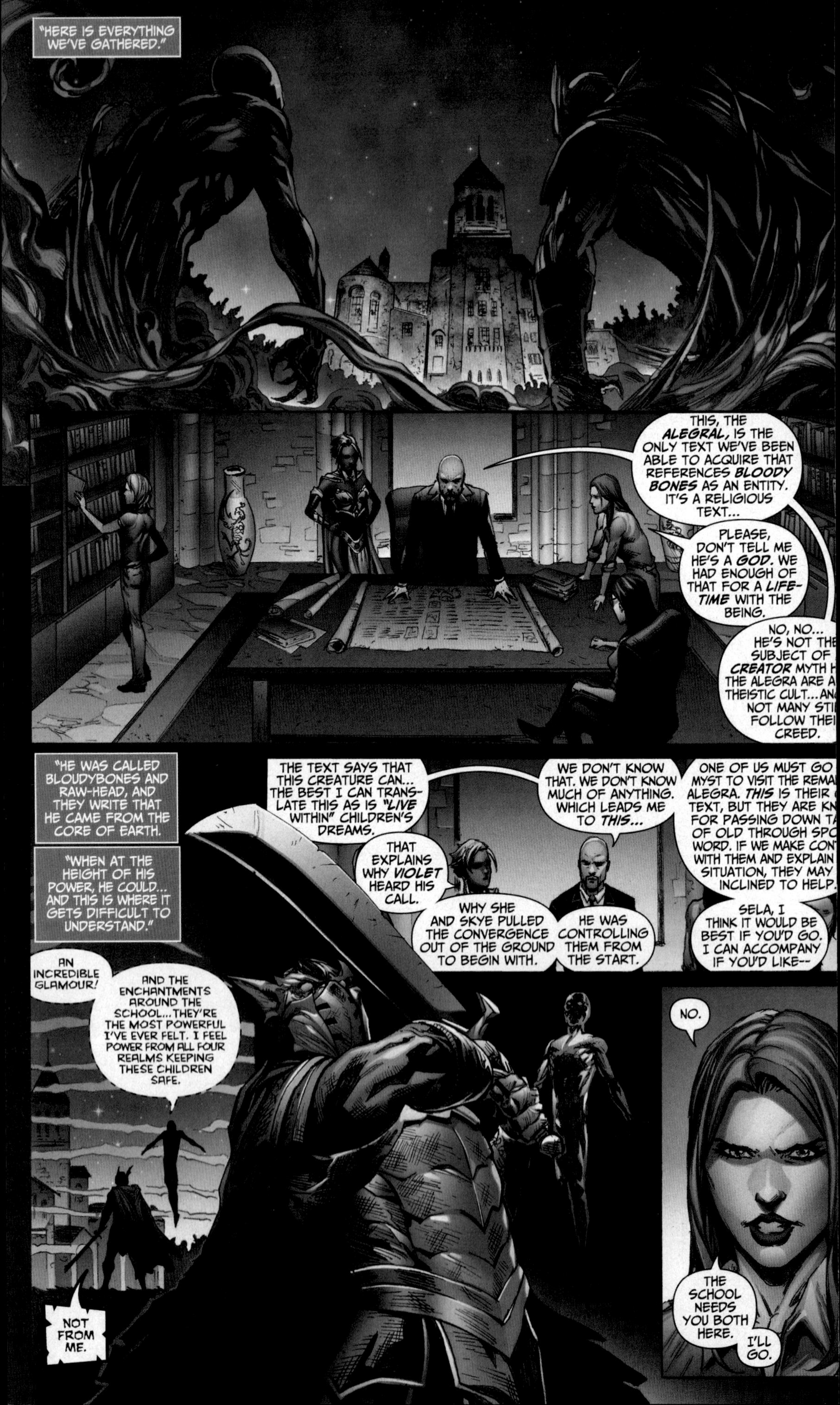
"HERE IS EVERYTHING WE'VE GATHERED."
THIS, THE ALEGRAL, IS THE ONLY TEXT WE'VE BEEN ABLE TO ACQUIRE THAT REFERENCES BLOODY BONES AS AN ENTITY. IT'S A RELIGIOUS TEXT...
PLEASE, DON'T TELL ME HE'S A GOD. WE HAD ENOUGH OF THAT FOR A LIFETIME WITH THE BEING.
NO, NO... HE'S NOT THE SUBJECT OF CREATOR MYTH H THE ALEGRA ARE A THEISTIC CULT...AN NOT MANY STI FOLLOW THEI CREED.
"HE WAS CALLED BLOUDYBONES AND RAW-HEAD, AND THEY WRITE THAT HE CAME FROM THE CORE OF EARTH.
"WHEN AT THE HEIGHT OF HIS POWER, HE COULD... AND THIS IS WHERE IT GETS DIFFICULT TO UNDERSTAND."
THE TEXT SAYS THAT THIS CREATURE CAN... THE BEST I CAN TRANSLATE THIS AS IS "LIVE WITHIN" CHILDREN'S DREAMS.
THAT EXPLAINS WHY VIOLET HEARD HIS CALL.
WHY SHE AND SKYE PULLED THE CONVERGENCE OUT OF THE GROUND TO BEGIN WITH.
HE WAS CONTROLLING THEM FROM THE START.
WE DON'T KNOW THAT. WE DON'T KNOW MUCH OF ANYTHING. WHICH LEADS ME TO THIS...
ONE OF US MUST GO MYST TO VISIT THE REMA ALEGRA. THIS IS THEIR TEXT, BUT THEY ARE KN FOR PASSING DOWN T OF OLD THROUGH SPO WORD. IF WE MAKE CON WITH THEM AND EXPLAIN SITUATION, THEY MAY INCLINED TO HELP.
SELA, I THINK IT WOULD BE BEST IF YOU'D GO. I CAN ACCOMPANY IF YOU'D LIKE--
NO.
THE SCHOOL NEEDS YOU BOTH HERE.
I'LL GO.
AN INCREDIBLE GLAMOUR!
AND THE ENCHANTMENTS AROUND THE SCHOOL... THEY'RE THE MOST POWERFUL I'VE EVER FELT. I FEEL POWER FROM ALL FOUR REALMS KEEPING THESE CHILDREN SAFE.
NOT FROM ME.

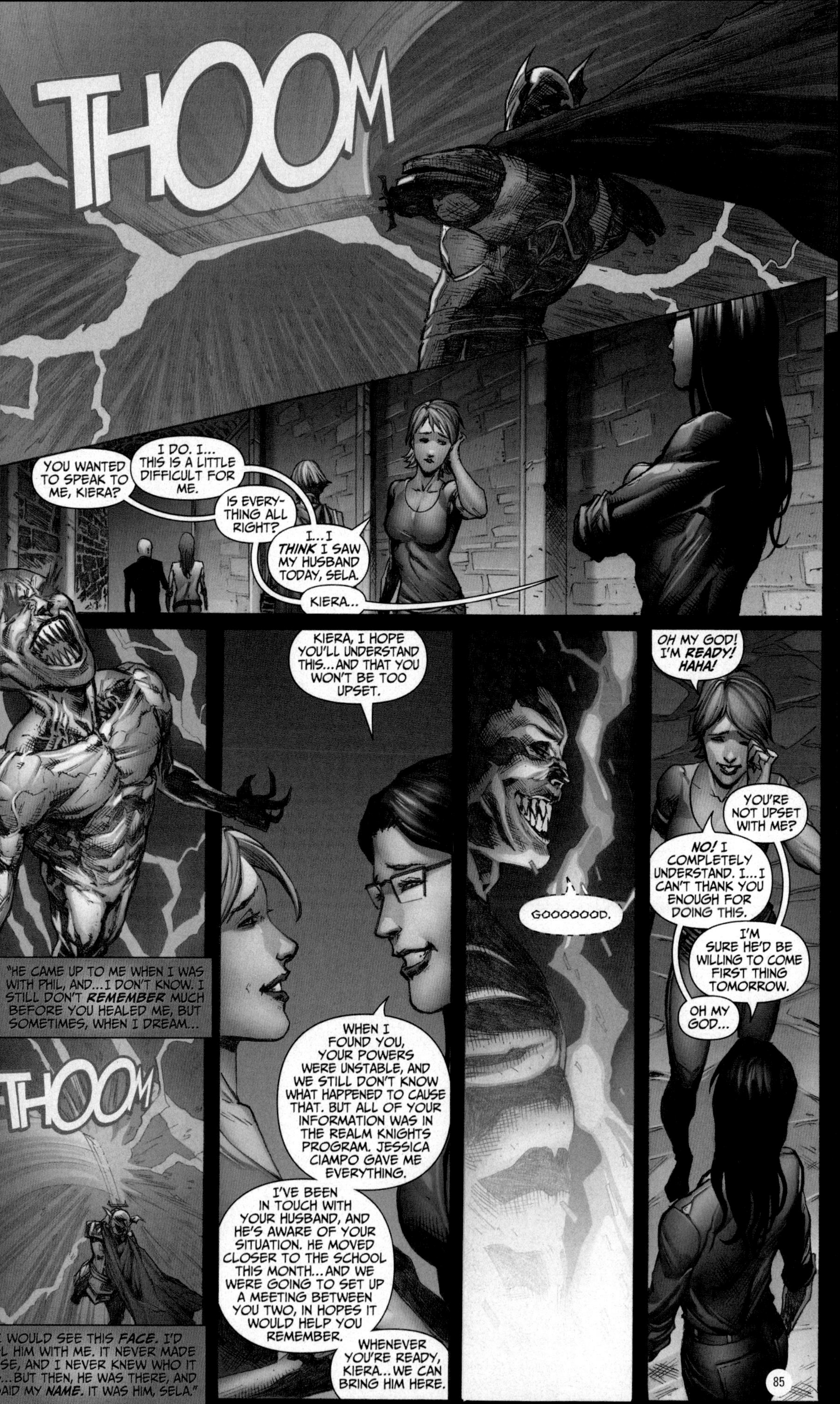
THOOM
YOU WANTED TO SPEAK TO ME, KIERA?
I DO. I... THIS IS A LITTLE DIFFICULT FOR ME.
IS EVERY-THING ALL RIGHT?
I...I *THINK* I SAW MY HUSBAND TODAY, SELA.
KIERA...
"HE CAME UP TO ME WHEN I WAS WITH PHIL, AND...I DON'T KNOW. I STILL DON'T *REMEMBER* MUCH BEFORE YOU HEALED ME, BUT SOMETIMES, WHEN I DREAM...
THOOM
E WOULD SEE THIS *FACE*. I'D
L HIM WITH ME. IT NEVER MADE
SE, AND I NEVER KNEW WHO IT
...BUT THEN, HE WAS THERE, AND
AID MY *NAME*. IT WAS HIM, SELA."
KIERA, I HOPE YOU'LL UNDERSTAND THIS...AND THAT YOU WON'T BE TOO UPSET.
WHEN I FOUND YOU, YOUR POWERS WERE UNSTABLE, AND WE STILL DON'T KNOW WHAT HAPPENED TO CAUSE THAT. BUT ALL OF YOUR INFORMATION WAS IN THE REALM KNIGHTS PROGRAM. JESSICA CIAMPO GAVE ME EVERYTHING.
I'VE BEEN IN TOUCH WITH YOUR HUSBAND, AND HE'S AWARE OF YOUR SITUATION. HE MOVED CLOSER TO THE SCHOOL THIS MONTH...AND WE WERE GOING TO SET UP A MEETING BETWEEN YOU TWO, IN HOPES IT WOULD HELP YOU REMEMBER.
WHENEVER YOU'RE READY, KIERA...WE CAN BRING HIM HERE.
GOOOOOOD.
OH MY GOD! I'M *READY!* *HAHA!*
YOU'RE NOT UPSET WITH ME?
NO! I COMPLETELY UNDERSTAND. I...I CAN'T THANK YOU ENOUGH FOR DOING THIS.
I'M SURE HE'D BE WILLING TO COME FIRST THING TOMORROW.
OH MY GOD...

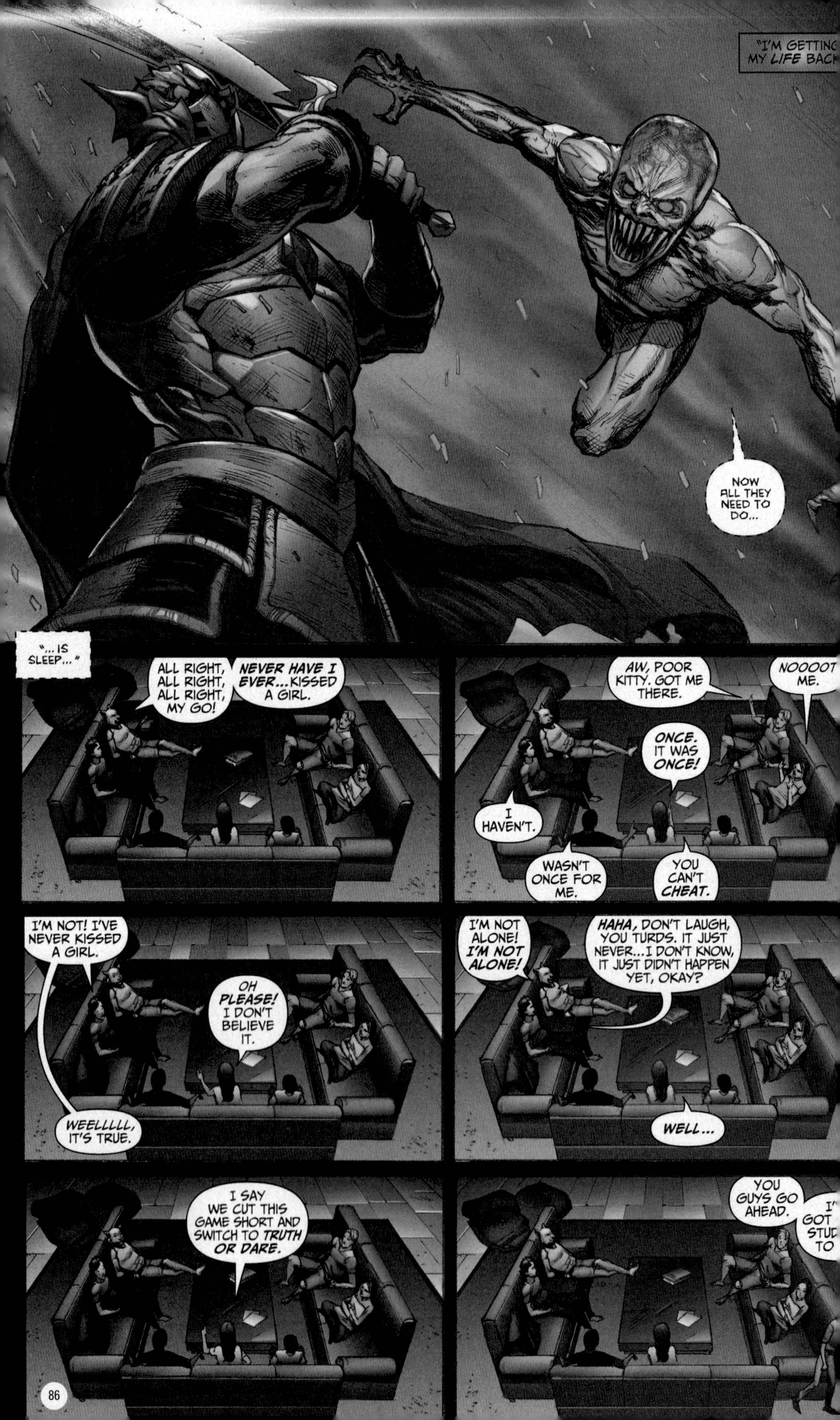
"I'M GETTING MY LIFE BACK
NOW ALL THEY NEED TO DO...
"...IS SLEEP..."
ALL RIGHT, ALL RIGHT, ALL RIGHT, MY GO!
NEVER HAVE I EVER...KISSED A GIRL.
AW, POOR KITTY. GOT ME THERE.
NOOOOT ME.
ONCE. IT WAS ONCE!
I HAVEN'T.
WASN'T ONCE FOR ME.
YOU CAN'T CHEAT.
I'M NOT! I'VE NEVER KISSED A GIRL.
OH PLEASE! I DON'T BELIEVE IT.
WEELLLLL, IT'S TRUE.
I'M NOT ALONE! I'M NOT ALONE!
HAHA, DON'T LAUGH, YOU TURDS. IT JUST NEVER...I DON'T KNOW, IT JUST DIDN'T HAPPEN YET, OKAY?
WELL...
I SAY WE CUT THIS GAME SHORT AND SWITCH TO TRUTH OR DARE.
YOU GUYS GO AHEAD.

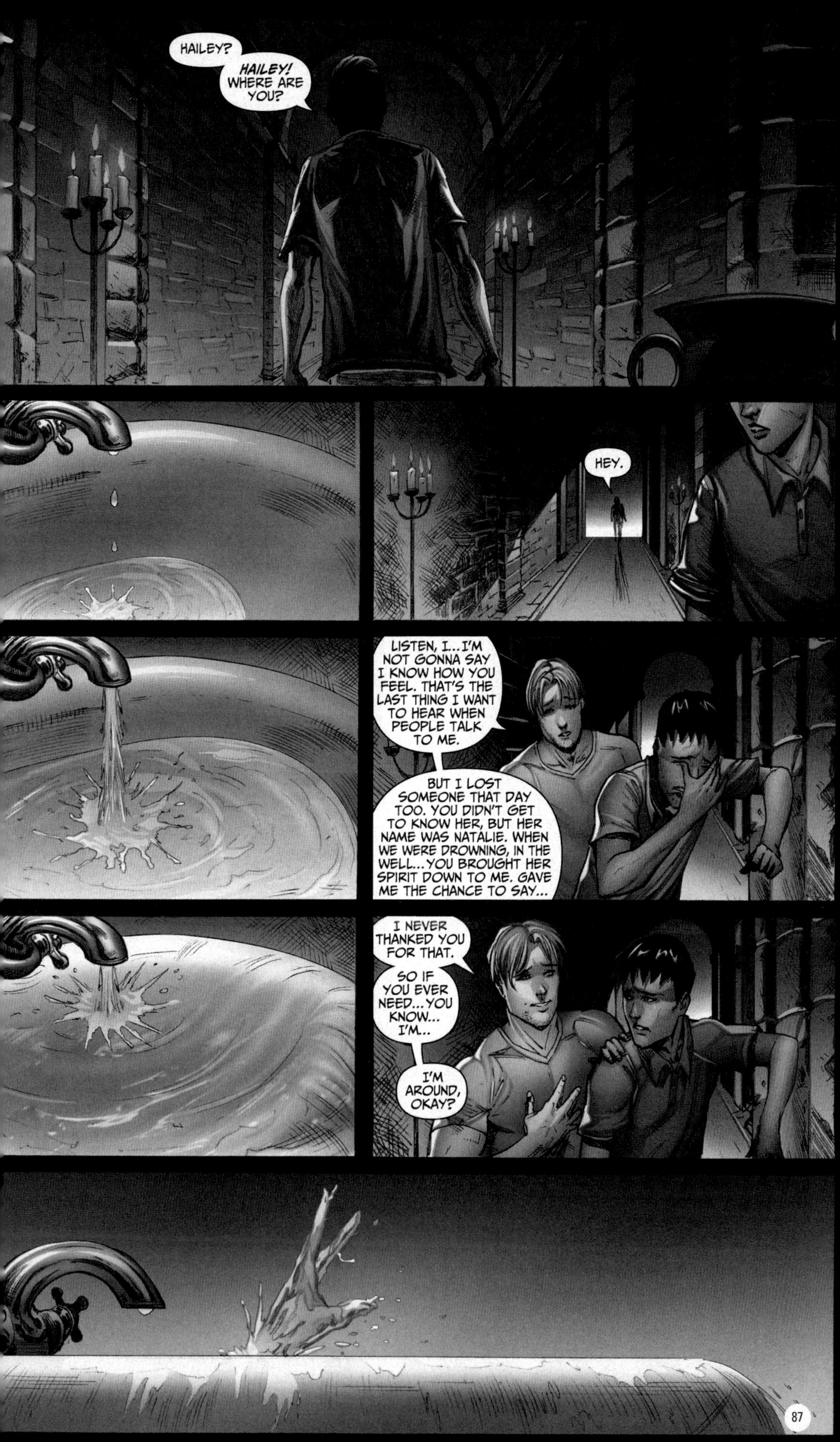
HAILEY?
HAILEY! WHERE ARE YOU?
HEY.
LISTEN, I...I'M NOT GONNA SAY I KNOW HOW YOU FEEL. THAT'S THE LAST THING I WANT TO HEAR WHEN PEOPLE TALK TO ME.
BUT I LOST SOMEONE THAT DAY TOO. YOU DIDN'T GET TO KNOW HER, BUT HER NAME WAS NATALIE. WHEN WE WERE DROWNING, IN THE WELL...YOU BROUGHT HER SPIRIT DOWN TO ME. GAVE ME THE CHANCE TO SAY...
I NEVER THANKED YOU FOR THAT.
SO IF YOU EVER NEED...YOU KNOW... I'M...
I'M AROUND, OKAY?

GOOD TO SEE YOU MAKING FRIENDS ALREADY, PHIL!

SO, ON A SCALE FROM ONE TO TEN, EXACTLY *HOW* MUCH TROUBLE AM I IN?

ZERO. LET SHE WHO HAS NOT PLAYED TRUTH OR DARE CAST THE FIRST STONE.

UGH.

FOR THE RECORD, IF I *COULD* KISS YOU WITHOUT KILLING YOU, THAT WOULD BE ME. I AM KISSING YOU VICARIOUSLY, RIGHT NOW.

TIME FOR LIGHTS OUT, YOU GUYS.

YOU CAN CONTINUE THE HORMONE HURRAH AFTER CLASS TOMORROW.

HEY, SKYE...DO YOU HAVE A MINUTE?

SURE.

YOU HAVE MY MOTHER'S BOOK. TAKING A TRIP?

OH. YEAH. THEY NEED SOME INFORMATION FROM A CULT IN MYST, SO...

GNARLY.

THEY'RE PEACEFUL. IT'S... THAT'S NOT WHY I WANTED TO TALK TO YOU.

EVER SINCE THE COURT- YARD, WITH MALEC, I--

HEY, OKAY, NO-- SORRY, BUT I CAN'T TALK ABOUT THIS NOW.

SKYE, YOU KNOW WHAT HE IS. YOU--

YOU VISIT HIS *GRAVE.* DO *YOU* KNOW WHAT HE IS?

IT'S NOT A BI DEAL. JUS LET ME KN WHEN YOU BACK.

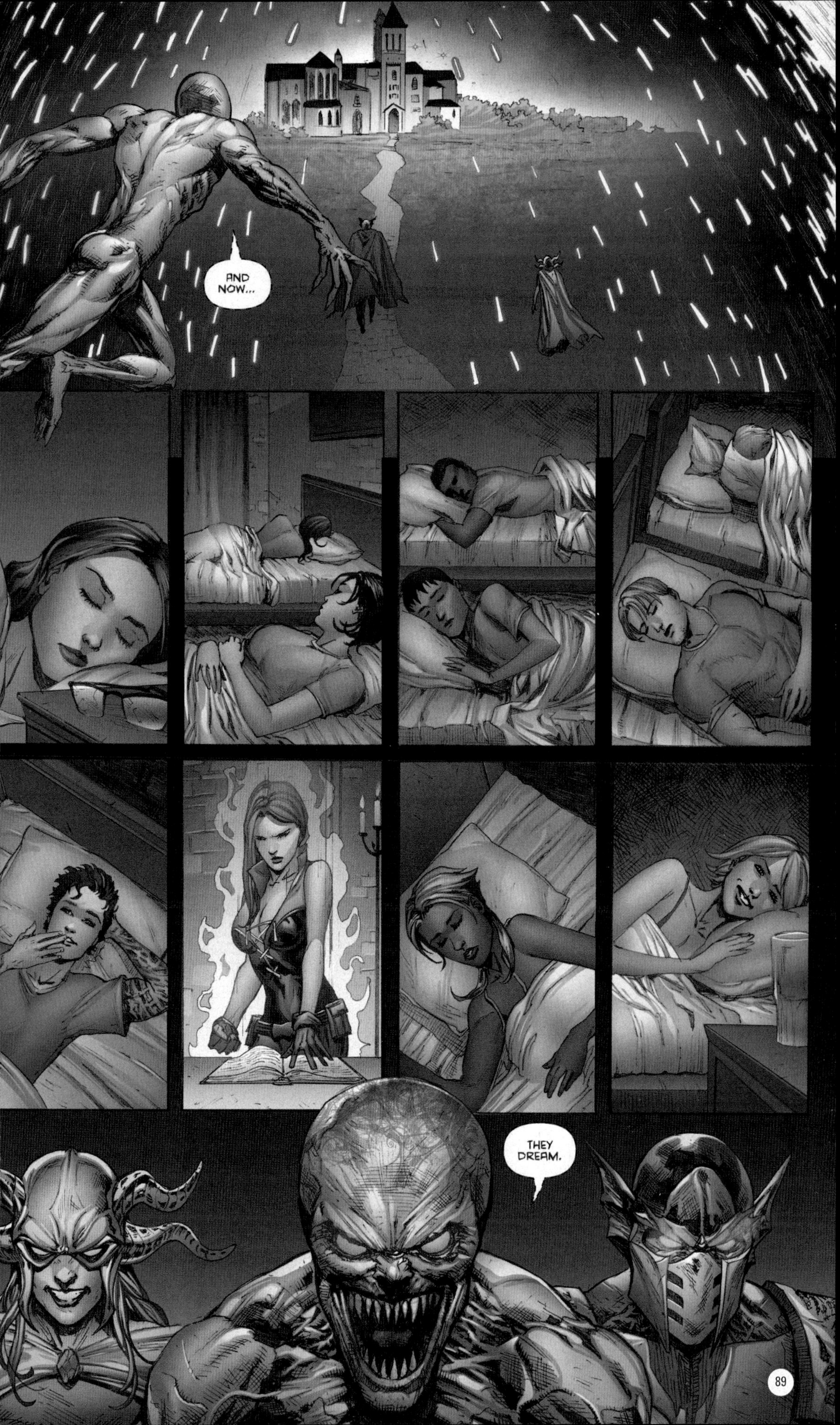
AND NOW...
THEY DREAM.

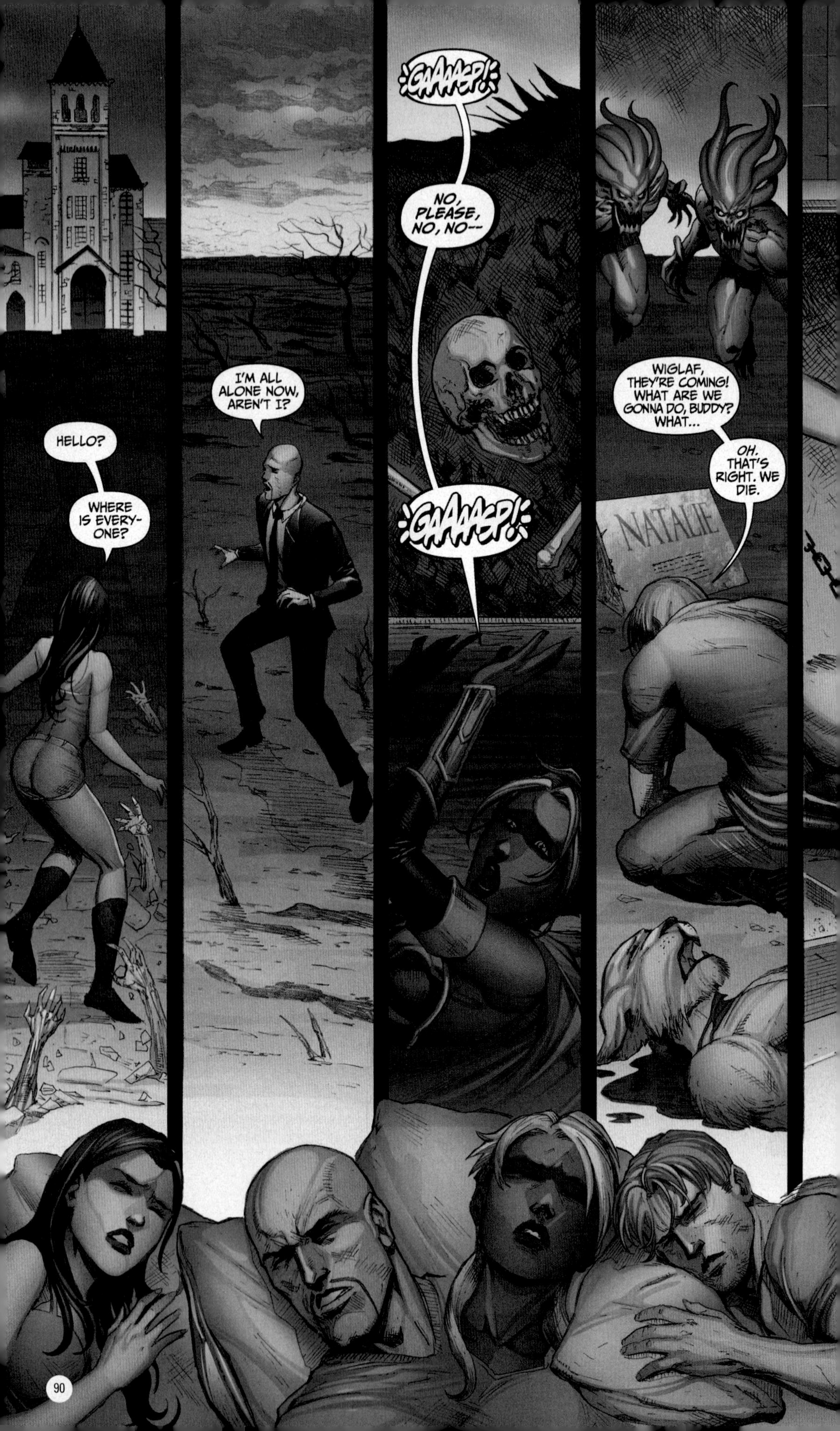
HELLO?
WHERE IS EVERY-ONE?
I'M ALL ALONE NOW, AREN'T I?
GAAAASP!
NO, PLEASE, NO, NO--
GAAAASP!
WIGLAF, THEY'RE COMING! WHAT ARE WE GONNA DO, BUDDY? WHAT...
OH. THAT'S RIGHT. WE DIE.
NATALIE

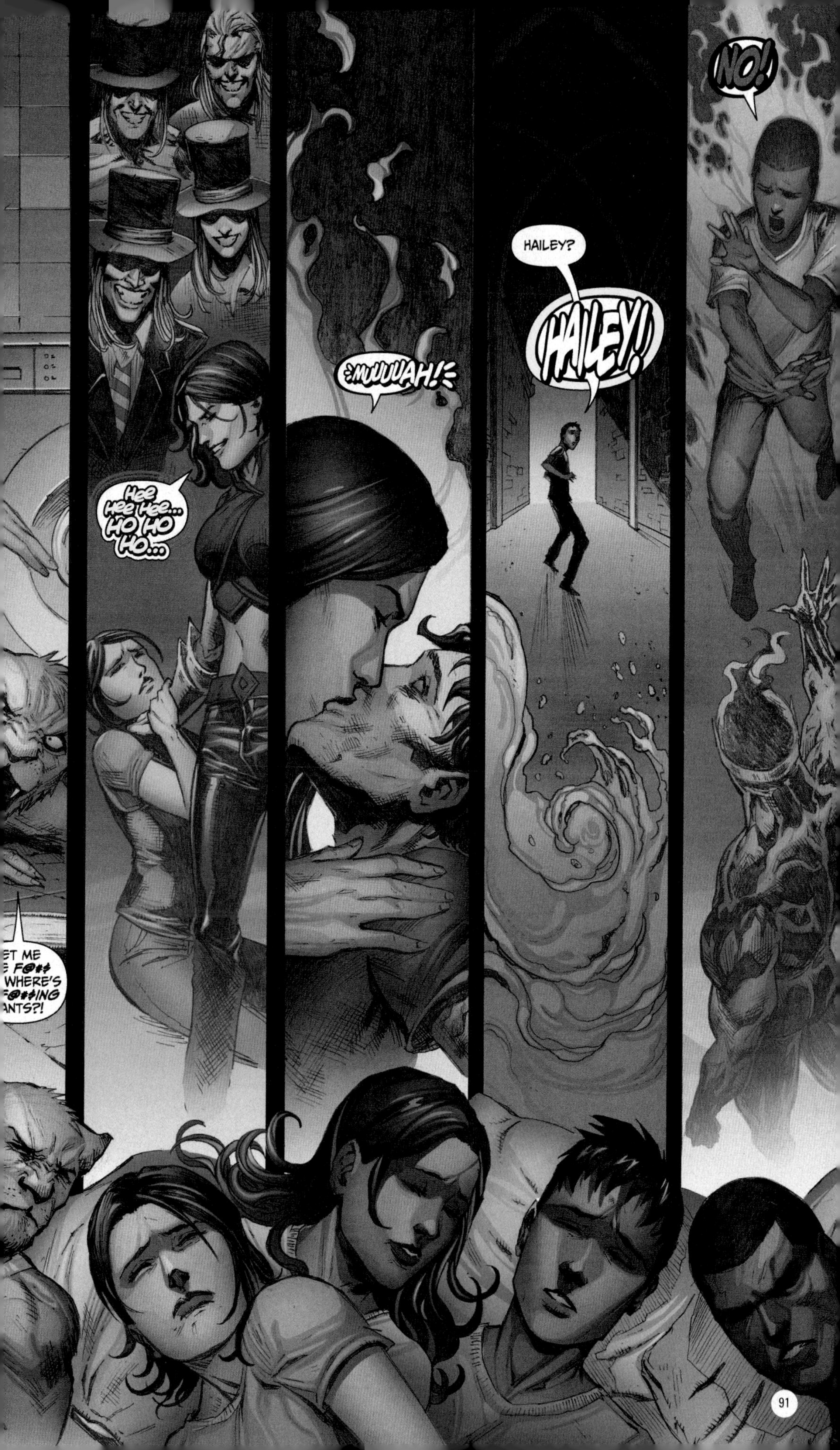
ET ME
E F@#$
WHERE'S
F@#$ING
ANTS?!
HEE HEE HEE... HO HO HO...
MUUUUAH!
HAILEY?
HAILEY!
NO!

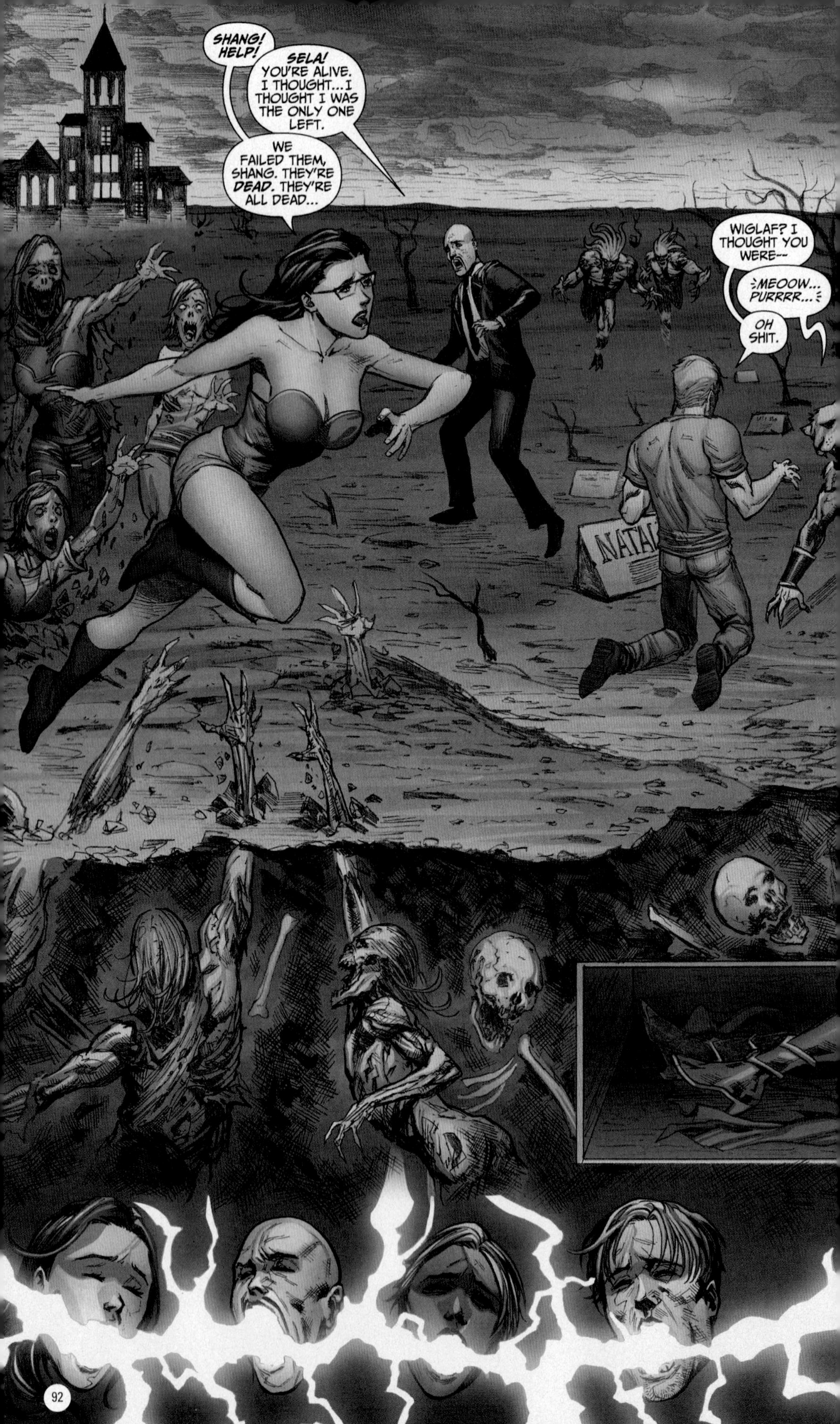
SHANG! HELP!
SELA! YOU'RE ALIVE. I THOUGHT... I THOUGHT I WAS THE ONLY ONE LEFT.
WE FAILED THEM, SHANG. THEY'RE DEAD. THEY'RE ALL DEAD...
WIGLAF? I THOUGHT YOU WERE--
MEOOW... PURRRR...
OH SHIT.

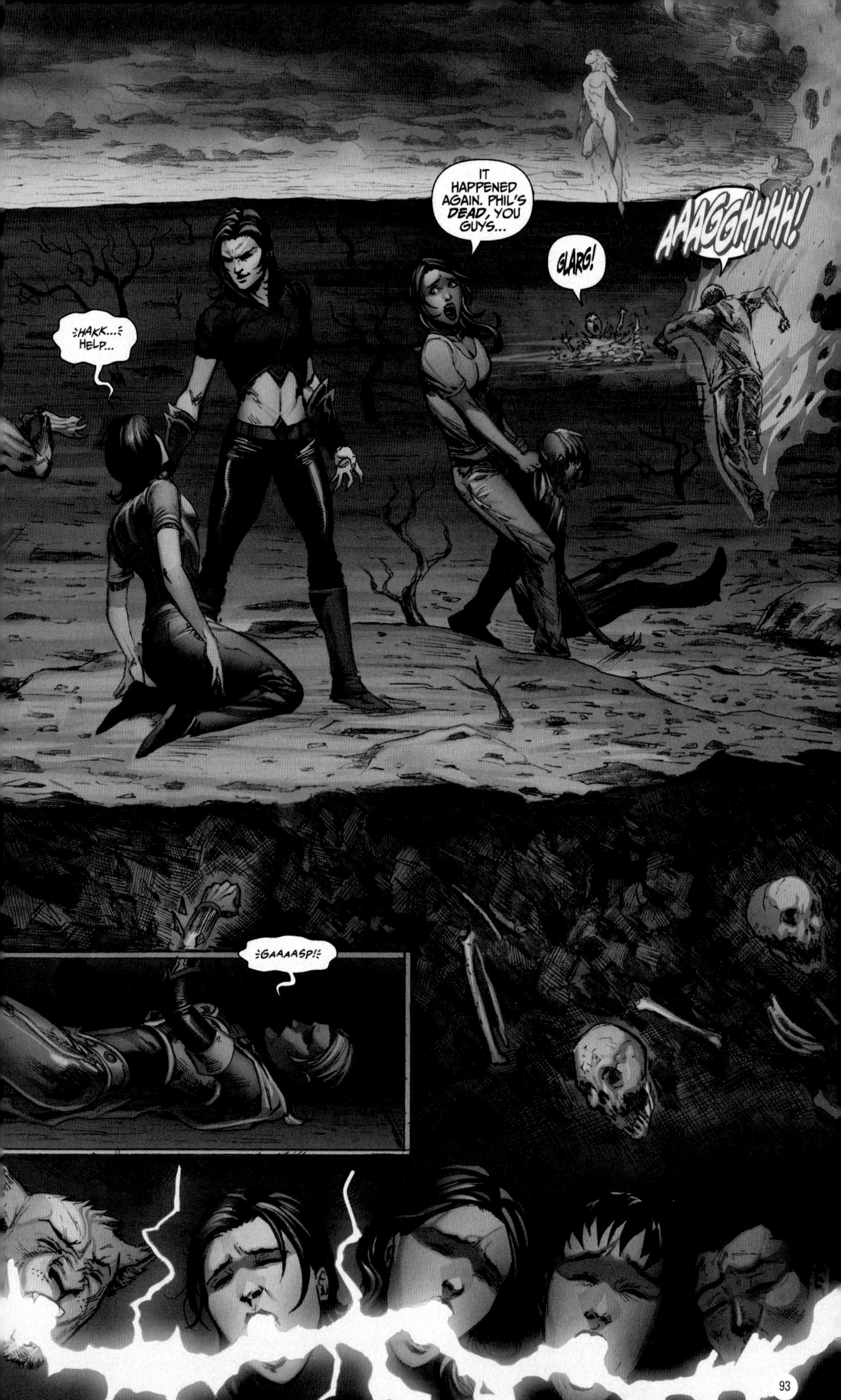
IT HAPPENED AGAIN. PHIL'S DEAD, YOU GUYS...
GLARG!
AAAGGHHHH!
HAKK... HELP...
GAAAASP!

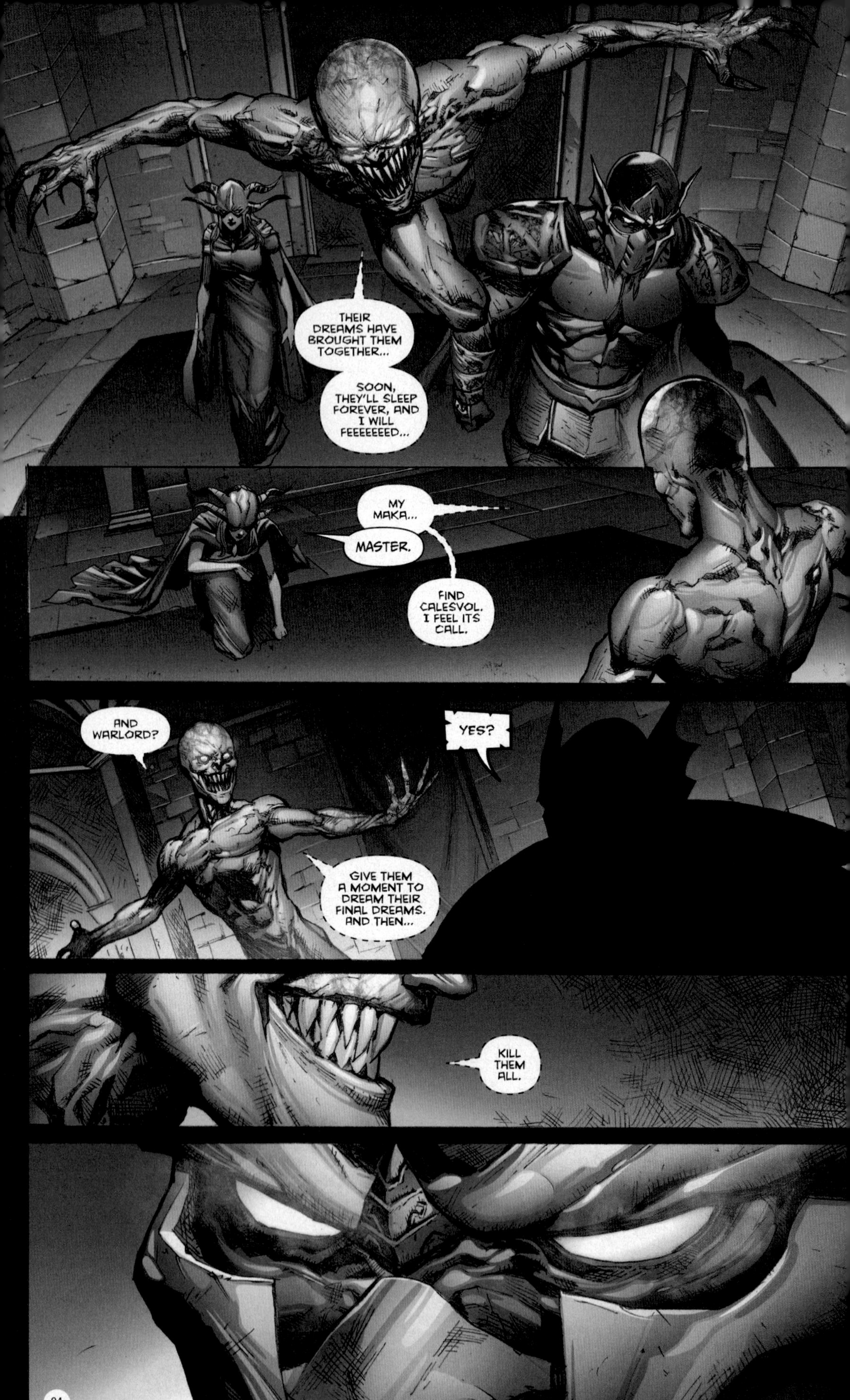
THEIR DREAMS HAVE BROUGHT THEM TOGETHER...
SOON, THEY'LL SLEEP FOREVER, AND I WILL FEEEEEEED...
MY MAKA...
MASTER.
FIND CALESVOL. I FEEL ITS CALL.
AND WARLORD?
YES?
GIVE THEM A MOMENT TO DREAM THEIR FINAL DREAMS. AND THEN...
KILL THEM ALL.

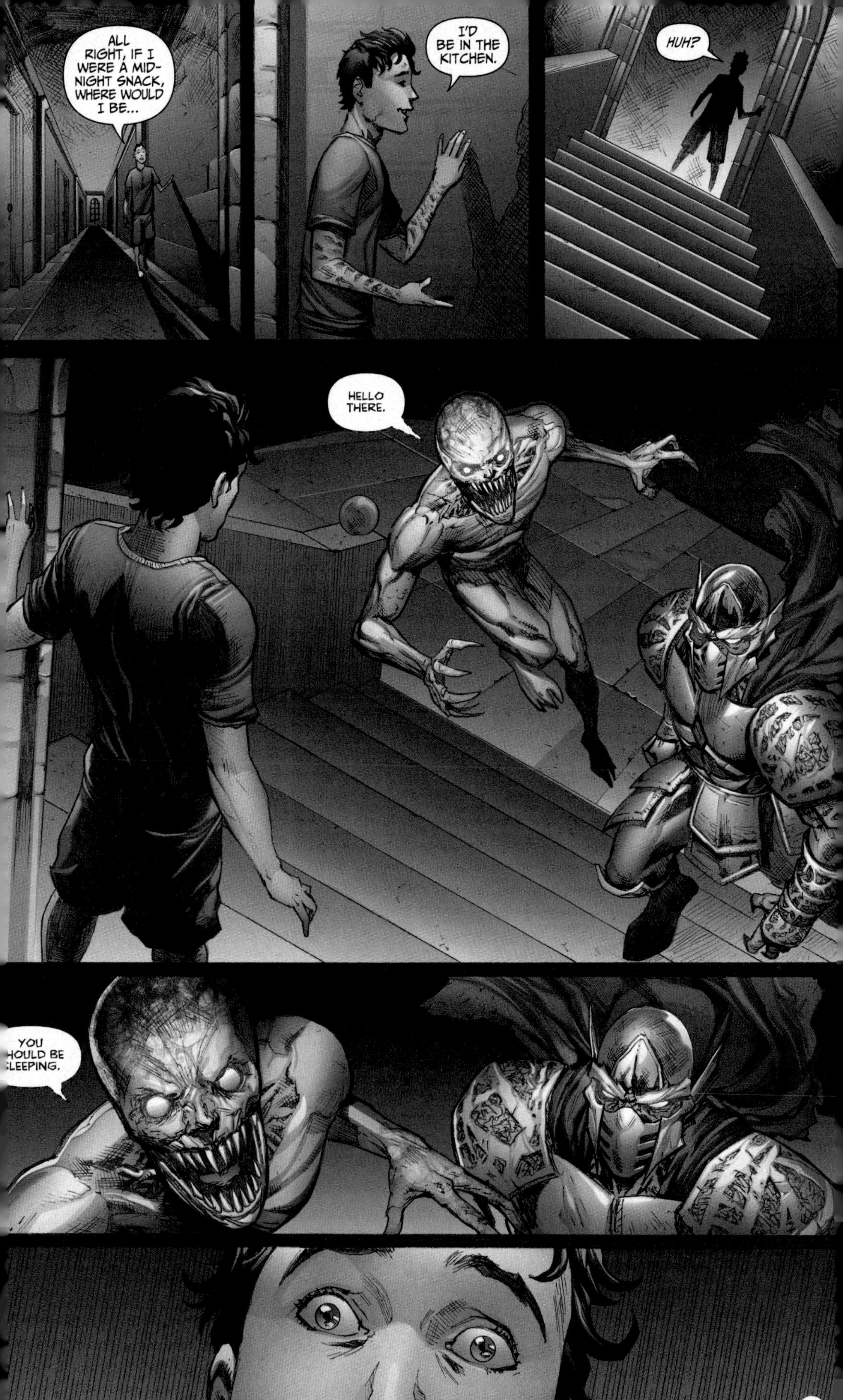
ALL RIGHT, IF I WERE A MID-NIGHT SNACK, WHERE WOULD I BE...
I'D BE IN THE KITCHEN.
HUH?
HELLO THERE.
YOU HOULD BE LEEPING.

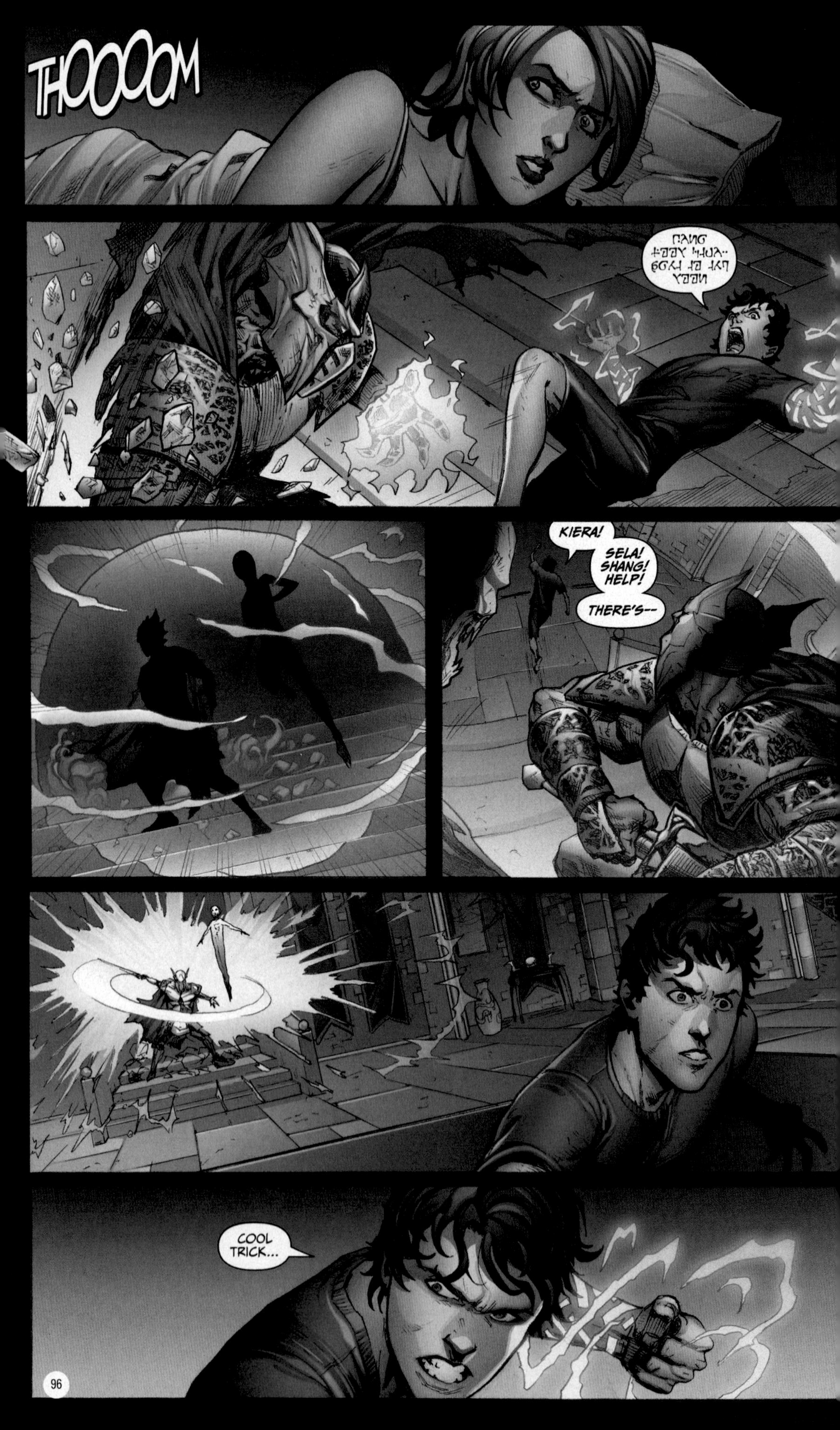
THOOOOM
KIERA!
SELA! SHANG! HELP!
THERE'S--
COOL TRICK...

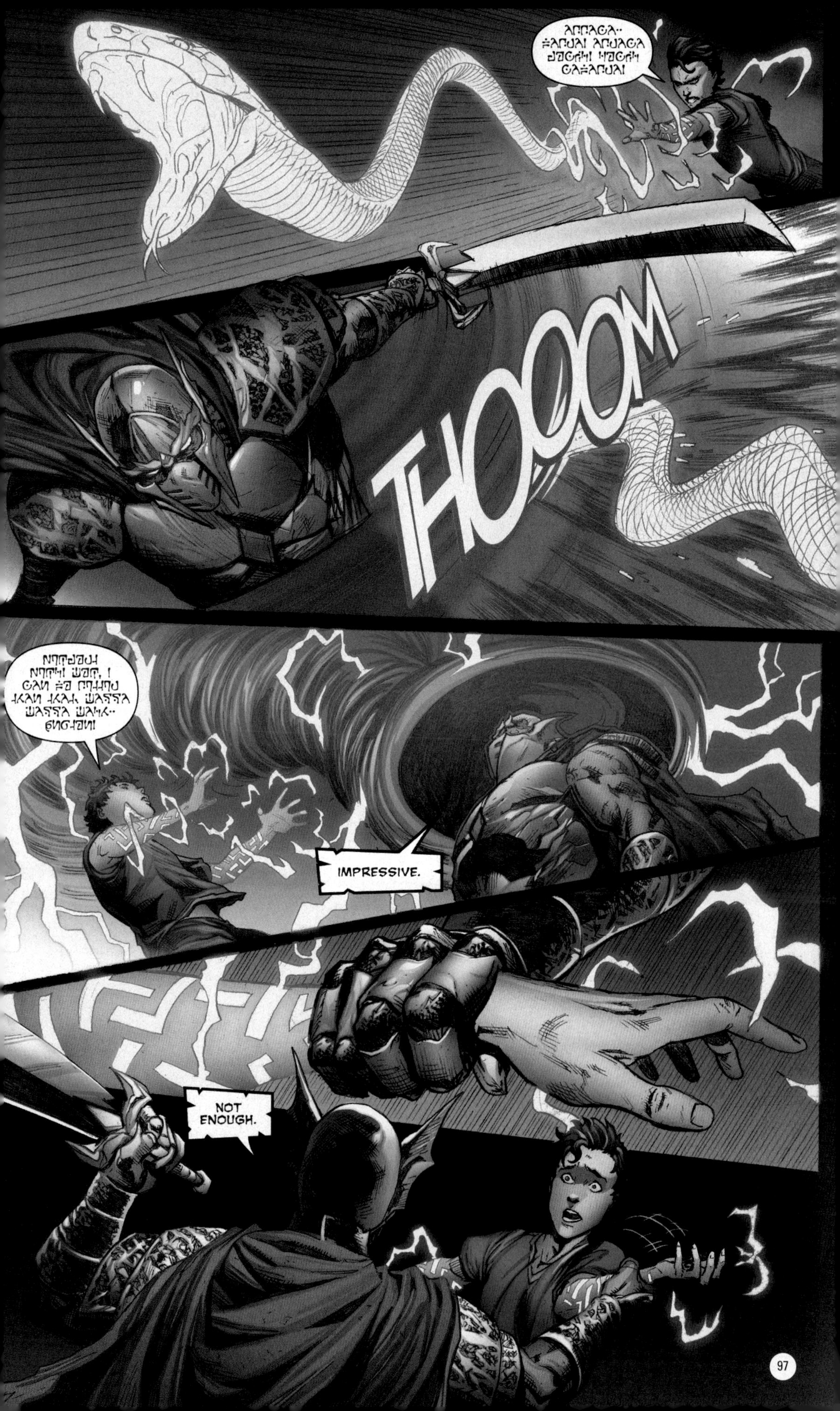
THOOOM
IMPRESSIVE.
NOT ENOUGH.

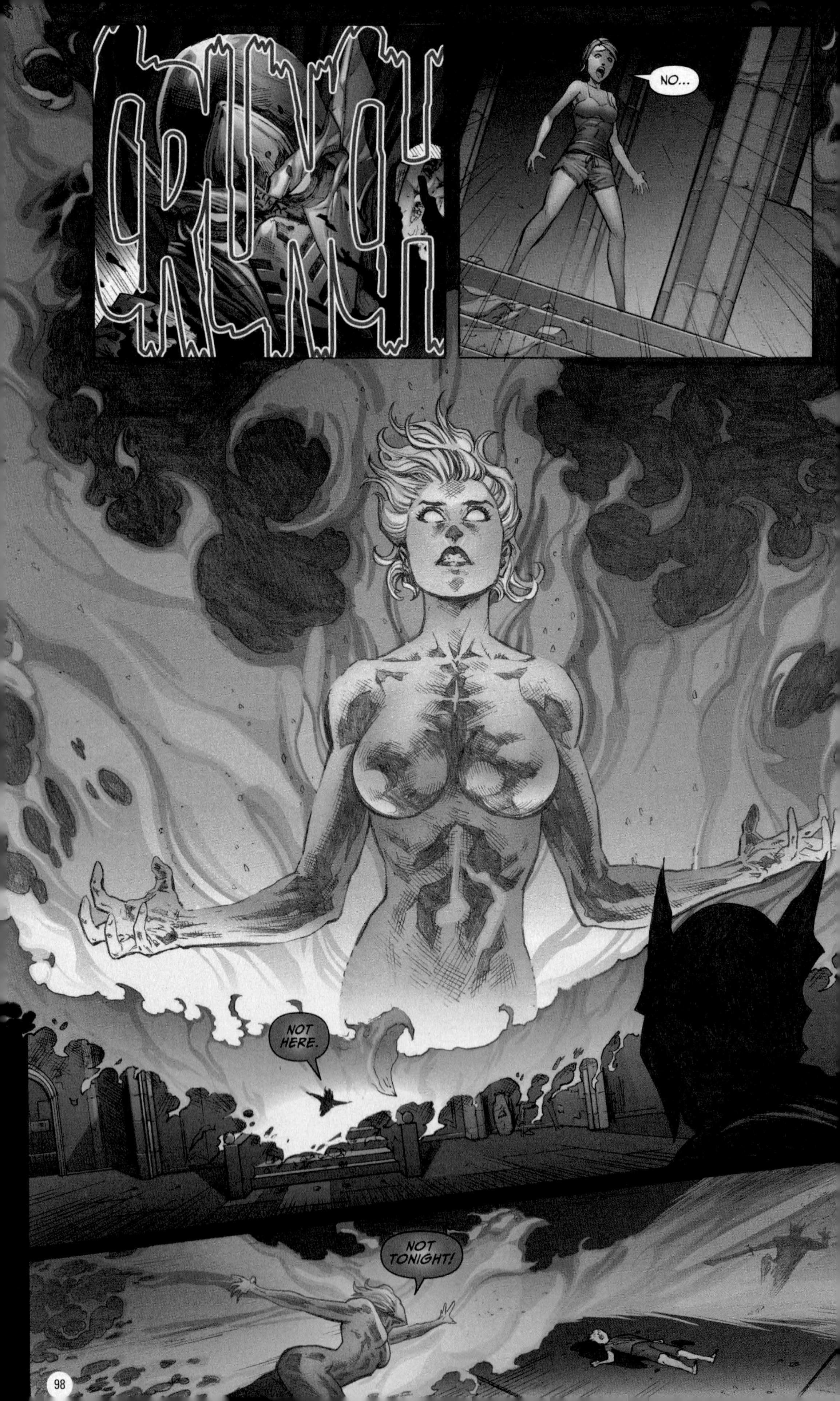
CRUNCH
CRUNCH
NO...
NOT HERE.
NOT TONIGHT!

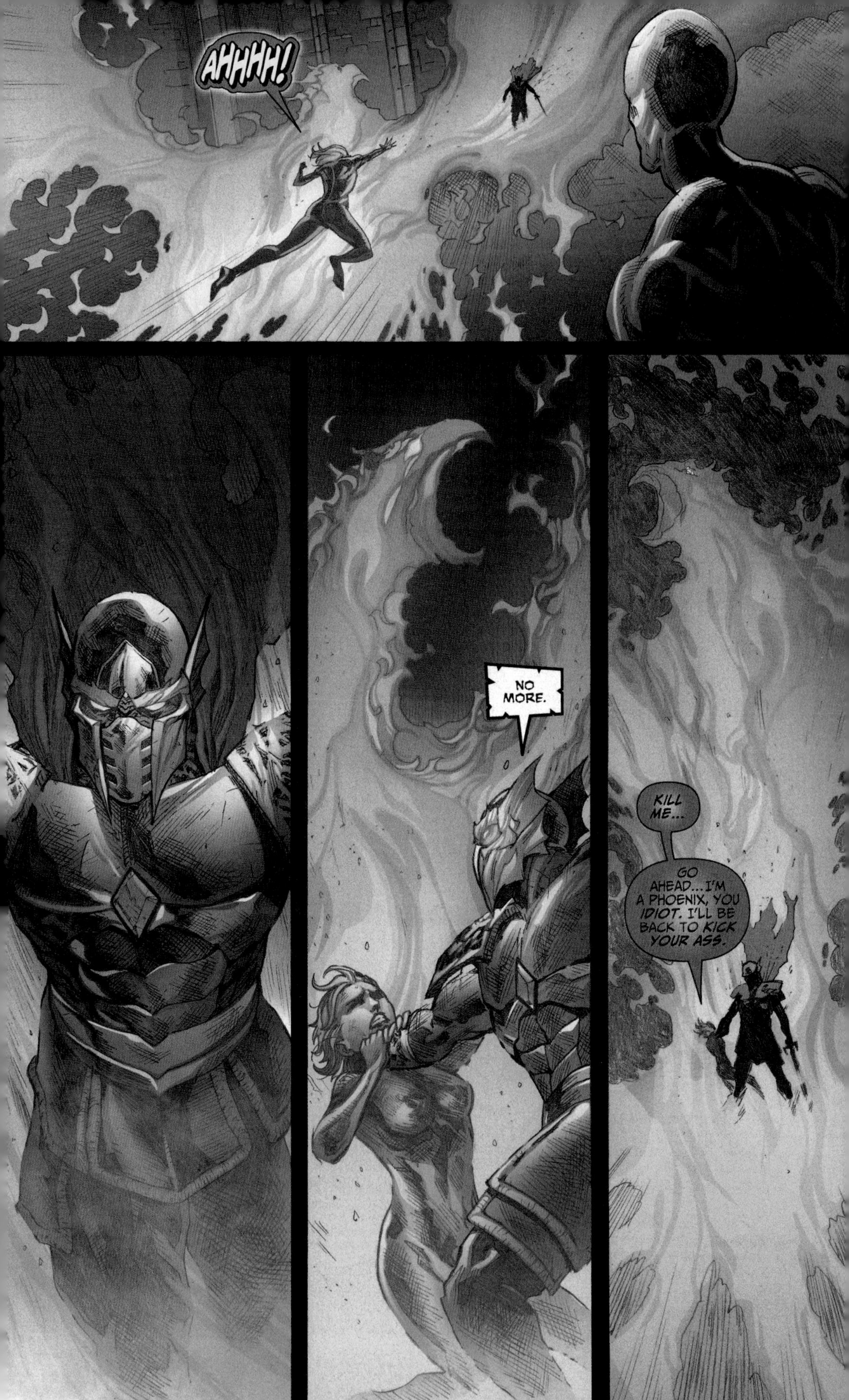
AHHHH!
NO MORE.
KILL ME...
GO AHEAD... I'M A PHOENIX, YOU IDIOT. I'LL BE BACK TO KICK YOUR ASS.

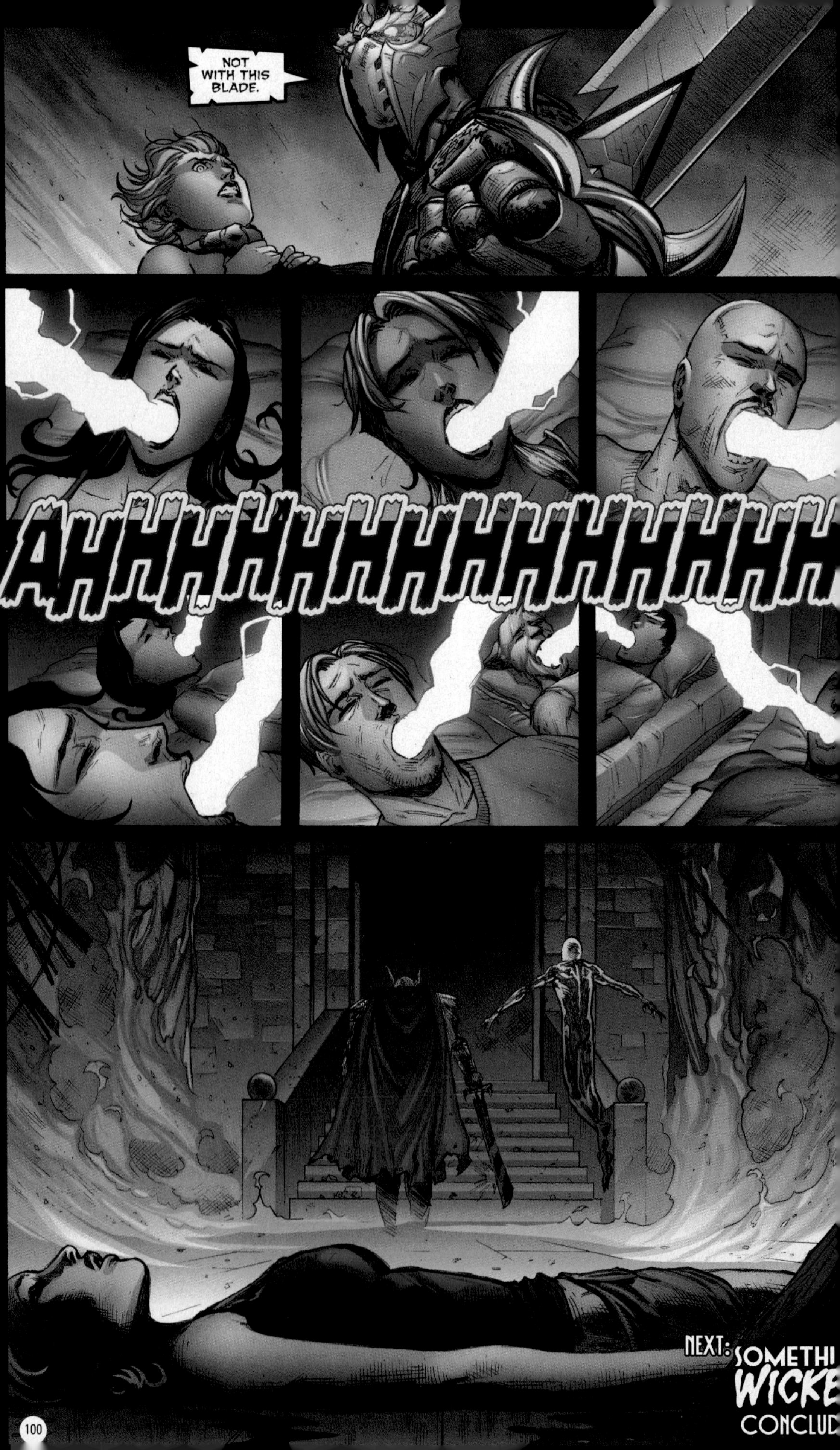
NOT WITH THIS BLADE.
AHHHHHHHHHHHHHHHHHH
NEXT: SOMETHI
WICKE
CONCLUD

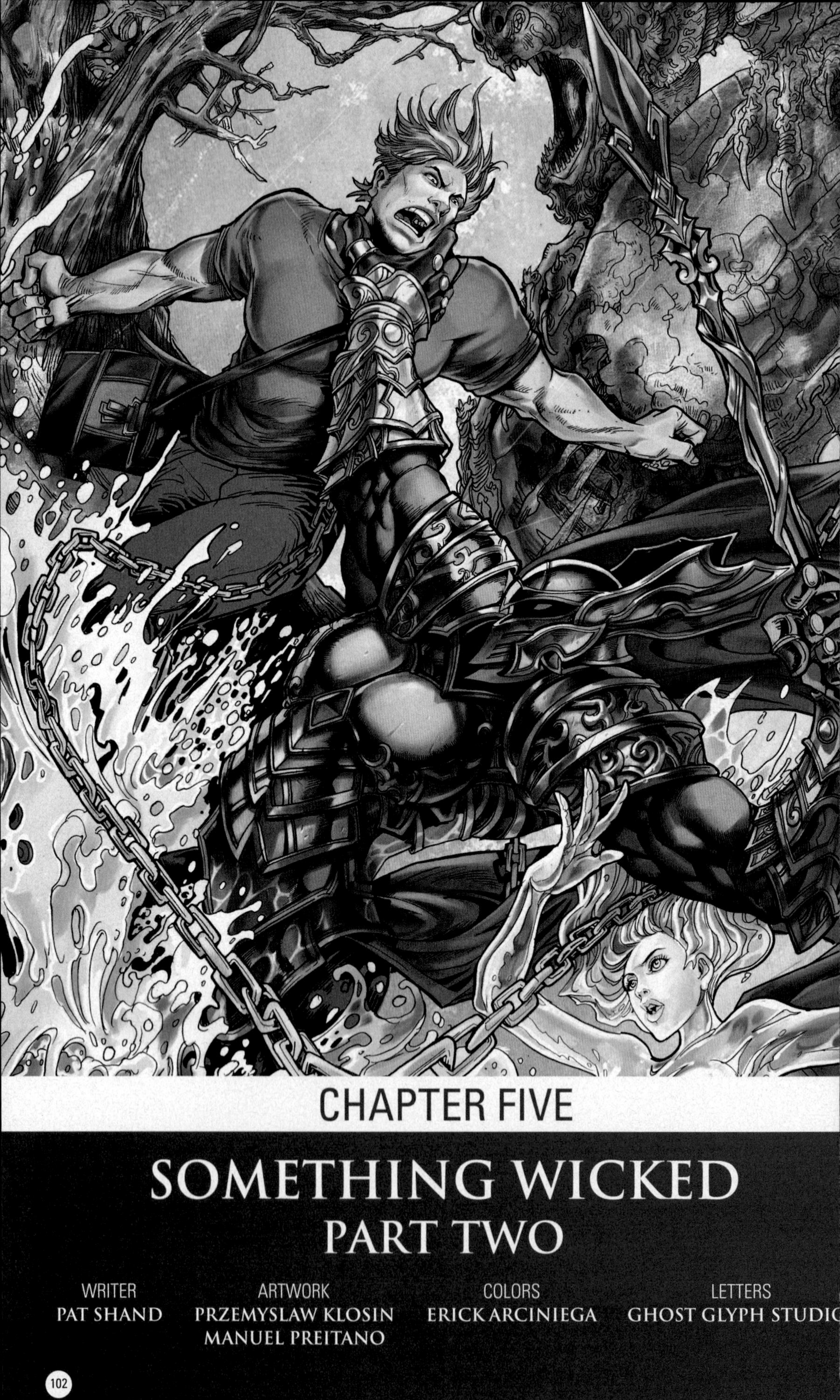

CHAPTER FIVE

SOMETHING WICKED
PART TWO

WRITER
PAT SHAND

ARTWORK
PRZEMYSLAW KLOSIN
MANUEL PREITANO

COLORS
ERICK ARCINIEGA

LETTERS
GHOST GLYPH STUDIO

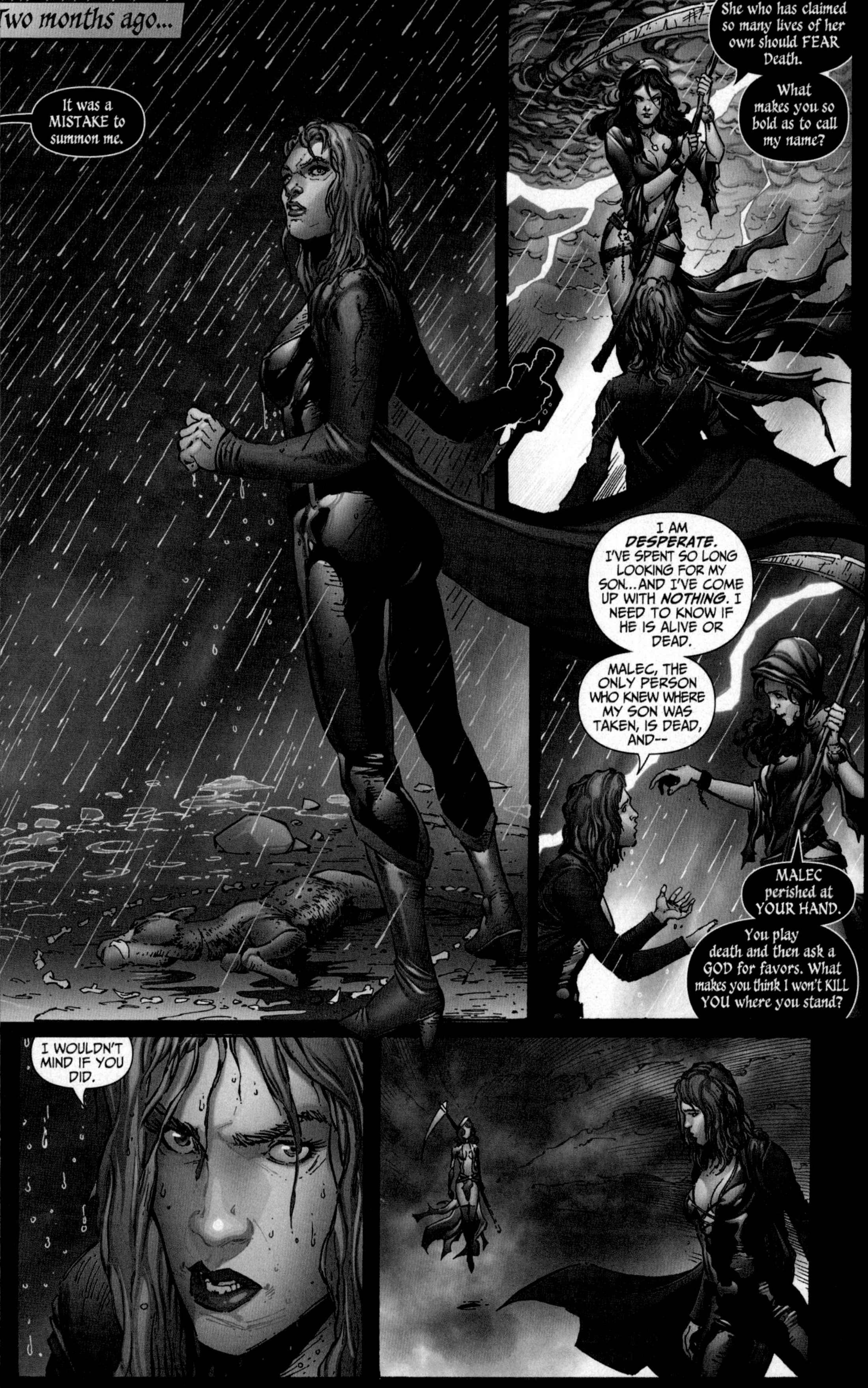
Two months ago...
It was a MISTAKE to summon me.
She who has claimed so many lives of her own should FEAR Death.
What makes you so bold as to call my name?
I AM DESPERATE. I'VE SPENT SO LONG LOOKING FOR MY SON...AND I'VE COME UP WITH NOTHING. I NEED TO KNOW IF HE IS ALIVE OR DEAD.
MALEC, THE ONLY PERSON WHO KNEW WHERE MY SON WAS TAKEN, IS DEAD, AND--
MALEC perished at YOUR HAND.
You play death and then ask a GOD for favors. What makes you think I won't KILL YOU where you stand?
I WOULDN'T MIND IF YOU DID.

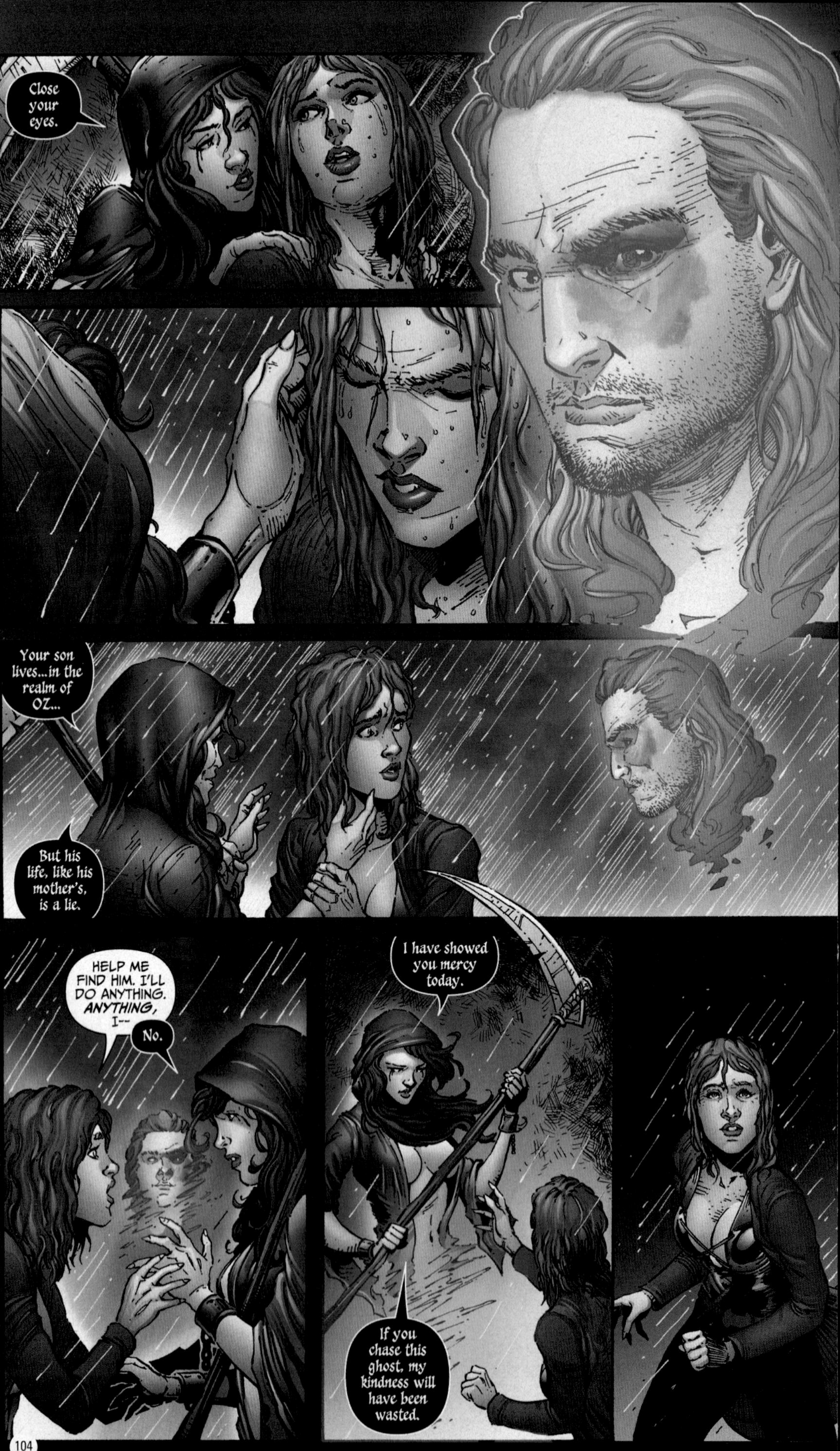
Close your eyes.
Your son lives...in the realm of OZ...
But his life, like his mother's, is a lie.
HELP ME FIND HIM. I'LL DO ANYTHING. *ANYTHING*, I--
No.
I have showed you mercy today.
If you chase this ghost, my kindness will have been wasted.

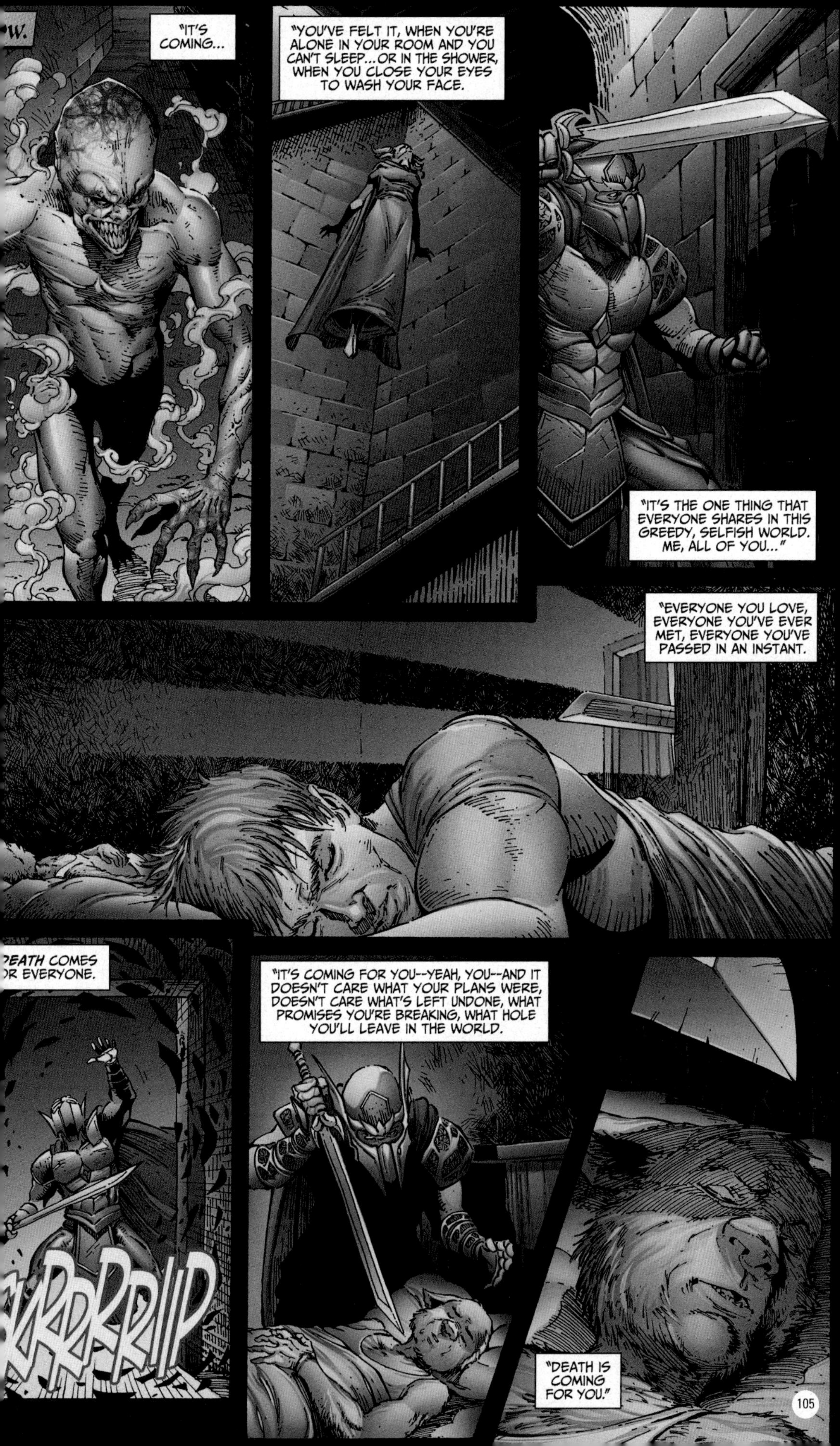

W.
"IT'S COMING...
"YOU'VE FELT IT, WHEN YOU'RE ALONE IN YOUR ROOM AND YOU CAN'T SLEEP...OR IN THE SHOWER, WHEN YOU CLOSE YOUR EYES TO WASH YOUR FACE.
"IT'S THE ONE THING THAT EVERYONE SHARES IN THIS GREEDY, SELFISH WORLD. ME, ALL OF YOU..."
"EVERYONE YOU LOVE, EVERYONE YOU'VE EVER MET, EVERYONE YOU'VE PASSED IN AN INSTANT.
DEATH COMES OR EVERYONE.
"IT'S COMING FOR YOU--YEAH, YOU--AND IT DOESN'T CARE WHAT YOUR PLANS WERE, DOESN'T CARE WHAT'S LEFT UNDONE, WHAT PROMISES YOU'RE BREAKING, WHAT HOLE YOU'LL LEAVE IN THE WORLD.
RRRRIIP
"DEATH IS COMING FOR YOU."

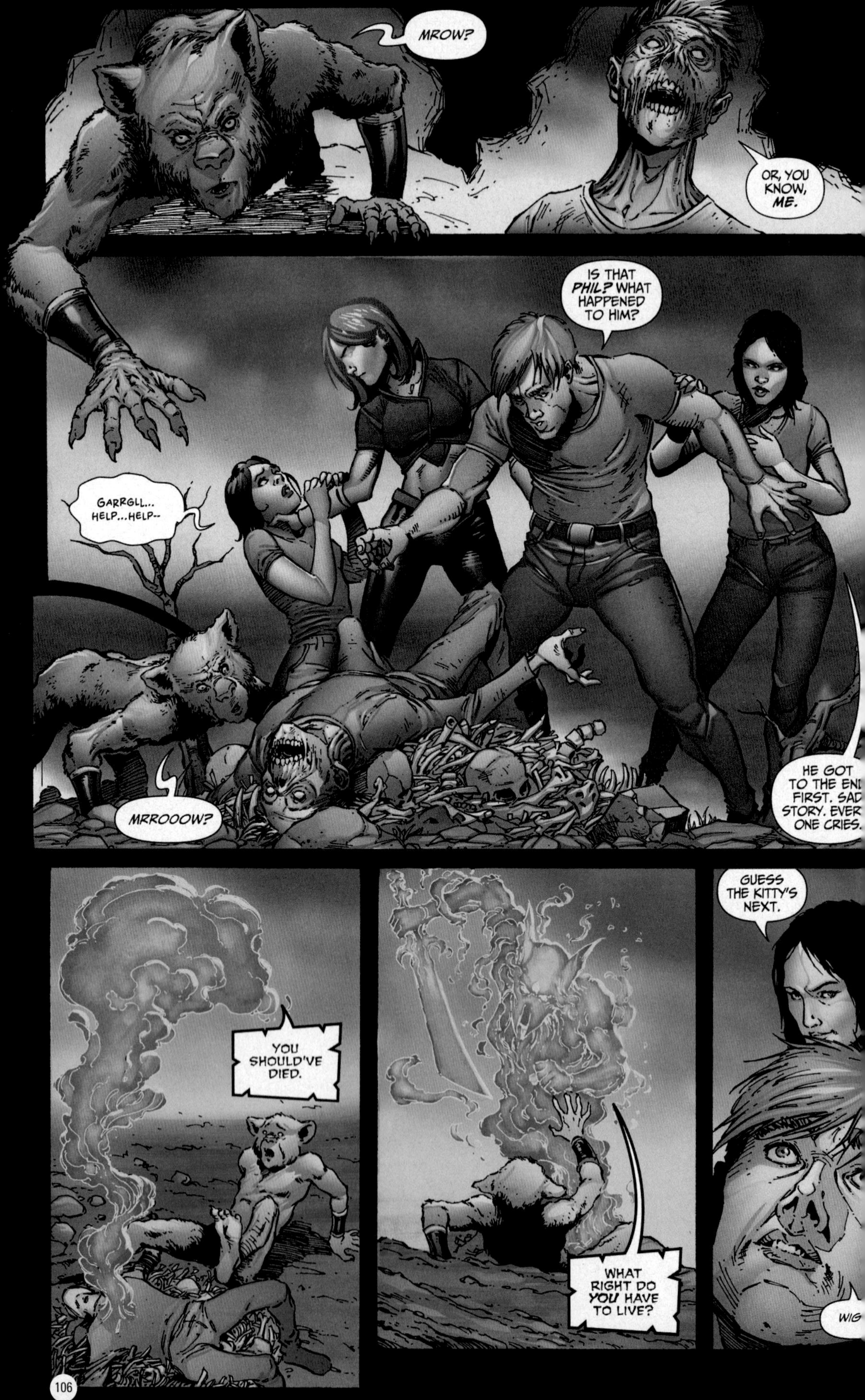

MROW?
OR, YOU KNOW, ME.
IS THAT PHIL? WHAT HAPPENED TO HIM?
GARRGLL... HELP...HELP--
MRROOOW?
HE GOT TO THE END FIRST. SAD STORY. EVERYONE CRIES.
YOU SHOULD'VE DIED.
WHAT RIGHT DO YOU HAVE TO LIVE?
GUESS THE KITTY'S NEXT.

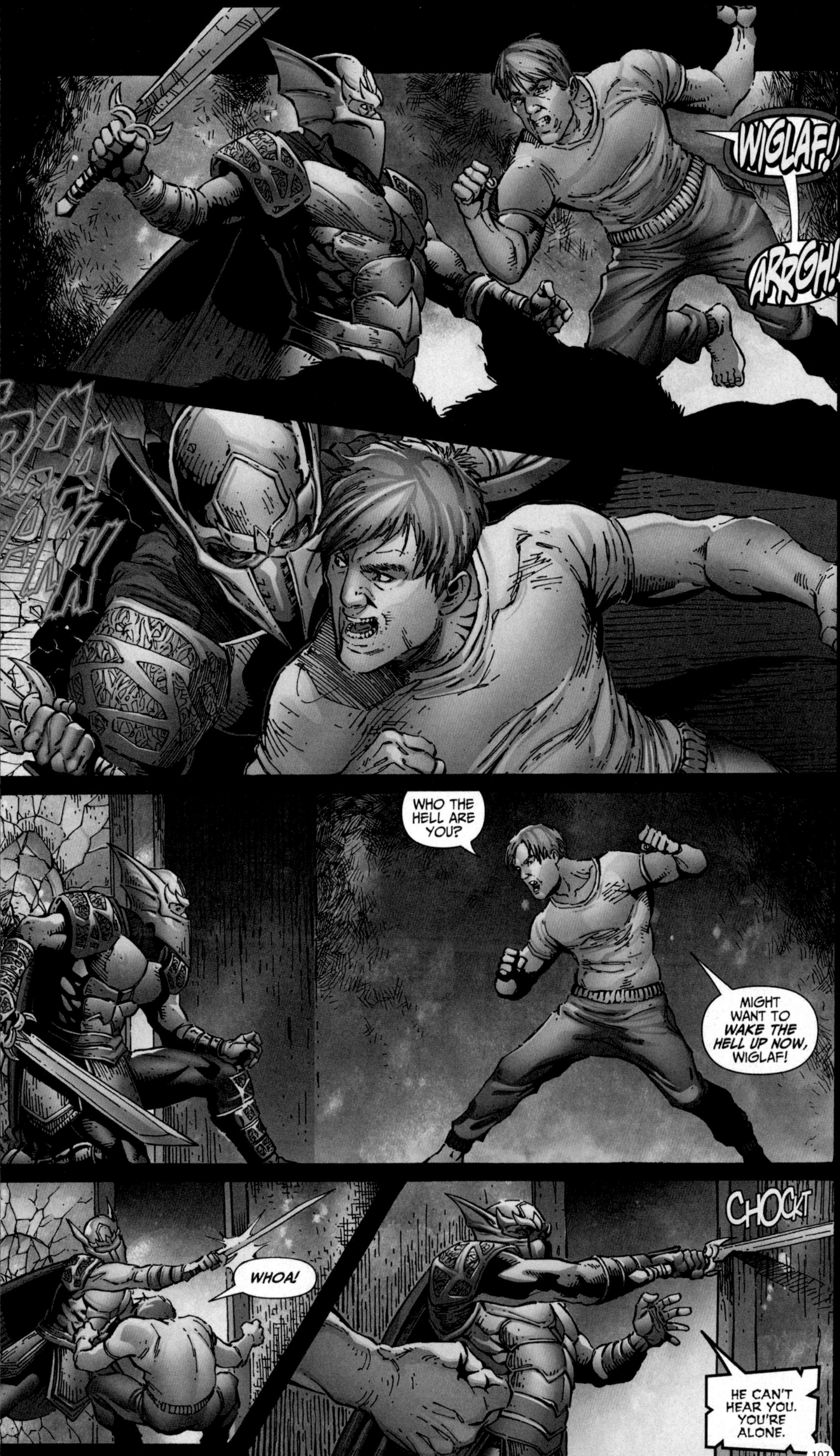
WIGLAF!
ARRGH!
WHO THE HELL ARE YOU?
MIGHT WANT TO *WAKE THE HELL UP NOW,* WIGLAF!
WHOA!
CHOCK
HE CAN'T HEAR YOU. YOU'RE ALONE.

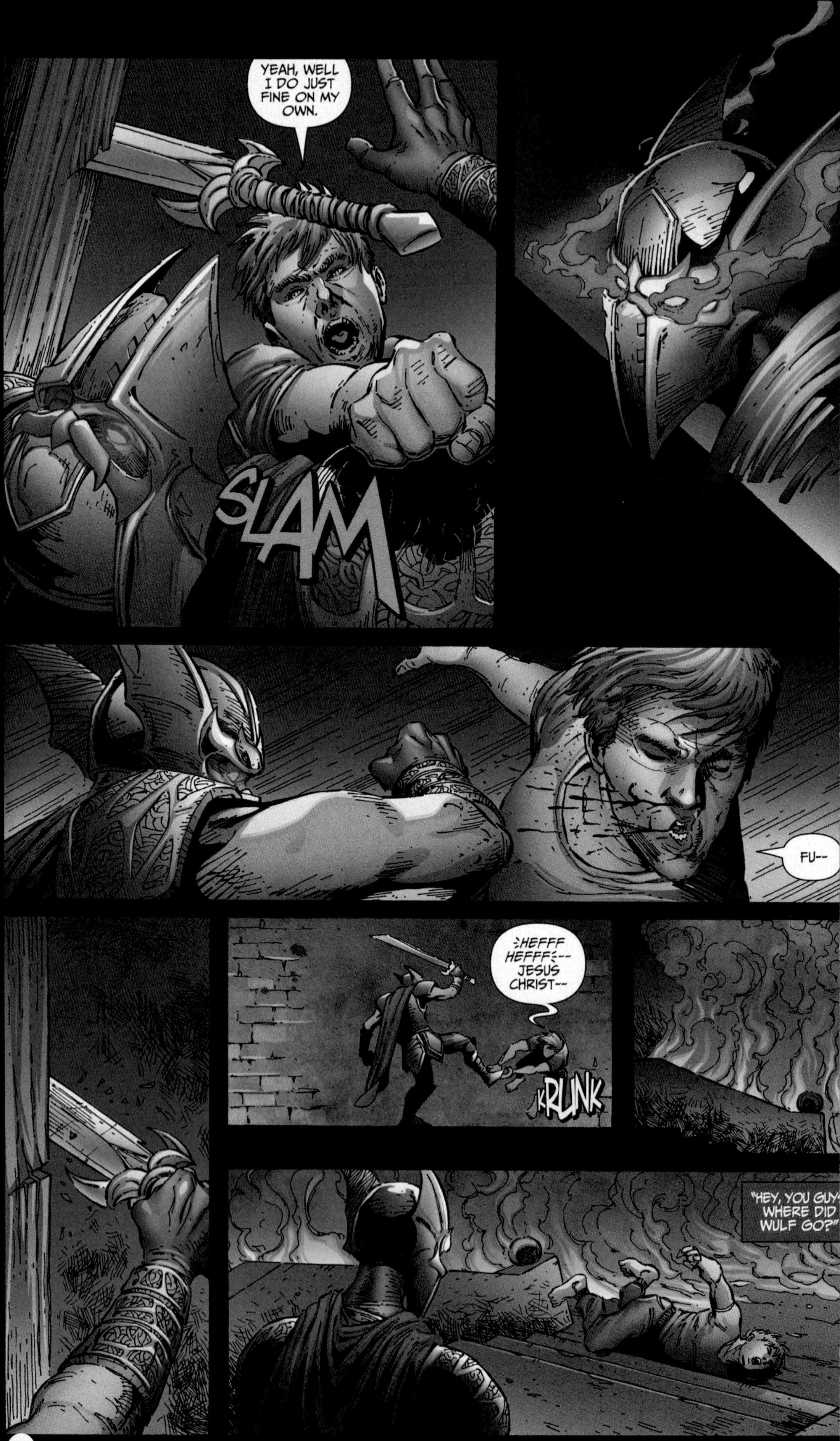
YEAH, WELL I DO JUST FINE ON MY OWN.
SLAM
FU--
HEFFF HEFFF-- JESUS CHRIST--
KRUNK
"HEY, YOU GUYS WHERE DID WULF GO?"

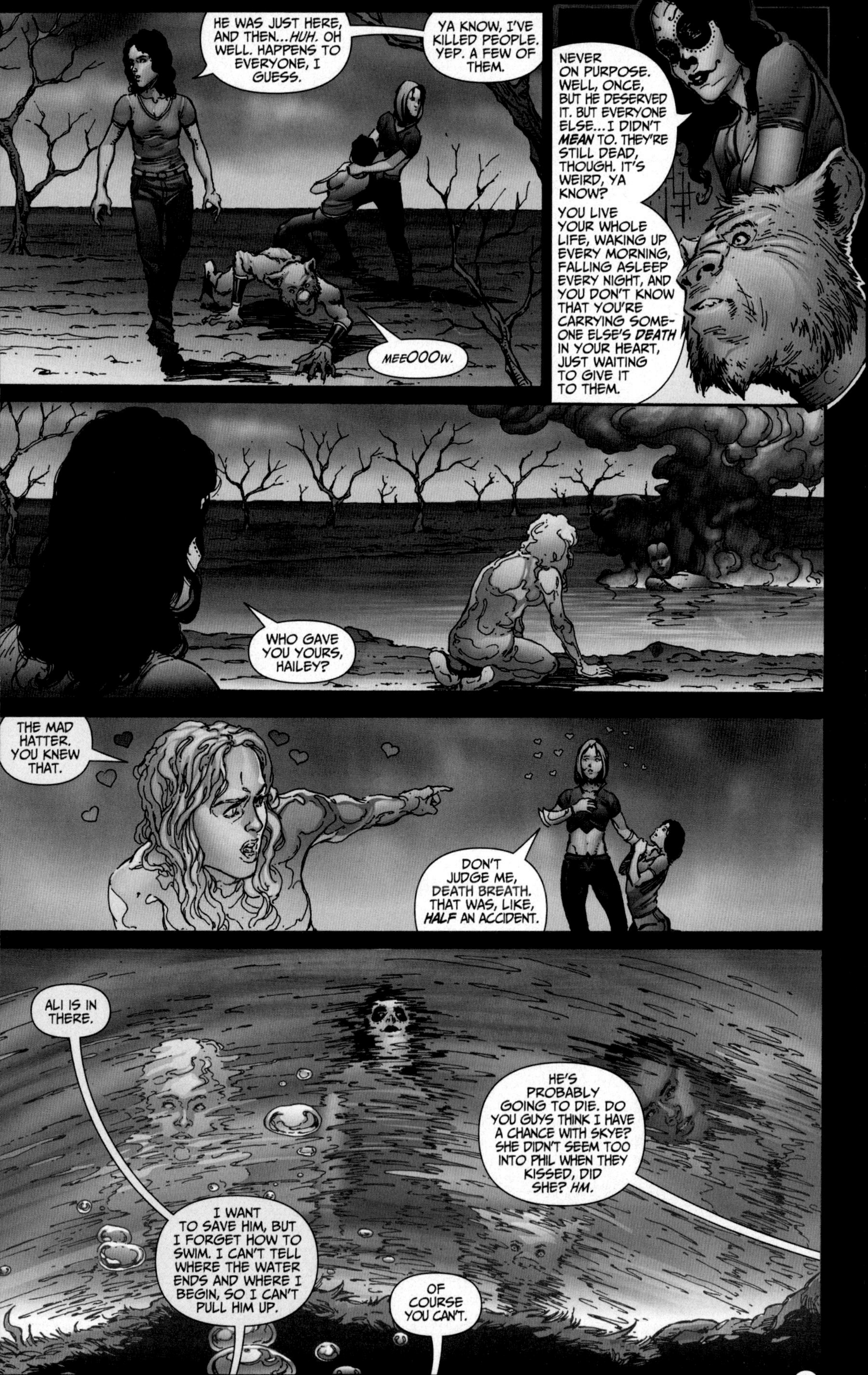

HE WAS JUST HERE, AND THEN...*HUH.* OH WELL. HAPPENS TO EVERYONE, I GUESS.
YA KNOW, I'VE KILLED PEOPLE. YEP. A FEW OF THEM.
MEEOOOW.
NEVER ON PURPOSE. WELL, ONCE, BUT HE DESERVED IT. BUT EVERYONE ELSE...I DIDN'T *MEAN* TO. THEY'RE STILL DEAD, THOUGH. IT'S WEIRD, YA KNOW?
YOU LIVE YOUR WHOLE LIFE, WAKING UP EVERY MORNING, FALLING ASLEEP EVERY NIGHT, AND YOU DON'T KNOW THAT YOU'RE CARRYING SOME-ONE ELSE'S *DEATH* IN YOUR HEART, JUST WAITING TO GIVE IT TO THEM.
WHO GAVE YOU YOURS, HAILEY?
THE MAD HATTER. YOU KNEW THAT.
DON'T JUDGE ME, DEATH BREATH. THAT WAS, LIKE, *HALF* AN ACCIDENT.
ALI IS IN THERE.
HE'S PROBABLY GOING TO DIE. DO YOU GUYS THINK I HAVE A CHANCE WITH SKYE? SHE DIDN'T SEEM TOO INTO PHIL WHEN THEY KISSED, DID SHE? *HM.*
I WANT TO SAVE HIM, BUT I FORGET HOW TO SWIM. I CAN'T TELL WHERE THE WATER ENDS AND WHERE I BEGIN, SO I CAN'T PULL HIM UP.
OF COURSE YOU CAN'T.

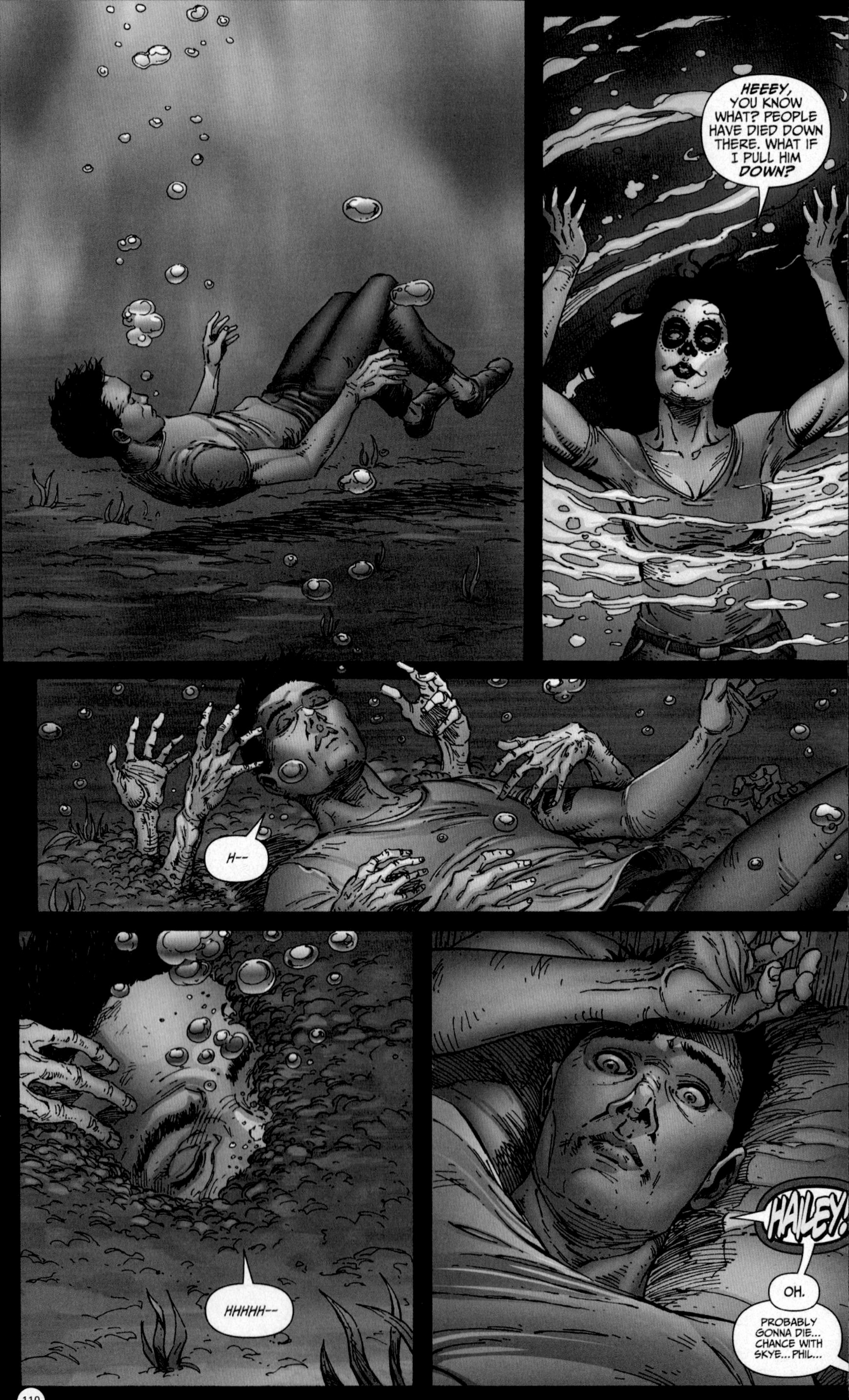
HEEEY, YOU KNOW WHAT? PEOPLE HAVE DIED DOWN THERE. WHAT IF I PULL HIM DOWN?
H--
HHHHH--
HAILEY!
OH.
PROBABLY GONNA DIE... CHANCE WITH SKYE... PHIL...

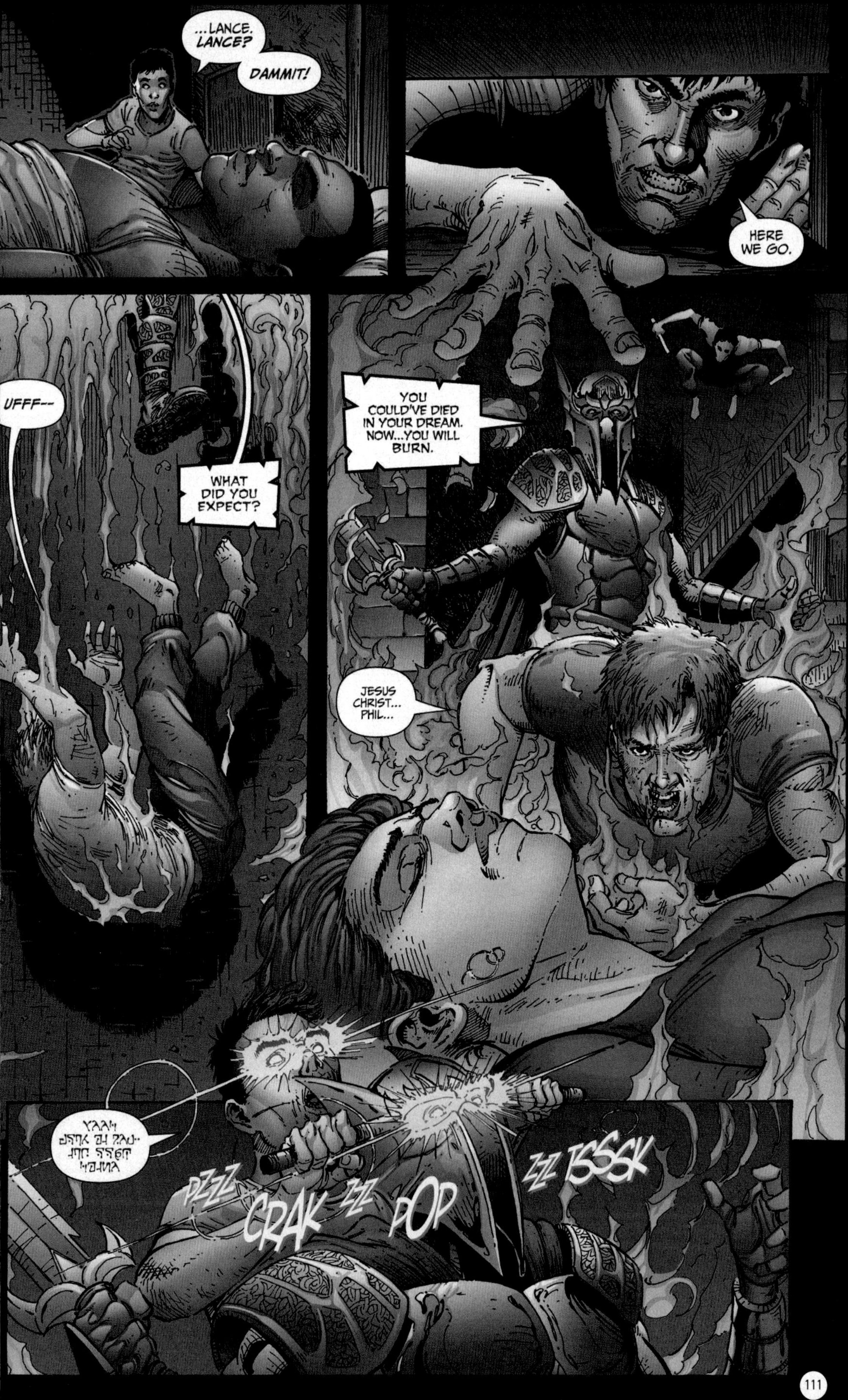
...LANCE.
LANCE?
DAMMIT!
HERE WE GO.
UFFF--
WHAT DID YOU EXPECT?
YOU COULD'VE DIED IN YOUR DREAM. NOW...YOU WILL BURN.
JESUS CHRIST... PHIL...
DZZZ
CRAK
ZZZ
POP
ZZZ
TSSSK

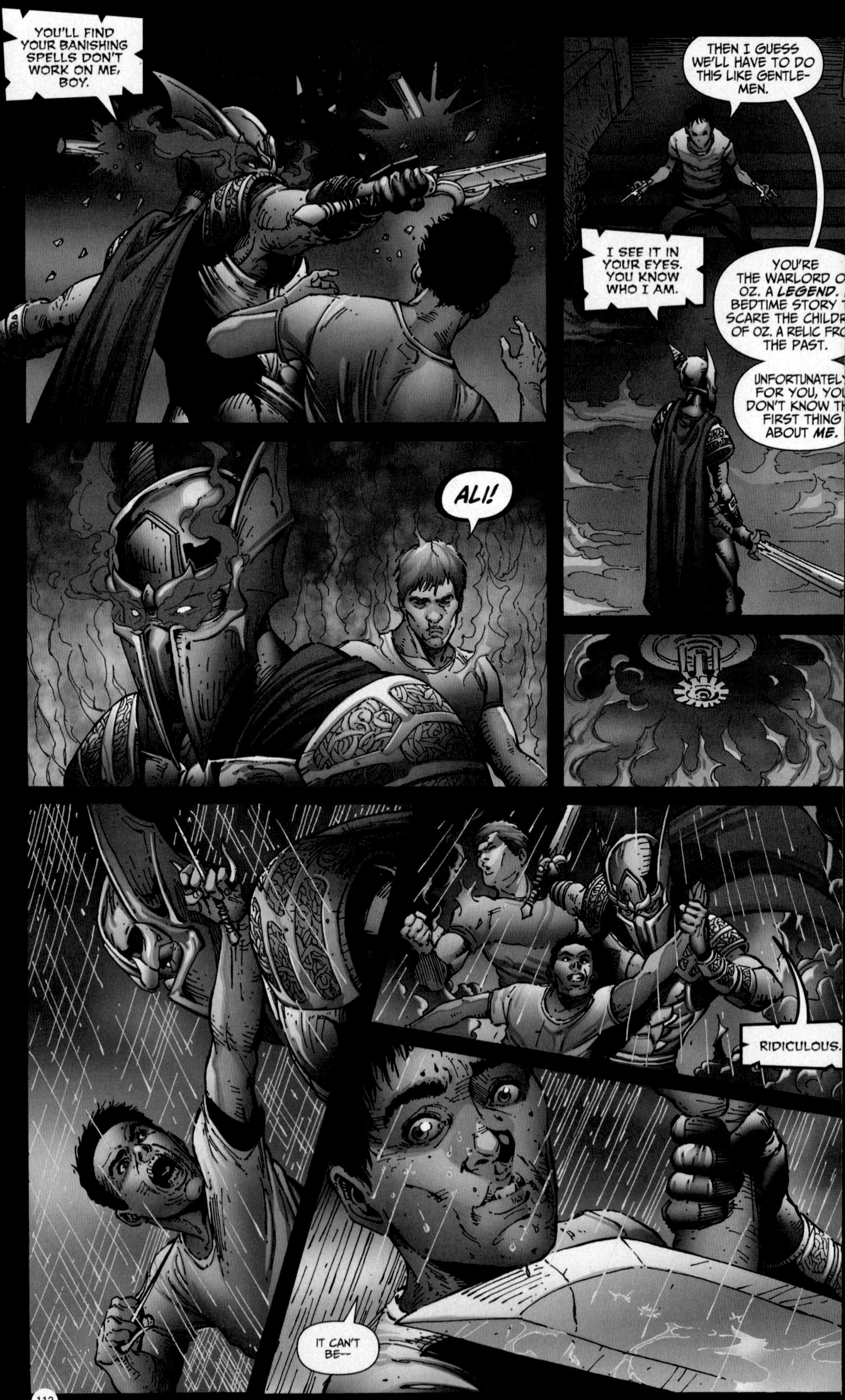
YOU'LL FIND YOUR BANISHING SPELLS DON'T WORK ON ME, BOY.
THEN I GUESS WE'LL HAVE TO DO THIS LIKE GENTLE-MEN.
I SEE IT IN YOUR EYES. YOU KNOW WHO I AM.
YOU'RE THE WARLORD O OZ. A *LEGEND.* BEDTIME STORY T SCARE THE CHILDR OF OZ. A RELIC FRO THE PAST.
UNFORTUNATEL FOR YOU, YO DON'T KNOW T FIRST THING ABOUT *ME.*
ALI!
RIDICULOUS.
IT CAN'T BE--

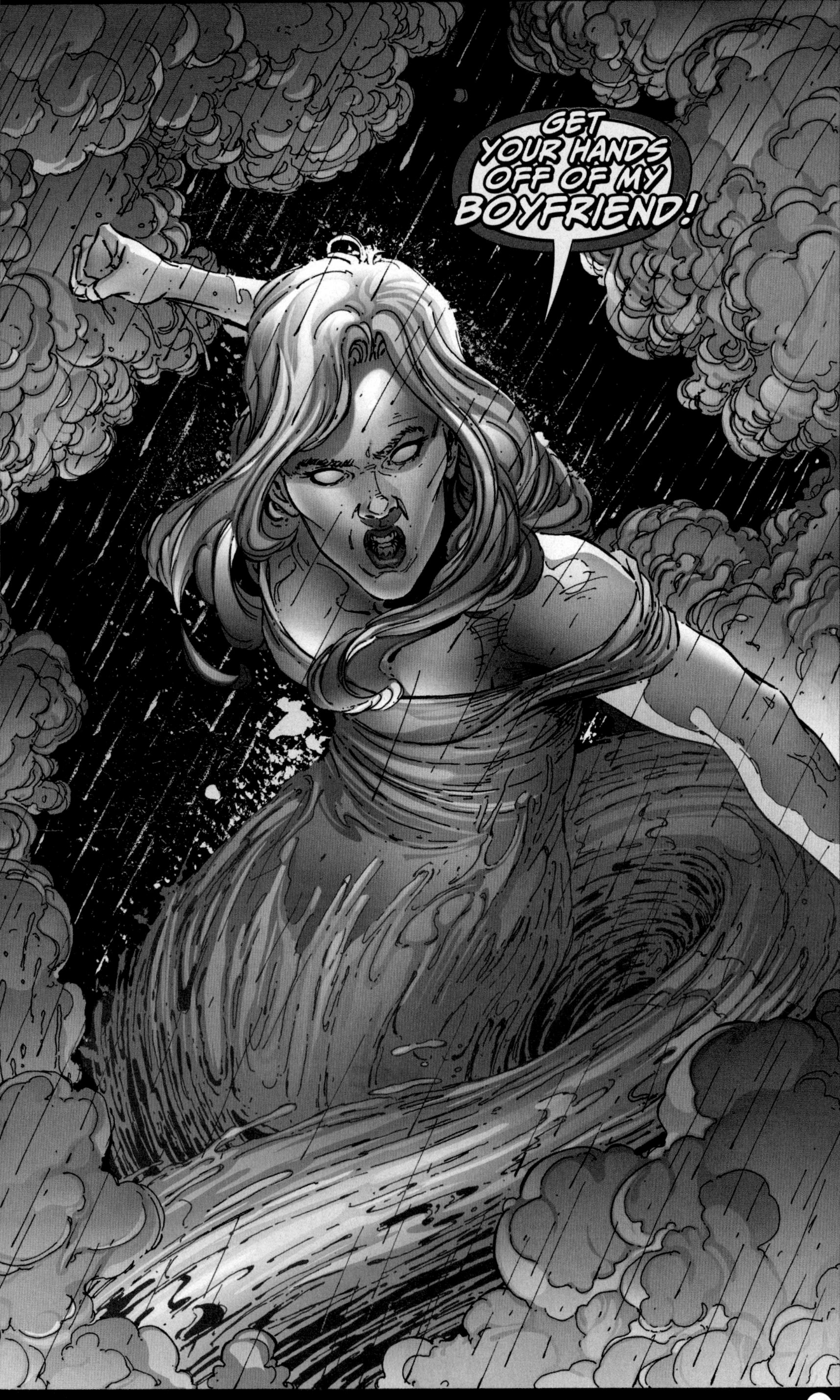
GET YOUR HANDS OFF OF MY BOYFRIEND!

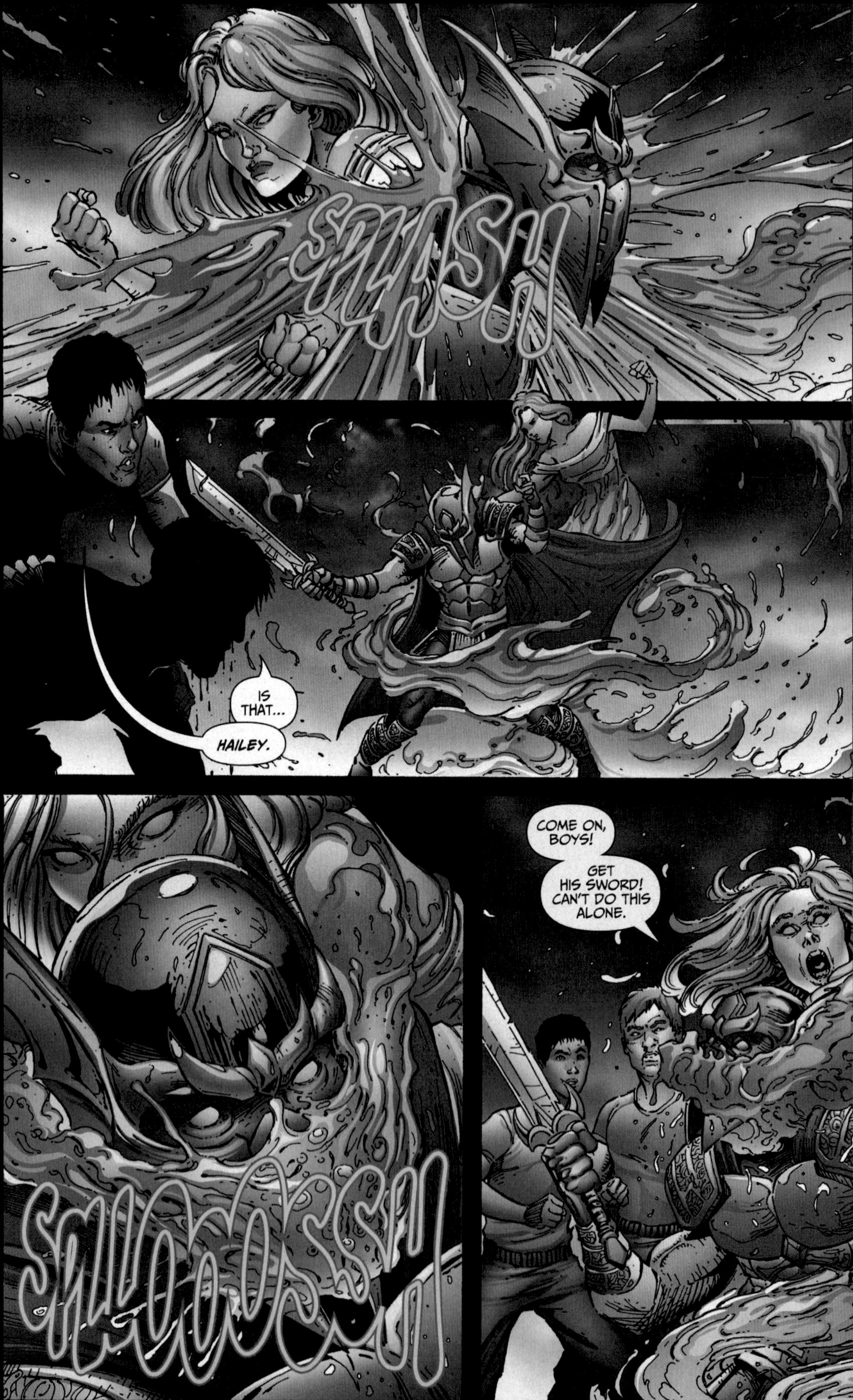
SPLASH
IS THAT...
HAILEY.
SPLOOOSSH
COME ON, BOYS!
GET HIS SWORD! CAN'T DO THIS ALONE.

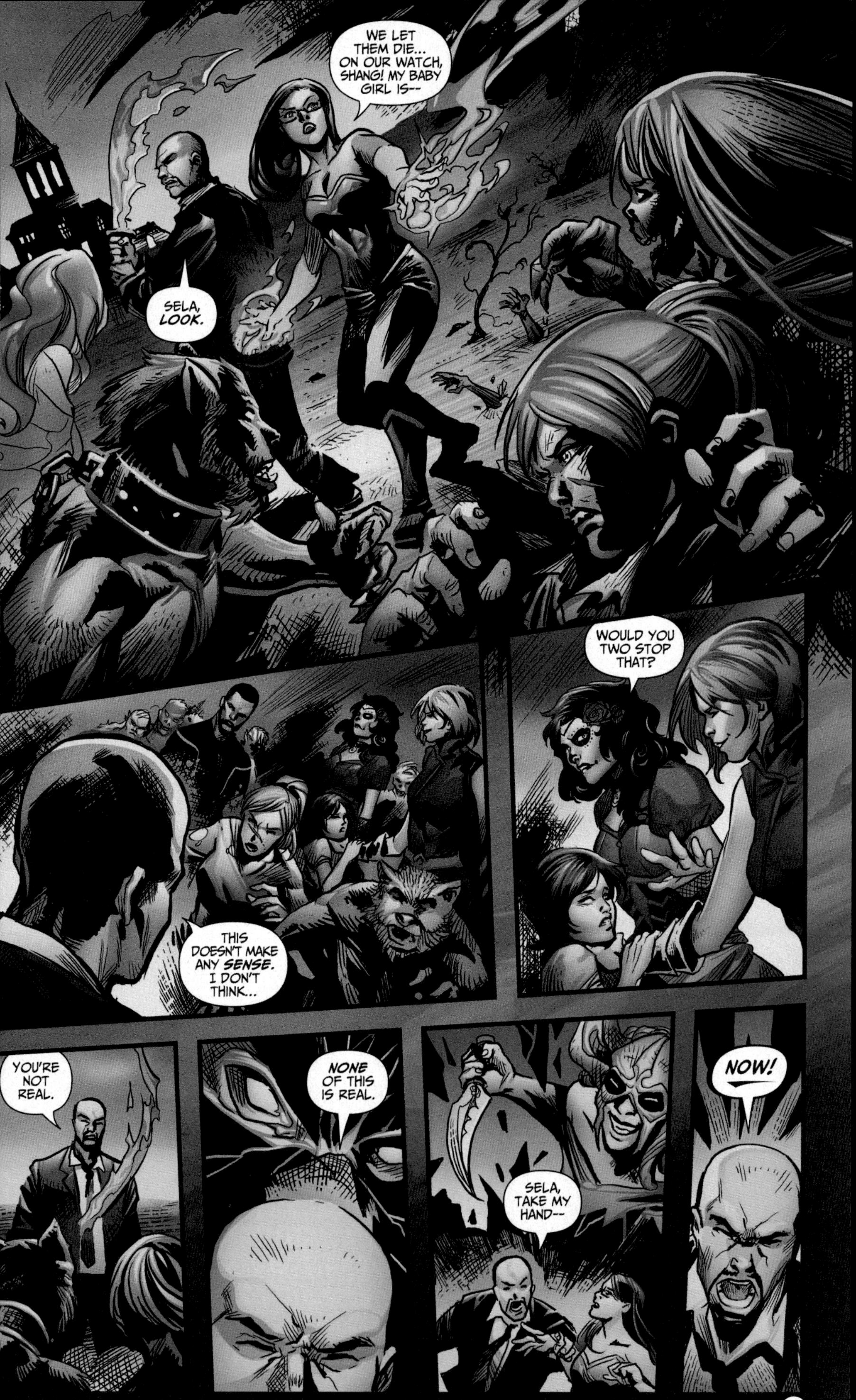
WE LET THEM DIE... ON OUR WATCH, SHANG! MY BABY GIRL IS--
SELA, LOOK.
THIS DOESN'T MAKE ANY SENSE. I DON'T THINK...
WOULD YOU TWO STOP THAT?
YOU'RE NOT REAL.
NONE OF THIS IS REAL.
SELA, TAKE MY HAND--
NOW!

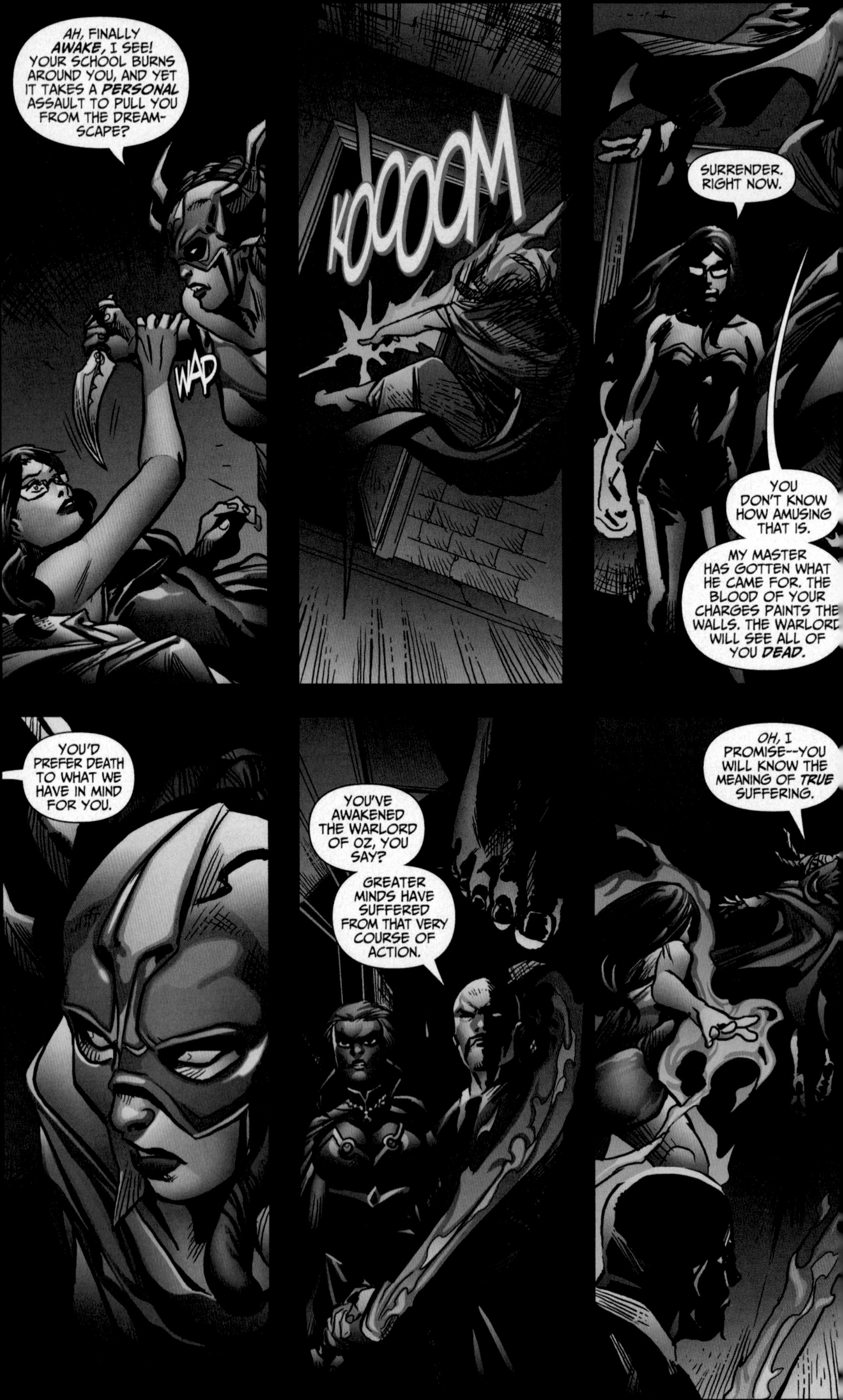
AH, FINALLY AWAKE, I SEE! YOUR SCHOOL BURNS AROUND YOU, AND YET IT TAKES A PERSONAL ASSAULT TO PULL YOU FROM THE DREAM-SCAPE?
WAP
KOOOOM
SURRENDER. RIGHT NOW.
YOU DON'T KNOW HOW AMUSING THAT IS.
MY MASTER HAS GOTTEN WHAT HE CAME FOR. THE BLOOD OF YOUR CHARGES PAINTS THE WALLS. THE WARLORD WILL SEE ALL OF YOU DEAD.
YOU'D PREFER DEATH TO WHAT WE HAVE IN MIND FOR YOU.
YOU'VE AWAKENED THE WARLORD OF OZ, YOU SAY?
GREATER MINDS HAVE SUFFERED FROM THAT VERY COURSE OF ACTION.
OH, I PROMISE--YOU WILL KNOW THE MEANING OF TRUE SUFFERING.

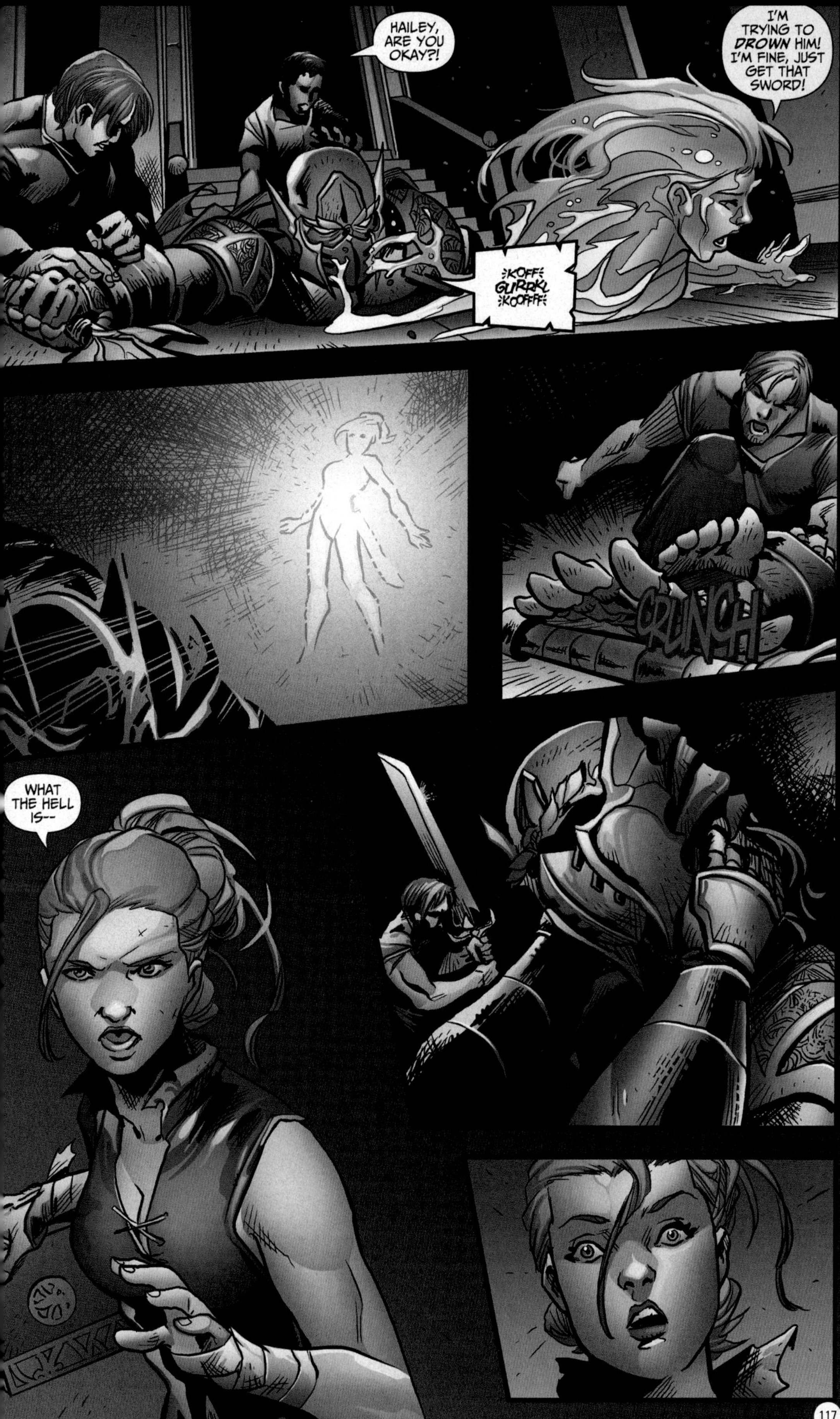
HAILEY, ARE YOU OKAY?!
I'M TRYING TO *DROWN* HIM! I'M FINE, JUST GET THAT SWORD!
KOFF GURRK! KOOFFF
CRUNCH
WHAT THE HELL IS--

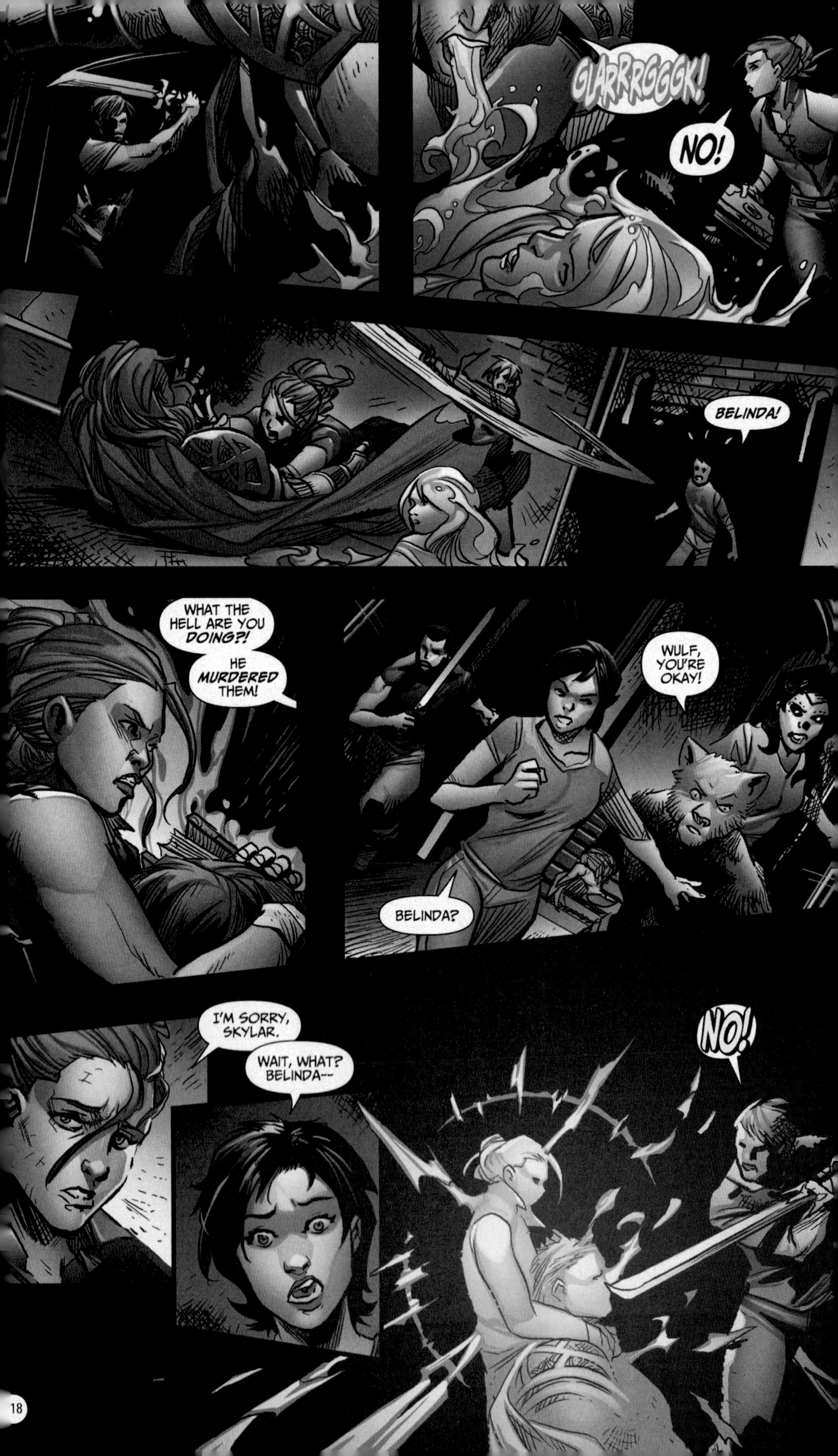
GLARRRGGGK!
NO!
BELINDA!
WHAT THE HELL ARE YOU DOING?!
HE MURDERED THEM!
WULF, YOU'RE OKAY!
BELINDA?
I'M SORRY, SKYLAR.
WAIT, WHAT? BELINDA--
NO!

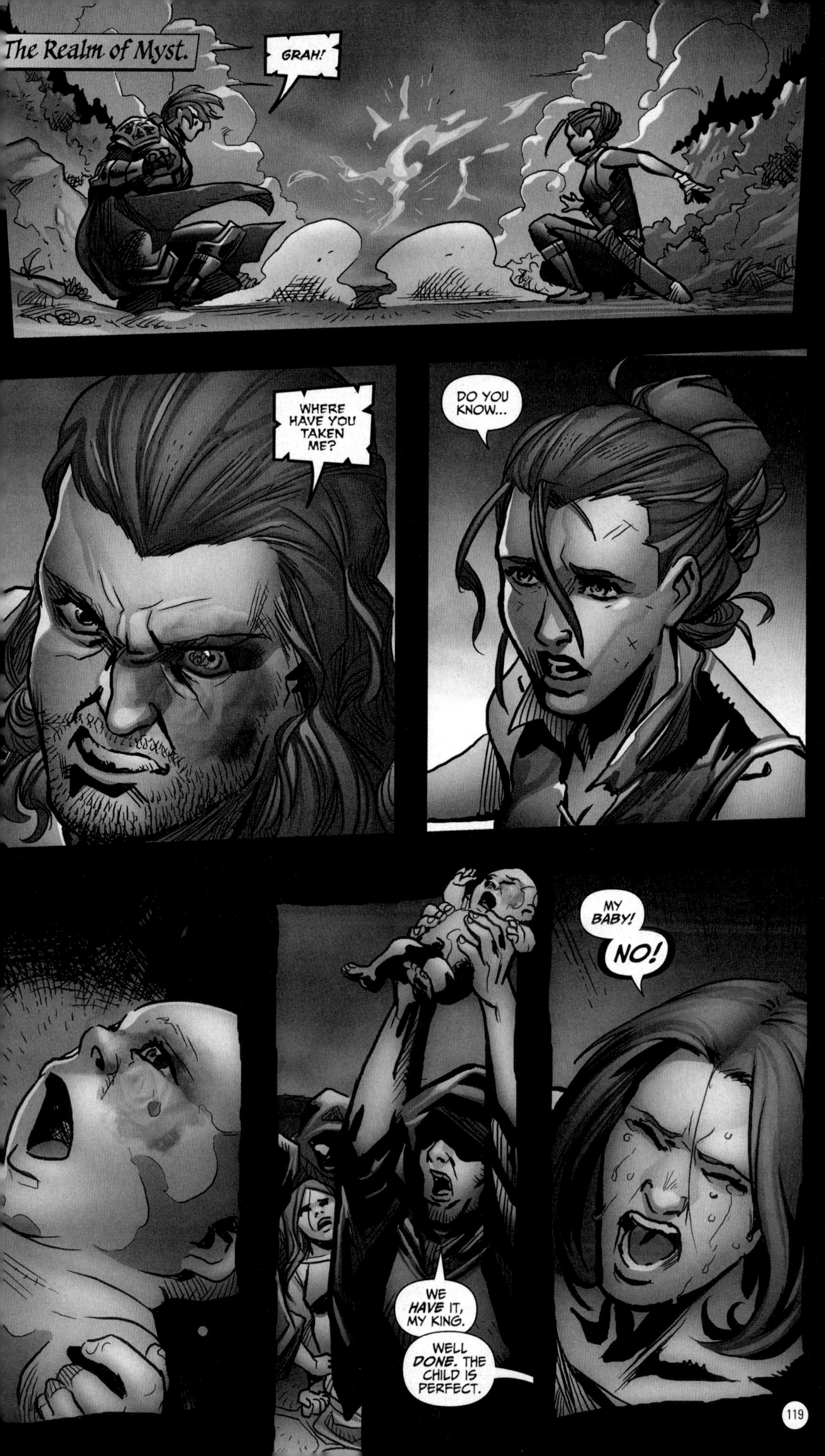
The Realm of Myst.
GRAH!
WHERE HAVE YOU TAKEN ME?
DO YOU KNOW...
MY BABY!
NO!
WE HAVE IT, MY KING.
WELL DONE. THE CHILD IS PERFECT.

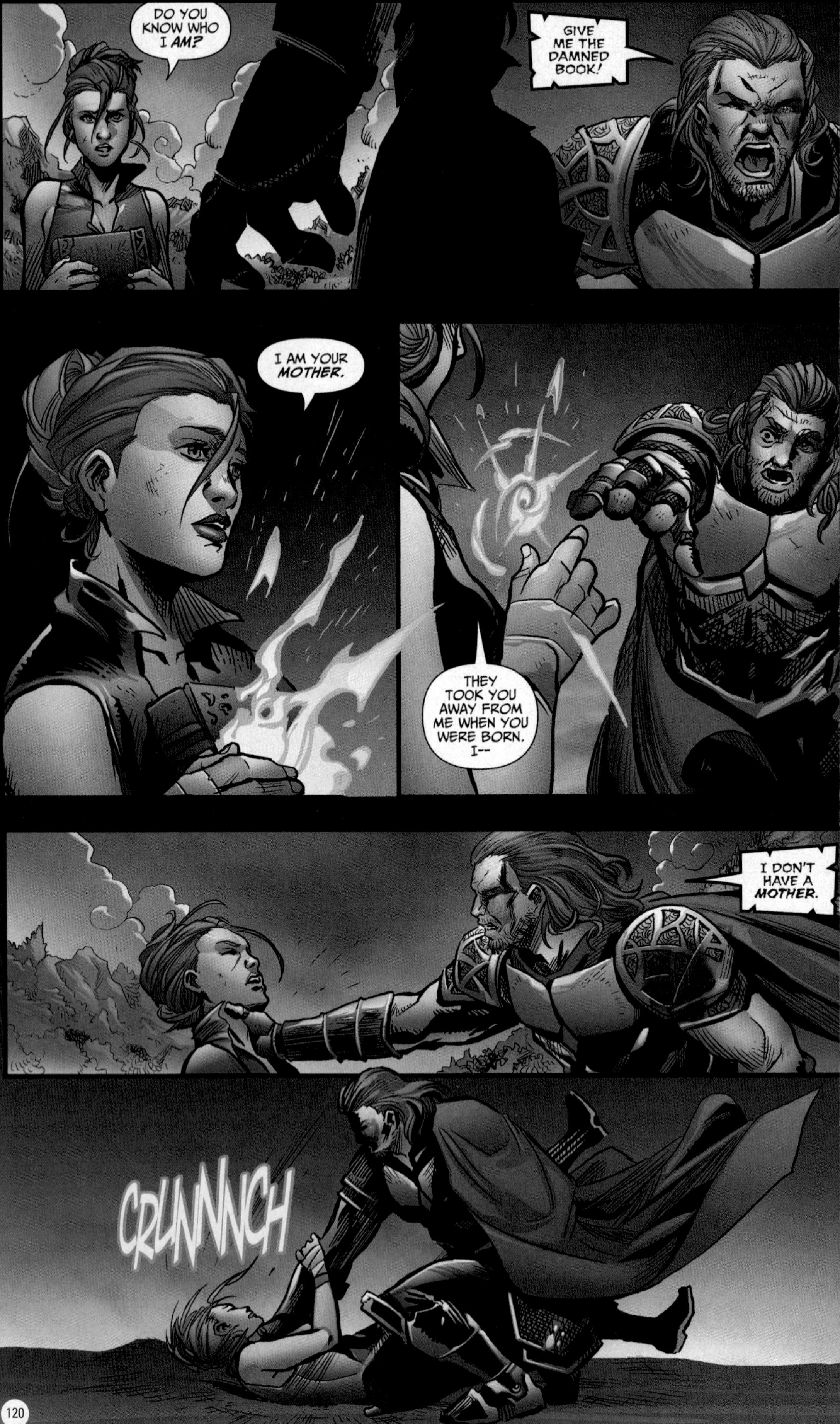
DO YOU KNOW WHO I AM?
GIVE ME THE DAMNED BOOK!
I AM YOUR MOTHER.
THEY TOOK YOU AWAY FROM ME WHEN YOU WERE BORN. I--
I DON'T HAVE A MOTHER.
CRUNNNCH

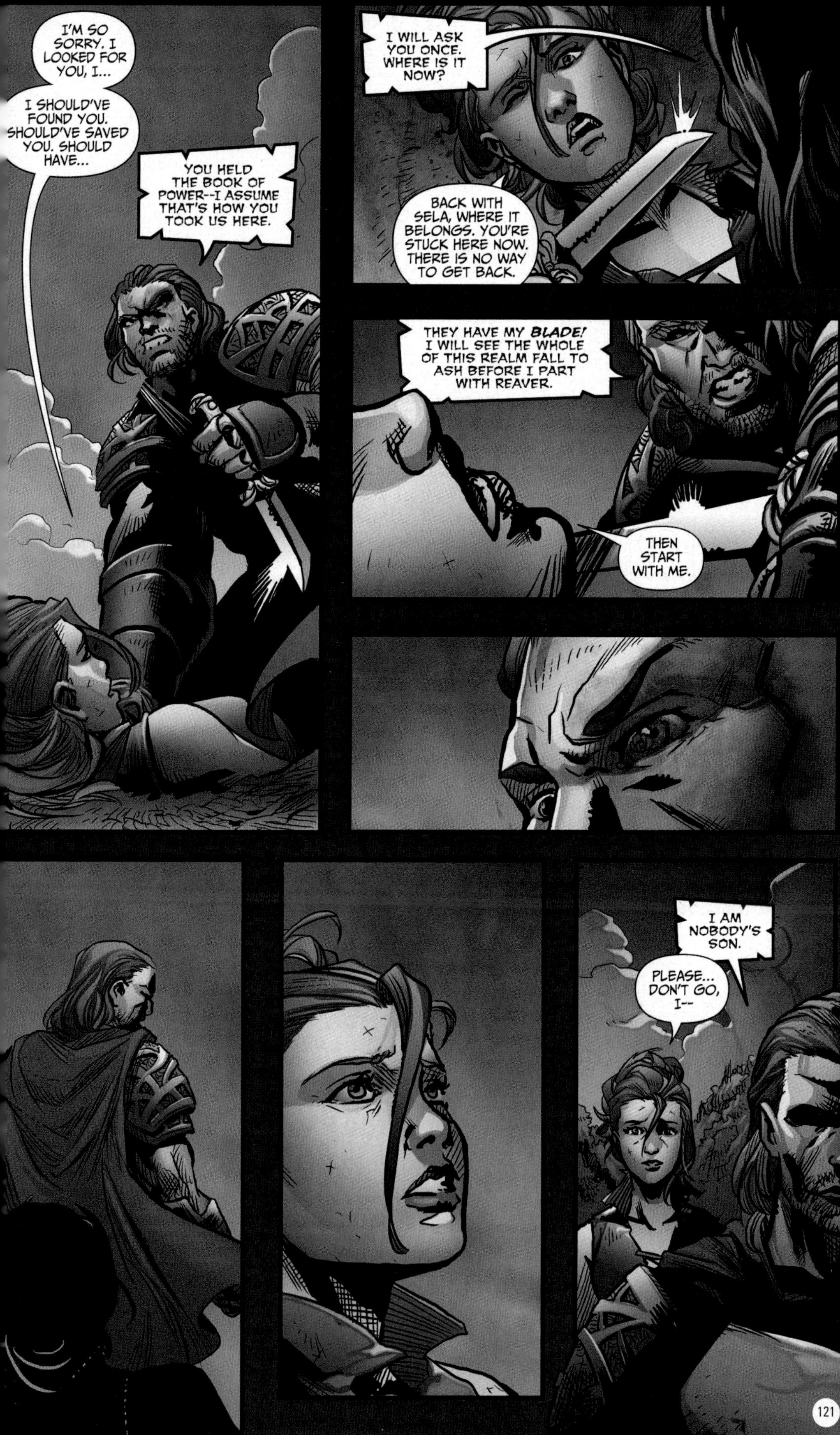
I'M SO SORRY. I LOOKED FOR YOU, I...
I SHOULD'VE FOUND YOU. SHOULD'VE SAVED YOU. SHOULD HAVE...
YOU HELD THE BOOK OF POWER--I ASSUME THAT'S HOW YOU TOOK US HERE.
I WILL ASK YOU ONCE. WHERE IS IT NOW?
BACK WITH SELA, WHERE IT BELONGS. YOU'RE STUCK HERE NOW. THERE IS NO WAY TO GET BACK.
THEY HAVE MY *BLADE!* I WILL SEE THE WHOLE OF THIS REALM FALL TO ASH BEFORE I PART WITH REAVER.
THEN START WITH ME.
I AM NOBODY'S SON.
PLEASE... DON'T GO, I--

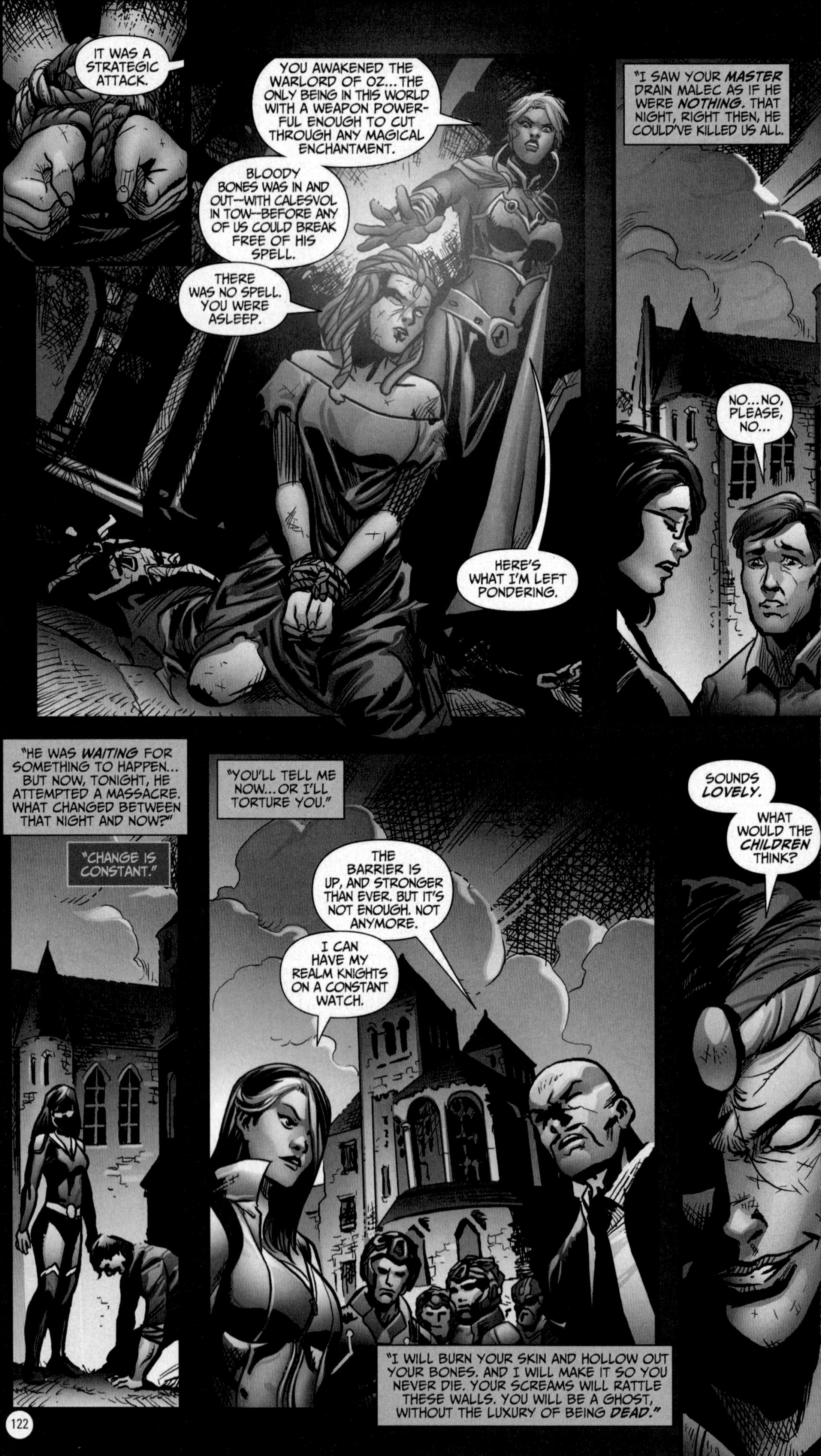
IT WAS A STRATEGIC ATTACK.
YOU AWAKENED THE WARLORD OF OZ... THE ONLY BEING IN THIS WORLD WITH A WEAPON POWERFUL ENOUGH TO CUT THROUGH ANY MAGICAL ENCHANTMENT.
BLOODY BONES WAS IN AND OUT--WITH CALESVOL IN TOW--BEFORE ANY OF US COULD BREAK FREE OF HIS SPELL.
THERE WAS NO SPELL. YOU WERE ASLEEP.
HERE'S WHAT I'M LEFT PONDERING.
"I SAW YOUR MASTER DRAIN MALEC AS IF HE WERE NOTHING. THAT NIGHT, RIGHT THEN, HE COULD'VE KILLED US ALL.
NO... NO, PLEASE, NO...
"HE WAS WAITING FOR SOMETHING TO HAPPEN... BUT NOW, TONIGHT, HE ATTEMPTED A MASSACRE. WHAT CHANGED BETWEEN THAT NIGHT AND NOW?"
"CHANGE IS CONSTANT."
"YOU'LL TELL ME NOW... OR I'LL TORTURE YOU."
THE BARRIER IS UP, AND STRONGER THAN EVER. BUT IT'S NOT ENOUGH. NOT ANYMORE.
I CAN HAVE MY REALM KNIGHTS ON A CONSTANT WATCH.
SOUNDS LOVELY.
WHAT WOULD THE CHILDREN THINK?
"I WILL BURN YOUR SKIN AND HOLLOW OUT YOUR BONES. AND I WILL MAKE IT SO YOU NEVER DIE. YOUR SCREAMS WILL RATTLE THESE WALLS. YOU WILL BE A GHOST, WITHOUT THE LUXURY OF BEING DEAD."

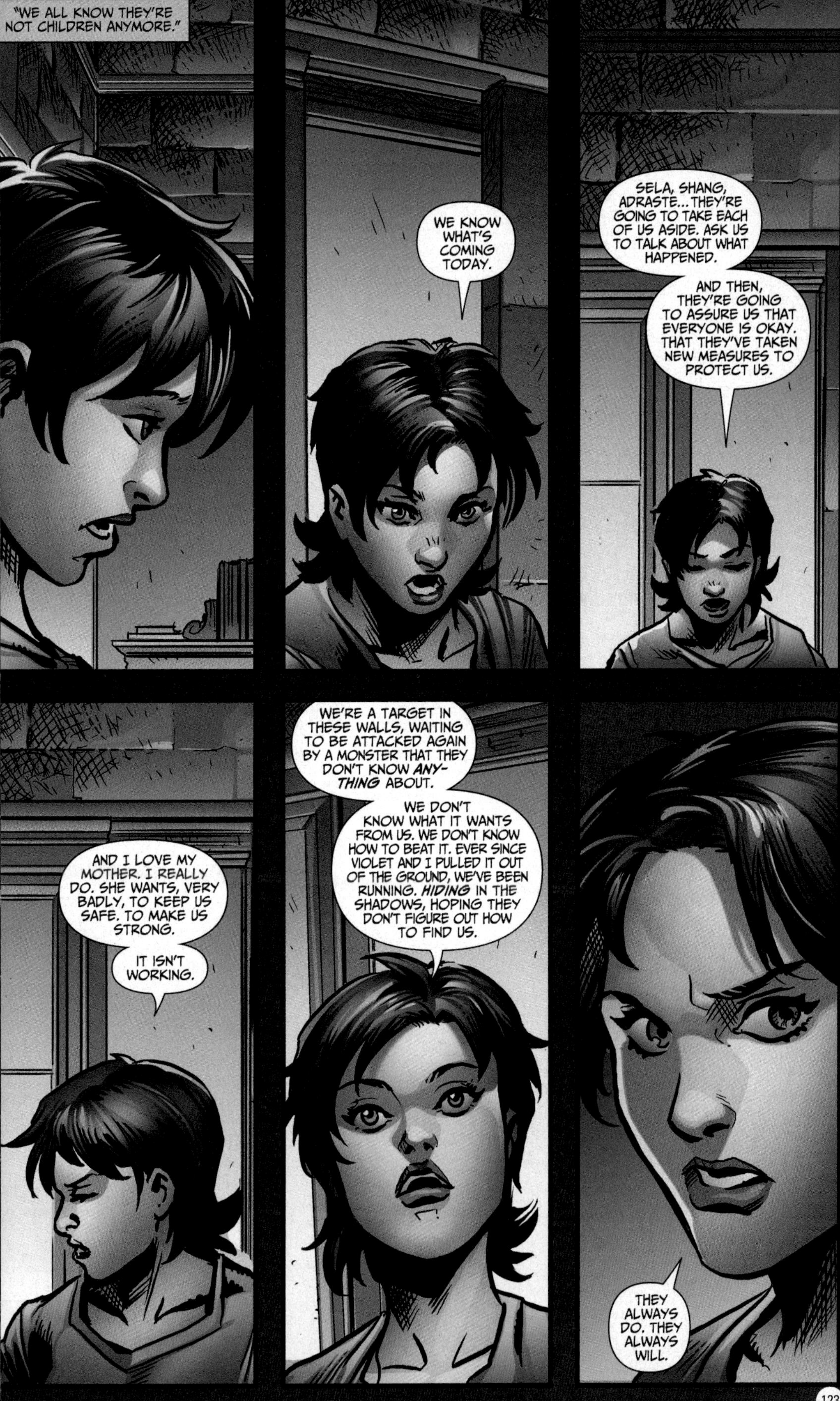
"WE ALL KNOW THEY'RE NOT CHILDREN ANYMORE."
WE KNOW WHAT'S COMING TODAY.
SELA, SHANG, ADRASTE... THEY'RE GOING TO TAKE EACH OF US ASIDE. ASK US TO TALK ABOUT WHAT HAPPENED.
AND THEN, THEY'RE GOING TO ASSURE US THAT EVERYONE IS OKAY. THAT THEY'VE TAKEN NEW MEASURES TO PROTECT US.
AND I LOVE MY MOTHER. I REALLY DO. SHE WANTS, VERY BADLY, TO KEEP US SAFE. TO MAKE US STRONG.
IT ISN'T WORKING.
WE'RE A TARGET IN THESE WALLS, WAITING TO BE ATTACKED AGAIN BY A MONSTER THAT THEY DON'T KNOW *ANY-THING* ABOUT.
WE DON'T KNOW WHAT IT WANTS FROM US. WE DON'T KNOW HOW TO BEAT IT. EVER SINCE VIOLET AND I PULLED IT OUT OF THE GROUND, WE'VE BEEN RUNNING. *HIDING* IN THE SHADOWS, HOPING THEY DON'T FIGURE OUT HOW TO FIND US.
THEY ALWAYS DO. THEY ALWAYS WILL.

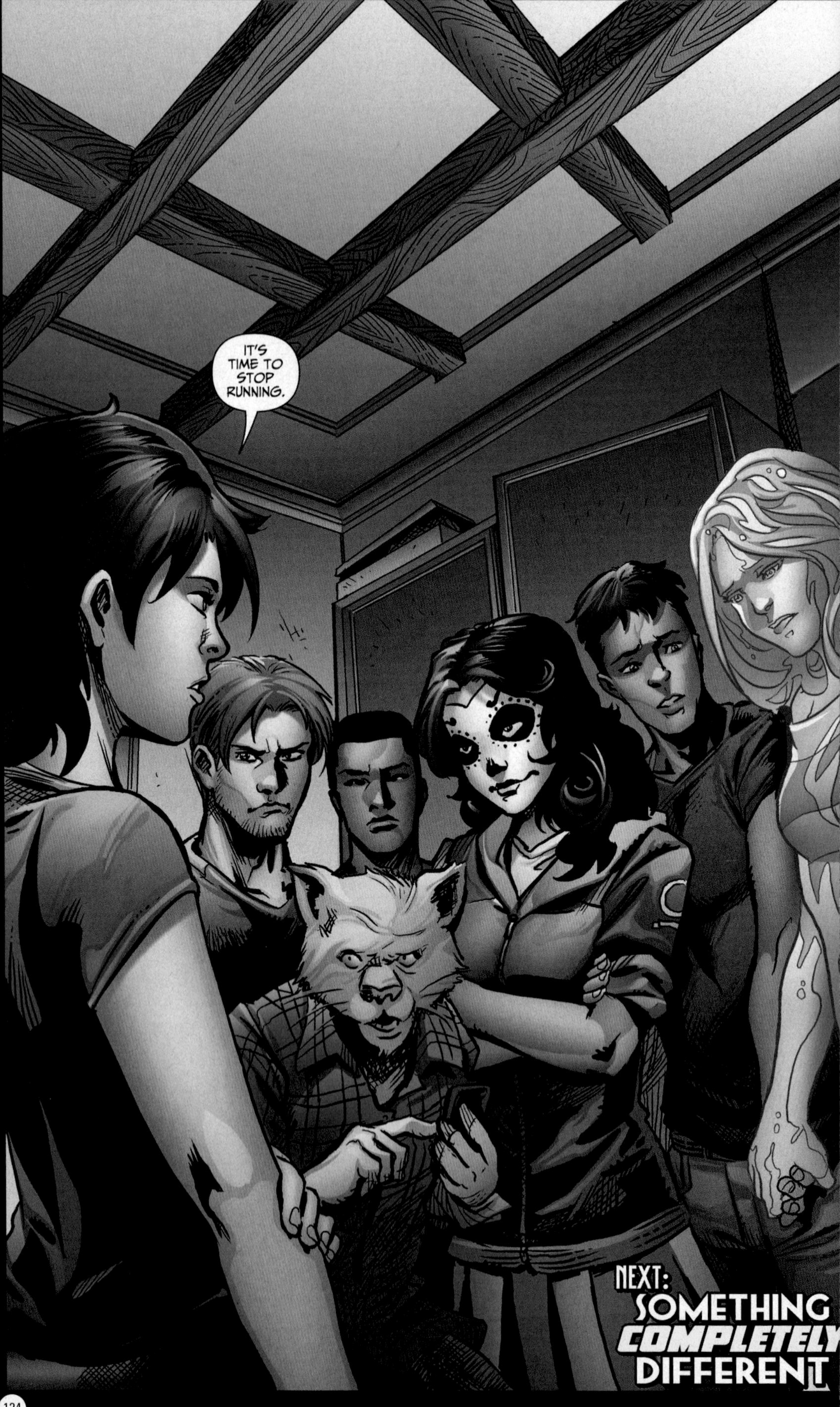
IT'S TIME TO STOP RUNNING.
NEXT: SOMETHING COMPLETELY DIFFERENT

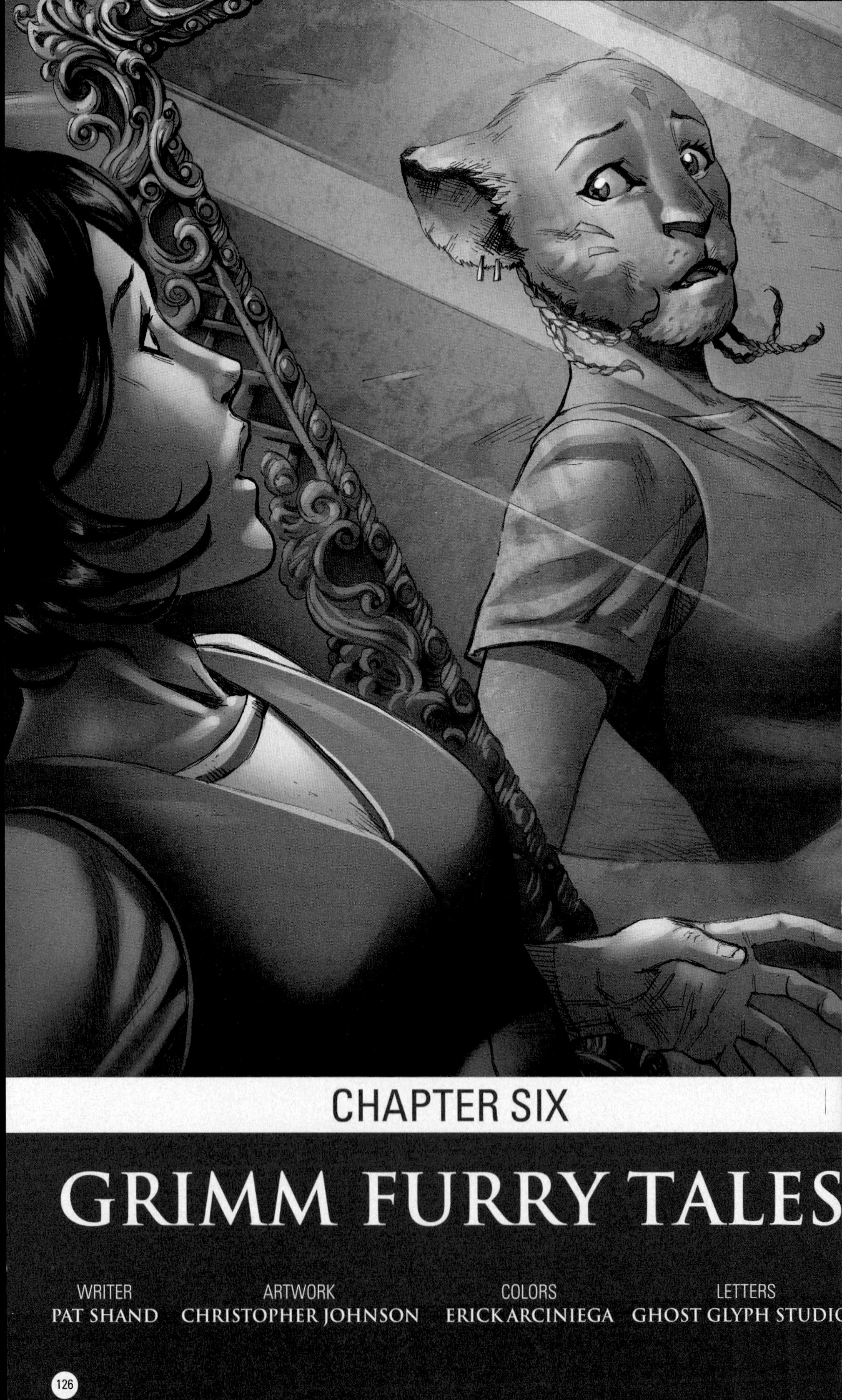

CHAPTER SIX

GRIMM FURRY TALES

WRITER
PAT SHAND

ARTWORK
CHRISTOPHER JOHNSON

COLORS
ERICK ARCINIEGA

LETTERS
GHOST GLYPH STUDIO

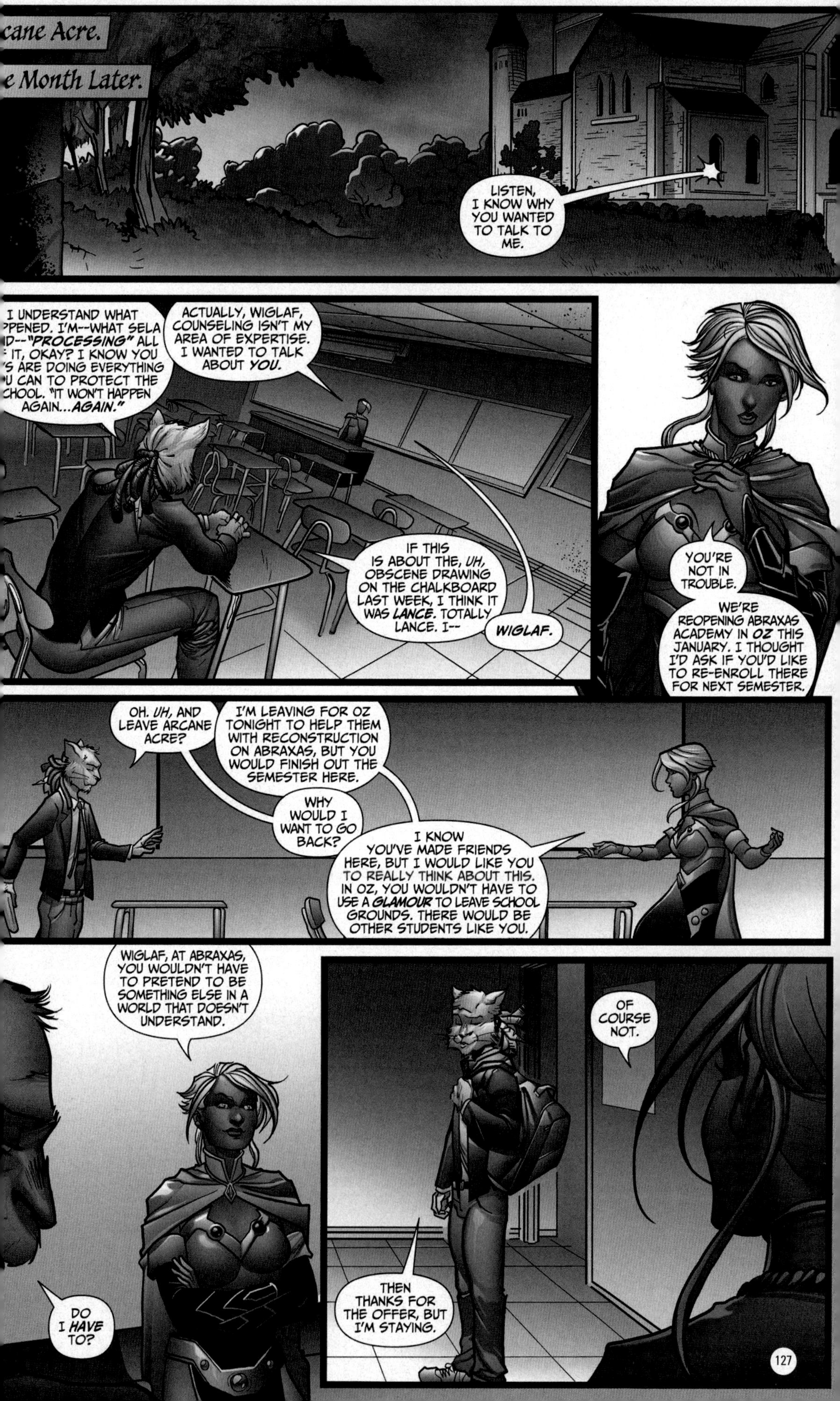
cane Acre.
e Month Later.
LISTEN, I KNOW WHY YOU WANTED TO TALK TO ME.
I UNDERSTAND WHAT PPENED. I'M--WHAT SELA ID--"PROCESSING" ALL IT, OKAY? I KNOW YOU 'S ARE DOING EVERYTHING U CAN TO PROTECT THE CHOOL. "IT WON'T HAPPEN AGAIN...AGAIN."
ACTUALLY, WIGLAF, COUNSELING ISN'T MY AREA OF EXPERTISE. I WANTED TO TALK ABOUT YOU.
IF THIS IS ABOUT THE, UH, OBSCENE DRAWING ON THE CHALKBOARD LAST WEEK, I THINK IT WAS LANCE. TOTALLY LANCE. I--
WIGLAF.
YOU'RE NOT IN TROUBLE.
WE'RE REOPENING ABRAXAS ACADEMY IN OZ THIS JANUARY. I THOUGHT I'D ASK IF YOU'D LIKE TO RE-ENROLL THERE FOR NEXT SEMESTER.
OH. UH, AND LEAVE ARCANE ACRE?
I'M LEAVING FOR OZ TONIGHT TO HELP THEM WITH RECONSTRUCTION ON ABRAXAS, BUT YOU WOULD FINISH OUT THE SEMESTER HERE.
WHY WOULD I WANT TO GO BACK?
I KNOW YOU'VE MADE FRIENDS HERE, BUT I WOULD LIKE YOU TO REALLY THINK ABOUT THIS. IN OZ, YOU WOULDN'T HAVE TO USE A GLAMOUR TO LEAVE SCHOOL GROUNDS. THERE WOULD BE OTHER STUDENTS LIKE YOU.
WIGLAF, AT ABRAXAS, YOU WOULDN'T HAVE TO PRETEND TO BE SOMETHING ELSE IN A WORLD THAT DOESN'T UNDERSTAND.
DO I HAVE TO?
OF COURSE NOT.
THEN THANKS FOR THE OFFER, BUT I'M STAYING.

"IN OZ, YOU WOULDN'T HAVE TO USE A *GLAMOUR* TO LEAV[E] THE SCHOOL." NYEAH, NYEAH, NYEAH! I WISH PEOPLE WOU[LD] STOP TALKING ABOUT ME LIKE I'VE GOT A @#$% GROWIN[G] OUT OF MY FOREHEAD! I'M JUST A LITTLE DIFFERENT IS AL[L].

AND ANYWAYS, WHEN [I'M] WEARING THAT GLAM[OUR] THING, I DON'T FE[EL] LIKE I'M *PRETEND[ING]*. IT'S JUST... ANOTH[ER] *VERSION* OF ME. A[ND] WHO'S TO SAY I'M [NOT] ALLOWED TO LIKE T[HAT] VERSION *BETTER*[?]

I MEAN, JUST LOOK AT HAILEY.

NONE OF US CAN FATHOM THE *TRAUMA* YOU'VE BEEN THROUGH. I WANTED TO LET YOU KNOW THAT IF YOU EVER NEED ANYTHING—SOMEONE TO TALK TO, QUESTIONS ANSWERED...BOTH SELA AND I ARE HERE FOR YOU.

THANK YOU, SIR.

SHE WAS A *GHOST*, AND ALI AND MARY MADE HER INTO A...LIKE, WATER-PERSON-THING, AND EVERYONE'S JUST GLAD TO HAVE HER BACK.

AND, COME ON, LANCE IS A DUDE MADE OF FLOWERS! THAT'S *WAY* WEIRDER THAN ME.

HOW GOES THE SECRET PLANNING, GUYS?

HUSH WIGLAF!

QUIET, MAN!

WIGLAF, REALLY...

I MISS WHEN [WE] ALL HATED H[ER].

AT LEAST WULF'S GOT MY BACK.

AND THEY WERE ALL, *"SHUT UP, WIGLAF!"* LIKE I'M GONNA MESS EVERYTHING UP JUST BY BEING THERE, YOU KNOW?

TWO-HUNDRED AND TWO...TWO-HUNDRED AND THREE...

THANKS FOR LISTENING, BRO.

AW, MAYBE ADRASTE IS *RIGHT*.

WHO AM I KIDDING ANYWAY?

MAYBE I SHOULD JU[ST] GO BACK TO OZ.

ADRAST[E,] *WAIT!*

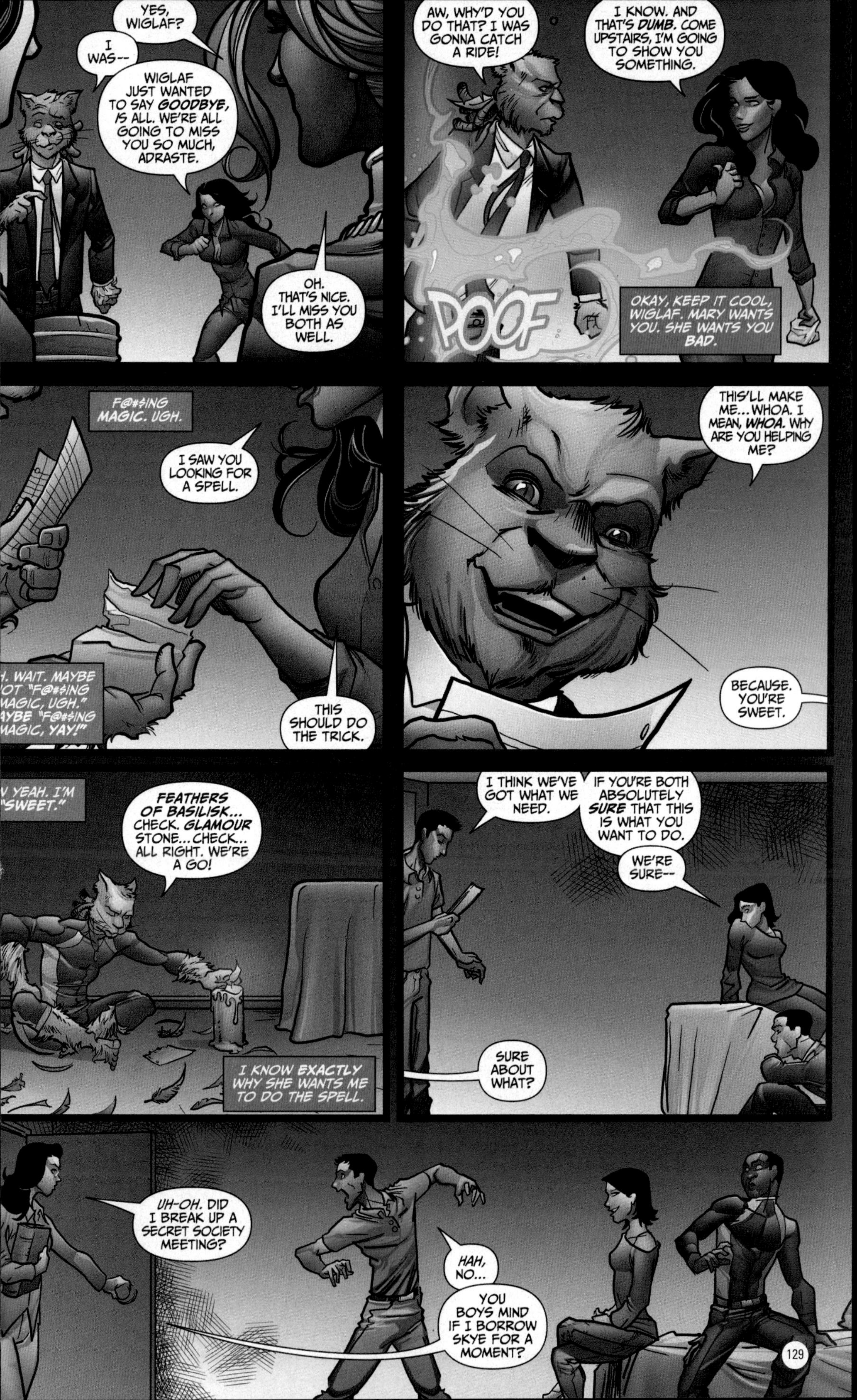
YES, WIGLAF?
I WAS--
WIGLAF JUST WANTED TO SAY GOODBYE, IS ALL. WE'RE ALL GOING TO MISS YOU SO MUCH, ADRASTE.
OH. THAT'S NICE. I'LL MISS YOU BOTH AS WELL.
AW, WHY'D YOU DO THAT? I WAS GONNA CATCH A RIDE!
I KNOW. AND THAT'S DUMB. COME UPSTAIRS, I'M GOING TO SHOW YOU SOMETHING.
POOF
OKAY, KEEP IT COOL, WIGLAF. MARY WANTS YOU. SHE WANTS YOU BAD.
F@#$ING MAGIC. UGH.
I SAW YOU LOOKING FOR A SPELL.
H. WAIT. MAYBE OT "F@#$ING MAGIC, UGH." AYBE "F@#$ING MAGIC, YAY!"
THIS SHOULD DO THE TRICK.
THIS'LL MAKE ME... WHOA. I MEAN, WHOA. WHY ARE YOU HELPING ME?
BECAUSE. YOU'RE SWEET.
V YEAH. I'M "SWEET."
FEATHERS OF BASILISK... CHECK. GLAMOUR STONE... CHECK... ALL RIGHT. WE'RE A GO!
I KNOW EXACTLY WHY SHE WANTS ME TO DO THE SPELL.
I THINK WE'VE GOT WHAT WE NEED.
IF YOU'RE BOTH ABSOLUTELY SURE THAT THIS IS WHAT YOU WANT TO DO.
WE'RE SURE--
SURE ABOUT WHAT?
UH-OH. DID I BREAK UP A SECRET SOCIETY MEETING?
HAH, NO...
YOU BOYS MIND IF I BORROW SKYE FOR A MOMENT?

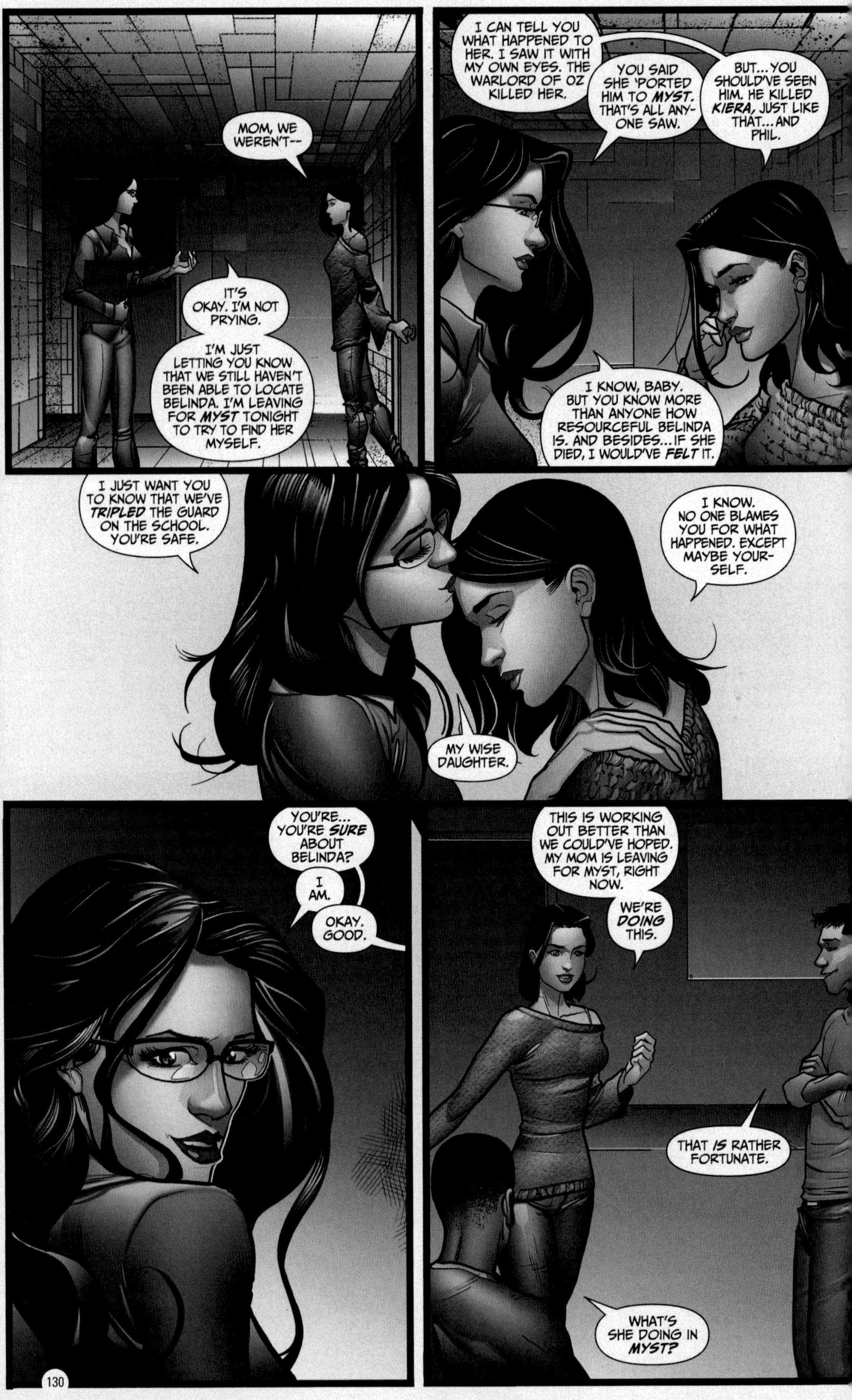
MOM, WE WEREN'T--
IT'S OKAY. I'M NOT PRYING.
I'M JUST LETTING YOU KNOW THAT WE STILL HAVEN'T BEEN ABLE TO LOCATE BELINDA. I'M LEAVING FOR MYST TONIGHT TO TRY TO FIND HER MYSELF.
I CAN TELL YOU WHAT HAPPENED TO HER. I SAW IT WITH MY OWN EYES. THE WARLORD OF OZ KILLED HER.
YOU SAID SHE 'PORTED HIM TO MYST. THAT'S ALL ANY-ONE SAW.
BUT... YOU SHOULD'VE SEEN HIM. HE KILLED KIERA, JUST LIKE THAT... AND PHIL.
I KNOW, BABY. BUT YOU KNOW MORE THAN ANYONE HOW RESOURCEFUL BELINDA IS. AND BESIDES... IF SHE DIED, I WOULD'VE FELT IT.
I JUST WANT YOU TO KNOW THAT WE'VE TRIPLED THE GUARD ON THE SCHOOL. YOU'RE SAFE.
I KNOW. NO ONE BLAMES YOU FOR WHAT HAPPENED. EXCEPT MAYBE YOUR-SELF.
MY WISE DAUGHTER.
YOU'RE... YOU'RE SURE ABOUT BELINDA?
I AM.
OKAY. GOOD.
THIS IS WORKING OUT BETTER THAN WE COULD'VE HOPED. MY MOM IS LEAVING FOR MYST, RIGHT NOW.
WE'RE DOING THIS.
THAT IS RATHER FORTUNATE.
WHAT'S SHE DOING IN MYST?

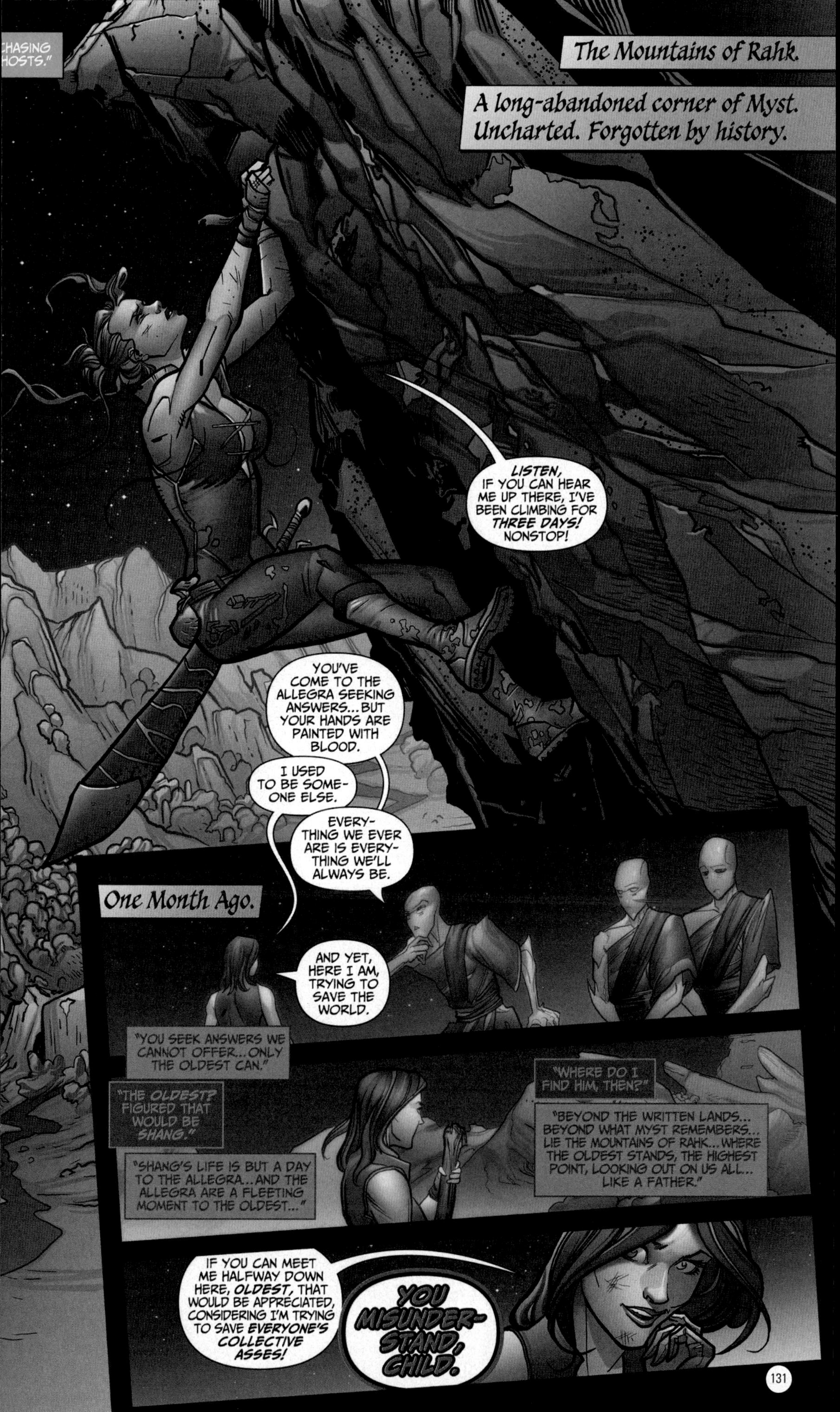
"CHASING GHOSTS."
The Mountains of Rahk.
A long-abandoned corner of Myst. Uncharted. Forgotten by history.
LISTEN, IF YOU CAN HEAR ME UP THERE, I'VE BEEN CLIMBING FOR THREE DAYS! NONSTOP!
YOU'VE COME TO THE ALLEGRA SEEKING ANSWERS... BUT YOUR HANDS ARE PAINTED WITH BLOOD.
I USED TO BE SOME-ONE ELSE.
EVERY-THING WE EVER ARE IS EVERY-THING WE'LL ALWAYS BE.
One Month Ago.
AND YET, HERE I AM, TRYING TO SAVE THE WORLD.
"YOU SEEK ANSWERS WE CANNOT OFFER... ONLY THE OLDEST CAN."
"THE OLDEST? FIGURED THAT WOULD BE SHANG."
"SHANG'S LIFE IS BUT A DAY TO THE ALLEGRA... AND THE ALLEGRA ARE A FLEETING MOMENT TO THE OLDEST..."
"WHERE DO I FIND HIM, THEN?"
"BEYOND THE WRITTEN LANDS... BEYOND WHAT MYST REMEMBERS... LIE THE MOUNTAINS OF RAHK... WHERE THE OLDEST STANDS, THE HIGHEST POINT, LOOKING OUT ON US ALL... LIKE A FATHER."
IF YOU CAN MEET ME HALFWAY DOWN HERE, OLDEST, THAT WOULD BE APPRECIATED, CONSIDERING I'M TRYING TO SAVE EVERYONE'S COLLECTIVE ASSES!
YOU MISUNDER-STAND, CHILD.

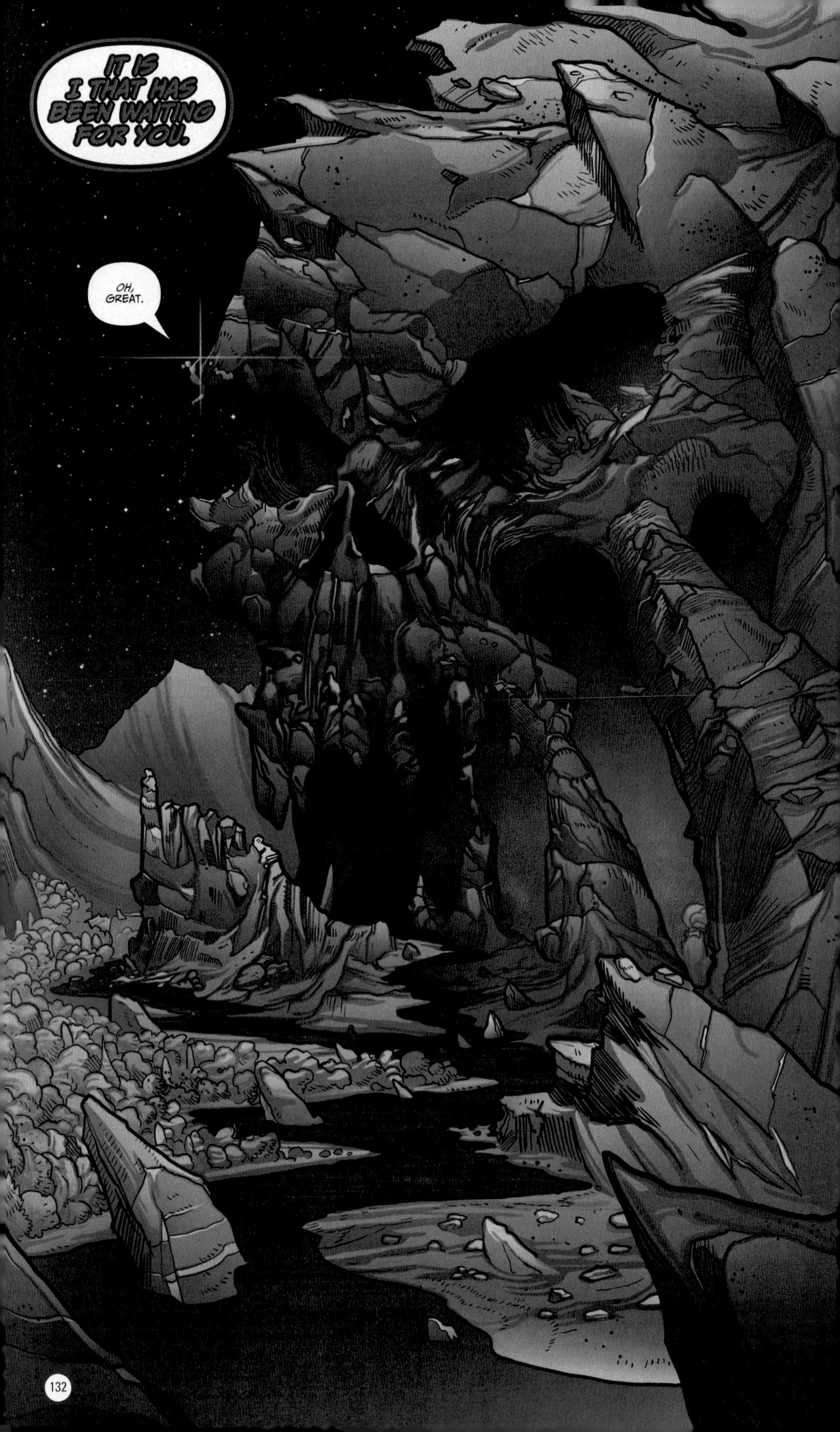
IT IS I THAT HAS BEEN WAITING FOR YOU.
OH, GREAT.

tside Arcane Acre.

NOTHING TO WORRY ABOUT. IT'S JUST A SHOOTING STAR.

I KNOW. IT'S JUST SO BEAUTIFUL.

...PLEASE BE QUIET.

"YOU'RE SURE IT'LL GET US PAST THEM?"

IF THE REALM KNIGHTS SEE US LEAVING, OR IF WE TRIP SOME KIND OF MAGICAL WIRE, WE'RE SCREWED.

I'VE TAKEN **VERY MEASURE** I **N** TO ENSURE A QUIET **EPORTATION.** THIS IS **WE CAN DO FROM DE** THE SCHOOL. WE **ST** HAVE TO HOPE.

HOPE ISN'T GOOD ENOUGH.

PERHAPS NOT. BUT IT'S ALL WE HAVE.

YOU'LL BEGIN TO FEEL A *TUG* IN YOUR STOMACH. NO CAUSE FOR CONCERN.

I JUST...I *WANTED* TO BE BACK. I THOUGHT IT WASN'T GOING TO WORK, AND THEN...THEN I JUST FELT MYSELF BECOMING *WHOLE.*

BUT I'M NOT WHOLE. I'M *MISSING* SOME-THING...

I, AH...I DON'T BELIEVE A *TISSUE* WOULD HELP, WOULD IT?

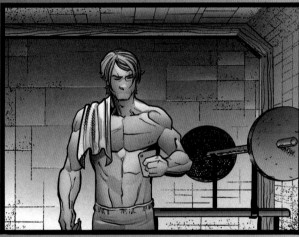

WHAT I WEAR, I WILL BE WHAT I AM, ALL WILL SEE CARNAG...

OH, COME ON, HOW THE HELL DO YOU SAY THAT?

CARNAGIO, AMILO-RAH

RAH-LODINE, A'DDAH-ME

F@#$ING GIBBERISH.

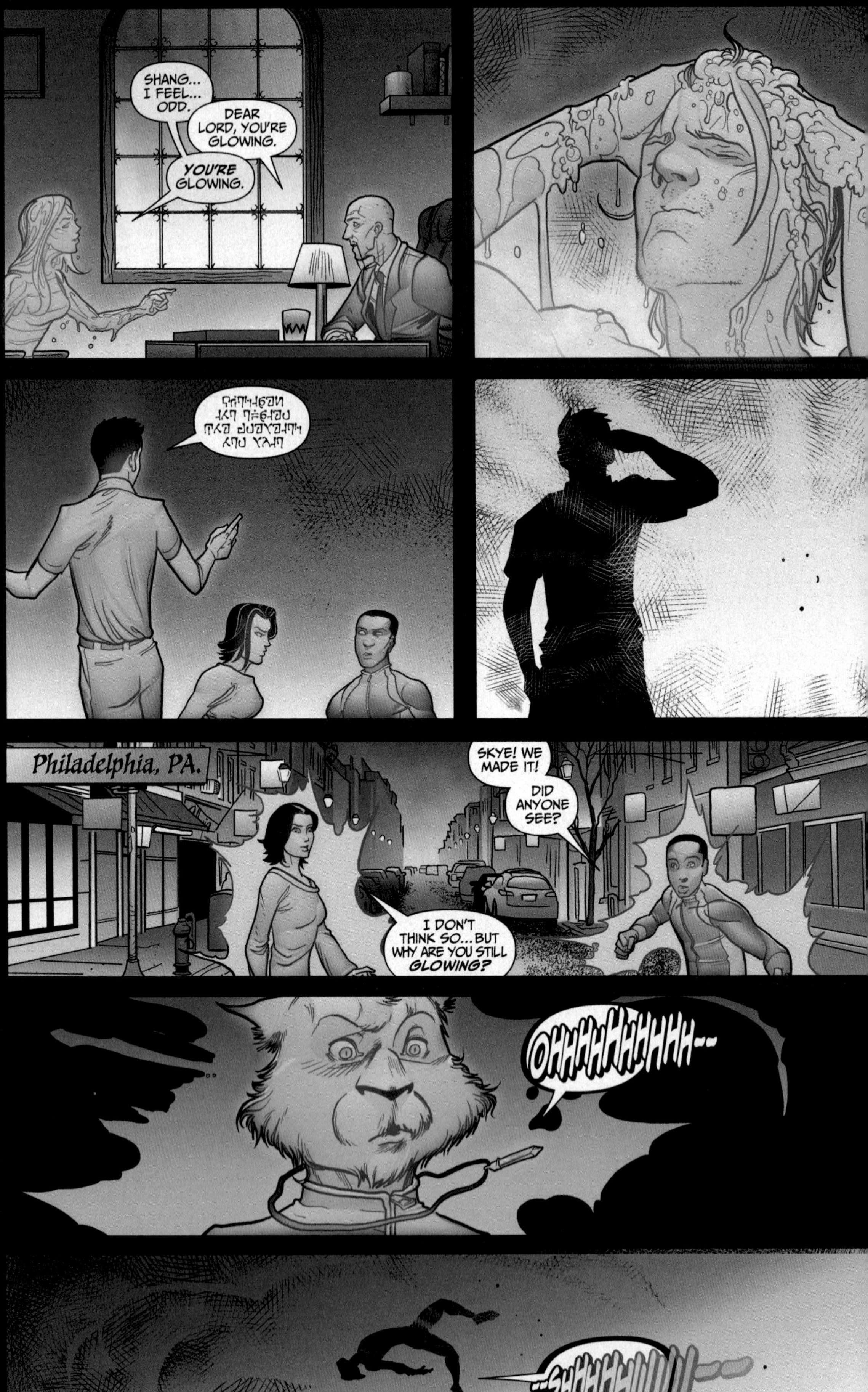
SHANG... I FEEL... ODD.
DEAR LORD, YOU'RE GLOWING.
YOU'RE GLOWING.
Philadelphia, PA.
SKYE! WE MADE IT!
DID ANYONE SEE?
I DON'T THINK SO... BUT WHY ARE YOU STILL GLOWING?
OHHHHHHHHHH--
--SHHHHH

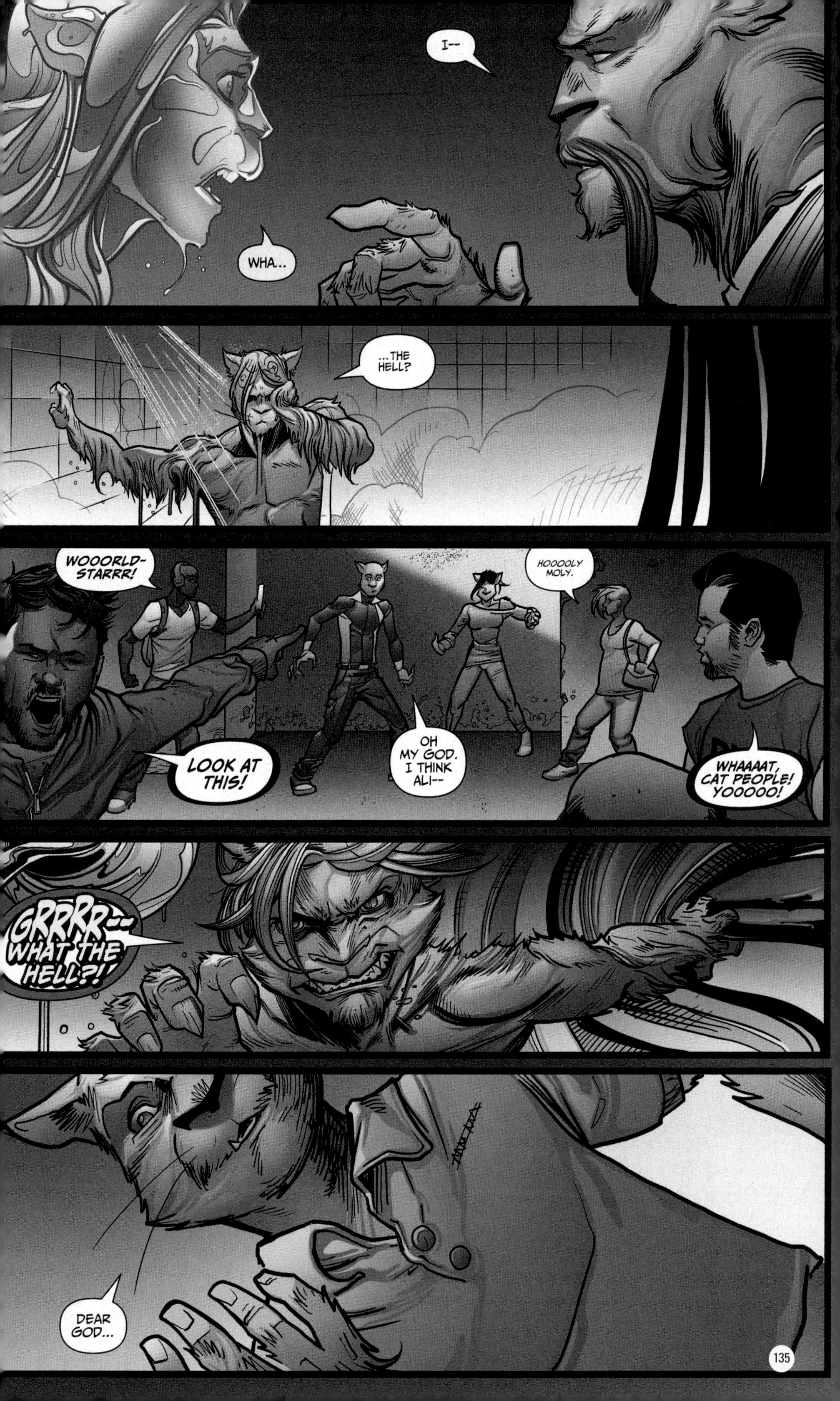
I--
WHA...
...THE HELL?
WOOORLD-STARRR!
HOOOOLY MOLY.
LOOK AT THIS!
OH MY GOD. I THINK ALI--
WHAAAAT, CAT PEOPLE! YOOOOO!
GRRRR-- WHAT THE HELL?!
DEAR GOD...

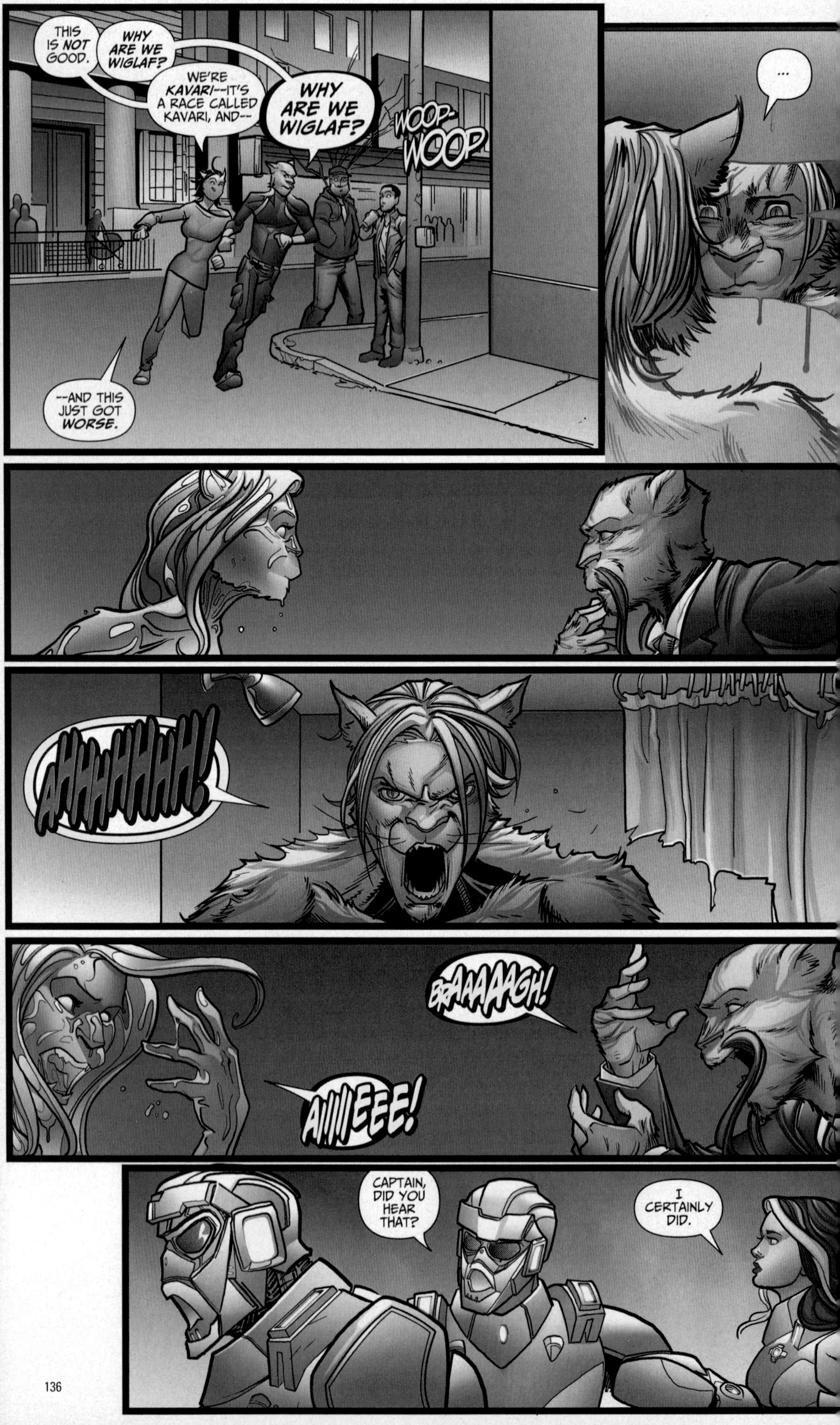

THIS IS NOT GOOD.
WHY ARE WE WIGLAF?
WE'RE KAVARI--IT'S A RACE CALLED KAVARI, AND--
WHY ARE WE WIGLAF?
WOOP-WOOP
--AND THIS JUST GOT WORSE.
...
AHHHHHHH!
BRAAAAAGH!
AIIIIEEE!
CAPTAIN, DID YOU HEAR THAT?
I CERTAINLY DID.

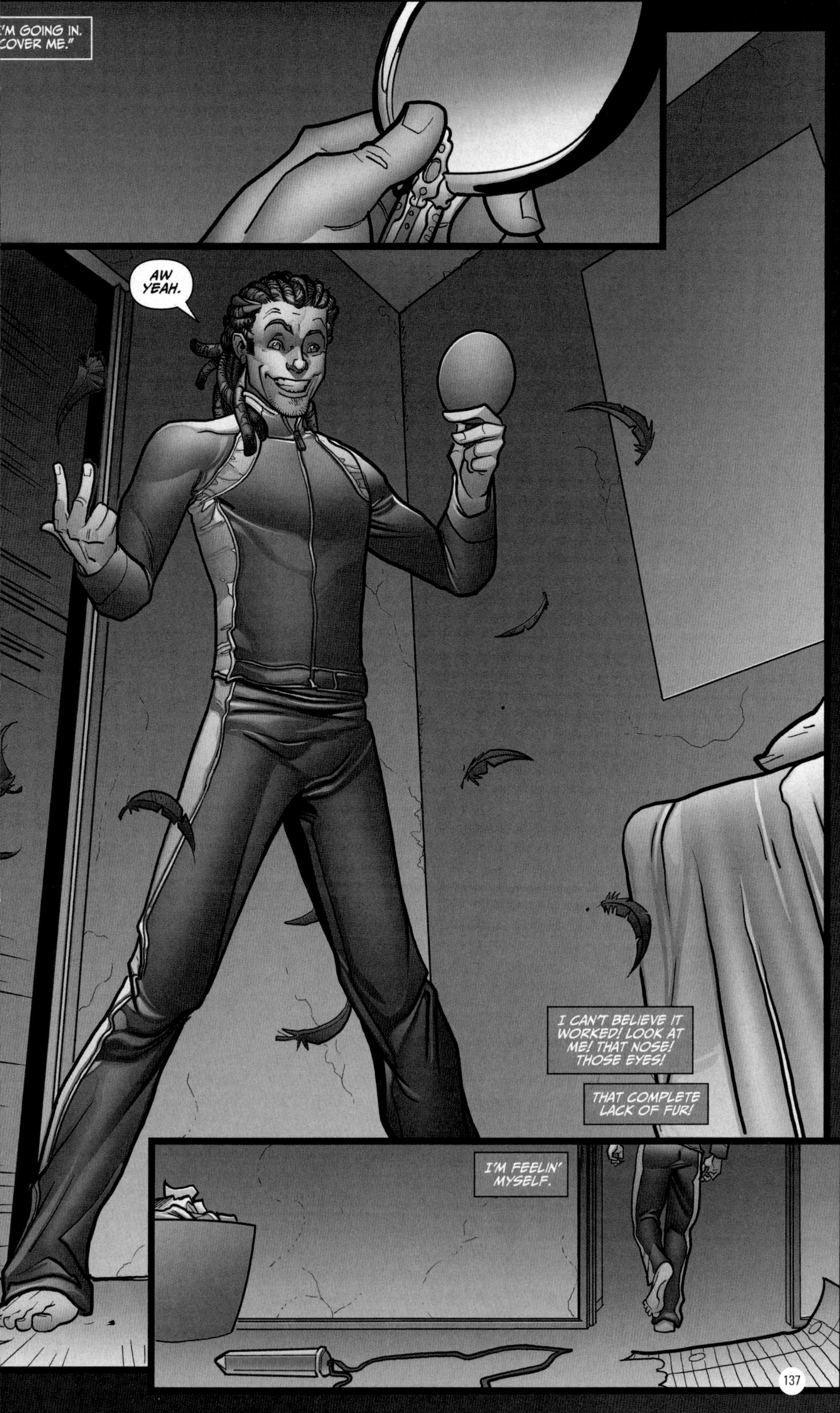
"I'M GOING IN.
COVER ME."
AW YEAH.
I CAN'T BELIEVE IT WORKED! LOOK AT ME! THAT NOSE! THOSE EYES!
THAT COMPLETE LACK OF FUR!
I'M FEELIN' MYSELF.

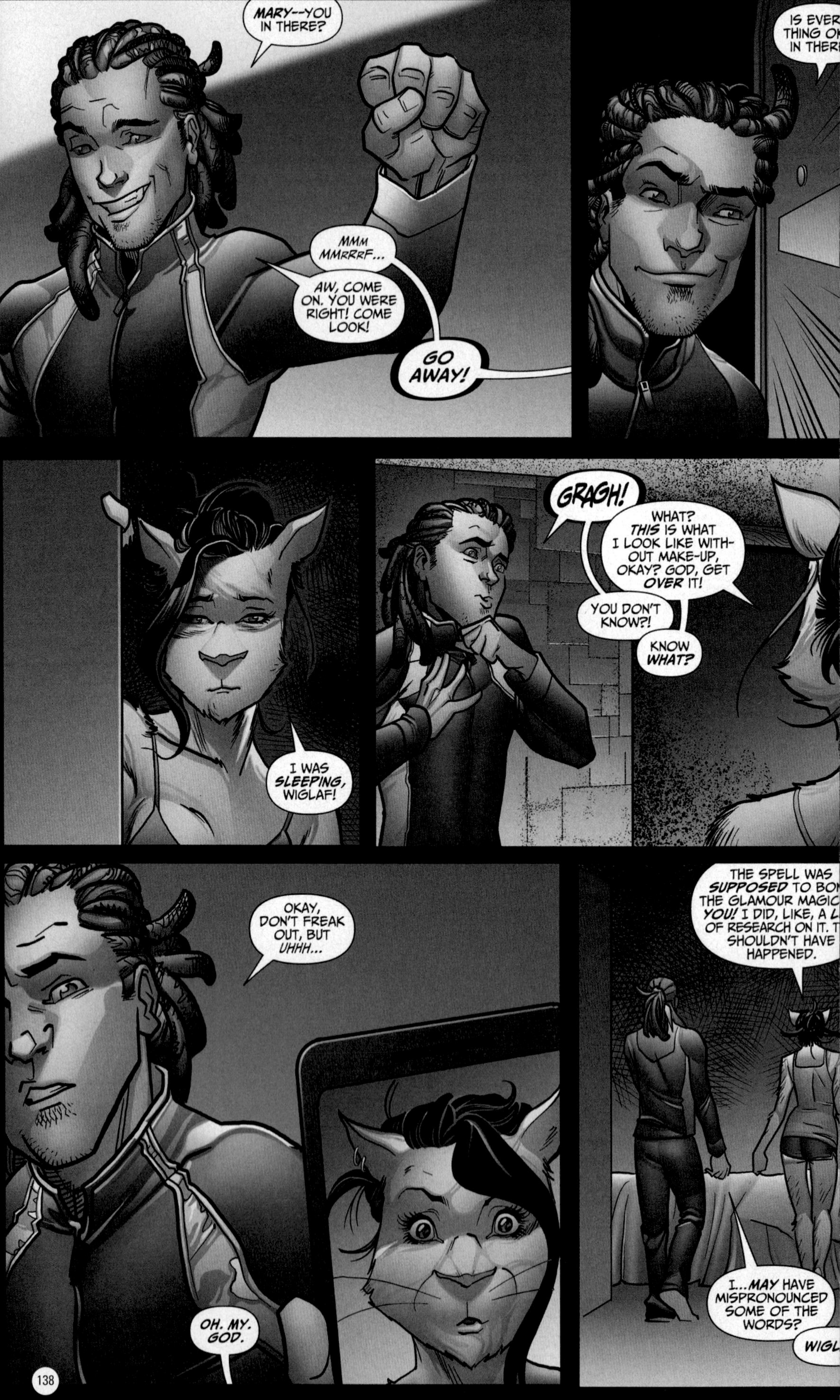

MARY--YOU IN THERE?
MMM MMRRRF...
AW, COME ON. YOU WERE RIGHT! COME LOOK!
GO AWAY!
IS EVER THING OK IN THER
I WAS SLEEPING, WIGLAF!
GRAGH!
WHAT? THIS IS WHAT I LOOK LIKE WITH-OUT MAKE-UP, OKAY? GOD, GET OVER IT!
YOU DON'T KNOW?!
KNOW WHAT?
OKAY, DON'T FREAK OUT, BUT UHHH...
OH. MY. GOD.
THE SPELL WAS SUPPOSED TO BON THE GLAMOUR MAGIC YOU! I DID, LIKE, A L OF RESEARCH ON IT. T SHOULDN'T HAVE HAPPENED.
I...MAY HAVE MISPRONOUNCED SOME OF THE WORDS?
WIGL

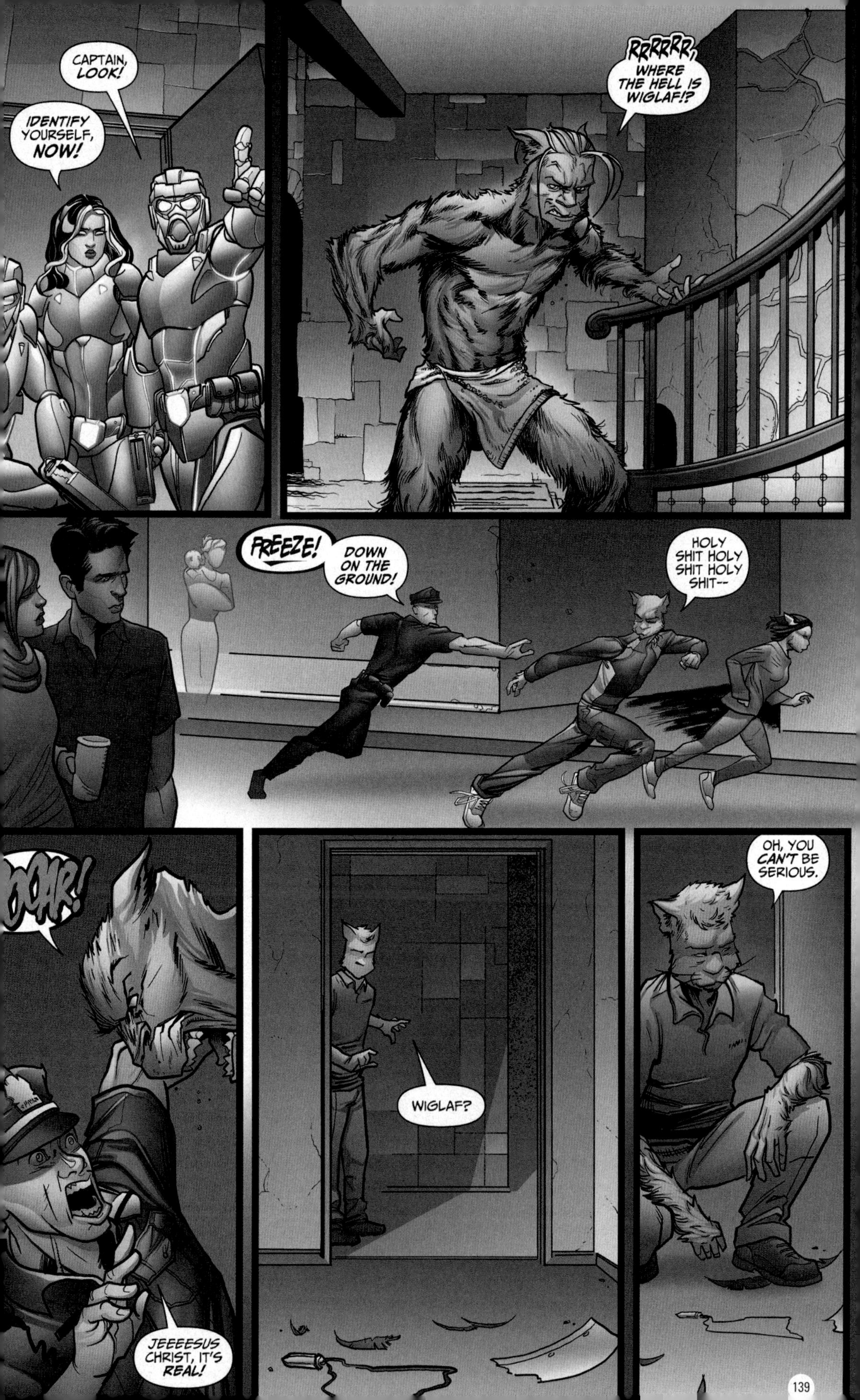
CAPTAIN, LOOK!
IDENTIFY YOURSELF, NOW!
RRRRRR, WHERE THE HELL IS WIGLAF!?
FREEZE!
DOWN ON THE GROUND!
HOLY SHIT HOLY SHIT HOLY SHIT--
OOAR!
JEEEESUS CHRIST, IT'S REAL!
WIGLAF?
OH, YOU CAN'T BE SERIOUS.

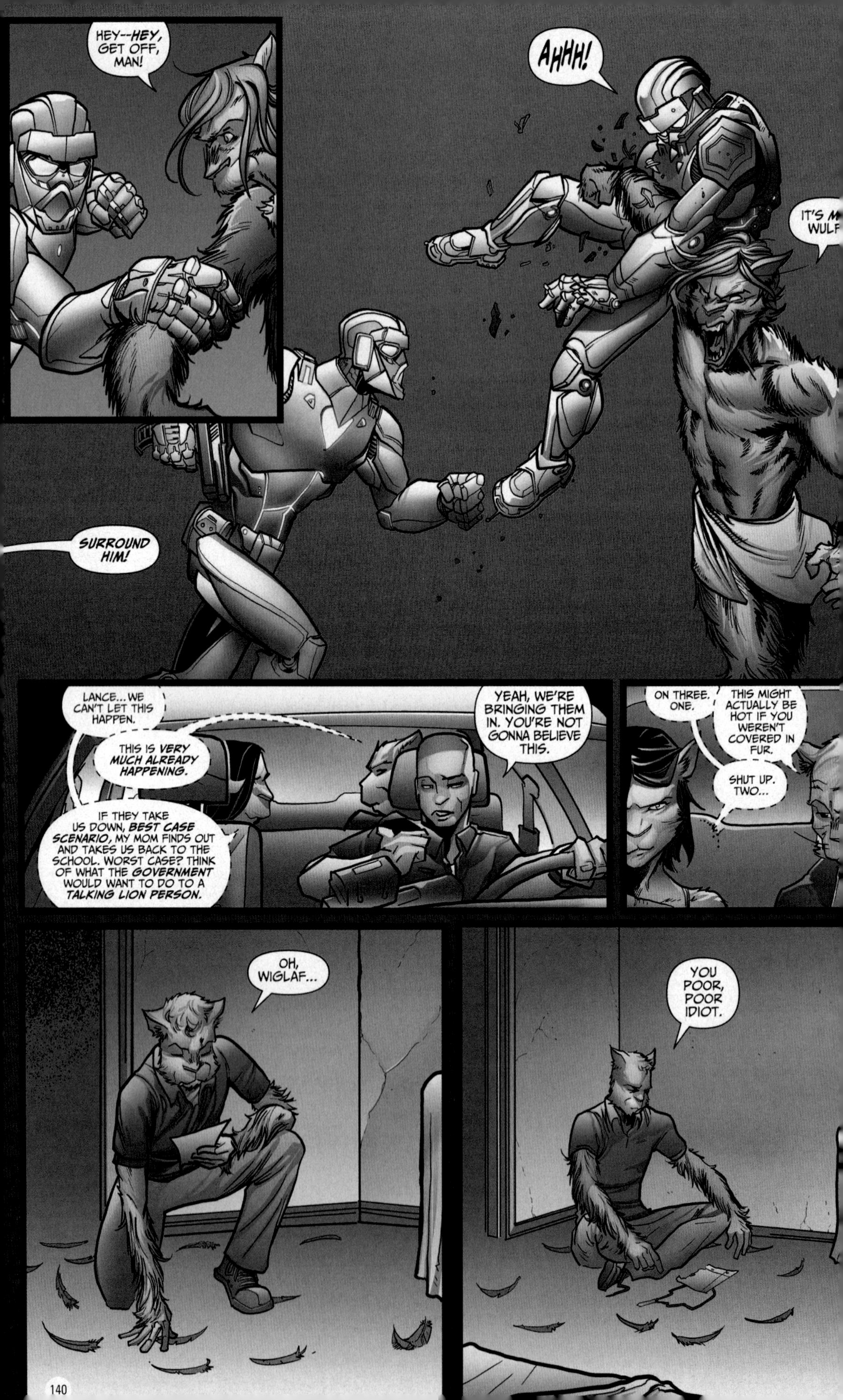

HEY--HEY, GET OFF, MAN!
AHHH!
IT'S M
WULF
SURROUND HIM!
LANCE... WE CAN'T LET THIS HAPPEN.
THIS IS VERY MUCH ALREADY HAPPENING.
IF THEY TAKE US DOWN, BEST CASE SCENARIO, MY MOM FINDS OUT AND TAKES US BACK TO THE SCHOOL. WORST CASE? THINK OF WHAT THE GOVERNMENT WOULD WANT TO DO TO A TALKING LION PERSON.
YEAH, WE'RE BRINGING THEM IN. YOU'RE NOT GONNA BELIEVE THIS.
ON THREE. ONE.
THIS MIGHT ACTUALLY BE HOT IF YOU WEREN'T COVERED IN FUR.
SHUT UP. TWO...
OH, WIGLAF...
YOU POOR, POOR IDIOT.

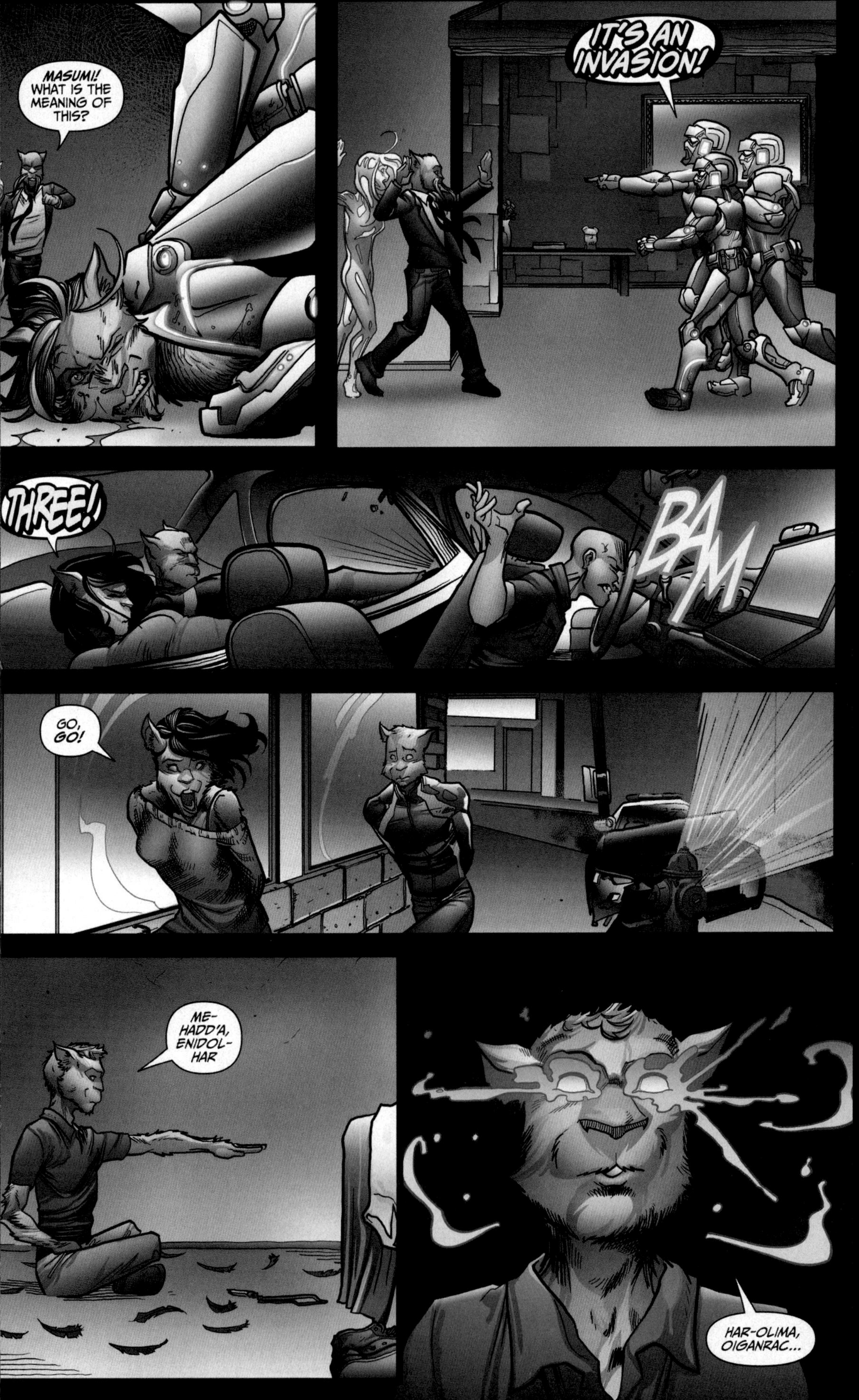
MASUMI! WHAT IS THE MEANING OF THIS?
IT'S AN INVASION!
THREE!
BAM
GO, GO!
ME-HADD'A, ENIDOL-HAR
HAR-OLIMA, OIGANRAC...

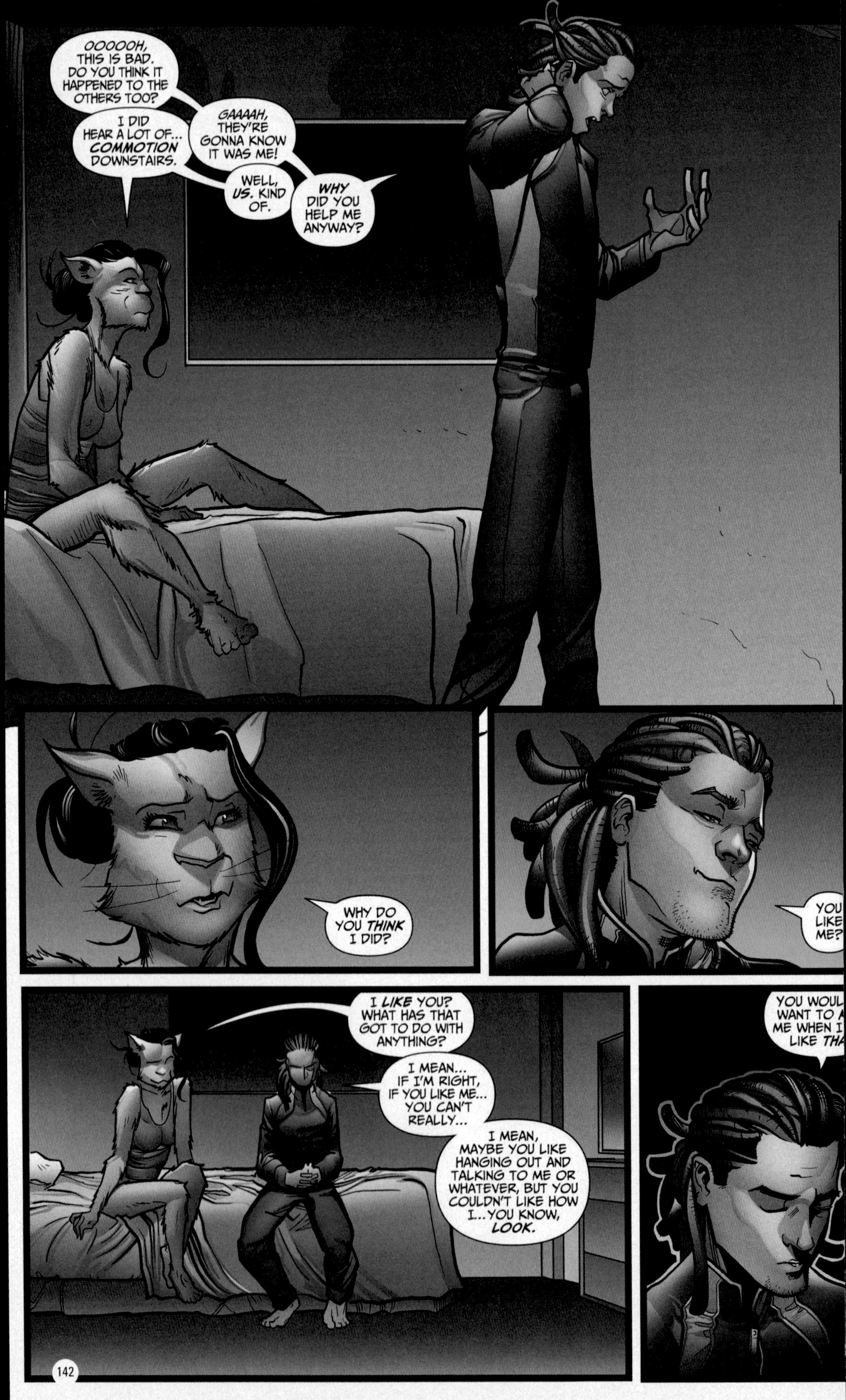
OOOOOH, THIS IS BAD. DO YOU THINK IT HAPPENED TO THE OTHERS TOO?
GAAAAH, THEY'RE GONNA KNOW IT WAS ME!
I DID HEAR A LOT OF... COMMOTION DOWNSTAIRS.
WELL, US. KIND OF.
WHY DID YOU HELP ME ANYWAY?
WHY DO YOU THINK I DID?
YOU LIKE ME?
I LIKE YOU? WHAT HAS THAT GOT TO DO WITH ANYTHING?
I MEAN... IF I'M RIGHT, IF YOU LIKE ME... YOU CAN'T REALLY...
I MEAN, MAYBE YOU LIKE HANGING OUT AND TALKING TO ME OR WHATEVER, BUT YOU COULDN'T LIKE HOW I...YOU KNOW, LOOK.
YOU WOUL WANT TO ME WHEN I LIKE THA

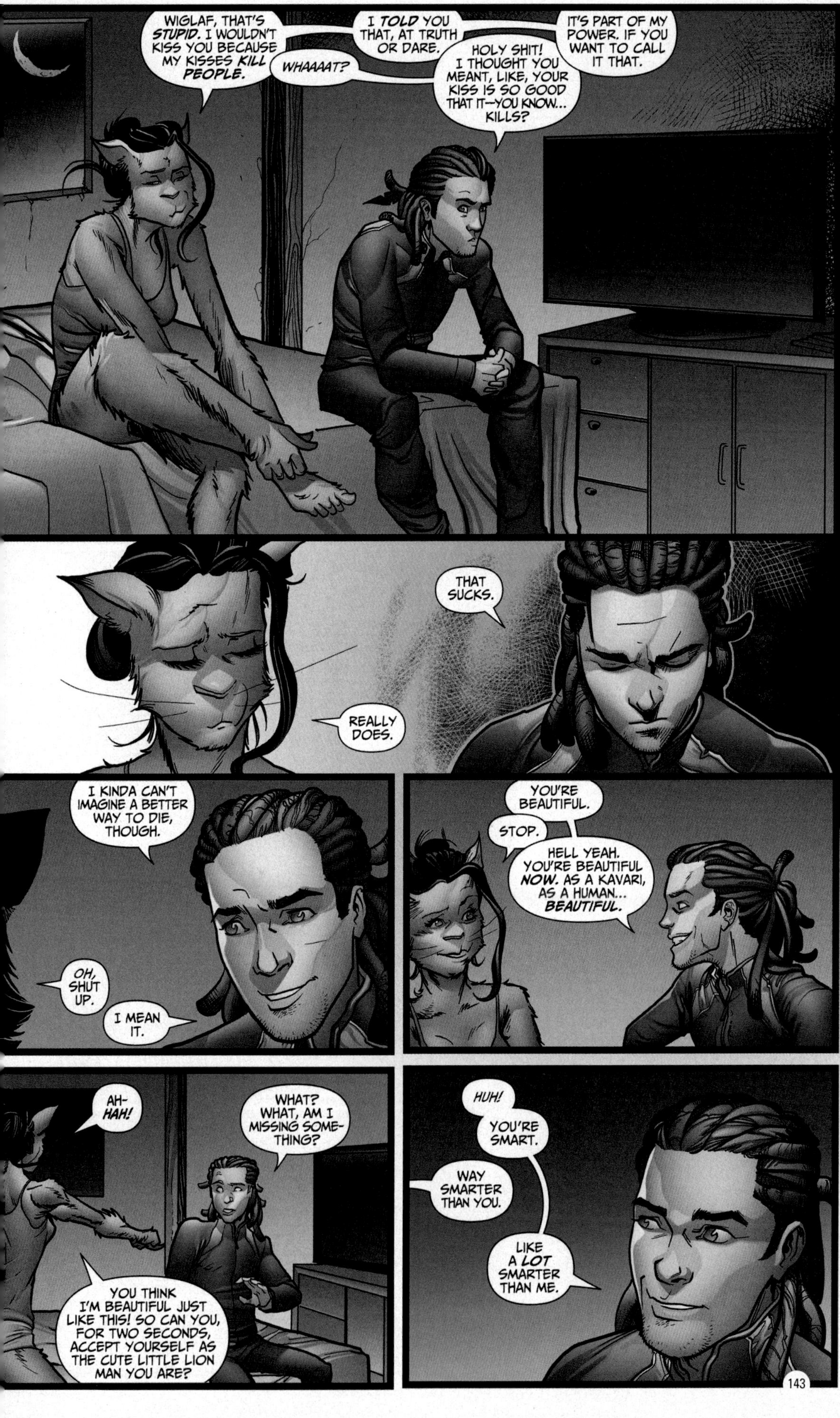

WIGLAF, THAT'S **STUPID.** I WOULDN'T KISS YOU BECAUSE MY KISSES **KILL PEOPLE.**
WHAAAAT?
I **TOLD** YOU THAT, AT TRUTH OR DARE.
HOLY SHIT! I THOUGHT YOU MEANT, LIKE, YOUR KISS IS SO GOOD THAT IT--YOU KNOW... KILLS?
IT'S PART OF MY POWER. IF YOU WANT TO CALL IT THAT.
THAT SUCKS.
REALLY DOES.
I KINDA CAN'T IMAGINE A BETTER WAY TO DIE, THOUGH.
OH, SHUT UP.
I MEAN IT.
YOU'RE BEAUTIFUL.
STOP.
HELL YEAH. YOU'RE BEAUTIFUL **NOW.** AS A KAVARI, AS A HUMAN... **BEAUTIFUL.**
AH-**HAH!**
WHAT? WHAT, AM I MISSING SOME-THING?
YOU THINK I'M BEAUTIFUL JUST LIKE THIS! SO CAN YOU, FOR TWO SECONDS, ACCEPT YOURSELF AS THE CUTE LITTLE LION MAN YOU ARE?
HUH!
YOU'RE SMART.
WAY SMARTER THAN YOU.
LIKE A **LOT** SMARTER THAN ME.

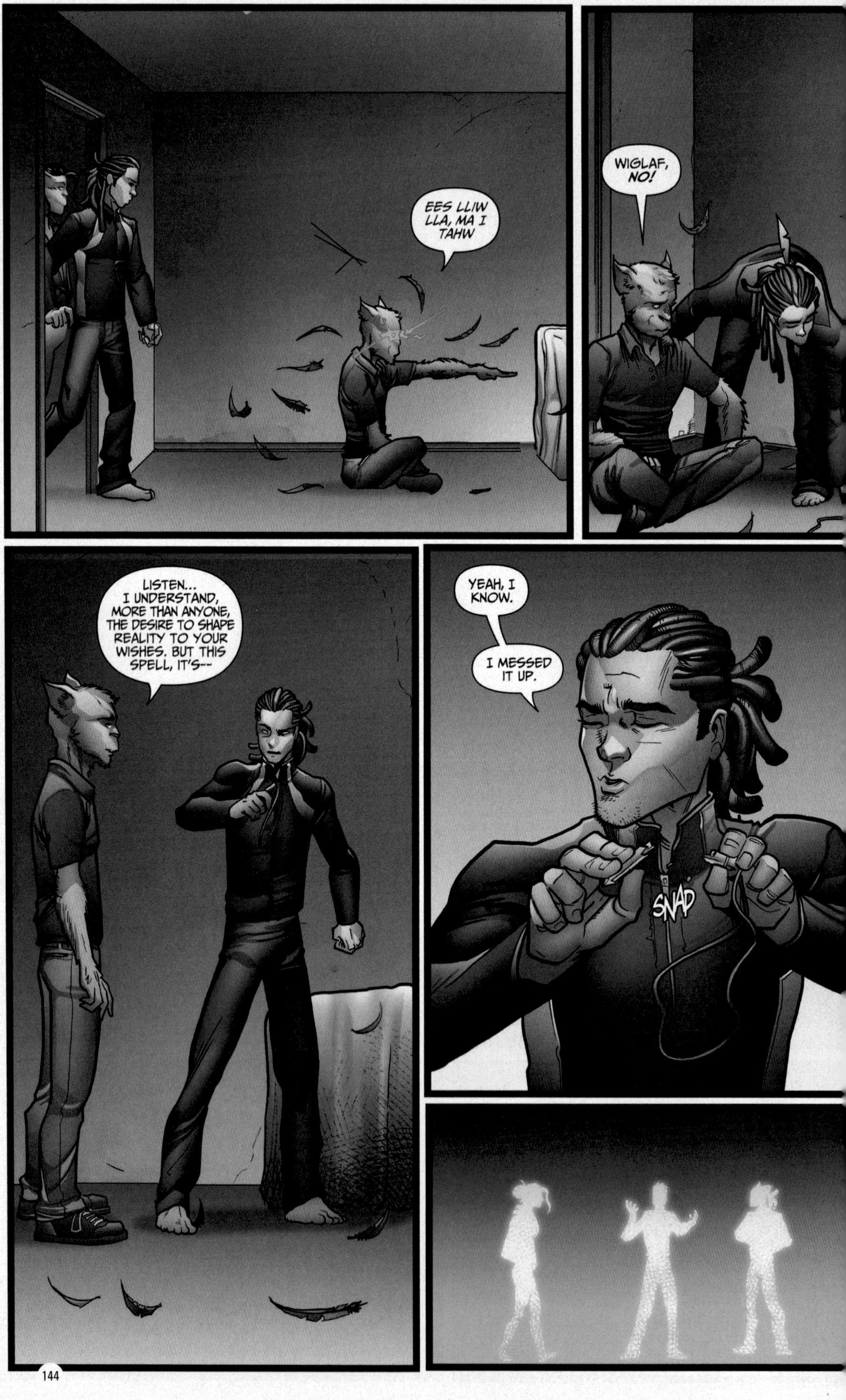
EES LLIW LLA, MA I TAHW
WIGLAF, NO!
LISTEN... I UNDERSTAND, MORE THAN ANYONE, THE DESIRE TO SHAPE REALITY TO YOUR WISHES. BUT THIS SPELL, IT'S--
YEAH, I KNOW.
I MESSED IT UP.
SNAP

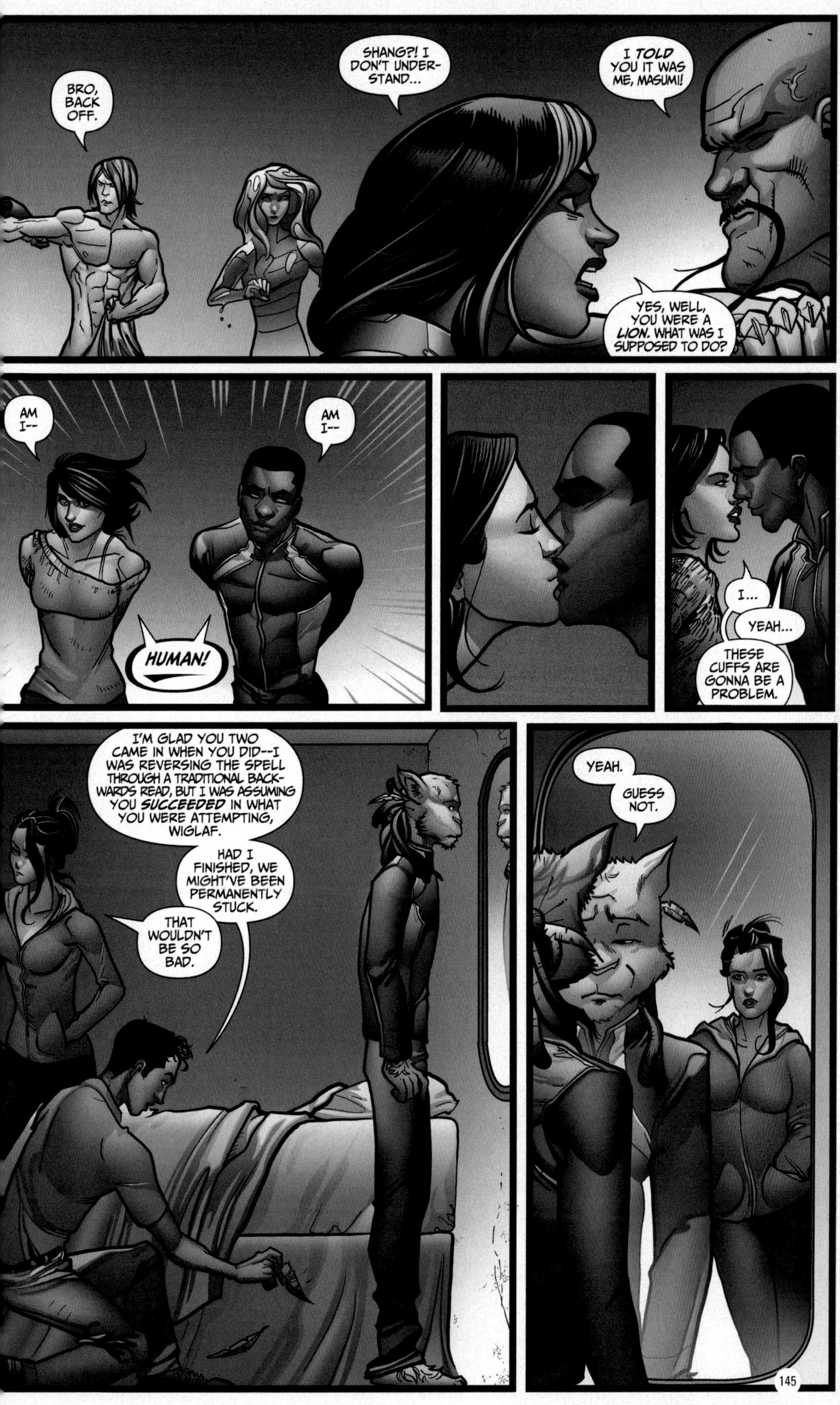
BRO, BACK OFF.
SHANG?! I DON'T UNDER-STAND...
I TOLD YOU IT WAS ME, MASUMI!
YES, WELL, YOU WERE A LION. WHAT WAS I SUPPOSED TO DO?
AM I--
AM I--
HUMAN!
I...
YEAH...
THESE CUFFS ARE GONNA BE A PROBLEM.
I'M GLAD YOU TWO CAME IN WHEN YOU DID--I WAS REVERSING THE SPELL THROUGH A TRADITIONAL BACK-WARDS READ, BUT I WAS ASSUMING YOU SUCCEEDED IN WHAT YOU WERE ATTEMPTING, WIGLAF.
HAD I FINISHED, WE MIGHT'VE BEEN PERMANENTLY STUCK.
THAT WOULDN'T BE SO BAD.
YEAH.
GUESS NOT.

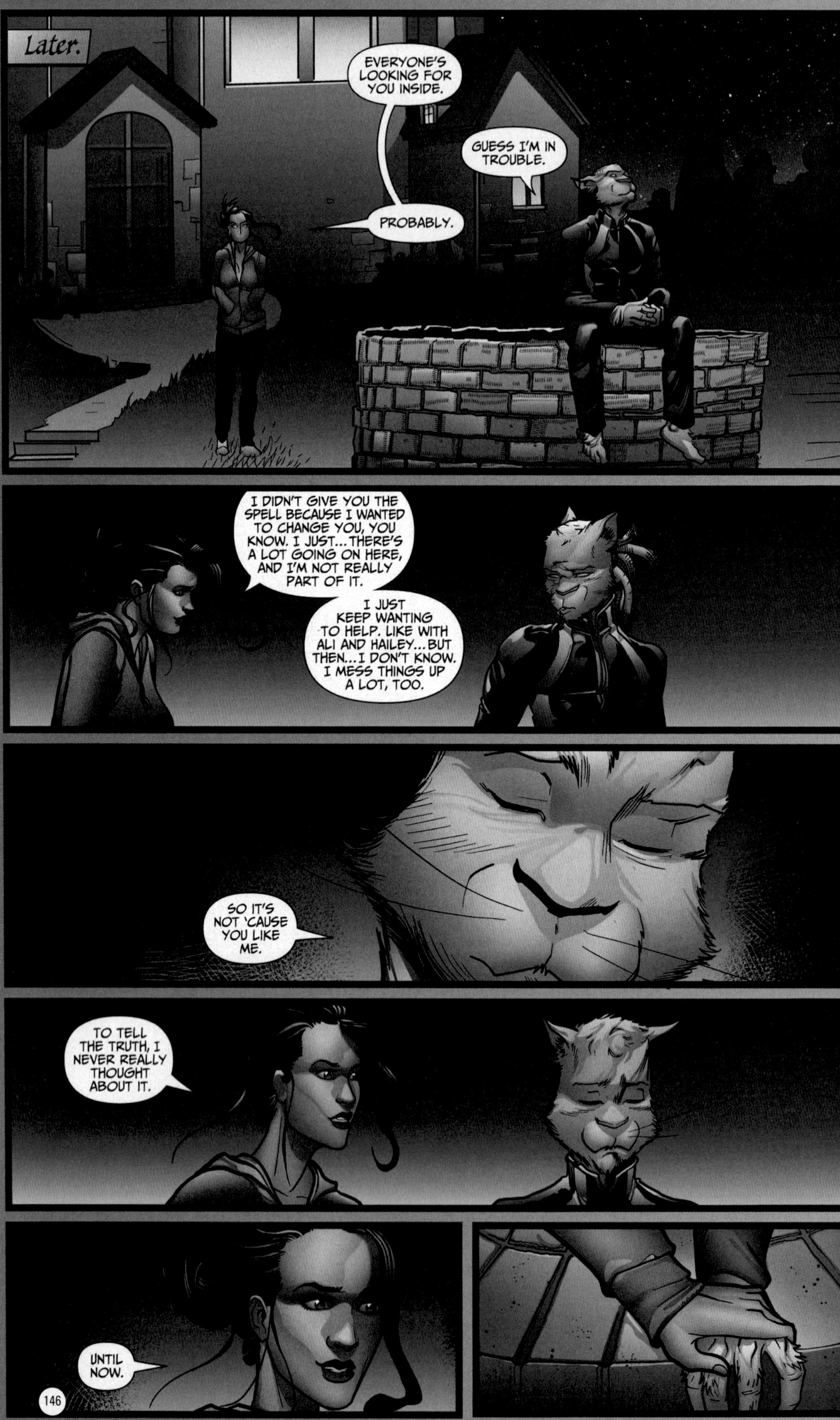

Later.
EVERYONE'S LOOKING FOR YOU INSIDE.
GUESS I'M IN TROUBLE.
PROBABLY.
I DIDN'T GIVE YOU THE SPELL BECAUSE I WANTED TO CHANGE YOU, YOU KNOW. I JUST... THERE'S A LOT GOING ON HERE, AND I'M NOT REALLY PART OF IT.
I JUST KEEP WANTING TO HELP. LIKE WITH ALI AND HAILEY... BUT THEN... I DON'T KNOW. I MESS THINGS UP A LOT, TOO.
SO IT'S NOT 'CAUSE YOU LIKE ME.
TO TELL THE TRUTH, I NEVER REALLY THOUGHT ABOUT IT.
UNTIL NOW.

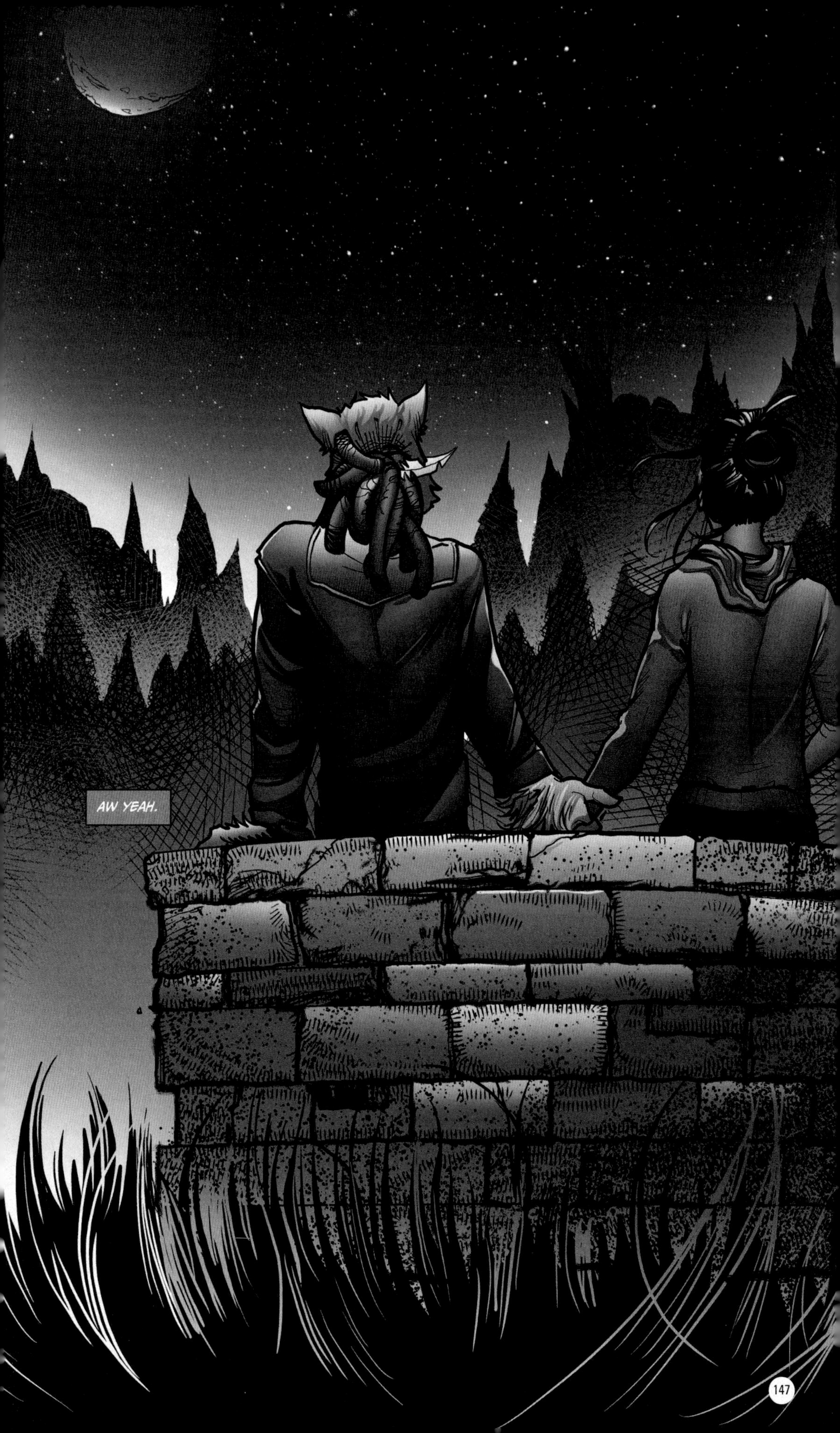
AW YEAH.

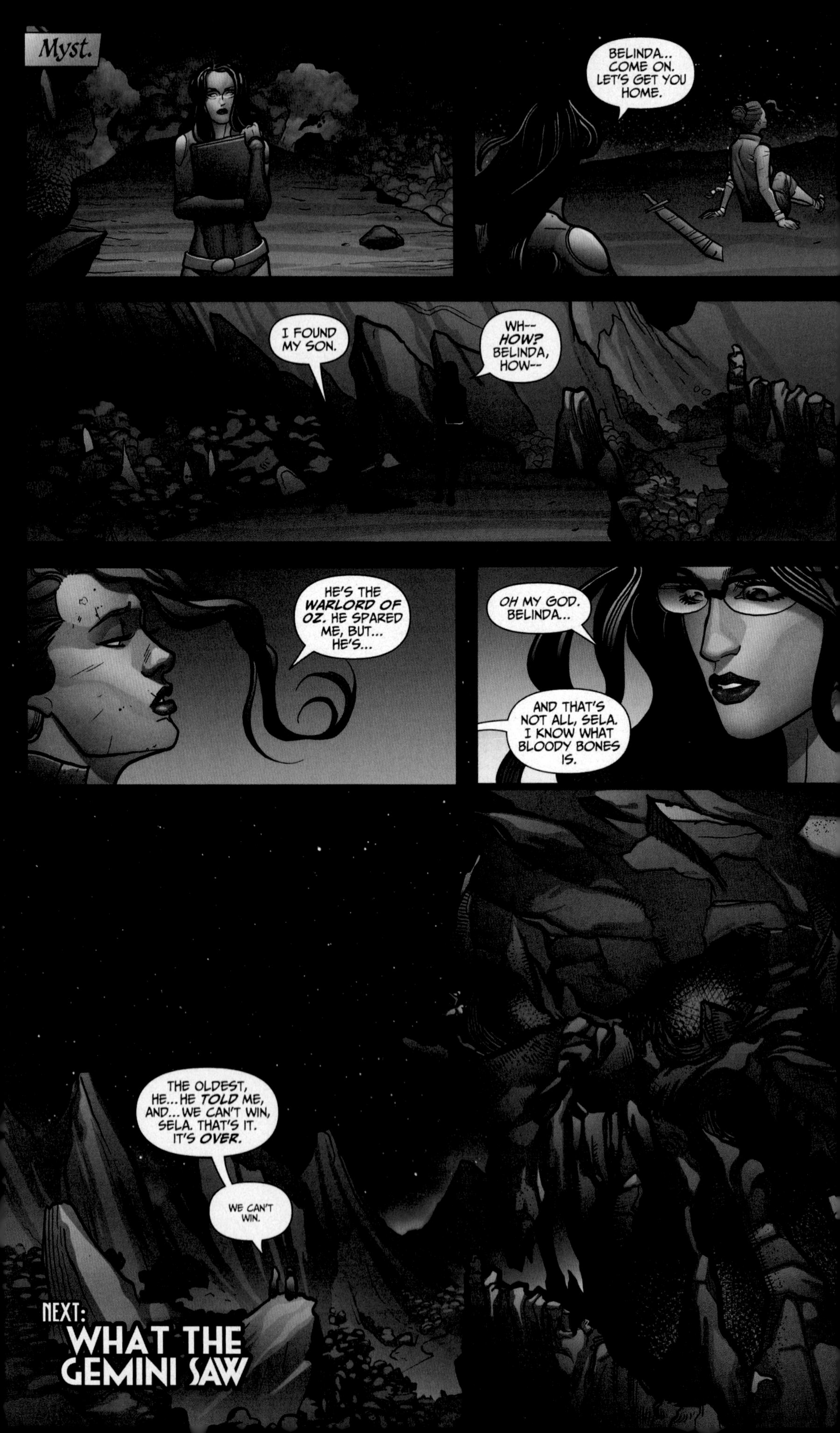
Myst.
BELINDA... COME ON. LET'S GET YOU HOME.
I FOUND MY SON.
WH-- HOW? BELINDA, HOW--
HE'S THE WARLORD OF OZ. HE SPARED ME, BUT... HE'S...
OH MY GOD. BELINDA...
AND THAT'S NOT ALL, SELA. I KNOW WHAT BLOODY BONES IS.
THE OLDEST, HE... HE TOLD ME, AND... WE CAN'T WIN, SELA. THAT'S IT. IT'S OVER.
WE CAN'T WIN.
NEXT:
WHAT THE GEMINI SAW

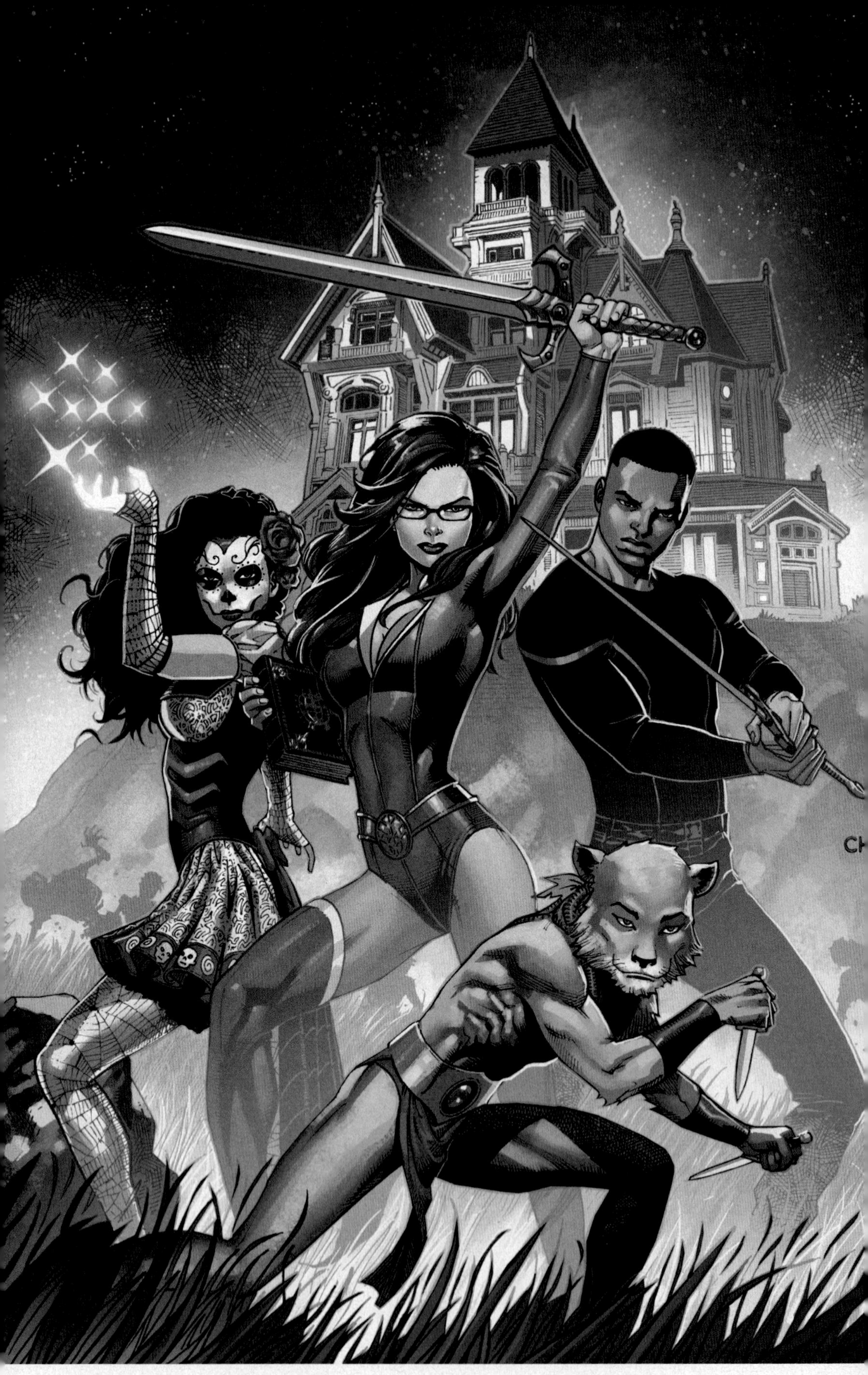
CH

GRIMM FAIRY TALES 113 • COVER A
ARTWORK BY SEAN CHEN • COLORS BY ROMULO FAJARDO JR.

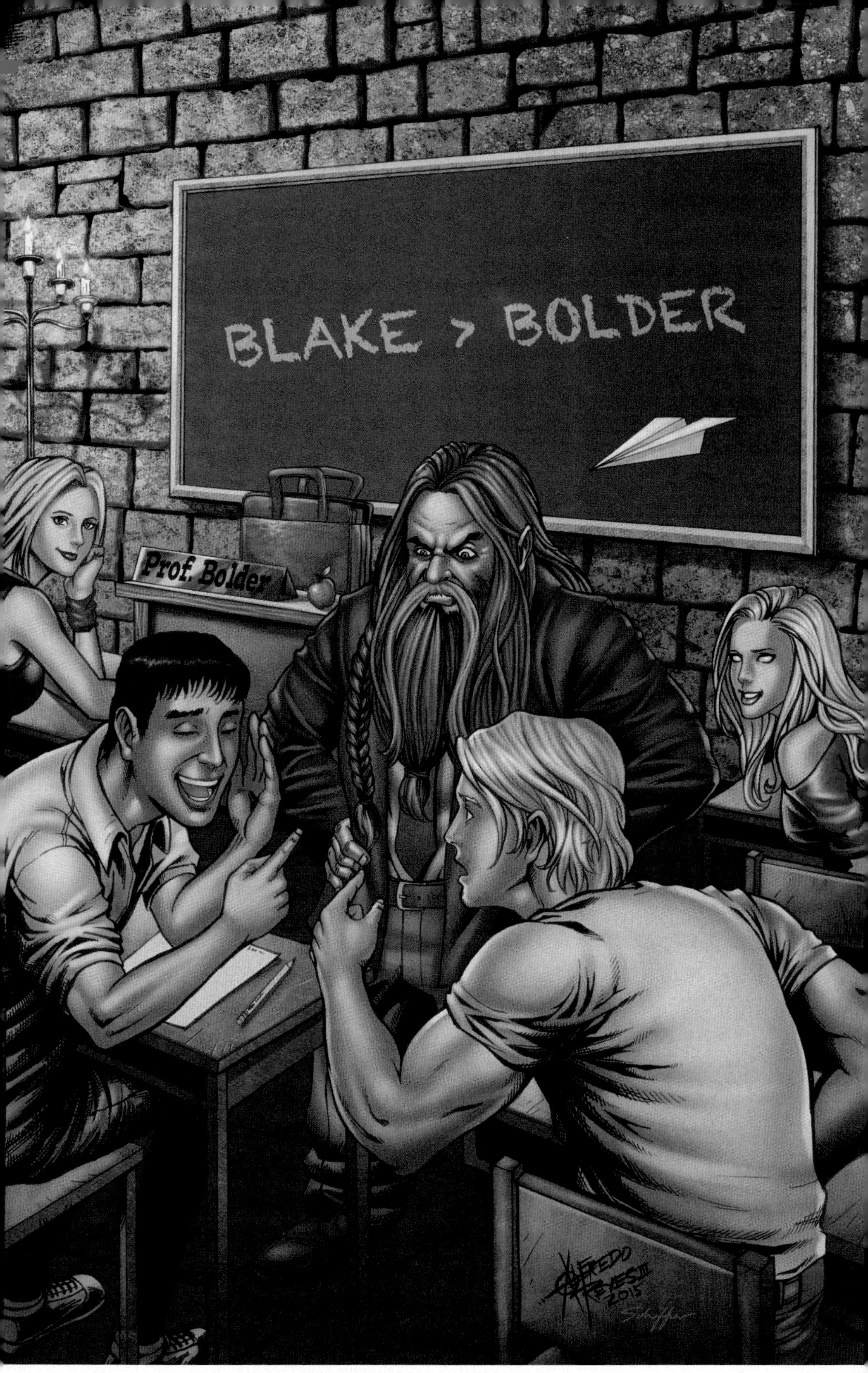
BLAKE > BOLDER
Prof. Bolder

GRIMM FAIRY TALES 113 • COVER B
ARTWORK BY ALFREDO REYES • COLORS BY STEPHEN SCHAFFER

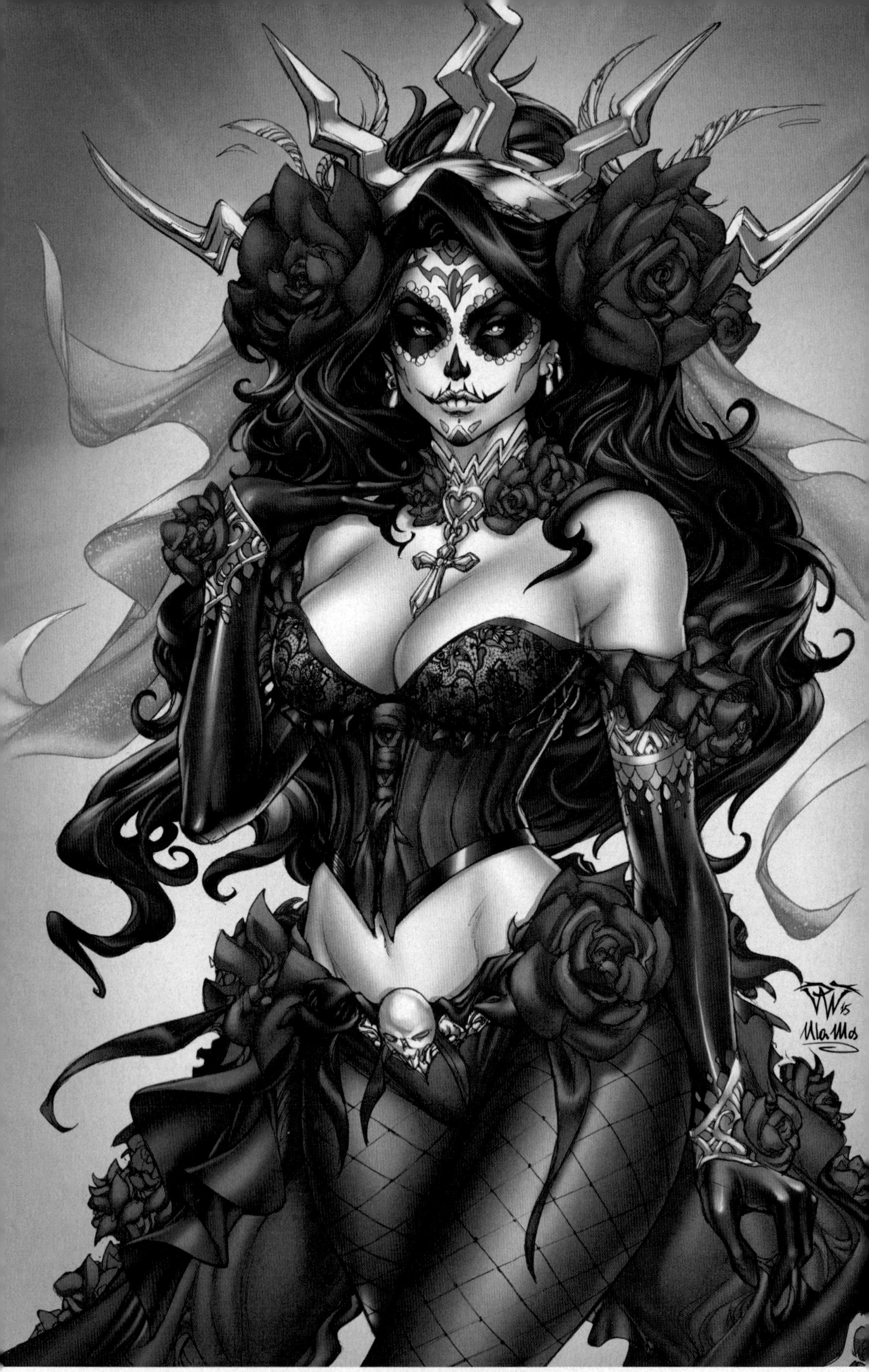
Ula Mos

GRIMM FAIRY TALES 113 • COVER C
ARTWORK BY PAOLO PANTALENA • COLORS BY ULA MOS

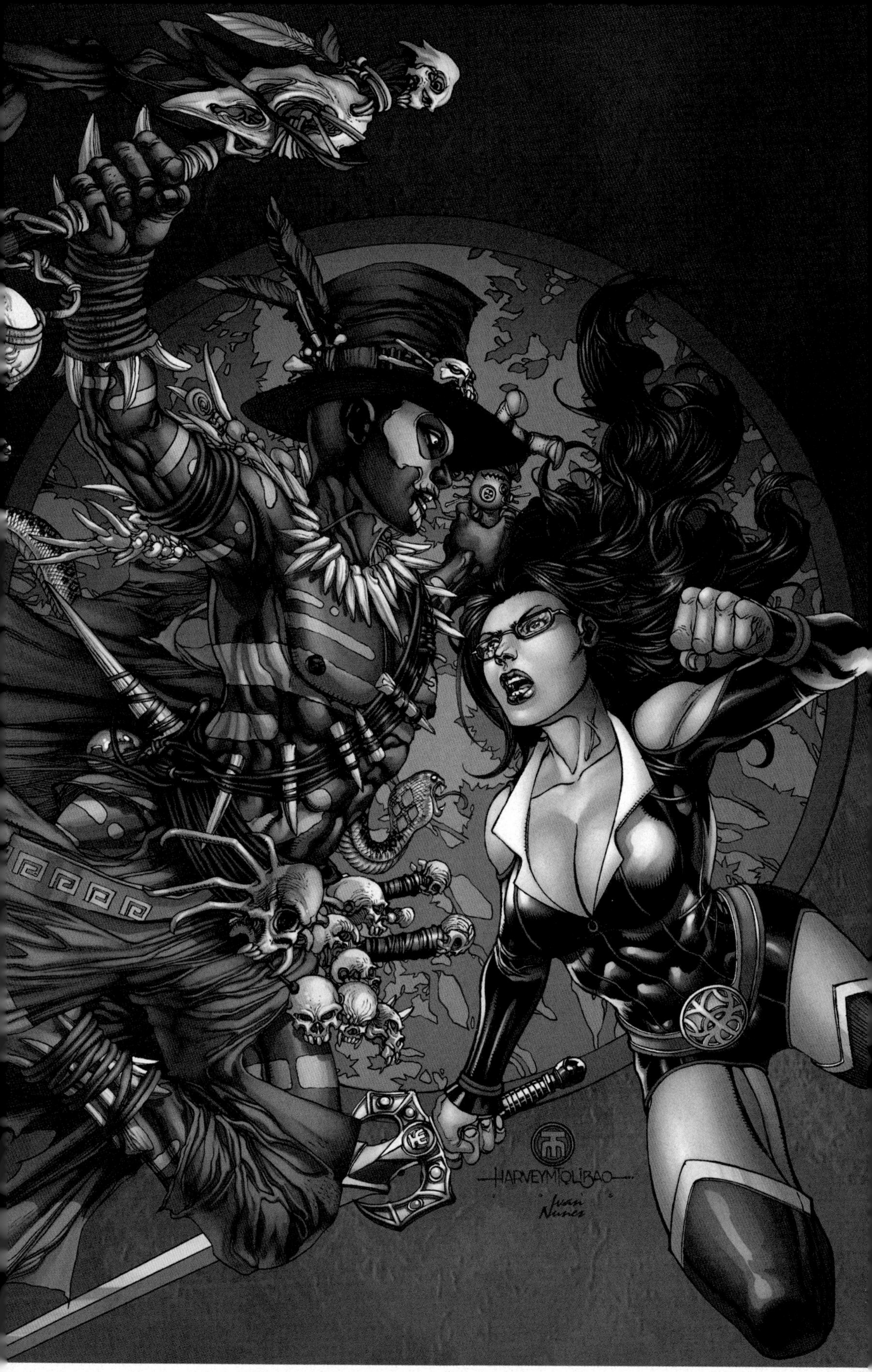
HARVEYMTOLIBAO
Ivan Nunes

GRIMM FAIRY TALES 114 • COVER A
ARTWORK BY HARVEY TOLIBAO • COLORS BY IVAN NUNES

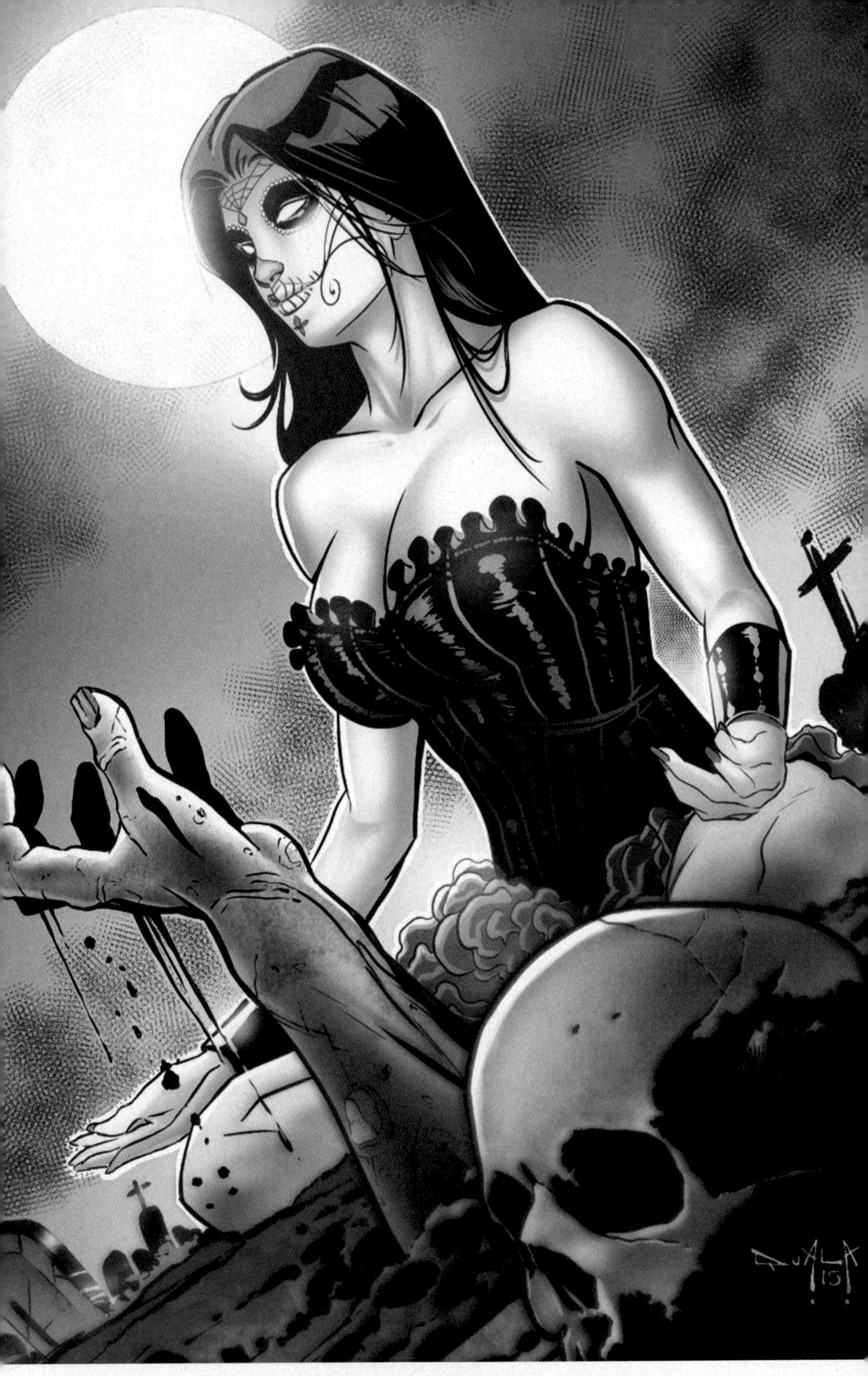

GRIMM FAIRY TALES 114 • COVER B
ARTWORK BY PASQUALE QUALANO • COLORS BY YLENIA DI NAPOLI

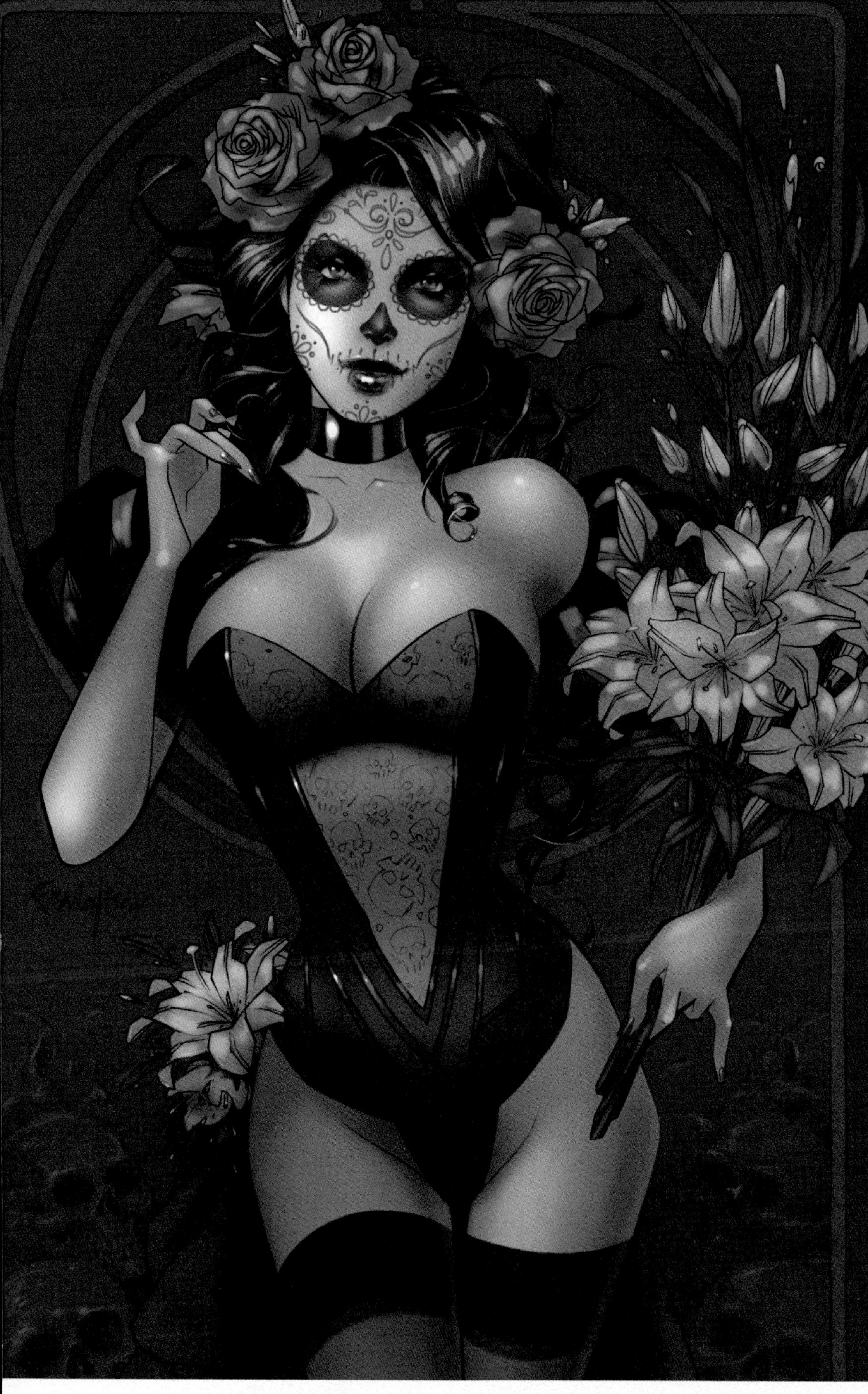

GRIMM FAIRY TALES 114 • COVER C
ARTWORK BY FRANCHESCO!

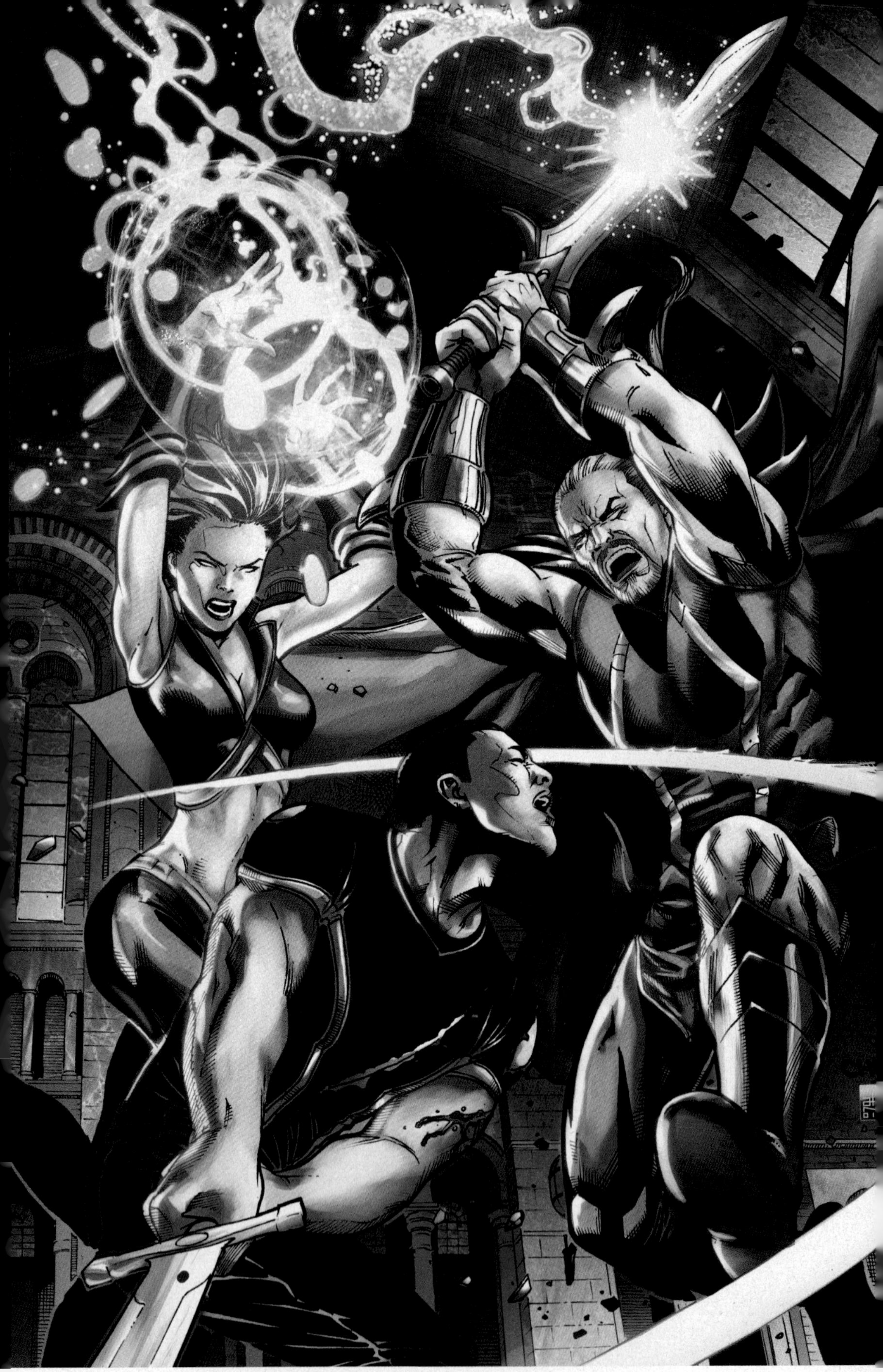

GRIMM FAIRY TALES 115 • COVER A
ARTWORK BY SEAN CHEN • COLORS BY ALESSIA NOCERA

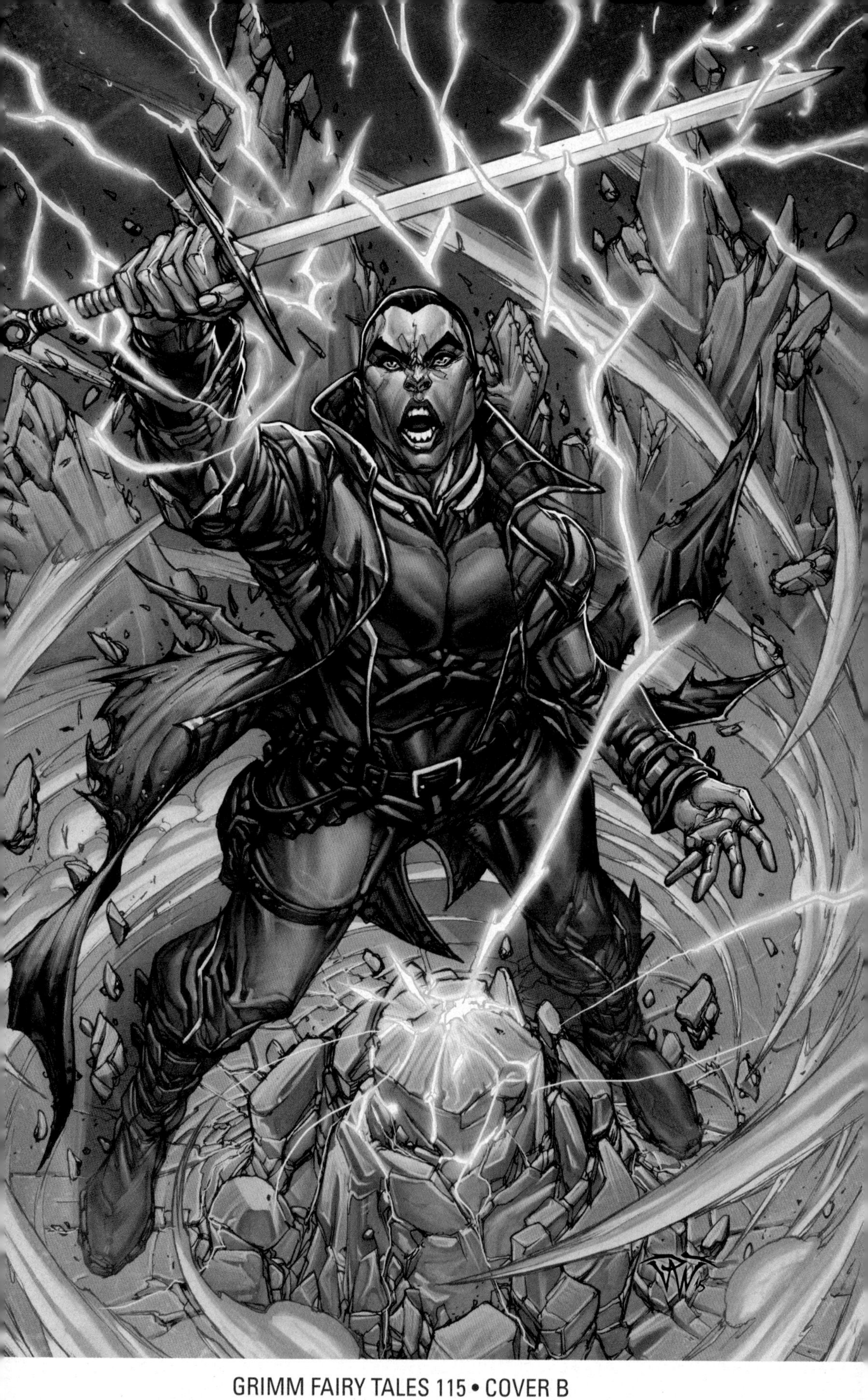

GRIMM FAIRY TALES 115 • COVER B
ARTWORK BY PAOLO PANTALENA • COLORS BY ROSS CAMPBELL

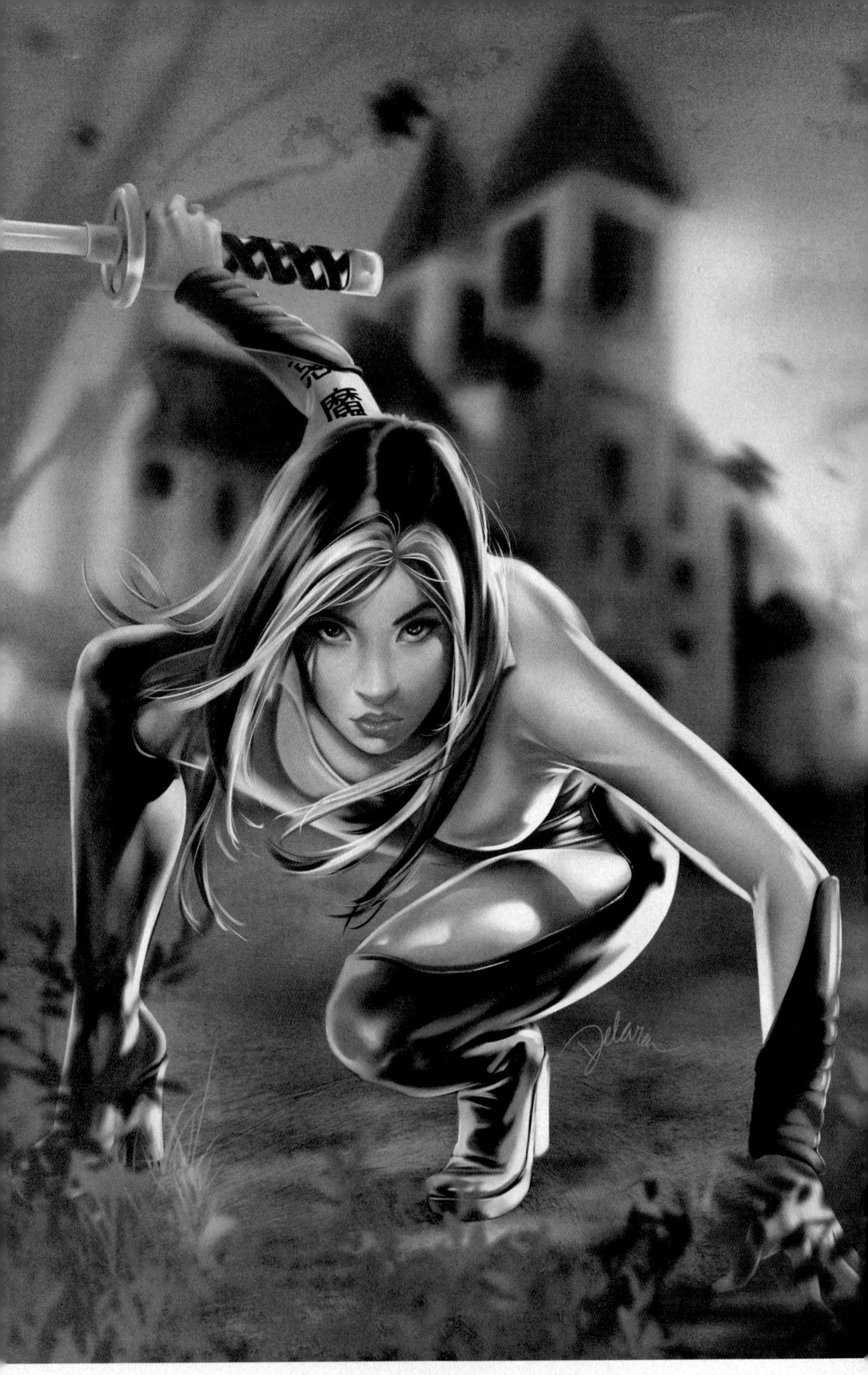
Delara

GRIMM FAIRY TALES 115 • COVER C
ARTWORK BY CRIS DELARA

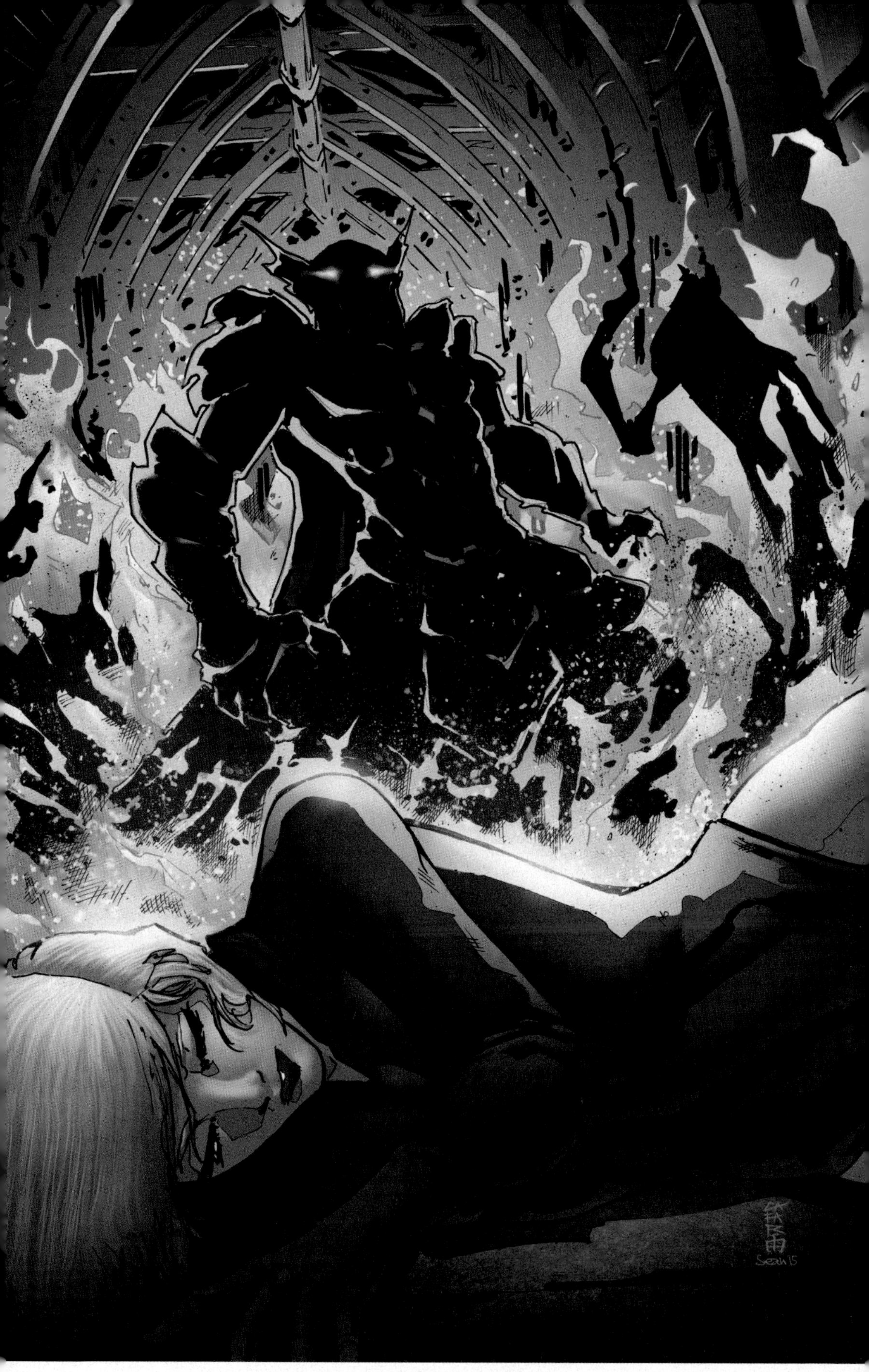

GRIMM FAIRY TALES 116 • COVER A
ARTWORK BY GIUSEPPE CAFARO • COLORS BY SEAN ELLERY

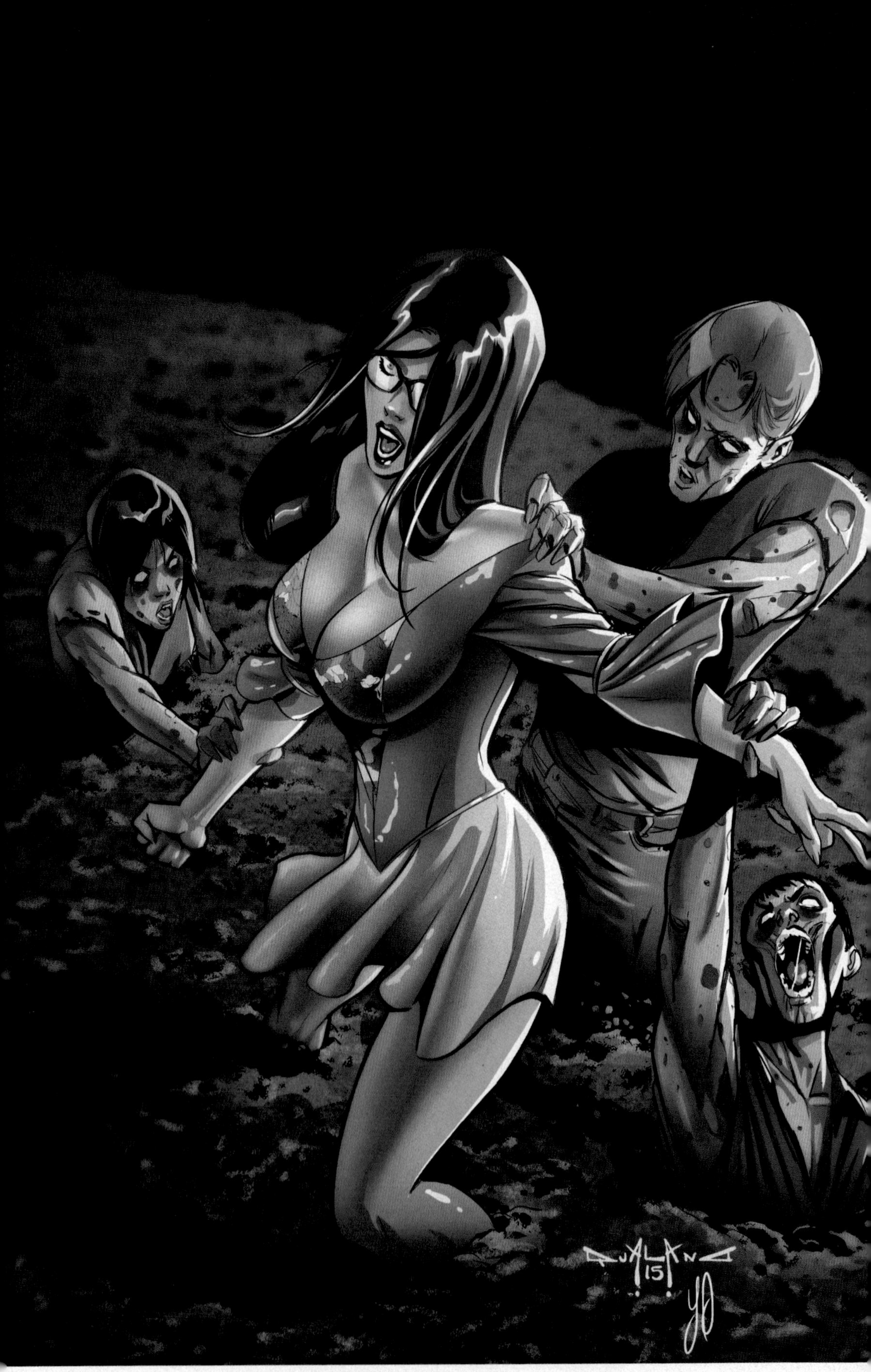
QUALANO 15

GRIMM FAIRY TALES 116 • COVER B
ARTWORK BY PASQUALE QUALANO • COLORS BY YLENIA DI NAPOLI

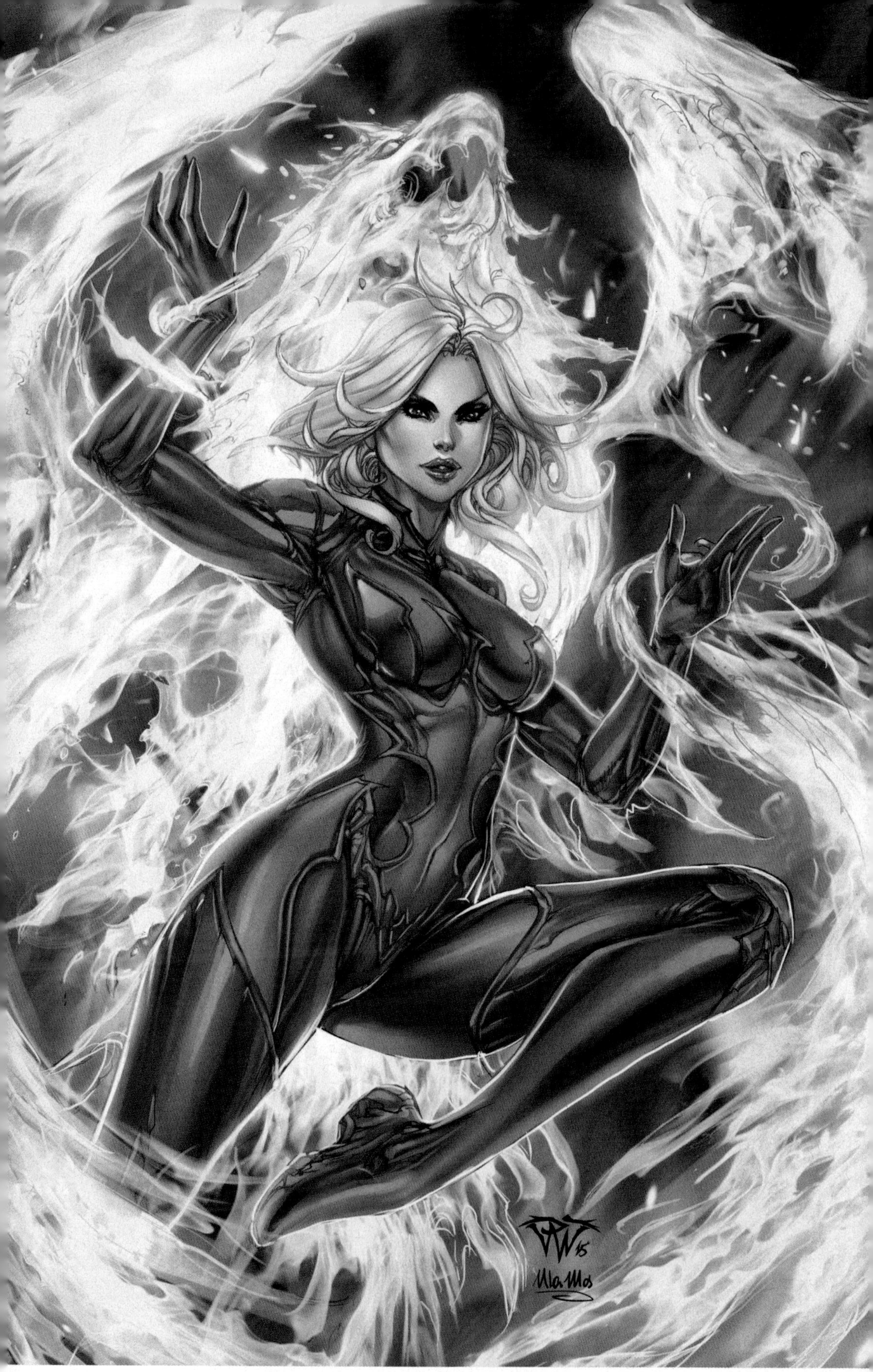

GRIMM FAIRY TALES 116 • COVER C
ARTWORK BY PAOLO PANTALENA • COLORS BY ULA MOS

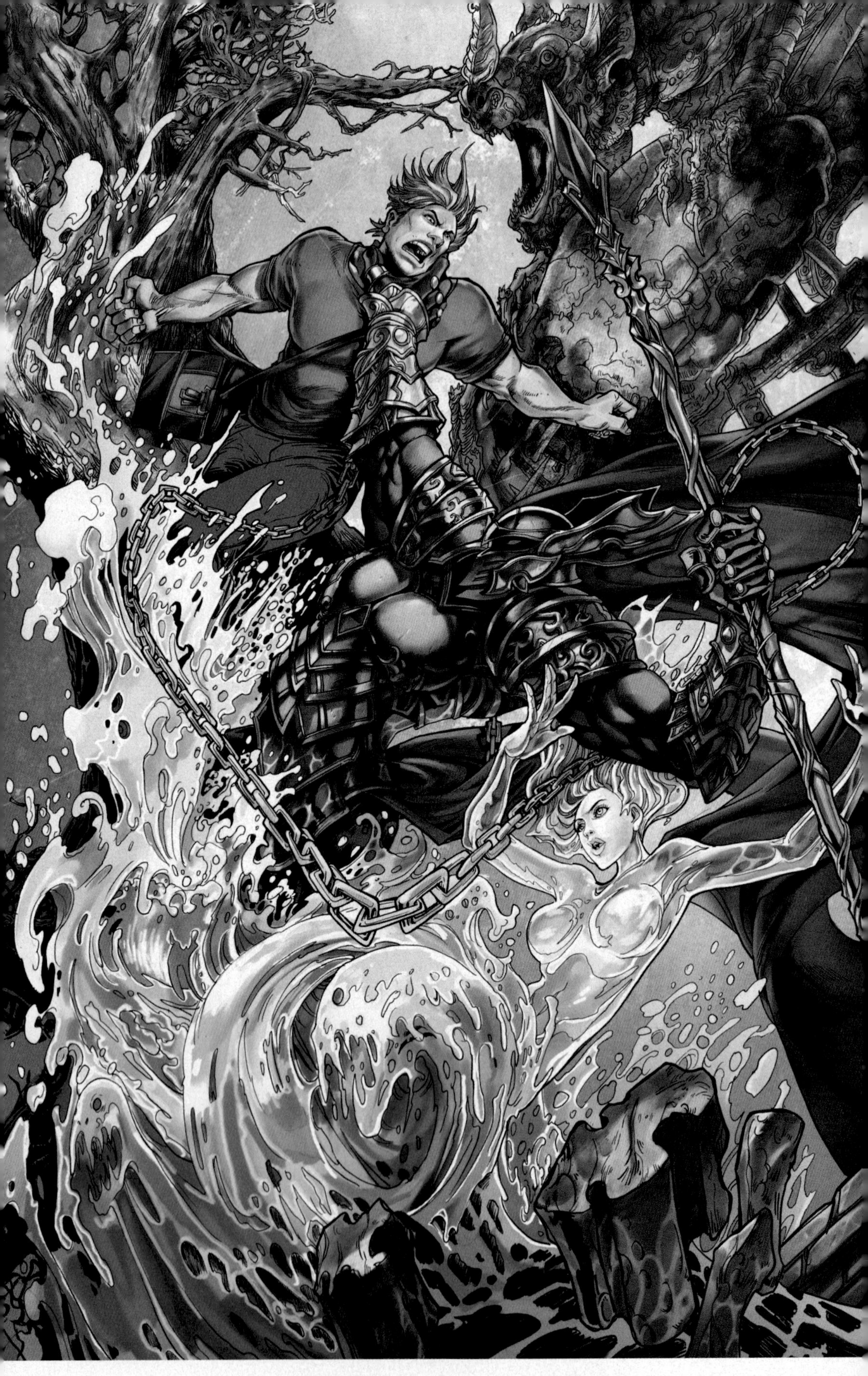

GRIMM FAIRY TALES 117 • COVER A
ARTWORK BY DAXIONG

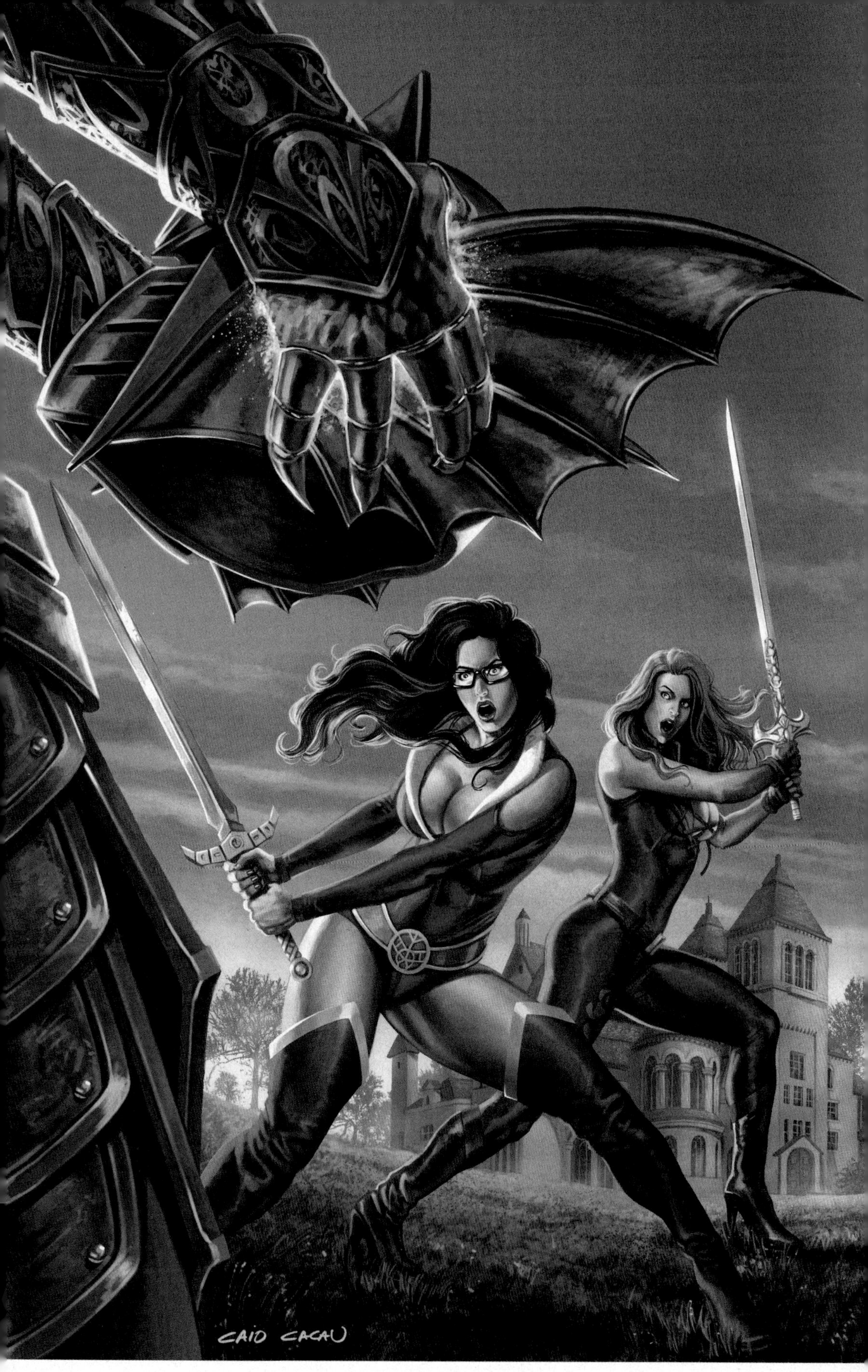
CAIO CACAU

GRIMM FAIRY TALES 117 • COVER B
ARTWORK BY CAIO CACAU

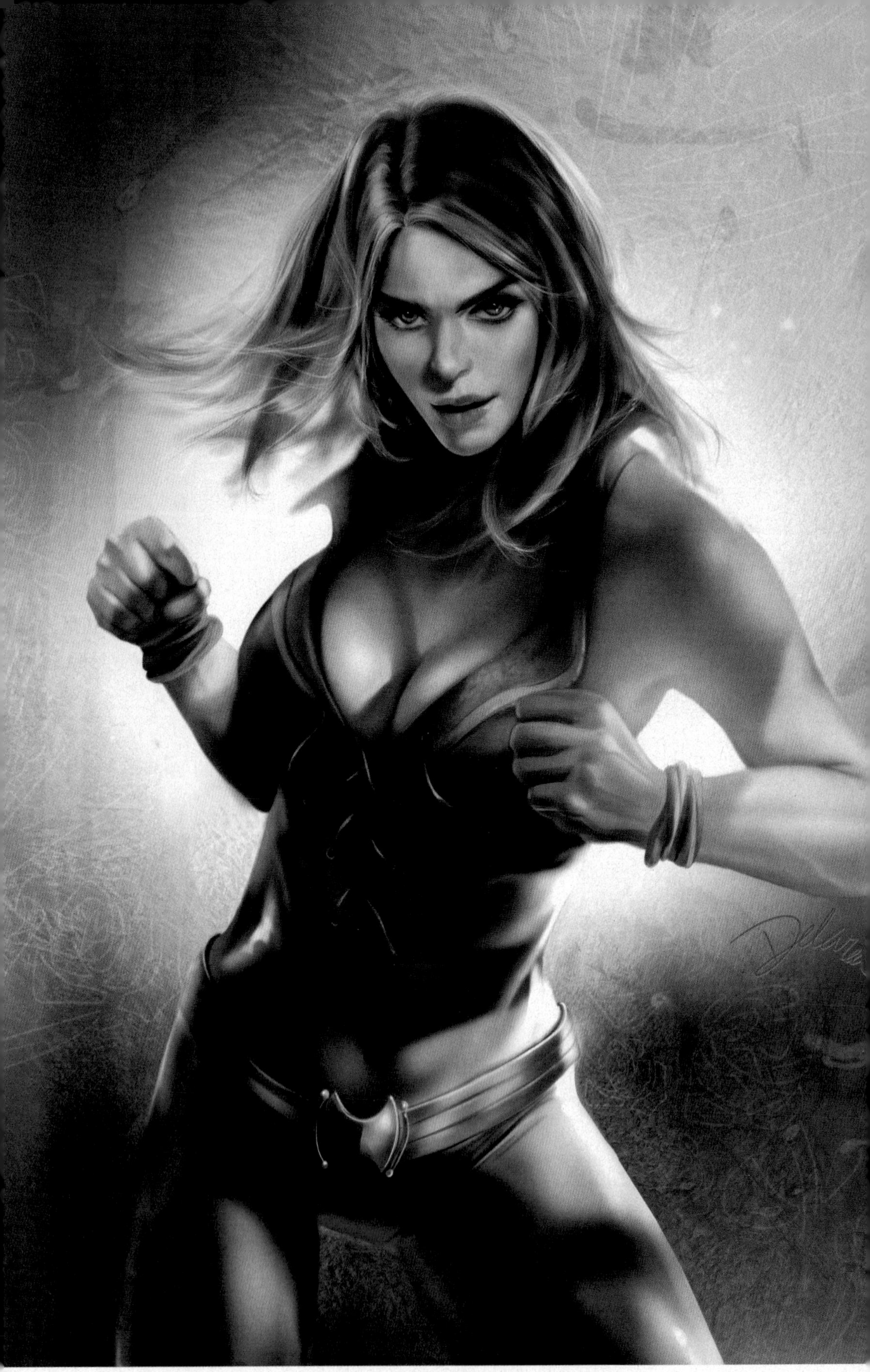
Delara

GRIMM FAIRY TALES 117 • COVER C
ARTWORK BY CRIS DELARA

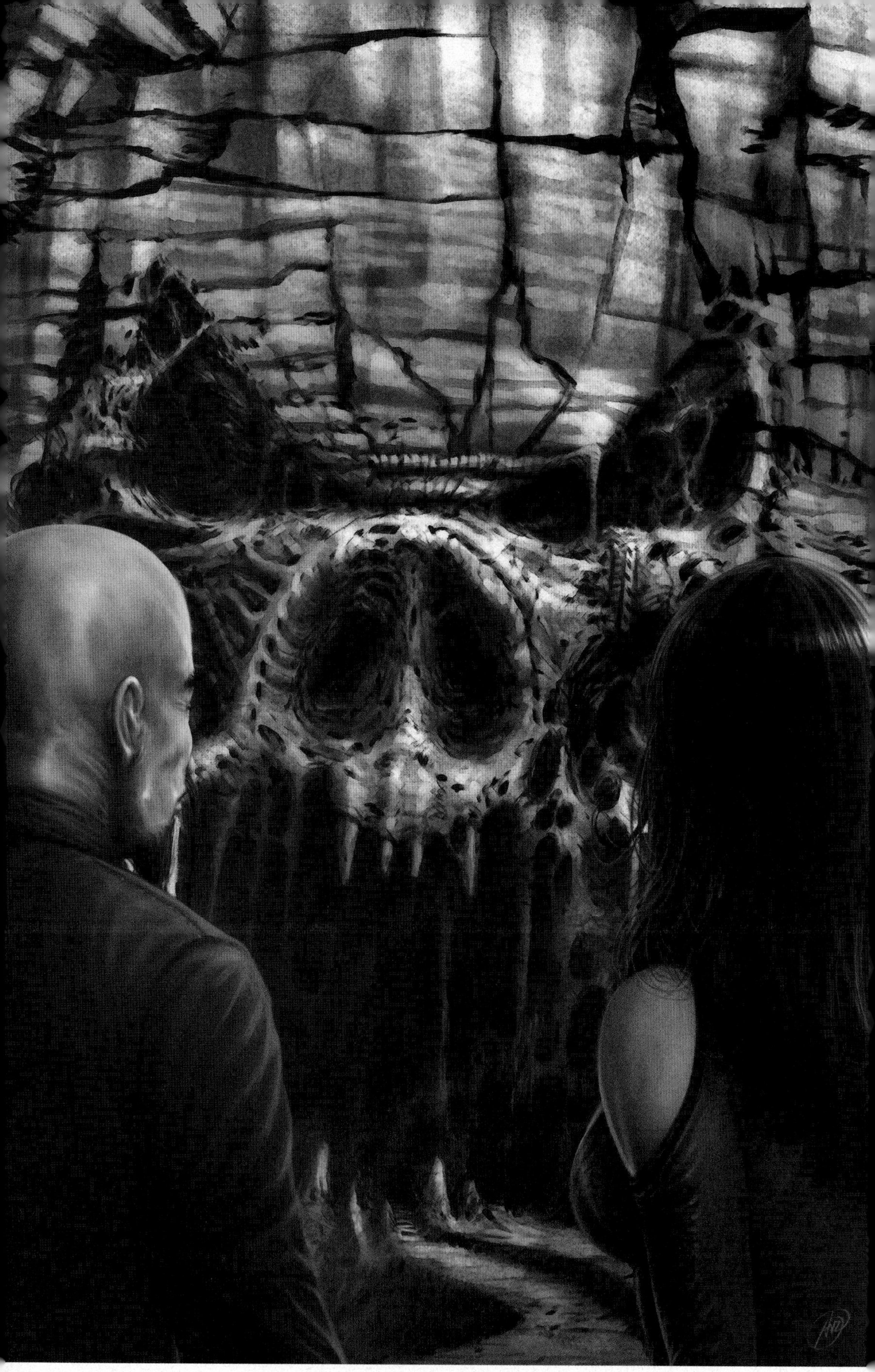

GRIMM FAIRY TALES 118 • COVER A
ARTWORK BY ED ANDERSON

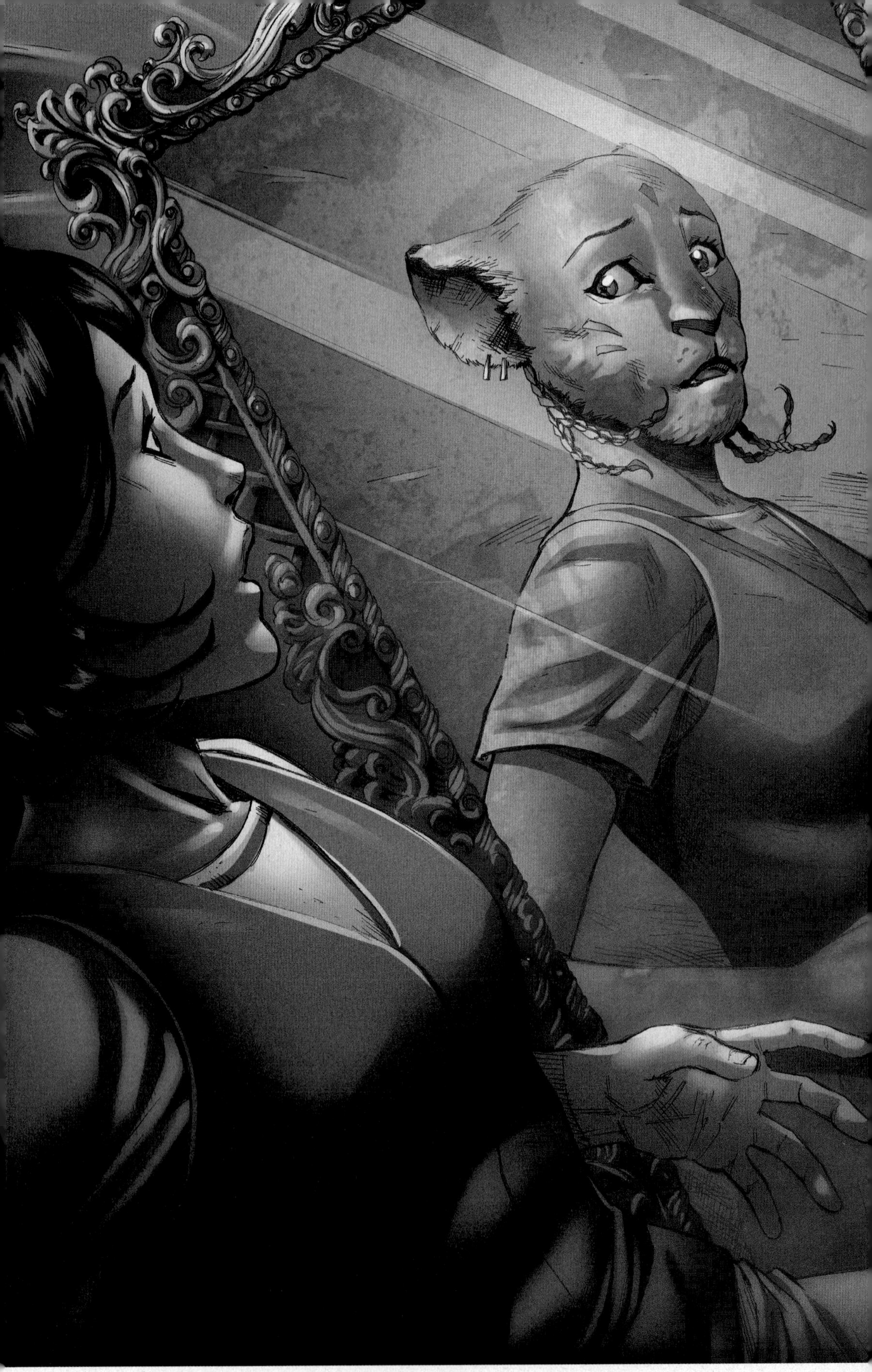

GRIMM FAIRY TALES 118 • COVER B
ARTWORK BY MIGUEL MENDONCA • COLORS BY YLENIA DI NAPOLI

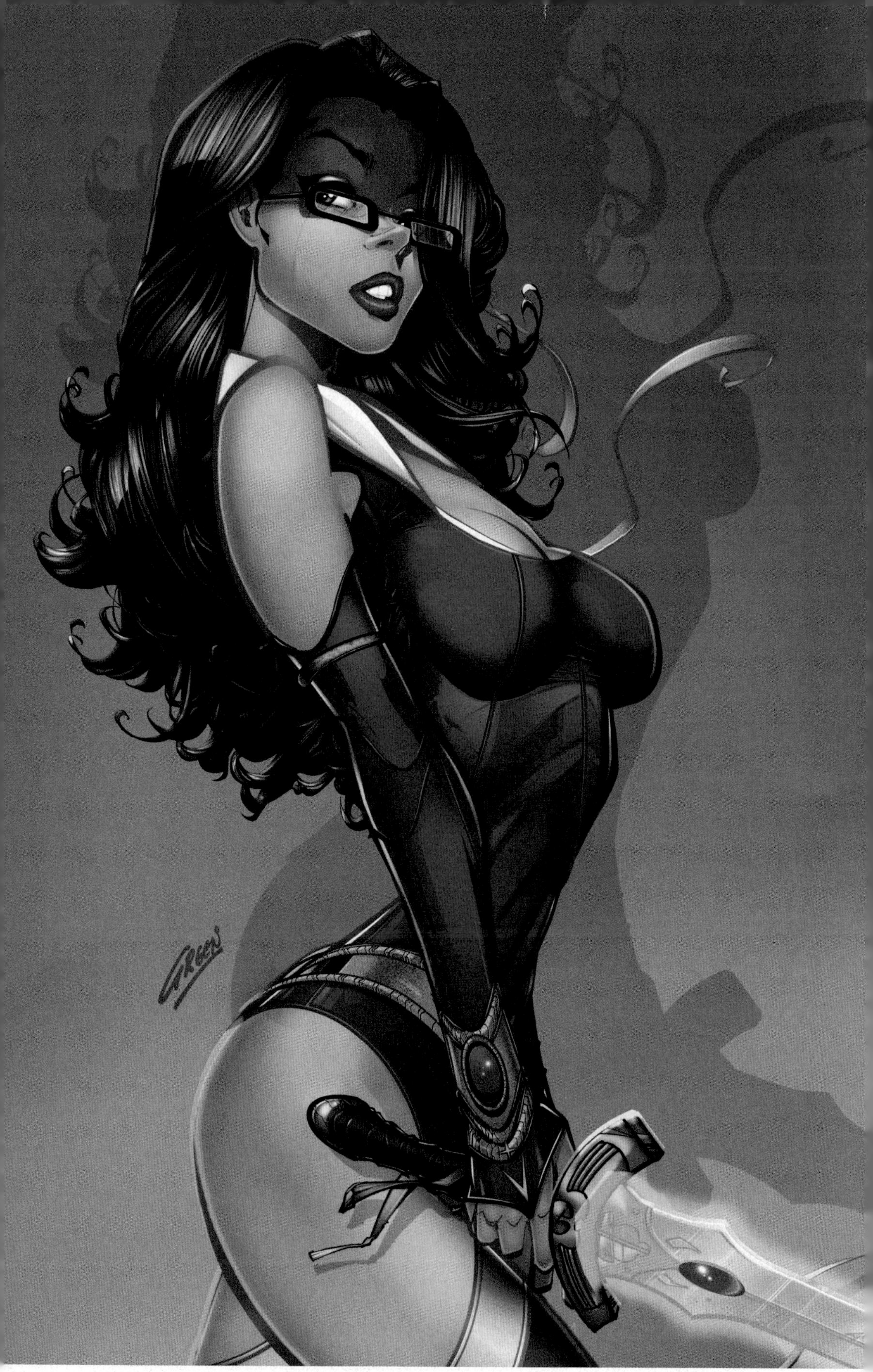

GRIMM FAIRY TALES 118 • COVER C
ARTWORK BY PAUL GREEN

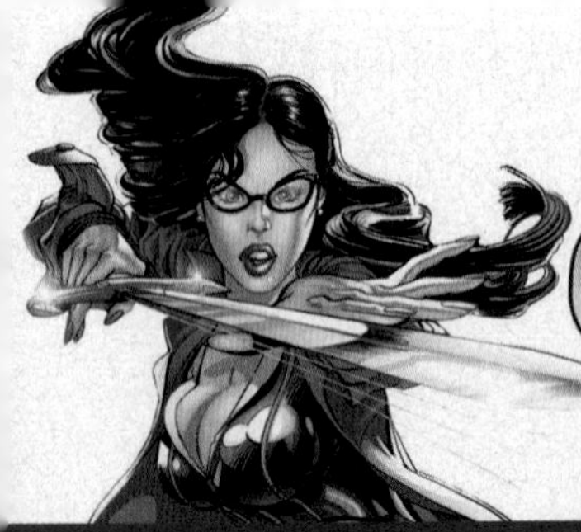